THE ROUGH GUIDE TO

Videogames

ROUGH GUIDES

www.roughguides.com

Credits

The Rough Guide to Videogames

Editors: Peter Buckley and Sean Mahoney
Design and layout: Diana Jarvis
Proofreading: Elaine Pollard
Cover: Peter Buckley and Chloë Roberts
Production: Rebecca Short and Vicky Baldwin

Rough Guides Reference

Reference Director: Andrew Lockett
Editors: Peter Buckley, Tracy Hopkins,
Sean Mahoney, Matthew Milton,
Joe Staines, Ruth Tidball

Cover credits

Halo image courtesy of Microsoft Game Studios; World of Warcraft image courtesy of Blizzard; retro alien graphic designed by Simeon Bradshaw; *Mario Kart* image courtesy of Nintendo Company Ltd.

Publishing information

This first edition published August 2008 by
Rough Guides Ltd, 80 Strand, London WC2R 0RL
345 Hudson St, 4th Floor, New York 10014, USA
Email: mail@roughguides.com

Distributed by the Penguin Group:
Penguin Books Ltd, 80 Strand, London WC2R 0RL
Penguin Putnam, Inc., 375 Hudson Street, NY 10014, USA
Penguin Group (Australia), 250 Camberwell Road, Camberwell,
Victoria 3124, Australia
Penguin Books Canada Ltd, Toronto, Ontario, Canada M4P 2YE
Penguin Group (New Zealand), 67 Apollo Drive, Mairongi Bay,
Auckland 1310, New Zealand

Printed in Italy by LegoPrint S.p.A

Typeset in Din, LLPixel and Myriad Pro

312 pages; includes index

A catalogue record for this book is available from the British Library

ISBN: 978-1-84353-995-7

1 3 5 7 9 8 6 4 2

THE ROUGH GUIDE TO

Videogames

by
Kate Berens & Geoff Howard

CONTENTS

Canon entries

Introduction

Videogames are poised on the brink of the cultural mainstream, widespread popular acceptance still lying just out of reach. Like any new medium in its formative years – film, TV, pop music – videogaming is an unremarkable fact of life for anyone younger than the technology (in this case around fifty) while older generations routinely dismiss, or even vilify it. Now, though, the kids who've grown up with gaming are on the verge of becoming the ones in power, taking over the reins of politics and the mass media, making this the perfect time to examine where games have got to so far.

No more than a great book or movie, a great game isn't newsworthy based solely on merit; it's more often sky-high sales figures or provocative content that catches the attention of those who don't already play games. In search of a headline, the media tend not to dwell on the work done by games charities, or the increased demand for music lessons thanks to *Guitar Hero*, but on the minuscule proportion of games aimed squarely at a mature audience, the massive amounts of money involved, or the assertion that school shootings are somehow caused by videogames, a link that has not been proven. Interestingly, the facts contained in the UK's 226-page Byron report, a UK government-sponsored study entitled "Safer Children in a Digital World", were repeatedly overlooked by the British press in favour of rabid comments by random celebrities. In the US, videogames have been a political hobby horse for decades, not that this is surprising when you consider how much easier it is to deal with games as a cause of gun crime than with, say, guns. Coverage of Nintendo's family-friendly Wii has made a welcome change to the hysteria, with positive accounts of its use in nursing homes; on the other hand, it can make other kinds of game seem more alienating by contrast. All in all, it's understandable that many people view videogaming as a thoroughly unwelcoming world they'd prefer not to enter. Meanwhile, going unnoticed is the fact that the variety of games on offer is wider than ever, and that many of the very people who would baulk at being called gamers are clocking up hours online playing *Peggle* or *Scrabulous*.

Even without mainstream approval, the videogames industry has grown so large that it now rivals the film industry in sheer money earned, and for many countries is an increasingly important source of national income. In Europe, British games industry veterans have been awarded OBEs by the Queen, while France is politically committed to supporting what it considers a homegrown cultural art form; across the Atlantic, tax breaks offered to games companies have encouraged developers to relocate to Canada. As the business grows, the cost of making games rises too, with *Halo 3* costing a rumoured $30 million, and Microsoft allegedly paying $50 million just for exclusive downloadable content for *Grand Theft Auto IV*. The fastest-growing cultural phenomenon of the last fifty years, the videogames industry is impossible to ignore.

About this book

The Internet is a fantastic resource for videogamers: never has it been easier to find the solution to a puzzle, to access instant games ratings and watch videos to help decide whether to buy a new game; or indeed to play a game, download it or simply shop for it online. With this book we're offering something different, a tangible, dip-in-and-out guide that talks to a broader audience, addressing games and the unique experience of playing them in the context of videogaming history and culture. Newcomers can certainly see it as an introduction, but it's written for anyone interested in videogames past and present – computer, console or handheld.

The book is divided into four main parts. Following this introduction is the Backstory, a history of videogames from the earliest mainframes to the present day, including brief reviews of key games along the way. The main section of the book is the Canon, our collection of classic games, old and new, in no order other than alphabetical. You may not agree with our selection – in fact we're sure you won't agree with all of them – but, among the many games covered in this book we're bound to have included your favourites somewhere (if not, let us know). Following the Canon is a section on the Players – the individuals, companies and characters who've left an indelible mark on videogames. Then comes the Peripherals section, gathering together additional pieces on some of the strange kit that's been created for games and the perpetually unhappy relationship between games and movies, plus a list of recommended books, magazines and websites. Finally, there's a comprehensive index.

Game over?

Our understanding of what videogaming is, of what it can do and how we engage with it, is being constantly and subtly reframed. It already embraces vastly different eras and experiences: *Donkey Kong*, for example, is just as much a videogame as *World of Warcraft*, yet the two seem barely related. And still, designers strive to invent new ways to engage us, beyond standard controller and disc-based games, from the Wii Balance Board to games delivered as monthly episodes, not to mention games that are increasingly user-generated. As a medium, it's proved itself endlessly adaptable and will no doubt continue down roads that are currently unimaginable. As for the players themselves, the once rigid line dividing hardcore and casual is becoming more broken and blurry, as the age and lifestyle of gamers extends over a broader range: according to the Entertainment Software Association, the average age of American gamers is 33, and nearly a third are women over the age of 18. This is yet more evidence for unbelievers that games are not just for kids, but can provide us with all sorts of experiences, of which the adrenaline charge of winning is but one; they are developing more mature ways of dealing with complex narrative subject matter all the time. Also changing are the mechanics of the gameplay experience – hardly surprising when it's so dependent on technology – particularly in the overlapping of games and other entertainment, both online (social networking-cum-MMORPGs) and offline (watching Blu-ray movies on a games console). In every way, this is a medium as much in transition as the society it serves.

It's hard to say what might happen next in videogames' inexorable march into maturity. One thing you can count on staying the same is that very thing that makes a game different from any other form of entertainment: you can't sit back and take a passive role. All videogames, however disparate they may otherwise be, depend on the player's involvement. They're nothing without you there to make things happen, whether it's swinging a baseball bat to score a home run or to smash a car window.

Ready? … Then press START.

About the authors

Kate Berens first experienced the thrill of videogaming playing the *Pong*-alike *TV Tennis* with her father in the 1970s; her first all-nighter was with *Secret of the Silver Blades* on the PC, and her introduction to handhelds came with *Sonic the Hedgehog* on the Game Gear. Passionate about videogames and their role in popular culture, she recently left her job as editorial director at Rough Guides Travel to concentrate on freelance writing and editing. Based in South London, she blogs at atypicalgamer.com.

Geoff Howard has been playing videogames since the mid-1970s, when his grandfather bought a broken Monarch CTX-4 Video Sporter from Tandy Shack, fixed it, and gave it to Geoff and his brother. He swiftly moved on to the Atari 2600 and hasn't been far from a console or PC since. A UK-based Rough Guides editor and writer for many years, he is now based in Melbourne, Australia, and is particularly keen to see an Australian game-ratings system introduced which recognizes that like films, games can be for adults as well as kids. This is the third book he has written with Kate on videogaming.

Acknowledgements

Kate: I would like to thank Sean Mahoney for commissioning the book, asking the right questions and keeping my spirits up when needed; Andrew Lockett for full-on support at Penguin HQ; Peter Buckley for pitching in and getting it all into perfect order; Ruth Tidball and Tracy Hopkins for expert assistance; Diana Jarvis for fabulous design work; Martin Dunford for graciously letting me cross the divide; Samantha Cook for writerly support; and my upside-down co-author for all the rest. Last but not least, thanks to Lydia, Andrew and the Greens for being interested, and to Richard for playing co-op right to the end.

Geoff: I would like to thank all the people who made this book happen, not least Kate for putting up with her co-author suddenly relocating to another continent, time zone and job in the middle of writing it, with all the stress it engendered: here's to the good times of Carlos del Sol and Miguel de Santa Clara. At Rough Guides I'd like to thank my erstwhile colleagues Sean Mahoney, for taking the idea from conception to fruition, Peter Buckley for support along the way, and Andrew Lockett for taking time out of his Australian schedule to meet up for some very spicy fish dishes. At home I'd like to thank Judith, without whose support I would not have found time to juggle work and writing, Miss Polly for being herself, and the Port Melbourne possums for luring me to Australia.

The
Backstory

The Backstory

Videogames aren't what they used to be. They're bigger, faster and vastly more complicated, and the lines between games and other forms of entertainment are blurring further year by year. In this chapter we summarize the evolution that's taken place over the last fifty or so years: from the clumsy, monochromatic cabinets of *Computer Space* to the multi-million-player *World of Warcraft*, from family-friendly Pikachu to computer games of the worst possible taste, it's a story that parallels changes in technology and society as a whole, with plenty of disastrous flops as well as high points of achievement. Throughout the chapter, we've picked out some key games past and present that didn't make it into our canon for a more in-depth look at their historical significance.

Once upon a time in the West...

The concept of using computers to play games has no single origin, but what is clear is that its pioneers were spurred on by developing postwar technologies. Some, such as Thomas Goldsmith and Estle Ray Mann, wanted to apply the new discoveries to the field of entertainment: their 1947 US patent for the never-constructed Cathode-Ray Tube Amusement Device described launching a missile at a target depicted on a plastic overlay upon a TV screen. For Ralph Baer, asked in 1951 by his employers to build "the best TV set in the world", it was about incorporating an interactive game into the set (the idea was turned down). For others it was about education: nuclear physicist William Higginbotham's interactive 1958 *Tennis For Two* (a spiritual precursor to *Pong*) was designed to instruct visitors to the Brookhaven National Laboratory on the effects of gravity; while Alexander S. Douglas had created his onscreen *OXO* (noughts and crosses, or tic-tac-toe) for his Cambridge thesis on human-computer interaction back in 1952.

These were mere evolutionary convulsions, however. The big-bang moment was MIT student Steve Russell's

1961 *Spacewar!* (see p.4), with its introduction of concepts still used today: in-game options, a two-player mode, a scoring system and limited resources (in this case missiles and fuel). Designed as a fun way of showcasing the institute's latest mainframe computer – a nine-kilo, phone-booth-sized machine with a price tag of well over $100,000 – the game was never patented and continued to be mimicked for decades, acting as the blueprint for even relative latecomers like *Asteroids*. It was also the slow beginning of videogaming's rise into the commercial stratosphere: where Ralph Baer had envisioned a gaming TV in every household, student Nolan Bushnell, inspired by his summer job as manager of a pinball arcade and misbegotten MIT semesters spent playing *Spacewar!*, dreamt instead of banks of coin-operated videogame machines under one roof. So began his quest to produce a machine compact and financially viable enough for the job.

Attack of the arcade machines

It was to take Bushnell, with help from programmer Ted Dabney and arcade-machine manufacturer Nutting Associates, the best part of a decade to produce the first-ever mass-produced coin-operated videogame. It came in the shape of 1971's *Computer Space*, whose genius lay in transferring *Spacewar!*'s computer-programmed gameplay into readily available, hard-wired logic circuitry, vastly reducing the scale and cost of the build. (Recognition for the very first coin-operated videogame should go to Computer Recreations for their *Galaxy Game*, another repurposed version of *Spacewar!* that existed as a single machine at Stanford University. It debuted two months before *Computer Space* but ventured no further than a campus coffee shop).

The trouble for Bushnell was that, mass-produced or not – and 1500 cabinets were manufactured – sales weren't numerous enough, something he blamed on both a lack of support from Nutting and the relatively complicated gameplay. Undaunted, he and Dabney parted company with Nutting in 1972 to set up Atari (an attacking manoeuvre in the Japanese board game, *Go*), and that year produced the iconic *Pong*. Problems with another mass-producer led Atari to build their own, single prototype for a local bar, who reported back within a fortnight that the machine had broken down. It hadn't: the sheer volume of quarters rolling through its pay-slot had simply stopped it working. Within twelve months Atari had sold around 8500 *Pong* units, inspiring myriad copycats; by 1973, these already included *Pong Tron* from the Japan-based, American-founded Sega, *Soccer* from Japan's own Taito (another traditional arcade machine supplier) and Midway's *Winner*. For a while, playing videogames meant playing *Pong*.

Within the space of a few years, arcades would hum to the sights and sounds of other classics-in-the-making. Atari's *Breakout* arrived in 1976, the same year Cinematronics' *Space War* introduced vector graphics. Trackballs and microprocessors started to appear,

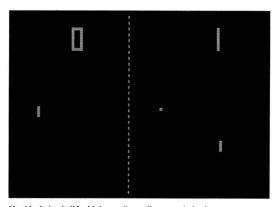

"Avoid missing ball for high score" was all you needed to know for a game of *Pong*.

Pong
Arcade; Atari; 1972

"Avoid missing ball for high score." Simplicity itself, this nugget of advice comprises the entirety of *Pong*'s instructions. Although some have seen it as the result of lessons learned from *Computer Space*'s user-unfriendliness, the simple bat-and-ball concept was originally designed to give Atari's new, inexperienced programmer Al Alcorn, something to cut his teeth on. When he saw the result, Bushnell realized that its idiot-proof playability could turn it into a very welcome cash-cow for funding future projects, and decided to put videogaming's first back-of-an-envelope stroke of genius into the public domain.

Space Invaders
Arcade; Taito, Midway; 1978

Designer Tomokado Nishikado had initially envisioned his space invaders as airplanes, but found that would be too technically difficult, and so reached to H.G. Wells' *War of the Worlds* for inspiration – giving us the iconic, hallucinogenic flying jellyfish-cum-octopuses. Appearing first in Japan and licensed to Midway in the US, the invaders' inexorable, malevolent descent from the sky towards humanity's sole defender, sliding for cover beneath just three, disintegrating shields, set players' hearts racing and caused many a sweaty palm to slip on the joystick. The game was alarmingly addictive, with Japan suffering coin shortages and US truancy rates sky-rocketing. Indeed, when no less a figure than Shigeru Miyamoto (see p.245) was asked in a 2007 *Time Magazine* interview which single game had revolutionized the industry, he was unequivocal: *Space Invaders*, because it alone had made him want to design games.

Asteroids
Arcade; Atari; 1979

Although *Pong* kick-started the industry, *Asteroids* actually proved to be Atari's bestselling arcade game, shifting over 50,000 machines worldwide. Originally a blatant copy of *Spacewar!*, for which Cinematronics would unsuccessfully sue for patent violation, it ironically went on to become one of the first two videogames to be copyrighted in the US. Even more in keeping with the still cottage-industry atmosphere, *Asteroids* was never conceived of as its own entity, being instead the black-and-white spin-off of a doomed, far fancier project involving holograms.

Pac-Man
Arcade; Namco, Midway; 1980

Creator Toru Iwatani originally called his character *Puck-Man*, after the Japanese phrase *paku-paku*, used to describe the sound of eating – though Iwatani has since contradicted his original claim that a pizza with a single missing slice was his inspiration. US distributor Midway, however, wisely changed the name for its cabinets, lest graffitists decided to intervene. But frankly, it was a moot point whether they'd be able to tear their eyes away from helping Pac-Man avoid the ghosts maniacally patrolling their maze: in fact, *Pac-Man* became the second game in history to cause a coin-shortage in Japan.

In this year...

1974 – The first game to use a steering wheel and gearstick: *Gran Trak 10*
1978 – The first trackball controller: *Atari Football*
1979 – The first game with different levels and a boss enemy: *Ozma Wars*
1979 – The first first-person game: *Tailgunner*
1980 – The first platform game: *Space Panic*
1980 – The first game with a bonus round: *Carnival*
1981 – The first game with selectable difficulty levels: *Tempest*
1983 – The first game with selectable viewpoints: *I, Robot*
1984 – The first game with an ending: *Marble Madness*

as did RGB colour in 1978's *Galaxians*, also the year Taito's *Space Invaders* landed. The first arcade beat-'em-up, *Warrior*, arrived in 1978, but the first game to be as popular with female gamers as it was with male gamers, *Pac-Man*, didn't appear from Japan's Namco until 1980, the year after *Asteroids* lodged itself in the public's consciousness. Along the way, such luxuries as selectable difficulty levels and multiple weapons debuted, alongside a decent whack of Betamax-style moments, such as flirting with laserdisc technology in the early 1980s.

But Atari stayed top dog throughout, and as early as 1976 was an attractive enough proposition for Warner Communications to buy, laying the financial foundations for Atari to sustain its dominant presence in the arcades while investing heavily in the last videogaming battleground of the 1970s: the home console market.

Consoles for kids

Ralph Baer, meanwhile, had persuaded his new em-ployers that TV-based gaming was the future, and in 1967 released a prototype that transmogrified into 1972's Magnavox Odyssey, the first home videogam-ing system. Its twelve games – all slight variations on the same basic one – included a precursor to *Pong*. Interestingly, a pre-*Pong* Bushnell is known to have at-tended the Odyssey's press launch and to have played it (Magnavox, who'd had the foresight to patent their version, would later collect $700,000 in damages from Atari). Confusing marketing led potential buyers to believe the system would only work on a Magnavox TV set, and Baer's vision of a twenty-dollar add-on had somehow become a $100 purchase, but it still sold around 100,000 units.

As with *Pong*, the Odyssey was a tipping point. By 1976, rivals included Coleco's Telstar and Fairchild

Camera & Instrument's breakthrough Video Entertainment System (later renamed Channel F), the first console to use cartridges to load games rather than hard-wiring them into the circuitry. It was a system first copied by RCA's negligible Studio II and then more importantly by Atari in 1977 with their Video Computer System (also known as the VCS and Atari 2600). But all featured games written exclusively for their platforms and fared poorly. In fact, the VCS did so badly that it lost Warner millions of dollars and prompted Bushnell's 1978 departure.

But as the decade turned, so too did Atari's fortunes – dramatically. In 1979, Fairchild withdrew from what they saw as a spent market, leaving Atari to sell a million consoles to an effectively undivided audience that year alone (Magnavox's Odyssey 2, while selling respectably, was a minnow in comparison). Then, in 1980, with the only serious competition being Mattel's Johnny-come-lately 16-bit Intellivision, the VCS became the first console to receive a licensed arcade game and hence the first to be able to claim exclusive content: *Space Invaders*. Just for bringing Namco's two-year-old arcade hit into the living room, and for adding over one hundred new gameplay options to it, sales and profits went through the roof, doubling every year until 1982.

The iconic Atari 2600 or VCS, bringing *Space Invaders* out of the arcade and into your living room for the first time.

The great US videogame crash and the rise of the PC

The boom years of the early 1980s wouldn't last long. The US console market was soon to nosedive, setting in motion a number of divestitures within a period now referred to as "the great videogame crash". The rise of home computing (see p.15) was certainly a factor, but poor judgement from Atari was the main culprit.

For starters, credit – both financial and professional – wasn't being given where it was due. Despite the vast amounts of money sloshing around, the company refused even to name-check developers in their games, and increasingly disgruntled staff left to form the first third-party development companies (the first and most significant being Activision, see p.223, a good indication of the level of talent being haemorrhaged). Secondly, Atari's quality control, for various reasons, went out the door, dragging videogames' (and by definition, Atari's) good name through the mud. The public were happy to shell out for Activision's excellent *Pitfall!* (1982) and *Stampede* (1981), but they were repulsed by Mystique's reprehensible *Custer's Revenge* (see p.50) and decidedly short-changed by Atari's flagship *E.T.* (see box). Atari even managed to stuff up their 1981 licensed port of *Pac-Man*.

Furthermore, the market was getting crowded. In 1982, Coleco not only released their superior Colecovision, they looked at the Atari-Namco alliance and raised the stakes, creating a formidable partnership with Sega, Konami, Universal and Nintendo (whose *Donkey Kong* would get its US debut in 1981); and the home PC market, Commodore especially, began to steal away great swathes of gamers (see p.15). Atari found itself deep in the red, and in 1984 Warner sold everything but the arcade division (renamed Atari Games) to

E.T. – THE GAME THAT PHONED IN ITS PERFORMANCE

Basing a game on the Spielberg megahit seemed like such a no-brainer that in 1982 Atari was willing to pay out a reputed twenty-odd million dollars for rights to produce *E.T. The Extra Terrestrial*. Only big sales could recoup the outlay, so it was vital that the game hit the shelves in time for Christmas. Unfortunately for developer Howard Scott Warshaw, the rights negotiations had lasted so long there were just six weeks left to achieve this.

All credit to Warshaw for making it happen, but no kudos to Atari for expecting anything other than the most basic of releases. Often cited as the worst game of all time for its excruciating dullness, the

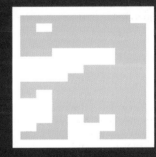

gameplay is thus: E.T. floats down into a hole to retrieve a telephone component; E.T. floats up and along to the next hole. Ad infinitum. Except for an occasional glitch that sees E.T. get stuck in aforesaid holes.

Sales of around one million were surprisingly good given its critical mauling, but Atari was still faced with the dilemma of what to do with the other four million copies it had optimistically produced. The answer, perhaps apocryphal, is that they were dumped the following year in a secure New Mexico landfill site at night, to prevent witnesses and deter scavengers. True or not, the story is vastly more intriguing than the game.

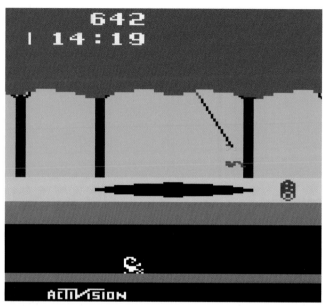

642
| 14:19

ACTIVISION

If not for Activision's *Pitfall!* there would be no *Tomb Raider*, no *Prince of Persia*...

1972) and the astonishingly foresighted *Maze War* (1974), which not only created the non-arcade, first-person-perspective game, it was also the very first networked game – but they remained well away from the public at large. Interim developments such as ARPAnet (the Internet's predecessor), Intel's evolving microchips, IBM's floppy disk format and the 1975 Altair, the self-build kit that popularized the concept of the Personal Computer (and for which Harvard freshman Bill Gates co-created BASIC), were surely leading up to something.

The arrival of the Apple I and Apple II, Radio Shack's TRS-80 and the Commodore PET continued the trend, but it took the PET's 1980 budget build, the VIC-20, to really set PC gaming on fire. The bargain price of $300, the fact that it was marketed as a grown-up home-office machine-cum-educational tool *and* took cartridge- and cassette-loaded games meant it ticked pretty much every requirement for each member of the household. It was also a cinch to programme and was taken to the bosom of an entire generation of budding game developers.

Jack Tramiel – the founder of nemesis Commodore – as Atari Corp. The shockwaves were catastrophic: third-party developers went bust; Coleco stopped fully supporting the Colecovision, which stalled; and Mattel sold off their electronics division, along with the Intellivision, after crippling losses.

Home computing geeks, unite!

Tramiel could tell which way the wind was blowing: his first act was to suspend production of the VCS in favour of making 16-bit computers. Ever since *Space-war!*, prohibitive costs had ensured that computers were for offices and institutions rather than the home. Games were written for them – such as the text-based adventures *Hunt the Wumpus* and *Adventure* (both

Almost simultaneously, a raft of other PCs made their way into gamers' hearts and minds: the first BBC Microcomputer (1981), Acorn's Electron (1983), Sir Clive Sinclair's super-low-budget (and tech) ZX80 (1980), ZX81 (the Timex Sinclair 1000 in the US; both 1981) and ZX Spectrum (1982), and the VIC-20's successor, the Commodore 64 (1982). Commodore continued to smother any of Tramiel's efforts at breaking into the PC market with its Amiga (1985), though there was some comfort for Atari: worldwide affection for the venerable VCS ensured it wasn't officially discontinued until 1992.

The number of games across all platforms consequently exploded and splintered in a fashion that was virtually impossible to measure. Genres, licences and rip-offs, and freeware and shareware abounded as hobby shops and department stores overflowed with colourfully packaged cassettes, floppies and carts and even hard-copy program code. Piracy, a relatively easy accomplishment in the PC world, was particularly prevalent, with many a teen uncovering the black arts of hacking in order to distribute copies of *Manic*

Miner, *Chuckie Egg* (both 1983) or *Sabre Wulf* (1984) to friends. Building on the long-established gaming fanzine scene (the equivalent of today's fansites and modding communities), the first consumer magazines began catering to gamers of all stripes with the UK's *Computer and Video Games* and the US's *Electronic Games Magazine*, sating a thirst for knowledge on the upcoming releases and hints and tips on the latest hits. In fact, unless you were a console manufacturer, the crash of 1983 was very much a blink-of-the-eye affair.

GAME, SET & WATCH

Despite falling prices, the cost of home consoles in the 1970s and 1980s was still prohibitive to many. Milton Bradley, recognizing this, had produced the handheld cartridge-based Microvision in 1979 with the rather tempting price tag of $50 or so, but a double-whammy of poor-quality hardware and a tiny library of games meant that it sank without trace in 1981 in the face of Atari's ascendancy.

Step forward Nintendo's Gunpei Yokoi who, so the story goes, on observing a bored commuter playing aimlessly with his digital calculator, decided to come up with a digital watch that would also play a game. The prosaically named Game & Watch that hit the shelves in 1980 was the size of small notepad, its simple LCD screen with its printed overlay playing just one game according to the version you purchased – but at a price that was within reach of a fortnight's worth of pocket-money savings. Not only was it a huge hit, its revolutionary d-pad system became the blueprint for console controllers thereafter, with the player manipulating the onscreen action with their left thumb and action buttons with their right. It also laid the groundwork for the Game Boy (see p.12), and in its various different guises introduced a new audience to such characters as Donkey Kong and the Mario brothers, in the form of a dual-screen Game & Watch that prefigured the layout of the Nintendo DS.

Nintendo's Game & Watch was the ultimate hi-tech toy, fought over in the back seat of cars the world over.

The invasion of Japanese videogames

It might have appeared to the US that the entire videogames industry had been pronounced dead after the crash of 1983, but this wasn't the case in Japan or indeed much of the rest of the world. In fact, the market looked positive enough for Nintendo to release its first home console in 1983, the 8-bit Famicom (short for Family Computer), a system whose overwhelming success changed the business of videogames forever.

The NES hits the US

The Famicom, which had sold around 3 million units by the end of 1984, was aided by decent home versions of favourite arcade games like *Donkey Kong*, played using a controller whose cross-button d-pad design has been echoed in every Nintendo controller since, including the Wii remote. Now that it had its own hardware, Nintendo stopped licensing its software to other console manufacturers – from now on, if you wanted to play a Nintendo game, you would have to buy a Nintendo machine.

Following on from its success at home, Nintendo attempted to work with Atari to market the system in the US, but the deal fell through in what was just one of many clashes between the companies. Left to its own devices, Nintendo's small American operation launched the Famicom, as the sophisticated-sounding Nintendo Entertainment System, or NES, in New York and Los Angeles in October 1985. Hard hit by the crash, retailers were reluctant to invest in what might be another short-lived fad, but as a point of difference the NES came with a light gun – the first "Zapper" – and, even better, Nintendo was offering it on a sale or return basis. The risk paid off well enough that the launch was extended nationwide in February 1986.

Believing it was the quality of games rather than the hardware that had torpedoed its predecessors, Nintendo maintained a strict control over the games released for the NES. As well as producing a limited number of its own titles, it introduced a system of licensing games from other developers such as Capcom, Konami, Namco and Taito. The way this worked was rather restrictive: developers were only allowed to produce five games per year and they had to be exclusive to Nintendo for two years after that, terms that were enforced by Nintendo's use of proprietary hardware and security chips that prevented anyone else from producing NES cartridges.

During the first few years of the NES, there may not have been as many games as there were for the Atari systems, but it was quality over quantity with titles like 1985's *Super Mario Bros.* (still the bestselling, not to mention most influential videogame of all time),

The basic NES controller, featuring the A, B and d-pad that still grace today's Wii remote.

Legend of Zelda, Metroid, Castlevania and, in Japan, *Dragon Quest* (all 1986) and *Final Fantasy* (1987) – all of which are still going strong more than twenty years later. By the strength of its games, Nintendo built a rock-solid brand identity. Its characters were household names and its own name became synonymous with the word videogames.

Sega enters the market

1986 was a very good year for Nintendo, but that didn't stop a new contender from entering the ring. Still primarily a successful arcade producer, Sega had loads of well-known properties to help sell its console, the 8-bit Master System. And even though the NES cost nearly fifty percent more and didn't look nearly as cool, Sega had nowhere near the marketing power of Nintendo and failed to make much of a dent in the US market. It was, however, a lot more popular in the UK, where it was released in 1987.

As with the Dreamcast in later years, technically Sega was ahead of the game, the Master System sporting a much faster processor and more RAM, but as Nintendo continued to prove, it was the quality of games that sold a system, not the hardware. Nintendo's practice of keeping its developers in handcuffs was soon to end,

Compare this recognizable, but pixilated early Mario to the later incarnation featured on p.190.

though. Having signed a licence to produce games for the NES, Atari had its developers secretly working on a way to circumvent the security chip, allowing it to release its own games for the system in 1988. It then promptly took Nintendo to court claiming the company's practices constituted an unfair monopoly. Nintendo won the case, but this was just one of several legal battles that no doubt influenced its eventual decision to drop the exclusivity clause in its licensing agreement.

Sega Mega Drive and the Game Boy

It wasn't long before Sega came back with a much stronger offering in the 16-bit Mega Drive (released as the Genesis in the US in 1989), based on its arcade-machine technology, which meant that arcade gamers could get home versions of favourites like Yu Suzuki's *Hang-On*, *Space Harrier* and *OutRun*. Now that they were free to do so, the companies working with

Nintendo, such as Capcom, began producing games for Sega's system, too, as did computer-game-oriented publishers like Electronic Arts, which brought with it strategic titles such as Bullfrog's *Populous* (1989). Boasting twice the power of its predecessor or the NES, it had a year's head start on Nintendo's next home console.

Its console may have been losing ground, but Nintendo was indisputable champion in the handheld arena. The Game Boy, released in Japan and the US in 1989 (the following year in Europe), was the first handheld to use changeable cartridges, and remains the biggest selling handheld to date. Crucial to its success was Nintendo's legal victory over Atari for the rights to publish a home version of the most addictive game in history, *Tetris*. Competitors Atari Lynx and Sega Game Gear may have had colour graphics and a glossy, hi-tech sexiness, but they were far less pocketable, their batteries ran out more quickly, and they were ultimately a footnote.

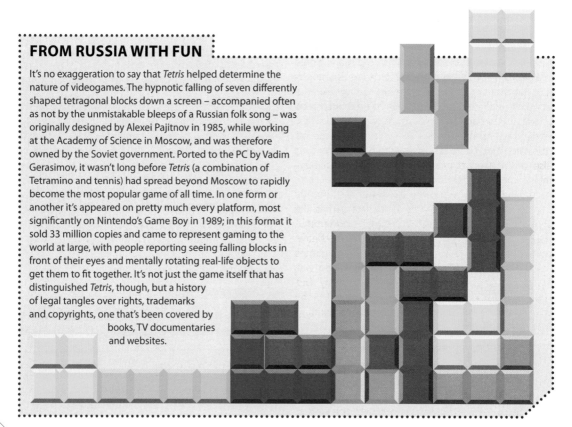

FROM RUSSIA WITH FUN

It's no exaggeration to say that *Tetris* helped determine the nature of videogames. The hypnotic falling of seven differently shaped tetragonal blocks down a screen – accompanied often as not by the unmistakable bleeps of a Russian folk song – was originally designed by Alexei Pajitnov in 1985, while working at the Academy of Science in Moscow, and was therefore owned by the Soviet government. Ported to the PC by Vadim Gerasimov, it wasn't long before *Tetris* (a combination of Tetramino and tennis) had spread beyond Moscow to rapidly become the most popular game of all time. In one form or another it's appeared on pretty much every platform, most significantly on Nintendo's Game Boy in 1989; in this format it sold 33 million copies and came to represent gaming to the world at large, with people reporting seeing falling blocks in front of their eyes and mentally rotating real-life objects to get them to fit together. It's not just the game itself that has distinguished *Tetris*, though, but a history of legal tangles over rights, trademarks and copyrights, one that's been covered by books, TV documentaries and websites.

SNES vs Sonic

The 16-bit Super Famicom or SNES was released in time for Christmas 1991. As expected, it got a new Mario game (*Super Mario World*) and *Legend of Zelda*, plus Rare's outstanding *Donkey Kong Country* (see p.251); it also played host to some of the best RPGs produced by Square and Enix. Nintendo's solid territories, however, had been eroded by the more powerful Mega Drive.

For the first time, armed with a new CEO with a marketing background, Sega was in the game, targeting a more mature and edgy market, as exemplified by aggressive advertising campaigns that bashed Nintendo, plus of course their antidote to Mario, Sonic the Hedgehog (see box). Whereas the podgy Italian plumber was a plucky underdog who never got the princess, Sonic was a spiky-haired ball of speed with a bad attitude and running shoes. Accompanied by yowling rock music, *Sonic the Hedgehog* showed off the speed and power of the Mega Drive like nothing else, and firmly positioned it as a system that boys might want once they'd outgrown Nintendo.

And it worked, for a while. In the end, though, Nintendo's brand loyalty, plus innovative games like *Super Mario Kart* (see p.241), won out. The addition of the Mega-CD, intended to give the system a technical boost, was an expensive flop without enough games to take advantage of it. Meanwhile, Nintendo was working on a CD-ROM drive, too, with Sony, but dropped it when Sega's version floundered. Sony continued working on it, however, with devastating results.

The rise of the arcade brawler

So many options for the home had put a damper on the popularity of arcade machines, but every now and then a game would come out with the kind of

SONIC'S CV

Yuji Naka and Sonic Team's spiky blue mascot has been almost as prolific as his rival Mario, his games ranging from the first 2D side-scroller (which had Game Gear owners desperately trying to reach the end before the batteries ran out); to kart-racing games; to party games such as *Sonic Shuffle*; and even an arcade beat-'em-up. There was also the Dreamcast's high-quality 3D *Adventures* series (which included the incongruous Tamagotchi-like "chao" farming feature) and games where Sonic takes second place to foxy sidekick Tails or Knuckles the Echidna.

Sonic games were never about the puzzles, the new moves, nor even fighting Dr Robotnik/Eggman, but about one thing: speed. The anarchic hedgehog's at his best when racing, bounding off springs in a pinball machine, whizzing across the lush Emerald zone, or grinding snow-rails to cross heart-stopping gaps, all the while collecting jingling gold rings. Historically, though, Sonic enjoyed equal billing with Mario for only a short time, and is now something of a faded star, best seen in his old games and a few select recent appearances.

Here's a conservative list of the main entries in Sonic's canon, not including compilations:

1991 – *Sonic the Hedgehog*
1992 – *Sonic the Hedgehog 2*
1993 – *Sonic CD*
1994 – *Sonic the Hedgehog 3*
1994 – *Sonic & Knuckles*
1996 – *Sonic 3D*
1999 – *Sonic Adventure*
2001 – *Sonic Adventure 2*
2002 – *Sonic Advance*
2003 – *Sonic Advance 2*
2004 – *Sonic Advance 3*
2005 – *Sonic Rush*
2006 – *Sonic The Hedgehog*
2007 – *Sonic and the Secret Rings*
2007 – *Sonic Rush Adventure*

appeal that saw cabinets sprout up everywhere. By far the biggest game of 1991, *Street Fighter II* packed out arcades and gave the SNES a welcome boost in sales when Capcom announced it as an exclusive title. Amongst the glut of arcade beat-'em-up conversions that followed there was another that would have a long-term impact on the industry – Midway's *Mortal Kombat*, whose characters' gory finishing moves were aptly known as "fatalities". Reproduced on the Mega Drive and SNES by Acclaim, the Nintendo version had been edited to remove the most offensive bits (with sweat droplets instead of blood, for example) and for this reason was less desirable than Sega's full version. This distinction formed an integral part of the 1993 US congressional hearings about violent videogames and the selling of them to children, a topic that has remained in the spotlight ever since. With so much at stake, the hearings quickly turned into a Nintendo vs Sega battle, with Sega claiming that its voluntary ratings system meant it was more, rather than less, responsible than Nintendo. One outcome of the hearings was the adoption of an industry-wide ratings system (the ESRB) still in existence today.

Mortal Kombat
Arcade, SNES; Midway, Acclaim; 1992

While *Street Fighter II* features combat as art form, *Mortal Kombat* provides exactly what it says on the tin. Liberal amounts of gore are integral to the game, since the fighters are only distinguished in gameplay by their special moves and fatalities, most memorably Sub-Zero's pulling off an opponent's head with dangling spine attached. Almost as intriguing as these fatalities was the existence of a secret ninja, Reptile, who would only appear under circumstances so rare that he was thought by many to be a myth. Later games in the series have adopted 3D and differing fighting styles, but for players who thrive on subtlety, *MK* is never going to be top of the pile.

It was the depiction of blood – or lack of it – that put *Mortal Kombat* at the centre of 1993's congressional hearings on violence in games.

The PC strides forth

While *Sonic* and *Mario* duked it out in the console wars, the battle for dominance in the land of the PC was no less frenetic. Heavy hitters such as Hewlett-Packard, IBM, Apple and Compaq strove against each other with their proprietary machines, while Intel and Microsoft rose to dominate the chip and operating-system markets, respectively. Often regarded as the second golden age of PC gaming, by today's standards things were still primitive and just installing games – especially before Windows' ubiquity – required a working knowledge of DOS. But the upshot for gamers was that processors had become fast enough to produce some then-impressive pixel-counts, allowing for improved graphics, while CD-ROM drives, in existence since 1984, had advanced enough to work in conjunction with sound cards – especially those from Creative Labs – to take PC games into the multimedia arena.

Indeed, full motion video (FMV) and pre-rendered graphics read straight from CD-ROMs – necessary as hard drives and RAM quantities were still minuscule – looked like the future for a while, something the astonishing success of 1993's *Myst* (see p.182) only served to endorse. Some learned the lesson well: Westwood's *Command & Conquer* (see p.71), whose cheerfully cheesy cut scenes propelled the plot forward at a preposterously enjoyable rate, was a great example of successful integration. Others stumbled, not least because creating FMV often meant producing movie-quality footage, with its attendant costs.

Big-bucks and high-end technology weren't everything, however. Despite being distributed via then-cutting-edge shareware, the huge success of *Doom* (see p.17) was actually a miracle of data compression and astute use of resources. The low-CPU-intensive *Lemmings* (see p.17) and the decidedly languorous *Sid Meier's Civilization* (see p.176), *SimCity*

Wing Comander III: Heart of the Tiger
PC, Mac; Origin Systems; 1994

The hugely popular Wing Commander space-combat series from Origin, in its 1994 incarnation *Wing Commander III: Heart of the Tiger*, came on like (and was often touted as) an interactive CGI movie. Its then unprecedented budget of $4 million gave it access to a cast that included Malcolm McDowell, Mark Hamill and Tim Curry and the kind of production technology that only George Lucas usually benefits from. Impressive as that was, its po-faced script and repetitive gameplay came off a distinct second.

(see p.260) from Will Wright (see p.258) and *Populous* (see p.248) from Peter Molyneux (see p.247) also showed that the low- to mid-range home PC was perfectly capable of capturing players' imaginations through gameplay alone. And ostensibly traditional games, such as the 1989 platformer *Prince of Persia* (see p.155), served notice that tweaking long-established conventions could produce results as enthralling as any multimedia package.

The popularity of roleplaying games (RPGs) too, a genre that had migrated from academic mainframes to the PCs at the turn of the 1970s with Automated Simulations' *Temple of Apshai* and *Akalabeth: World of Doom* from Richard Garriot, was now booming. Along the way, seminal titles such as the *Wizardry* series from Sir-Tech, beginning in 1981, *Might and Magic* (1986) from New World Computing, Dynamicro's *Dungeons of Daggarath* (1982) and SSI's *Pools of Radiance* (1986) all helped lay the foundations for the first fully 3D RPG, *Ultima Underworld* (1991), itself a massive influence on the open-world gameplay of 1994's *Elder Scrolls* (see p.78).

Myst
Mac, PC; Brøderbund; 1993

The product of a new digital era, *Myst* was the first game to push contemporary home-computing multimedia capabilities to the max. It was also the antithesis of the kind of adrenaline-fuelled, violence-driven gameplay promoted by the likes of its contemporary *Doom*, reaching out well beyond the hardcore audience to create gamers from those who had once viewed their Mac or PC as a mere home-office tool. But the lack of a driving narrative and some wilfully obtuse puzzles, all presented with a minimum of documentation, led to accusations that it was merely an interactive slideshow. Others pointed to its unprecedented, beautifully rendered setting inspired by Jules Verne's *The Mysterious Island*, and its evocative soundtrack, arguing that its immersive, hypnotic universe was its very *raison d'être*. Ultimately, its notorious challenge and renowned atmosphere proved an irresistible combination, with over twelve million copies of the game and its sequels sold to date across a variety of platforms.

Myst's isolated, atmospheric islands boast a leisurely trail of puzzles to help you solve the brothers' mystery. This aerial view offers a good frame of reference for any given location.

WHAT PLACE, NOSTALGIA?

Sometimes it pays to be harsh on history. Back in the 1990s, for example, gamers were raving about contemporary superhits as the greatest ever invented – and there were several that, at the time, fitted that label. Things move on, however: while it owes its very existence to *Doom*, there's no way *Half-Life 2* would cede its place in the canon to the former in terms of gameplay and design. Such titles are interesting from an historical perspective, but only those looking for a nostalgia hit will really derive much value from them; others will most certainly get more out of later games.

Likewise, the point-and-click adventure, while receiving a massive boost from *Myst*'s success, had been bending the minds of gamers for years before. LucasArts in particular had been instrumental in popularizing the genre thanks to their admirable quest to constantly reframe gameplay and their healthy injections of knowing humour. Their 1990-debuting *Loom* and the *Monkey Island* series (see p.141) whetted the public's appetite for further bestsellers, including their *Indiana Jones* franchise and *Sam & Max Hit the Road*, and the adventure-cum-puzzler *Gabriel Knight* series from Sierra. Usually featuring colourful 2D artwork, and so remaining processor friendly, the genre was to reach its apotheosis in the mid-1990s with the great *Broken Sword* games (see p.66), the superlative *Grim Fandango* (see p.103), and *Discworld* (1995), the game many felt the genre was born for.

Wolfenstein 3D
PC, Mac; id Software; 1992

Of id Software's two defining moments in the history of the first-person-shooter (FPS), it was *Wolfenstein 3D* that first put them and the genre firmly on the gaming map (see below for the second). The testosterone-fuelled gameplay proved so popular that the PC game was ported to over half-a-dozen other platforms.

For all its heady mix of weaponry, buckets of blood and high body count, the tongue-in-cheek campness running throughout – from its opening instruction "You're William J. 'B.J.' Blazkowicz, the Allies' bad boy of espionage and terminal action seeker" to selectable difficulty levels named "Can I Play Daddy" and "I Am Death Incarnate" – heavily mitigated its violence and use of Nazi imagery, but not to the satisfaction of all. Completely banned in Germany in 1994, even the US SNES release saw the blood substituted for sweat, and Nazi guard dogs replaced by mutant rodents after complaints from animal rights activists. Human rights groups, conversely, were mute.

Doom
PC; id Software; 1993

Buoyed by the success of *Wolfenstein 3D*, creators John Carmack and John Romero set about making, in the latter's words, "the most badass game in the history of the planet Earth". They succeeded with the monster-splattering fest *Doom*, with its vast range of weaponry (including the fondly remembered BFG 9000, which does *not* stand for Big Friendly Giant), zombies and satanic imagery, a heavy-metal soundtrack, the replacement of the health bar with an increasingly bloodied face icon, and difficulty levels labelled "Nightmare!" and "Ultra Violence".

Single-player mode was a blast, and its relatively low-spec requirements certainly helped spread its popularity, but it was the introduction of *Doom's* network gaming that really saw it take off. While not the first multiplayer FPS, it was the first to do it by LAN, enabling the estimated ten million users who downloaded the freeware version to take part in deathmatches across educational and office networks worldwide. In a fitting act of bravado, id had predicted that *Doom's* release would become "the number one cause of decreased productivity in businesses around the world". They weren't far off. One of the first institutions to ban staffers from playing it was the company providing the game's very lifeblood: Intel.

Lemmings
Amiga, PC; Psygnosis; 1991

Ostensibly a puzzle game, *Lemmings* also verges into platform and real-time strategy (RTS) territories by virtue of the way players exert immediate control over the cute-but-dim creatures across landscapes strewn with fatal dangers. Hazards can be removed or circumvented – individual lemmings can be put to the greater good by building bridges across chasms and digging tunnels under mountains, or even, and more entertainingly, by blowing themselves up – but shepherding their relentless advance entails the kind of multitasking more normally associated with air-traffic control duty. Or perhaps something more fiendishly addictive: even the prolific Terry Pratchett clearly found his productivity affected by the game: "Not only did I wipe *Lemmings* from my hard disc, I overwrote it so's I couldn't get it back."

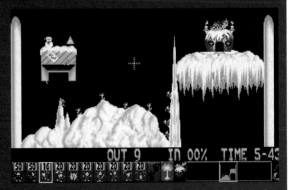

Screens may have varied in theme and difficulty, but the task was always the same: to save the little red lemmings from themselves.

The battle of 32-bits and the last cartridge console

For a while it seemed that gorgeous-looking games were the sole prerogative of computer gamers, but with a shift to 32-bit processors, console games were once again in the limelight. With the new generation of consoles, developers benefited from more colours and faster processing speeds, allowing for more detail, more realistic textures, genuine 3D, and basically a lot more stuff happening onscreen. And with CDs as the medium there was now space for video scenes, bigger worlds and crisper sound. When a successful home electronics manufacturer entered a market still dominated by companies with a background in arcade machines, it was clear that console gaming was primed to enter the mainstream in a way it hadn't since the birth of the NES.

Sega's 32-bit offerings

Sega was giving its fans ever more ways to spend money. On top of the Mega Drive CD, in late 1994 it released the 32X, a contraption that plugged into the cartridge slot and allowed higher-spec games to be played on either cartridge or, with the add-on, CD. Bizarrely, at almost exactly the same time, the company released its first genuine 32-bit CD-based console, the Saturn, in Japan, where massive demand was fuelled by ports of various arcade titles, including *Virtua Fighter*. In the US, Sega announced the Saturn's launch as anticipated in May 1995 at the first Electronic Entertainment Expo (the trade show later known as E3); completely unexpected, though, was the revelation that a number of consoles had already shipped, four months early, in a bid to beat Sony's PlayStation. This merely added to the confusion, however, as no one now wanted the 32X at all, and the following year Sega stopped making games for the Mega Drive altogether. Developers, on the other hand, weren't entirely happy with the new console, considering it unnecessarily rushed and, thanks to its two processors, difficult to program for.

"Do not underestimate the power of PlayStation"

Nintendo may have left Sony stranded with an unwanted SNES CD attachment, but in doing so it unwittingly opened the door to a new contender, and one that would dominate the industry for years to come. Turning the disaster to its advantage, Sony took the brave decision to go it alone in a market where many had fallen by the wayside, taking on not just Sega but Nintendo itself with a new CD-based console, the PlayStation. But the company was blessed with one of the most reliable names in electronics and its confidence turned out to be well founded. When it was released in Japan, just after the Saturn – with a fraction of the press clamour and public demand – no one would have predicted that Sony had an even greater, more significant success on its hands than it had enjoyed with the Walkman.

September 1995 was the launch date in the US and Europe, but unlike the Saturn, there was no shortage of either consoles or games, and as if that wasn't enough, the console was 25 percent cheaper than the competition. Third-party developers, offered access to brand-new, programmer-friendly technology (the PlayStation processor was built primarily to optimize 3D graphics) had queued up to work with Sony, giving

WIPEOUT

WipEout is the game credited with taking consoles out of teenage boys' bedrooms and into the Ecstasy-fuelled clubworld of the mid-90s. An exhilarating racer developed by Sony-owned Psygnosis, it was the epitome of cool, not least due to a licensed soundtrack featuring the likes of Chemical Brothers, Prodigy, Leftfield and Orbital.

Anonymous pilots represented teams such as United Europe's Feisar or the USA's Auricom Research Industries in the Anti-Gravity Racing Federation of 2105, zooming round desertscapes and snowscenes, but most memorably neon-lit, darkly urban racetracks. The delicate craft were prone to crashing and exploding in flames if not handled with enough skill around the heartstopping switchbacks and corkscrews, picking up speedboosts, missiles and shields along the way. Even if the gameplay wasn't entirely dissimilar, the character-driven karts of the

Several iterations down the line, *WipEout*'s urban nighttime tracks still make for a uniquely exhilarating experience.

Mushroom Kingdom were culturally a million light years away. Stylized right down to the instruction booklet created by The Designers Republic, the series has never been able to repeat its astonishing first appearance, but has still continued to pump out high-quality games, featuring new weapons, bigger and better multiplayer technology, plus new takes on favourite tracks – the Special Edition version of *Wip3out* even lets you race around blueprint sketches of unbuilt courses.

1995 – WipEout (PS, also on PlayStation Network)
1996 – WipEout 2097/WipEout XL (PS)
1999 – Wip3out (PS)
2002 – WipEout Fusion (PS2)

2005 – WipEout Pure (PSP)
2007 – WipEout Pulse (PSP)
2008 – WipEout HD (PlayStation Network for PS3)

the PlayStation significantly more titles than any of its competitors. And while Sega's games were aimed at giving hardcore gamers their fix of arcade and Japanese console favourites, Sony was aiming for a broader base, not even bothering to produce minority-appeal RPGs (see p.22). Early games like *Ridge Racer* (1994), *Tekken*, *Mortal Kombat 3* (both 1995) and *WipEout* (see box) were joined in 1996 by the crowd-pleasing *Crash Bandicoot*, *Formula One* and *Tomb Raider*.

Despite press attempts to set *Crash* up alongside *Sonic* and *Mario*, Sony refused to adopt a character mascot, opting instead for a more revolutionary style of marketing, often subverting popular prejudices, for example in the SCEE commercial, where people of diverse ages, genders and abilities talked about having "commanded armies and conquered worlds" in their double lives, or the infamous SAPS (Society Against PlayStation) ads. Sega may have said that games

Sony denied him as their mascot, but the Bandicoot's anarchic style and lush backdrops spoke volumes about the PlayStation all the same.

weren't just for kids, but now Sony shouted it, the ubiquitous square, circle, triangle and cross icons on clothing, TV, and at sponsored sports events bringing gaming into the sphere of those who had never even seen a videogame, let alone played one. Add into the mix the extensive games library, and suddenly, from out of nowhere, everyone either had or was planning to get a PlayStation.

Nintendo's belated reply

Meanwhile, over at Nintendo, 1995 saw the release of the Virtual Boy, a thrilling-sounding but impossibly flawed contraption, designed by Gunpei Yokoi, creator of the Game Boy, to deliver genuine 3D gaming. Resembling an optometry-testing machine more than a console, it was pricey and the LED graphics gave people headaches; it never got as far as the UK.

As with the SNES, Nintendo were late entering the race with their next main console, which underwent several name changes before it was released in Japan in mid-1996 as the Nintendo 64, reaching the US in September, and Europe six months later. Surprisingly, the move to 64-bit processing was not accompanied

by a move to the disc-based media used by Sony and Sega; instead, Nintendo intended to continue producing games on cartridge. The explanation was that the format allowed game speed to be maintained (and it's true, there were no whirry loading screens on the N64) and would prevent games being copied. But proprietary cartridges were obviously far more expensive to produce than mass market discs, and this was one reason for a fall in the number of third-party games developed for the N64.

Another was the appeal for developers of working in a format that gave them more storage space. In a famously acrimonious split, Square, the company responsible for the *Final Fantasy* series, announced it would be working with Sony exclusively in order to pursue an artistic vision of cinematic roleplaying games that simply wasn't possible with a Gamepak. In many ways, though, the N64 was revolutionary: boasting four controller slots for multiplayer gaming, and with a weird-looking controller that sprouted the first analog stick, plus a plug-in rumble feature, both quickly adopted by Sony.

The Pokémon phenomenon

There may not have been a whole lot of titles for the N64 – although they did include, in *GoldenEye 007* (see p.95) *Legend of Zelda: Ocarina of Time* (see p.122) and *Super Mario 64*, (see p.190) some of the best games ever made – but in 1996 Nintendo had Japan at its feet regardless, with a cute, monochrome RPG for the Game Boy, called *Pocket Monsters*. From the outset it came in two versions, *Green* and *Red*, so that players could use the Game Boy link cable to trade monsters – the designer, Satoshi Tajiri, was famously influenced by his own childhood hobby of catching insects, plus the desire to swap with his friends items found in the *Dragon Quest* game (see p.255).

This early *Pokémon* screen is barely comparable with today's multi-million-dollar franchise, although gameplay has stuck to a successful RPG-lite formula.

With an unprecedented sleeper hit on its hands at home, Nintendo's marketing departments took their time preparing for the international launch of *Pokémon Red* and *Pokémon Blue* (US 1998, Europe 1999), and with the Saturday morning cartoons, which started a few weeks earlier, racking up massive viewing figures, plus comics, a trading card game, lunchboxes and all manner of related products in place, Nintendo was able to fully exploit what became a worldwide craze. Pikachu and his fellow *pokémon* were barely out of the newspapers: cards were banned in schools for causing playground fights, religious scrutiny focused on the game's notions of evolution, but *Pokémon* was also graced with papal approval for its message of friendship. In many ways the game itself, despite selling over 140 million copies in its first ten years, has been overtaken or at least equalled by its own spinoffs.

Pokémon Diamond and Pearl
DS; Nintendo; 2007

Maybe it's not the phenomenon it once was, but the DS versions of Pokémon still sold over 1.5 million copies in their first week. Retaining the familiar, mostly 2D style but with some graphical embellishments, it exploits DS technology without doing anything to alienate fans of the long-running series. When the media's all about marketing and materialistic fervour, it's easy to overlook the fact that Pokémon is in many ways a classic (if simplified) Japanese RPG, as much about world exploration, and nurturing these monsters with their cleverly localized names, as about collecting them.

Travelling through Sinnoh, there are constant choices about how to develop your *pokémon*: upgrading them, breeding them, putting them into frequent turn-based battles to level up. All this to achieve a balanced fighting team that will eventually help save the world from the big bad gym leaders. And even when the main game is finished, there are more monsters to collect to complete the Pokédex (heading towards 500 in total, including those from earlier games), some rarer than others. Uniquely, this fourth generation utilizes the DS's Wi-Fi connectivity to give the social side of the game the prominence it's always sought, and as well as allowing play with friends, it provides a kind of automated swap shop for the trading of *pokémon* all around the world.

Shinx is a leonine pokémon with the power to dazzle enemies with its electric glow.

MADE IN JAPAN

Many of the geeks programming computer games in the early 1980s grew up playing paper-and-dice *Dungeons & Dragons* in the late 1970s, so it isn't entirely surprising to see how much roleplaying games influenced the early home computer era. There was no equivalent for console gamers, though, who weren't necessarily so technically adept.

Being a fan of computer RPGs, Yuji Horii, a designer at Japanese publisher Enix, decided to create a simplified roleplaying game for the Famicom (NES), one that was designed to appeal to the mainstream Japanese audience and provide them with the kind of experience enjoyed by players of *Ultima* and the like. *Dragon Quest*, the first Japanese console RPG, released in 1986 (in the US as *Dragon Warrior* in 1989), marked the beginning of a new genre and of a schism in RPGs that continues until today. Not long

Elemental spells cast by pointy-hatted mages have been *Final Fantasy* stalwarts since the early days of the series.

The biggest RPG series in Japan, *Dragon Quest* has only sporadically been accessible to English-speaking gamers.

after, Hironobu Sakaguchi produced what he thought would be his last game before leaving Squaresoft, *Final Fantasy* (1987, in the US 1990; see p.83), and together these two series have dominated console RPGs, long one of the pre-eminent genres in Japan.

During the Famicom era, *Dragon Quest* was so popular that kids skived off school to buy the third in the series, leading the Japanese parliament to decree that subsequent instalments could only be released on Sundays or holidays. Meanwhile, Western gamers were still mostly wed to their computer RPGs, but this scenario began to change as more games made it across the Pacific to the US and eventually Europe. The two companies shared the market until a merger in 2003 (see p.255). Nowadays, the latest releases by Square Enix are an evolution of those early games – some might say not quite evolved enough – and while they show the influence of Western RPGs (vice versa is also true), they also adhere firmly to the elements that made them distinct in the first place.

Worlds apart

Thanks to BioWare and more recently Bethesda, computer RPGs have been expanding into the console environment, not coincidentally since the Xbox came onto the scene, but it would be difficult for anyone to confuse the two types. For a start, they look completely different. Japanese RPG characters, even in the latest games where they are designed and animated to look like real people (for instance in *Final Fantasy XII*), retain some level of manga/anime styling. Typically cute, ill-proportioned characters were a necessity back when realism was technologically impossible, and however alien they might have seemed to a neophyte *Final Fantasy VII* player, this had always been the accepted graphic style in their native territory. On the other hand, early games were firmly entrenched in the D&D-style medieval European world setting, only later shifting into sci-fi and steampunk futures.

More fundamental than looks, however, is the Japanese RPG's much stronger focus on character and story; they really aren't roleplaying games in a traditional sense at all, since the characters are not of the player's choosing. Since they don't rely on the player for cues, games tend to feature more dramatic stories, and can boast an emotional power that's absent from many Western RPGs. By the same token, there's not quite as much freedom to explore the world: as the characters are directly involved in the storyline, there has to be a prescribed (if not strictly linear) route through the game – you can't ignore the plot, as you can in many Western offerings. Even though characters are pre-written and often pre-named, tweaking them is a significant part of levelling up, deciding what spells to focus on, which abilities to prioritize, but still nothing like rolling your own from scratch. This kind of player choice is nonetheless crucial to combat, which tends to feature group rather than one-on-one battles, and asks the player to strategically build a party and come up with team tactics – the origin of *Final Fantasy Tactics* and other so-called tactical RPGs that have emerged from the genre.

Console by console

With *Dragon Quest* and *Final Fantasy* the NES was the cradle of JRPGs, and its successor, the SNES, was built to optimize precisely this kind of gameplay. *Final Fantasy* and *Dragon Quest* continued, though games didn't always to make it to North America and rarely any further afield. *Final Fantasy IV* was only the second of the series to be released in the US where it was renamed *Final Fantasy II*. *Final Fantasy V* took seven years to reach the West and ten before it was available in Europe. The SNES was also home to one of the genre's classic titles: a collaboration between the greatest talents of *Final Fantasy* and *Dragon Quest*, the time-travel epic *Chrono Trigger* was released in Japan and the US in 1995 but never made it to the UK (see p.256).

Meanwhile over at Sega, the hot JRPG property was *Phantasy Star* for the Master System (1988), followed by *Phantasy Star II* for the Mega Drive CD (1989; available via Wii Virtual Console), a series that was clearly influenced by the galaxy-spanning *Star Wars* movies. Another successful series for Sega was *Grandia* (1997), although it didn't appear in the West until a PlayStation port in 1999. Taking a

In a typical example of localization, *Grandia* reached the West with its visible gameworld intact, as shown here, but with all mentions of alcohol removed from its script.

Blue Dragon

Xbox 360; Mistwalker, Microsoft; 2007

Traditional JRPG in stunning high definition, produced by Hironobu Sakaguchi's studio, with characters designed by *Dragon Quest*'s Akira Toriyama and music by *Final Fantasy*'s Nobuo Uematsu. Unsurprisingly, one of the fastest-selling Xbox 360 titles when released in Japan, although it's not as innovative in gameplay as might have been expected.

Dragon Quest VIII: Journey of the Cursed King

PS2; Level 5, Square Enix; 2005

Unbelievably the first *DQ* game to hit the UK and a crescendo of achievement for the team, this is an enchanting, traditional JRPG, with lots of (pretty tough) random encounters, a funny script and superb voice acting by a cast of British actors (including Cockney comedian Ricky Grover). Characters are drawn in cel-shaded 3D style by Akira Toriyama, the manga artist who devised the series look, and the music is scored by Yoichi Sugiyama, whose *DQ* pieces have been committed to dozens of CDs and are performed regularly at live concerts in Japan.

different approach to its contemporaries, it was a far more lighthearted game than the darkly dramatic *Final Fantasy VII*.

Sony's PlayStation was the console that popularized JRPGs, just as it did gaming altogether. The marketing for *FFVII* was effective, resulting in colossal sales figures and perhaps slightly unrealistic expectations based on the stunning cut scenes. Once people had accepted the difference between these and the in-game action, cutesy characters and all, it was as absorbing as any game, and more so than most. Previously, JRPGs in the West were restricted to a niche market, but by focusing on the technology and design, Square and Sony effectively broke into the mainstream. The PlayStation hosted two further *Final Fantasy* games, plus a *Chrono* sequel, *Chrono Cross* (which again didn't make it to Europe).

The Dreamcast wasn't the best console for JRPG fans, featuring *Phantasy Star Online*, the first online console RPG, which could be played solo but was more fun online, plus the non-RPG that was *Shenmue* (see p.257). One bright spot was *Skies of Arcadia*, a sort of airborne *Pirates of the Caribbean* by the same developer as *Phantasy Star I* and *II*, with memorable characters, ship battles and gorgeous environments.

The Xbox 360's first RPG, *Blue Dragon*, was Microsoft's answer to *Final Fantasy*, created by JRPG veterans Hironobu Sakaguchi and Akira Toriyama. Many of the characters, such as Zola (pictured here), were instantly recognizable as Toriyama's creations.

Past meets future

The number of games that never make it out of home territory highlights the difficulties and prohibitive cost involved in translating the lengthy script of a roleplaying game. Enix produced no *Dragon Quest* games outside of Japan between the first NES titles and *Dragon Warrior VII* for the PlayStation; in Europe, the only game of the series to appear was *Dragon Quest VIII*, by which point *Final Fantasy* had the market completely sewn up. And while *Grandia* changed all instances of alcoholic drinks to coffee, to avoid causing offence, it was easier to avoid localization altogether. Luckily, now that so many old console games have found their way onto new systems by official means, many of these missing JRPGs are being reworked for release in the West, with the bonus of new cut scenes. Handheld gamers have always had *Pokémon*, but now they've the stirring stories from the first six *FF* episodes playable on the Game Boy Advance or DS, with the *DQ* series not far behind.

While many of the old games are getting a new audience, the genre continues to develop at a sluggish pace, treading some new ground in game dynamics and artwork, and continuing in many cases to blur the edges with Western games, although some unapologetically bizarre titles, such as *Eternal Sonata*, still make it out of Japan. Inevitably, Japanese RPGs have also had some influence on Western RPGs and, coming full circle, they've even begun to make their mark on the pen-and-paper *Dungeons & Dragons* game.

Eternal Sonata
XBox 360; Tri-Crescendo, Namco/ Atari; 2007

Originality abounds in this charming game whose story takes place in Chopin's mind while he's on his death bed. There's some exciting combat, which gets progressively harder, but that should be set against the slices of Chopin biography, designed to highlight parallels with the real world. The music is, obviously, a key feature.

Final Fantasy Tactics: The War of the Lions
PSP; Square Enix; 2007

A remake of the original PlayStation game from 1998, this turn-based strategy RPG starts off hard and gets more difficult. Set in Ivalice and with gorgeous pencil-shaded cut scenes and an involving, typically epic tale, it looks fantastic, but isn't as forgiving as the earlier spinoff *Final Fantasy Tactics Advance* (2003).

Its anime character stylings verge into too-cute territory, but *Eternal Sonata*'s uniquely bizarre premise adds weight to the visual candy.

Multimedia aspirations

In the late 1990s and early 2000s, the console battle became literally a fight to the death, with the next generation offering a chance for the combatants to re-invent their products in an attempt to win over the gameplaying public. A new contender was to enter the fight in the form of computer software giant Microsoft, with its lossmaking Xbox raising the odds substantially. Meanwhile, Sony's success had demonstrated that it was no longer just about kids' games; instead, the new consoles offered a chance to stake out space at the centre of the home as all-in-one entertainment systems, offering movies, music and the Internet.

Sega gets ahead of itself

Sega hadn't been sleeping while the PlayStation was taking over the market, but working on the world's first "next-generation" console, the 128-bit Dreamcast. It launched in late 1998 in Japan, along with a much anticipated new Sonic game and the usual high-quality arcade conversions, this time *Virtua Fighter 3* and

SoulCalibur. In the West, where it came out in September 1999, it was the Sega Sports titles, and in particular *NFL2K1*, that proved to be the bestsellers.

Not content with merely upping the graphics processor on the PlayStation, Sega had added a built-in modem and announced with plenty of fanfare the dawn of console online gaming via SegaNet, its own dedicated service; despite the marketing, this took a long time to get off the ground, especially in Europe, where the full service never materialized. Although it was pioneering in many ways, the Dreamcast managed to be both ahead of its time and too late, and it had far too little time to consolidate before the arrival of the PS2. Indeed, Sony execs were spoiling the party as soon as it had begun, promising as early as April 1999 a new generation of PlayStation with "supercomputer" specifications, thereby condemning the Dreamcast to death before it had launched – something that even its sponsorship of the Arsenal football team's shirts couldn't help it withstand.

Sales were boosted in late 2000 by massive price cuts and initial shortages of the PS2 (see below), and while five million consoles had been sold by the end of the year, Sega had invested so much in the project that it wasn't enough. The Dreamcast had fallen victim to its own ambition, and just a quarter into 2001 Sega halted production in all territories (although the console emerged again in Japan briefly in 2006). Over its short lifespan,

So beloved was Sega's Dreamcast that rumours of its resurrection regularly appear online even today.

the Dreamcast had boasted some groundbreaking Sega-developed games, and it was in software that the company opted to stake its future. Development departments such as Yuji Naka's Sonic Team and Yu Suzuki's AM2 were allowed to make the games that had so proudly shown off the Dreamcast's capabilities, but now for the PlayStation 2, and later for the Xbox.

PlayStation 2: "the future of entertainment"

Not merely the future of videogames – or so proclaimed Kaz Hirai, then head of Sony Computer Entertainment America, at the E3 event in 2000. Sony wanted their matte black machine – it didn't even look like a games console – to do everything, equipping the PlayStation 2 with the 128-bit "Emotion Engine" and the ability to play DVDs out of the box. At the time, a DVD player was an expensive luxury, and it's thought that this feature was responsible for a good amount of the console's success, especially when it launched in Japan in March 2000 – the console itself sold out in just a few hours but the software wasn't doing as well as expected, though that could also have been due to the so-so quality of the launch titles. Technically, the larger storage space afforded by the DVD format allowed much bigger games, with higher-quality graphics and sound, plus there were new controllers with analog buttons, all of which was very exciting to both consumers and developers. On the downside, the latter were forced to learn a powerful new system in record time – it would be some years before the PS2's engine was fully tested.

After what seemed to be an interminable buildup, the console's arrival in the US in October 2000 was a resounding anticlimax. Manufacturing shortages meant that a pitifully small number of units were available and only half the planned million were rolled out, distributed by advance order. In the UK, it wasn't only the shortages that infuriated, but the fact that Brits were paying £300 and Americans only $300. This unavoidably slow introduction of the console into the market didn't ultimately harm sales, but it did mean a far slower return for the games publishers and developers who'd ploughed money into rushing out PS2 titles for the launch.

Contrary to expectations, the original PlayStation wasn't dropped by Sony, but re-engineered and positioned as the entry-level, child-friendly PSOne. Hardcore PlayStation fans were encouraged to upgrade to the new console not just with the promise of better games, but also because the PS2 was backwardly compatible, something Sega had signally failed to provide with its short-lived consoles and a huge relief to those who had by then built up a decent-sized library of PlayStation games.

Standing vertically, the PS2 (depicted here with additional hard drive) certainly looked like gaming's future, if not the future of entertainment as a whole.

Microsoft muscles in

Hirai's 2000 E3 announcement about the PS2's all-encompassing abilities was a broadside aimed at Microsoft, who had spent the 1990s warily watching Sony's multimedia ambitions creep up on its digital turf. Its response, announced earlier that year, was the long-rumoured development of the X-box (sic), which Bill Gates claimed would be three times more powerful than the PS2 (Hirai's remark referred pointedly to the PS2's out-of-the-box DVD playability, something the Xbox couldn't match without add-ons). Microsoft fired back at Hirai with tech demos during the very same E3, where it would also sign up a little-noticed PC title, *Halo*.

The industry's response was mixed. Not only did this come in the face of the Dreamcast's dire straits and Sony's trouncing of Nintendo, but plans to launch it on home turf in late 2001, a full year after the PS2's US release, seemed remarkably generous to Sony. But Microsoft was determined to proceed, and if that meant taking a whopping financial hit in the name of establishing itself as a console manufacturer, so be it – though whether anyone could have predicted just how much cash was needed to shore them up along the way is debatable. By the time production stopped in 2005 – there was to be no Sony-style extended existence for this console – Microsoft had written off a \$4 billion loss on its baby.

Boasting an internal hard drive (a first for consoles), a NVIDIA graphics chip, a broadband Internet port and a Windows 2000-based OS, it drew immediate criticism for simply being a stripped-down PC, an impression its bulky presence did little to negate. But Microsoft spent its time wisely in the interim, launching a formidable publicity drive to counter negative press and marshalling an impressive line-up of big-name developers, culminating with giants EA and a newly refocused Sega. With a varied batch of appealing launch titles, not least the aforementioned *Halo*, even if the console had tanked completely it wouldn't have been because Microsoft had rested on its laurels.

Still, the Xbox was never going to overtake the PS2, but one area where Microsoft had a leg up on their rivals was in the world of online gaming, thanks to the launch of Xbox Live in late 2002. Exploiting its unrivalled presence in the Internet business to set up dedicated hosting around the world, the online environment quickly became a key element of the Xbox experience, a service that migrated smoothly over to the Xbox 360 in 2005. Not only could broadband-enabled gamers sample the (prepaid) multiplayer delights of frag-fests such as *Unreal Championship* and the highly anticipated *Halo 2*, they also got a standardized voice communication protocol – and in this respect, Microsoft's Xbox was well ahead of the game.

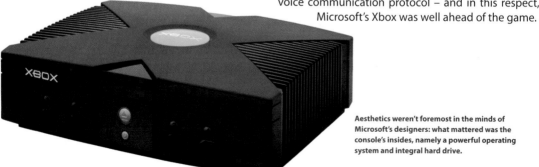

Aesthetics weren't foremost in the minds of Microsoft's designers: what mattered was the console's insides, namely a powerful operating system and integral hard drive.

WHAT'S IN A GAME:
HARD-SELLING THE HARDWARE

Ever since the Channel F debacle (see p.6), console manufacturers have recognized that no matter how cutting-edge their tech, the games on offer are a major factor in what makes people buy one system over another. Early adopters are always likely to be hardcore gamers who have made their minds up in advance, but the press coverage of a console's launch list can affect its take-up among casual gamers thereafter: so-called killer apps, like *Halo* (see p.110) and *Ridge Racer* (see p.31), are therefore highly prized; a Mario-based title, for example, has accompanied every Nintendo handheld and console launch since the Famicom except the Wii (which did in fact make previous *Mario* offerings available through the Virtual Console).

For newcomers to the market, starting lineups often seek to cover as many bases as possible, a strategy the Xbox's US launch list explicitly acknowledged with

Both Microsoft consoles have had *Dead or Alive* games in their launch lineup, showing off the Xbox graphics in inimitable style.

Halo: Combat Evolved turned out to be the Xbox killer app; with its beautifully designed environments and iconic visored hero, it was the beginning of a console-selling series.

Halo: Combat Evolved (a shooter), *Dead or Alive 3* (a beat-'em-up), *Oddworld: Munch's Oddysee* (a puzzle platformer), *NFL Fever 2002* (a sports title) and *Project Gotham Racing* (a driving sim). Problems can arise, however, from the conflict of interest between the game publishers and hardware manufacturers. The former need time to familiarize themselves with the machine; but the latter want to get it onto the market as soon as possible, especially if a rival has plans to do the same (though over-ambition here can backfire; witness the Xbox 360's woes, p.46).

The upshot can be that many launch games under-utilize the new hardware, as happened with the PS2 (see p.37), and come across as underwhelming. Or they can just be plain shocking: Namco's *Mobile Suit Gundam: Crossfire* on the PlayStation 3 inspired such critical put-downs as "I even hate the menu screen" from *Game Informer*. Sometimes though, it can be just a matter of months before coders crack the formula: Psygnosis's stock-car racing *Destruction Derby*, released the month after the PlayStation hit stores, and *WipEout* (see p.19) were two of the first games to be re-released to the market as reduced-price Greatest Hits (Platinum in the UK).

NFL 2K
Dreamcast; ESPN, Visual Concepts, Sega; 1999

The release of *NFL 2K* proved two things to the videogaming world: that the Dreamcast had a killer app; and that there was NFL videogaming life outside of EA's juggernaut *Madden* series (see p.130). In fact, *NFL 2K* was commissioned by Sega in response to EA's refusal to publish their game on the Dreamcast, something EA regretted the moment Visual Concepts' game started splitting their formerly consolidated market base: incredible visuals, fluid animation, intuitive controls, teams that played in the style of their real-life contemporaries, a master-class in sporting commentary and an online mode made *NFL 2K* so popular that EA's only recourse was to buy exclusive rights to both the NFL and ESPN franchises.

Panzer Dragoon
Saturn; Sega; 1995

The Saturn's earlier-than-expected launch must have been daunting for developers, but Sega's in-house team came up with one of the best games the ill-fated platform was to receive. An on-the-rails shooter that had its roots in Sega's arcade classic *Space Harrier*, *Panzer Dragoon*'s attractions were twofold. First was the hardcore simplicity of piloting a dragon through swarms of bugs with just two weapons – a lock-on laser or a rapid-fire handgun. Second was the artwork: one of the first games to take full advantage of the Saturn's hardware, the quick-fire action was set against one of the best-looking game environments to date and included such delights as reflections on water, all of which could be admired (battles permitting) thanks to a rotatable camera.

PilotWings 64
N64; Paradigm Entertainment, Nintendo; 1996

PilotWings 64 was as close to a flight simulator that console games got in 1996 – actually, thanks in part to its fluoro-graphics, playing the game was closer to acting out your dreams about flying than it was about physically strapping yourself into a cockpit. Set across a series of open-world environments, its key motif of exploration by flight, whether that be by plane, gyrocopter or even by being fired out of a cannon, was ostensibly given purpose through a series of goals: but ultimately the whole thing felt like spaced-out meditation-by-videogame, with gamers taking as much time to check out, say, Mario's depiction on Mount Rushmore while doing a lazy loop-the-loop, as to complete the tasks. If there was one game to convince unbelievers of the benefits of the N64's new-fangled analog stick, this was it.

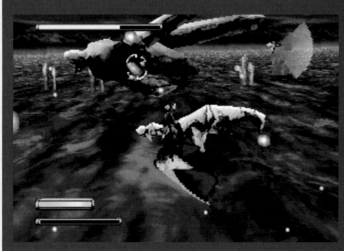

One of the titles available at the Saturn's surprise launch, the first *Panzer Dragoon* game presented a post-apocalyptic setting for a dragon-back shooter on rails.

Ridge Racer
PlayStation; Namco; 1994

The PlayStation's original racer par excellence, *Ridge Racer* confirmed many people's hopes that home consoles had finally reached a level of technology on a par with arcade machines. Namco's (then) blisteringly fast arcade port soon became synonymous with the console, matching handbrake-powerslide racing to the all-important high-polygon count to such success that Sony aligned Namco's series with the launch of both the PS2 and PS3 with *Ridge Racers V* and *7* respectively (Microsoft nabbed *6* for the launch of the Xbox 360). Unsurprisingly for such a veteran series, quality has waxed and waned with each release; to capture the adrenaline rush of the original game in an updated format, check out the 2006 PSP version.

Super Monkey Ball
GC; Amusement Vision, Sega; 2001

Sega's *Super Monkey Ball* remained a GameCube console exclusive from its launch in 2001 (2002 in the UK) until 2005 when the Xbox and PS2 attempted to wrest market share from Nintendo using their own ports. Playing it stokes the kind of nervous tension experienced by the first players of *Donkey Kong*. Its vertiginous, frustrating and dizzyingly addictive gameplay, involving overly cute banana-collecting monkeys rolling about in indestructible see-through balls, seems less and less bizarre as each level is determinedly fought and refought through. Throw in its wealth of minigames, multiplayer modes and arm-length list of sequels and their combined sales of several million, and you can understand Sony's and Microsoft's covetousness.

The market further divided

Despite the gulf between the technical abilities of the two machines, the Xbox was fighting an uphill battle against the GameCube. Nintendo's machine didn't play DVDs (apart from a rare, Japan-only model); it didn't have online capabilities (at least not without a latterly available adaptor); it had a smaller, proprietary 1.6GB disk format (as opposed to the Xbox and PS2's 4.7GB DVDs), and about half the processing power of the Xbox, meaning its games were never going to look as good or be as big as its rivals'. But it was far cheaper and it came with Nintendo's pedigree of producing legendary games, and enticingly, a promise to extend that particular genius to a more mature audience.

But the GameCube's launch list proved distinctly underwhelming, and seasoned adult videogamers never fully signed on. Though quality games did eventually come, most notably in the *Metal Gear Solid* franchise, and later, the remarkable *Resident Evil 4* (see p.166), *Killer7* (see p.116), and horror masterpiece *Eternal Darkness* (see p.229), the Cube never truly moved beyond its family appeal, proving ultimately unable to reclaim the market share lost since the glory days of the SNES.

The GameCube's limited success masked a strategic change of direction for Nintendo. While its promotion as an affordable platform for gaming excellence obviously prefigures the Wii, it simultaneously marked Nintendo's decision to remove itself from the intense battle of technological one-upmanship. Although the N64 had trounced the PlayStation and Saturn in pure processing power, and had cartridge-based games that loaded instantly (and were pretty much indestructible compared to its rivals' easily scratched CD-ROMs), it had still singed Nintendo's gaming fingers badly, losing much of the market gains the SNES had captured. While the GameCube didn't retake them, it was another stab at doing for platforms what Nintendo have always excelled at doing for the games themselves – redefining expectations.

THE CONTINUING SAGA OF VIDEOGAME CENSORSHIP

Games didn't exist for very long before becoming a subject of controversy. In 1976, just four years after *Pong*, the arcade game *Death Race* got societal guardians so hot under the collar that it was banned. Graphics were contemporarily basic, but this driving game based on running down "gremlins" – though its working title of "Pedestrian" rather gave the game away – established the mutually assured relationship between censors, games publishers and media outrage. Rockstar, creators of the *Grand Theft Auto* series (see p.100) and *Bully* (see p.252), are no doubt mightily grateful.

Offensiveness takes myriad forms according to the eye of the beholder, and censorship can come from surprising quarters. Some of the most voracious self-censorship came from Nintendo of America, for example, who were notoriously strict about the content they allowed to appear on their 1980s and early 1990s platforms, censoring even parent-company Nintendo of Japan's releases (not all manufacturers are so concerned; see the box on bad-taste games, p.50, for more). On top of a ban on violence, which went to such involved linguistic lengths as referring to a gamer's numbers of "chances" (rather than "lives"), their policies encompassed excluding religious imagery (*Castlevania III*'s vamp-slaying crosses were acceptable only as boomerangs), any vague suggestion of sex (*Castlevania*

The violence, noirish settings and crime of *GTA4* remain key elements of both the gameplay and mythology of the franchise.

IV's semi-naked classical statues became fully clothed), and any reference to alcohol and tobacco. It was violence, in the form of *Mortal Kombat* (see p.19) that would both bring NoA's moral guardians to their knees and provide them with a get-out clause.

Games sold in the UK display an age rating and indication of content provided by the European trade body PEGI, but there's also a legal requirement for any game featuring sexual content or excessive violence – a requirement that may be extended to every game with an age rating of twelve upwards, whatever the content – to be rated by the BBFC (British Board of Film Classification), which has the power to inhibit distribution by refusing classification. The first title to receive such treatment was SCI's 1997 *Carmageddon*, effectively a 3D update of *Death Race*: where its predecessor's disingenuous gremlins failed to persuade most of their veracity, SCI's original depiction of pedestrians and blood was transformed into green-ooze spouting zombies and the BBFC overturned their ruling.

While games like *Carmageddon* and *Grand Theft Auto* pretty much have the power to offend universally, there are cultural differences around the world. In Germany, laws banning the depiction of Nazi symbology often catch out World War II games: *Wolfenstein 3D* (see p.17) was one of the first to be banned, and many like the *Medal of Honor* and *Call of Duty* (see p.271 and p.223) titles, simply edit out any Nazi motifs. Germany's also pretty hardline on violence, refusing to classify the Xbox 360's *Dead Rising* (see p.229) as well as *Gears of War* (see p.91).

Australia is prone to banning titles containing violent or sexual content thanks to a games-rating system that tops out at fifteen-years-plus, presumably on the misplaced, rather quaint understanding that games are just for children. This has led to some mixed messages from the Classification Review Board. Initial bans on various *Grand Theft Auto* titles have been lifted after the offending content was removed; while the equally controversial *Manhunt* was rated as 15+ on its release in 2003, then issued a Refused Classification ruling the following year.

In Japan, sexual violence in games was hitting the headlines further back even than *Mortal Kombat*; as hard as it is to believe, in 1986, *177* posited the gamer as a rapist. The Japanese parliament became involved and it was recalled.

Debate around the link between violence in videogames and violence in society will forever be a part of the scenery, occasionally spilling into real-life events. Both *Manhunt* and *GTA* have been referenced in murder cases in the US and the UK, but never have the courts nor the police found any causality at play. And as was noted at the time, the perpetrators of the shocking 1999 Columbine High School massacre had been fans of *Doom* – but then they were also fans of Oliver Stone's *Natural Born Killers* and goth culture. Indeed, since *Doom* put 3D shooters into the mainstream, violent crime has actually dropped, according to the US Department of Justice. As research elsewhere supports, the fraction of the population who both play videogames and have also committed heinous crimes may simply represent that percentage of natural born killers already in our midst.

Manhunt
PS2, PC, Xbox; Rockstar; 2003

The controversy surrounding Rockstar's *Bully*, *Grand Theft Auto* series and *State of Emergency* (a game that involved inciting riots) simply doesn't compare to the reception of its most controversial videogame to date: *Manhunt*. The specialist press was faced with a dilemma: how to responsibly review a game with great mechanics but a disturbing setting – one that posited the player as forced into killing for a snuff-movie. The mainstream reaction was mixed, and many were repulsed. The slasher-movie imagery wasn't for those without strong stomachs: some of the executions the lead character makes are disturbing in the extreme, making *Mortal Kombat*'s fatality moves look like kids' stuff (needless to say, it wasn't published for the GameCube).

It did win respect in the gameplay stakes for pulling no punches with its stealth-based action, being very much a hardcore gamer's experience: the only two difficulty modes on offer, for example, were "Fetish" and "Hardcore". But ultimately it made more of a name for itself for its inclusion of a host of immensely unpleasant characters (not least the lead character) and actions that included death by castration and disembowelling. By the time *Manhunt 2* was ready for release in 2007, providing more of the same, the various classification boards around the world were so acutely aware of the original's public profile that it either received the highest-possible adult rating, effectively banning it from shops, or none at all.

Videogaming's equivalent of the slasher movie, *Manhunt* and its sequel are by far the most controversial of Rockstar's mature-rated properties.

The handheld evolution continues

Nintendo's GameCube may have been losing ground in the home-console market, but the company hadn't taken its eye off the handheld market, and with good reason. Not only was Sony's PSP just over the horizon, more immediate competition was already present in the form of a previously unknown market: the mobile phone.

The Game Boy advances

The dominance of Nintendo in the handheld arena allowed it to swat away temporary competition from the Neo Geo Pocket (launched by SNK in 1998) and Neo Geo Pocket Colour (1999) and focus on the successor to the Game Boy Colour. In 2001, the Game Boy Advance became the first to successfully put 32-bit cartridge-based gaming, literally, into gamers' hands. Offering a larger screen than its predecessor, and able to display more complex, more colourful graphics, US sales of the $100 gadget reached one million within just six weeks.

Nintendo then strengthened their hold on the market with the Game Boy Advance SP (SP standing for special) released in 2003. The upgrade was significantly different in looks: instead of a small

With its integral backlighting and neat clamshell look, the GBA SP was the ultimate Game Boy design.

and perfectly formed single plastic "brick", it now came as a slimline, metallic clamshell case that was about half the size of the GBA when folded. It also offered a much-needed brighter screen, meaning gamers were no longer forced to behave like vampires scurrying from shadow to shadow to avoid screen glare. The only false note was that the reduced size meant Nintendo had to do away with the original's headphone socket, meaning socially responsible gamers had to turn the volume off in public, while irresponsible ones simply annoyed everyone in the vicinity.

Supporting the theory that games sell hardware, *Pokémon Ruby* and *Sapphire* (see p.34) provided the GBA with its biggest selling titles, shifting around 13 million copies; both models also offered backwards compatibility with Game Boy and Game Boy Color carts. Still selling strongly up through 2007, they had by then merited such official add-ons as the Wireless Adaptor, which was of particular benefit to purchasers of *Pokémon FireRed* and *Pokémon LeafGreen*; Play-Yan, an MP3/4 cartridge-based player, initially on sale in Japan, and later released in Europe (with MP3-only functionality); and the e-Reader, a device that unlocks extra content in games by scanning cards, which received a Japanese and US release.

The very last incarnation of the GBA was the post-DS launch of the 2005 Game Boy Micro, which proved to be something of a lemon by Nintendo's standards. Announced to the world at the same time as the Wii, it looked like a vaguely modern Game & Watch (see p.9). It was certainly discreet, but that was all it did by way of improvement. In fact, it wasn't compatible with any pre-GBA games or previous GBA adaptors and cables, and the reduced size meant a smaller screen to boot.

Mobiles mobilize

By the early noughties, gaming was making its way onto a platform that reached people who wouldn't go near a handheld gaming device: the mobile phone. Step forward Nokia, who thought they could reach both markets simultaneously through the convergent N-Gage, launched in 2003. A hi-tech piece of kit even by today's standards, it was a mobile phone, a solo and multiplayer device (it was the first 3D-enabled portable, too, pipping the PSP and Nintendo DS to the post by a few months) with USB and wireless connections, as well as an MP3-, movie- and radio-

player. Unfortunately for Nokia, an inability to envisage the design as anything more than a complicated mobile phone led to some seriously awkward gameplay for its mostly underwhelming games.

The N-Gage aside, mobile phone gaming has seen an explosion in popularity since technology moved on from the monotone screens and basic graphics of the late 1990s. While these were fine for cloning old-school classics – usually arcade puzzle games like *Snake* and *Breakout* – the new millennium's third generation (3G) models' multimedia capabilities, especially the use of Flash and Java, have put the kind of games on mobiles that wouldn't have looked out of place on the Mega Drive. Onboard-memory and keypad limitations mean they tend to be much simpler and shorter affairs – minigames, effectively – which helps explain their popularity with casual gamers. This in turn is reflected by the kind of games available: in

THE GIZMONDO AFFAIR

Some really far-out business "strategy" was behind the Gizmondo (pictured below), a handheld that launched in spring 2005. It was touted with unprecedented hyperbole, much to the games press's bemusement, with mega-bucks lavished on its star-studded launch by out-of-the-blue manufacturer Tiger SEC. It was to be all things to all people: a gaming handheld; an in-car GPS navigation aid; a child-safety device (the argument being that as a games machine, your child would voluntarily carry the GPS tracking device around); a GPRS and Bluetooth-enabled SMS device; and a music and movie player. It was mediocre on all fronts, not to mention ludicrously expensive, and was met with shrugged shoulders on its release; the company went bankrupt in January 2006.

In February that year came news that one of Tiger SEC's Swedish founders had survived a high-speed car crash while driving an ultra-rare Ferrari Enzo in Los Angeles County. The media, curious as to what a recently bankrupted, UK-based businessman was doing in the US with such a luxury item, started to dig deeper and within weeks uncovered a labyrinthine tale of embezzlement, Swedish mobsters, extortion rackets and bizarre links to an anti-terrorist organization. Then, in 2008, much to the press's astonishment, came an announcement that it was to receive a second lease of life: seasoned gamers didn't even wait to reserve judgement. (Note that gizmodo.com has no relation whatsoever to the affair, other than perhaps being the unfortunate inspiration for the name.)

addition to the standard retro-looking scrolling shooters and arcade driving titles are games reflecting the current appetite for online gambling and television gameshows. Ease of distribution and a low pricing system are further factors in the dramatic expansion the market has experienced since its early days.

The big-name game publishers have been quick to realize the easy returns to be made from these relatively low-tech products. While engaged on expensive projects for consoles and PCs, they're also able to take the same intellectual properties – especially crossover brands like *Tomb Raider* and household names like Tony Hawk – and transport them, perhaps bringing some of their hardcore customers along with them, to a very different experience.

Meanwhile, back on the PC

The never-to-be-underestimated power of PlayStation was in part related to its cutting-edge polygonal graphics, something that was also at play in the world of the PC. Three-dimensional gaming was already huge, but the ever faster and denser pixel counts required for games like *Quake* (see p.224) meant that PCs' motherboards, CPUs and RAM were being taxed heavily. From 1995, the 3D graphics card was dedicated to taking the strain of making games look pretty.

Coders made the switch to the new graphics accelerators pretty swiftly, but there were issues. Gamers who already owned PCs were faced with buying another rig or fitting the expensive cards into their machines themselves, requiring specialist knowledge as well as finances. Once installed, they could be a pain to integrate with the operating system, let alone the games themselves: many only supported certain makes of card. Patches helped, but in the early days of home Internet access, not many were willing to suffer the cost of a then-whopping 2MB download by dial-up. Then there was the frightening pace of change: faster and more powerful cards would arrive on a nearly monthly basis, leaving less-hardcore gamers further and further behind.

The occasional publisher eased the pace for those who hadn't levelled up; one of the earliest genres to require the technology was the tactical shooter, yet developer Novalogic held out for years with their proprietary Voxel CPU-rendered 3D graphics across their entire, highly popular combat sim series. Likewise, Westwood realized that the runaway popularity of *Command & Conquer* (see p.71) owed more to its ability to run on mid-level PCs than it did to its looks, and continued

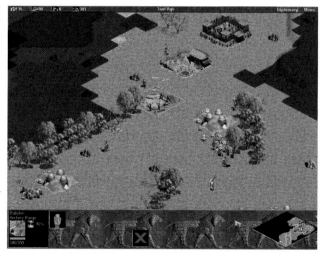

Featuring a typical isometric viewpoint of the action, Microsoft's *Age of Empires* series is one of the PC's classic RTS games from the 1990s.

to publish sequels and expansions at the same level for several years, as did Microsoft with *Age of Empires*. Ultimately, natural selection took its toll: the market levelled out, moving inexorably towards graphics cards supplied by the two big hitters of today, ATI and NVIDIA. Nowadays, you'd be hard pressed to buy even a low-end laptop without a graphics card inside it, let alone a big-release game that doesn't require one.

Strategy takes flight

Emboldened by new 3D capabilities powered by faster processors and ever-larger amounts of onboard RAM, software developers began exploring new frontiers, with a noticeable boom in worthy combat-based flight simulators in the late 1990s. EA even persuaded the strategic defence heavyweight Jane's to put its name to a couple of titles, and the latter end of the movement saw a couple of cracking games for propeller-heads in Ubisoft's *IL-2 Sturmovik* (see p.120) and Microprose's *B17 Bomber: The Mighty Eighth* (2000), the latter also notable for its heavy strategic emphasis.

If anything, the games that best captured the zeitgeist of the late 1990s and early 2000s PC scene are those that were either full-on strategy games – the aforementioned *Age of Empires*, or *Starquest* and *Homeworld* (see p.73), for example – or ones that meshed resource management and tactical awareness into their own fabric, such as Activision's *Battlezone* (1998). The FPS itself was redefined by Valve's 1998 *Half-Life* (see p.250), whose single-player mode required a very different mindset to that of *Quake* and *Unreal*; it also spawned *Counter-Strike* (see p.38), which added a level of strategic nuance previously lacking from online multiplayer frag-fests.

Within a few years of Tom Clancy's *Rainbow Six* (1998), the squad-based tactical shooter had established itself as a force to be reckoned with, something the PS2

and Xbox embraced with open arms (the PlayStation lacked the oomph to do justice to its port). *The Sims* (see p.182), a title that could hardly be described as hardcore and alienating, was also tactical at heart, falling into the god-game side of strategy, a genre also furthered around this period by *Black and White* (see p.64).

Multiplayer, moddings and Rockstars

Back in the 1970s, university-based networks enabled text-adventure and MUD (Multi User Dungeon) gamers to hook into access points across campus simultaneously. Later games like *Doom* only achieved such great popularity because local network access became even more refined and user-friendly (thanks again to universities). As Internet technology developed across the 1990s, making its way into homes and offices, the ability to log into servers around the world became a reality with which millions could engage. By 1996, a simple dial-up connection and a *Quake* disc allowed players on opposite sides of the world to compete in the same deathmatches. Yet despite the popular perception that shooters were the dominant attrac-

Quake
Mac, PC, N64, Saturn; id Software; 1996

Not content with creating two of the most influential shooters, Carmack and Romero took FPS gameplay a step further with *Quake*, most notably in the multiplayer department, with the original deathmatches involving players either teaming up or going solo in a hell-for-leather elimination of opponents. With moves such as bunny-hopping and strafe-jumping, light-speed hand-eye coordination is needed to bring opponents down: offline, veterans are invariably twitchy eyed bundles of nerves.

The *Star Wars: Warlords* mod for *Homeworld 2* featured some impressive renderings of familiar spacecraft from the original movie franchise (such as this Imperial Star Destroyer), whilst developers also took the time to put together custom vehicles that offer a few extra surprises.

tion for online gaming at the time, it was MMORPGs that mushroomed most: where shooters might have dozens of players in a single game, MMORPGs hosted head counts well into the thousands.

Modding (modifying), or customizing games, was also becoming a large part of the online PC gaming experience. It's a simple enough concept, involving independent coders taking a developer's commercial release and extending its gameplay, perhaps through the creation of extra levels and character models, and then posting them online for public consumption: this is referred to as partial conversion. More extreme, and potentially more exciting, is total conversion, in which the game in question is so thoroughly made-over that it becomes its own entity. This may be because the setting has been completely transformed, as in the *Battlefield 1942* mod *Battlefield 1862*; or it may be because the gameplay has been

so thoroughly revised, a case best exemplified by *Counter-Strike*, which in fact proved more popular than its parent, *Half-Life*. Publishers usually support this practice and freely publish the editing tools needed, as it extends the shelf life of their original product (an original copy of the game is needed to run the mods).

Because of its history, stemming from *Doom* and *Quake*, modding is most often associated with the FPS but has in fact a far broader reach. Unauthorized franchise mods, such as *Star Wars*-style makeovers are popular, with players of RTS *Homeworld 2* able to download a free *Star Wars: Warlords* adaptation (franchise holders will take a dim view of copyright breaches, but as in this case, toleration is often practised towards not-for-profit mods); while RPGs, which already inhabit vast worlds, usually benefit from new quests and non-player characters (NPCs).

StarCraft

PC, Mac, N64; Blizzard Entertainment; 1998

Still going strong over a decade on, Blizzard's contribution to the RTS world offered a strong enough narrative-driven challenge to solo gamers, but it was StarCraft's multiplayer modes that set online gaming alight. Mixing several parts *Command & Conquer*, *Age of Empires* and early *Warcraft* games together in an atmospheric sci-fi setting, its low-res pixels look dated by today's standards but the gameplay is anything but: witness its popularity in South Korea, whose residents were responsible for purchasing around half of its near ten million copies sold by 2007 and where it is regarded as the definitive game for professional gaming championships.

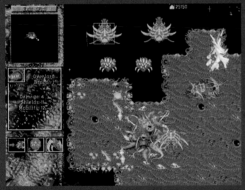

Sophisticated multiplayer gaming – rather than cutting-edge graphics – is the hallmark of Blizzard's sci-fi classic *StarCraft*, still massively popular after all these years.

Homeworld

PC, Mac; Relic Entertainment, Sierra Entertainment; 1999

The first truly 3D RTS, *Homeworld* took elements of the genre you thought you knew and showed you how different they looked when played out in 360-degree deep space. All the familiar mechanics were there – from resource gathering to unit and base building – but small touches like being able to continue exploring your cinematic galaxy long after the core mission was completed gave it a real sense of exploring the final frontier. It was as though *Battlestar Galactica* had been directed as a game.

Counter-Strike

PC, Xbox; Valve Software, Vivendi Universal, Microsoft; 1999

The mod that kept getting modded, Counter-Strike, initially developed from *Half-Life*, and morphed its way through PC incarnations *Condition Zero*, *Anthology* and *Source* alongside an Xbox version. The original redefined multiplayer shooters by emphasizing teamwork, putting players together as a unit of counter-terrorists or terrorists up against either specific objectives or opposing forces in a fight for survival. The basic aims hold true for *Source*, the 2004 version alongside *Half-Life 2*: expect short, sharp battles and to be killed frequently by teenagers in far-away locations.

With its exotic locations, the *Half-Life* mod *Counter-Strike* took on a life of its own, eventually ending up on the Xbox as an official release.

THE WORLD BEFORE WARCRAFT

While *World of Warcraft* (see p.216) isn't actually the biggest MMORPG in the world – that honour goes to South Korea's *Lineage II* – it's the one Western gamers know best. By blurring the lines between social networks and traditional roleplaying, and throwing in the concepts of virtual currencies, *Warcraft* predates *Second Life* by quite some distance – and is frankly more exciting to boot.

The history of MMORPGs, by definition, follows that of the Internet's. In the 1970s, they were only available as MUDs (Multi User Dungeons) on mainframes; in the 1980s to early 1990s they were limited to proprietary North American networks like QuantumLink (which then became AOL) and CompuServe, which charged fairly pricey rates. These companies were in turn restricted by the National Science Foundation Network, which controlled commercial access to the Internet until relaxing their rules in the mid-

1990s. From that point on, individual MMORPGS were to attract the kind of population figures of real-life villages, towns, and ultimately cities: by 2007, *Perfect World* and *Fantasy Westward Journey* could claim over one million concurrent users. PC gamers traditionally dominate, but the Dreamcast's *Phantasy Star Online* (2000) brought the genre to the console, while Square's 2002 *Final Fantasy XI* merged the two, allowing PC and console users to game together.

Other advances came in the fields of gameplay and gaming concepts. In 1996, 3DO's *Meridian 59* became the first 3D MMORPG. While it was highly influential on subsequent developers in the field, it was 1997's isometric *Ultima Online*, from Richard Garriot that really popularized the concept of multiple players interacting through avatars via in-game socio-economic systems: it ultimately had a subscription base of over 200,000, confirming the public appetite for further *Ultima* sequels. It was also the first to allow actual social behaviours, such as the tendency of experienced players to gang up against newer ones (known as Player-killing, or PKing), as well as the obvious technical strains of sustaining such a large number of clients.

Virtual economies, virtual lives

It was Sony's *Everquest* (see opposite) that brought the MMORPG into mainstream awareness, not least through the media's incredulous reporting on virtual objects selling for real-world money on eBay. A practice actually begun with the lower-profile *UO* and one that continues today, it's a divisive issue. Firstly, it appeals to gamers with limited playing time (see also below), who can literally buy into more advanced stages of the game; which in turn is unfair to players who've got through things by their own skill and effort.

More seriously, selling a product that is technically someone else's intellectual property construes a breach of copyright, so Sony asked eBay to ban all such sales. The sheer scale of them made it difficult, however, and merely kick-started a roaring black market. Some *Everquest*ers gave up their day jobs to turn pro, building up virtual

With its impressive gothic castles central to the gameplay, South Korean MMORPG *Lineage II* is at the top of the online gaming heap, more popular even than *World of Warcraft*.

collections to sell; real-to-virtual world exchange rates were calculated; specialized auction sites were set up; one company created from scratch and then sold levelled-up characters; while another set up an inter-game exchange rate mechanism for different series. So much actual money was being made that a study by the Center for Economic Studies and Institute for Economic Research in 2001 would conclude, astonishingly, that "the exchange rate between [*Everquest*'s] currency and the US dollar is determined in a highly liquid (if illegal) currency market, and its value exceeds that of the Japanese yen and the Italian lira."

To outsiders, this was starting to look like a distillation of all the things that turn gamers' minds into mush; players themselves even acknowledged its addictive qualities through nicknaming it *NeverRest* and *EverCrack*. But it had done the job of dragging what was once considered nerdy into the arena of the mainstream – at one point there were 2.5 million subscribers. The last big MMORPG of the decade was Microsoft's *Asheron's Call*, which effectively piggy backed on *Everquest*'s success. It was to be five years until the next big revolution in the genre came: *World of Warcraft* (see p.216). By then the appeal and concept of massive multiplayer games had been more than proven.

Everquest
Sony Online Entertainment; 1999

Prettier than *Ultima* and requiring more brains than *Asheron's Call* – and more the preserve of maturer gamers than the latter – *Everquest* wholeheartedly encouraged in-game social interaction in the name of simultaneously shutting yourself out of the real world for months at a time (hence its nicknames NeverRest and EverCrack). It effectively eliminated the issue of Player Killing, it rewarded teamwork, and it brought all the traditional aspects of RPGs to bear in a beautifully rendered variety of land- and townscapes. Even better, it did so effectively even over a 56K modem, with very little lag time, and it was endless – something that really made you consider caving in to the black market to speed things along.

Partial conversions can also be as minor as cheats that give players the upper hand in multiplayer games (which is a definite no-no in modding etiquette) and don't necessarily affect actual gameplay: witness the infamous Lara Croft in-the-nude patches that infrequently crop up across various *Tomb Raider* releases. Perhaps the most notorious of all mods is the so-called hot coffee sex-based minigame on both the PC and console versions of *Grand Theft Auto: San Andreas* – though Rockstar's claim that it was a mod created by hackers was swiftly rejected by the hacking community, who adamantly maintained it was Rockstar's own in-game code that they had merely unlocked.

Into the digital age

Convergence, the buzzword of the new century, could easily describe the ambitions of the current generation of consoles and handheld systems, still tagged "next-gen", at least until a new generation peeks over the horizon. Technological advances in digital storage, image processing and widespread access to broadband have seen gaming leap into territory long ago promised by the likes of the Dreamcast. It's possible to do all sorts of stuff with your gaming system – make phone calls, record TV, inhabit virtual gameworlds – that has little in common with computer games as envisaged by Nolan Bushnell and his contemporaries. Still, games themselves are bigger business than ever, and the console war therefore harder fought than ever, with every corporate statement and sales prediction picked over by financial analysts on a daily basis. With nowhere much left to go in terms of improving how games look and sound, development has turned to re-examining and redefining the gaming experience.

Smaller packages: Nintendo's DS

By 2004, sales of games in Japan were on an unmis-takable downwards trajectory, and with the Game Boy owning the handheld market, Nintendo or any-one else wanting in on mobile gaming in the iPod age were going to have to offer something different, something palpably next-gen. While Sony focused on giving the world multimedia on a portable scale (see p.44), Nintendo, as ever, remained fixed on the gaming – but still managed to come up with a revolutionary product.

Launched in the US in November 2004, a week later in Japan – one of several firsts for the system – the Nintendo DS was a chunky plastic clamshell that opened up to reveal two screens. It made the tidy little Game Boy Advance SP look positively sexy. It did, however, boast some distinctive features – a touch screen and a microphone, plus Wi-Fi capability – a list that left the press initially unconvinced. Star amongst a small bunch of launch games was undoubtedly *Super Mario 64 DS*, the bait to get the Nintendo fanbase hooked; it was the second half of 2005 before trademark touch-screen titles like *Nintendogs* (see p.149) or even *Mario Kart DS* (see p.132) made an appearance. The latter was the first to take advantage of the system's Wi-Fi Network, providing not just head-to-head "ad hoc" connections, for which a single game card sufficed, but multiplayer racing worldwide.

Lots of old games were adapted for the DS, boasting suffixes with the "D" and "S" initials, often as not, and with the dual screens and stylus sometimes used rather spuriously. Unsurprisingly, developers as well as the press had at first believed the design a gimmick, and so hadn't invested much in producing new games for the system. But the slow release calendar for new titles wasn't too much of a hardship anyway, as the system was compatible with the hundreds and hundreds of available Game Boy Advance cartridges. Then, just over a year later, to the dismay of early adopters, many of whom felt compelled to buy it all over again, a new DS Lite arrived; with a cleaner, slimmer, perhaps more Apple-like design, it came in black, white and pink (with regional differences) and sported a far brighter screen. It would become the top-selling games system in all the major markets, in the US reportedly selling one every five seconds through 2007, accompanied by an avalanche of titles of widely varying quality.

The market may have been shrinking, but Nintendo had scored a runaway success that wasn't dependent on their established customer base. They would continue to provide for hardcore fans, but the only way the industry could sustain itself was by growing the market and reaching those who didn't consider themselves videogame players. According to Satoru Iwata, President of Nintendo, games had become too difficult for the average person to be able to – or even want to – play. The DS was designed to change all that, mainly through the so-called *Touch! Generations* games, often lower-priced titles with simple controls that were aimed at people of any age with no real gaming experience.

Officially, the brand includes *Nintendogs* (see p.149), *Tetris DS* (2006), *Big Brain Academy* (2005), *Picross DS* (see p.43) and *Sudoku Master* (2006), among others, but the most visible and radically different title was *Brain Age* (known in the UK as *Dr Kawashima's Brain Training*). A sensational PR campaign had Nintendo sending copies of the console and game to anyone who mattered, including President George W. Bush on his sixtieth birthday, promising that "just a few minutes a day with more than 15 daily training tests will help keep your mind sharp". Bizarre to think that there's a "Health and Fitness" genre of DS games; although the games available in the West account for just a fraction of those released in Japan, where there are games

devoted to music, makeup, poetry and anything else you can think of, many of them offering an experience that simply couldn't occur on any other platform. Of course, the DS also has online functions, as well as a TV tuner attachment (in Japan), and has even provided GPS-enabled interactive tour guides at Walt Disney World, but it's by no means a media player. For that, you need to look to Sony.

Brain Age (US); Dr Kawashima's Brain Training (UK)
DS; Nintendo; 2006

Less a game, more a uniquely DS experience. The disembodied head of the doctor puts you through various tests – reading aloud, counting, simple maths and puzzles – to measure the age of your brain from 20 to 80 years old. With daily training of the prefrontal cortex, you can watch on a graph as it regains its youthful vigour. A decent Sudoku game comes included.

Cooking Mama
DS; Majesco Games, 505 Games; 2006

Selling a million just in Europe, *Cooking Mama* is evidence all on its own of a new type of gameplayer. Essentially, a

collection of recipe-themed minigames involving chopping, slicing, stirring and so on with the stylus, it's definitely low-cal fun: good for whiling away a few minutes, but not enough to really satisfy.

She's smiling now, but wait until you mess up a recipe: Mama's flaming eyes are enough to scare you out of the kitchen altogether.

Phoenix Wright: Ace Attorney
DS; Capcom; 2005

Manga-style, interactive cases featuring a rookie defence attorney. Whether searching crime scenes, questioning witnesses or presenting evidence in court, the script is offbeat, the characters entertaining, and the mysteries – not to mention moral dilemmas – intriguing. It was thought the original GBA games wouldn't cut it in the West, but their translation to the stylus-enabled DS has dismissed that theory for good.

Picross DS
DS; Nintendo; 2007

Newspaper-style logic puzzles along the lines of Sudoku, where pictures are gradually revealed by working out which squares to fill in on the grid according to the clues. Absorbing and addictive, the puzzles ramp up in size and therefore difficulty, and it would take a good while to get through the 300 grids included, after which you can design your own to challenge friends.

Trauma Center: Under the Knife
DS; Atlus Co, Nintendo; 2005

More futuristic hospital drama than Operation, *Trauma Center* sits alongside *Phoenix Wright* in the new genre of stylus-based storytelling/puzzle games. The star of the piece is Dr Derek Stiles, who requires superquick reactions and a steady hand to avoid losing patients on the operating table: despite instructions from the scary nurse on the top screen, procedures can be insanely difficult.

The PlayStation Portable

Sony's first foray into the handheld market since the short-lived PocketStation add-on (1998, available only in Japan) was always going to be an event, and the PlayStation Portable, with its sleek design (pictured below), did not disappoint. A stunning piece of hardware, less a handheld gaming device and more a sort of minicomputer, with a price to match, its launch at the end of 2004 coincided with that of the DS in Japan; it arrived in the US in March 2005, but was delayed six months in the UK to make sure that US launch demands were met. Ten years earlier, Sony had overturned the market with the original PlayStation, and at first it looked as though they might be about to do it again. After selling many times faster at launch, though, sales of the PSP steadied out, and the DS started to overtake it.

A surprisingly heavy, glossy black machine (pictured below), there was no mistaking the PSP for a child's toy; it had just the one screen, but a superb, sharply defined screen – as you'd expect for a machine built as much for watching movies and slideshows as for playing games; appropriately, the buttons and controls, including the nub of an analog stick, faded out discreetly around it. With no onboard hard drive, it relied on getting content from either a flash Memory Stick or via Sony's new Universal Media Disc, a PSP-exclusive format designed to be used for both games and movies. People were used to Memory Sticks, which they already had in their Sony cameras and

phones, and they were accustomed to spending thirty-odd pounds (or forty bucks) on a game; on the other hand, DVDs were getting a lot cheaper, and paying the same or more for a UMD movie that could be played only on the PSP and watched by one or at most two people at a time didn't seem particularly good value – far better value, if not necessarily legal, to find a way to rip your own DVDs onto the Memory Stick. Movie studio support for the format gradually slowed down, and UMDs have been reported to be on the critical list regularly ever since.

There are plenty of theories as to why the PSP didn't sell in as big numbers as the DS. Justifiably more expensive, its hi-tech nature also meant that people didn't feel comfortable using it on public transport – you could hide an iPod in your pocket, but the PSP was too large, and keeping it out of reach, carefully cushioned from damage, meant losing much of its functionality. Primarily, though, it just didn't compete as a games machine. A kind of pocket PS2, its launch titles were dominated by remakes of existing games, one notable exception being the brilliant *Lumines* (see p.128). Plus, with the new disc format, there was no chance of backwards compatibility, so unless they were willing to hack the hardware (see box on p.45), PSP owners needed to build up a games library from scratch – not especially appealing when so many titles were iterations of those they'd played before. Whereas the DS could encompass both the classic gaming of *Super Mario Bros.* and new-fangled stylus-based gameplay, the PSP was restricted to orthodox single-player plus online gaming, although that's not to say there weren't a few flashes of originality, such as *LocoRoco* (see p.215).

Part of the PSP's *raison d'être*, though, was to work in tandem with the PlayStation 3, and PSP owners who got themselves a PS3 were soon able to download some original PlayStation games from the PlayStation

Network. Later, with the arrival of the PSP Store, these could be downloaded from a computer too. With more original games promised for the future, perhaps Sony's longer term strategy was finally starting to pay off. In terms of the DS, by 2008 there wasn't much scope for new functions. But when Sony released a reworked Slim and Lite version of the PSP in late 2007, it made it clear that the PSP as a multimedia do-it-all device was far from finished, offering Skype and video-out ports (so you could plug it into a big screen), not to mention the ability to use the device as a PVR/DVR (again with the PS3), an Instant Messaging service, and a GPS add-on (for Europe) – more evidence that Sony's ambitions have always been bigger than the gaming market.

The Xbox 360

The Xbox 360 hit the shelves in November 2005 with unseemly haste, a full year ahead of the PS3 and Wii. Just two months after the production lines had started whirring, and preceded by a seven-month publicity blitzkrieg, its near-simultaneous launch in Europe, the US and Japan looked like an outstanding success, selling out immediately in the first two regions, where units instantly reappeared on eBay at twice the original asking price (once again, Japan remained wary of the Western interloper). Within a year it had been rolled out in over thirty countries. With stock levels soon restored, it was the only "next-gen" machine on the shelves, it had a cheaper pricing model than the PS3's was projected to be, and its high-definition video potential made Nintendo's output appear positively retro.

The Xbox 360 was also Microsoft's pre-emptive strike against the multimedia capabilities of Sony's machine. Mindful that the PS2's popularity was due in part to being a cheap DVD player, Microsoft duly added out-of-the-box DVD capability to its new machine, though a little bit of history did repeat itself: just as the original Xbox had required an upgrade to play DVDs, so too did the Xbox 360 in order to play HD-DVDs, something of a cost-cutting, hedge-betting move in preparation for the upcoming battle between that for-

The harbinger of high-definition gaming, Microsoft's Xbox 360 boasted a lighter, more refined design than its predecessor and was launched well before its rivals.

mat and Blu-ray (see p.49). Instead, Microsoft staked the greater part of the Xbox 360's fortune on an area in which it had already proved itself: online, via Xbox Live.

In 2005 this was limited to gaming, but it was still an impressive example of how to create a digital community. On the day of the Xbox 360's US launch, Microsoft took Xbox Live offline in a well-organized, 24-hour stroke to upgrade their previously subscription-only service. Henceforth, users could create either a free Silver account to access voice and video chat through Windows Live Messenger; or subscribe to the paid-for Gold service, which added multiplayer functionality. The real innovation at both levels, though, lay in the Xbox Live Marketplace, where extra content – both free and paid-for – could be downloaded to expand shop-bought games, as well as demos, trailers and even complete games, ranging from card and board games to classic arcade titles, a growing range of Xbox Originals and Xbox Live exclusives. Suddenly it became clear why anyone should invest in the version of the system that came with a hard drive.

The community aspect of Xbox Live was furthered by a system of Achievement points, awarded in all Xbox 360 games. These accumulate to a player's Gamerscore, providing players with an instant online ranking (and bragging rights) and giving players seeking online competitors an indication of participants' skill levels.

So far so good for gaming, but Microsoft's ambitions were grander: having made the Xbox 360 a communications hub, they sought to bring online multimedia into the living room. Partially sidestepping the Blu-ray versus HD-DVD debate, this move was launched in the US in 2006 on Xbox Live through downloadable standard- and high-definition TV and movies from the likes of MTV, CBS, Warner Brothers and Disney. This was followed in 2007 by an announcement that Microsoft would bring Internet Protocol Television to the console. It was looking more and more like the Xbox 360 was yet another PC in a box. Unfortunately for Microsoft, while these drives broke new console ground, vast numbers of the platform they needed – the Xbox 360 – kept breaking down.

The Red Ring of Death

Right from the first consoles shifting in 2005, reports emerged of a failure known as the Red Ring of Death, a reference to the circle of green lights on the console – which indicate which wireless controllers are active – turning red due to critical hardware failure (pictured). Microsoft initially claimed that this issue affected just 3–5 percent of all consoles bought (an industry standard for new technology, they insisted), but retailers put returns closer to an embarrassing 30 percent. Over-heating appeared to be at fault in most cases, causing, it's thought, permanent damage to the solder-ing of the circuitry. Microsoft refused to acknowledge this right up until mid-2007, when they issued an open letter of apology and extended the guarantee from one to three years – for that defect only.

In the meantime, much customer-relations damage had been done. The initial ninety-day guarantee had only been pushed out to a full year after twelve months of complaints; and even then, consoles continued to fail outside of the new guarantee period. Comments from a senior exec that complainants were simply a "vocal minority" rubbed salt into the wounds, and even the 2007 apology masked the fact that consoles might

BACK TO THE OLD-SCHOOL FUTURE

Retro, or old-school gaming, is now the videogaming industry equivalent of the Slow Food movement: faced with increasingly complicated and expensive games that take ever longer to play, a large body of interest has developed in going back to basics. Quite why owners of twenty-first-century technology should want to play the kind of games that a hamster-wheel could power speaks strongly to the draw of nostalgia and the demographics at work – and not least the enduring attraction of simpler gameplay.

The rise of casual gaming is in part responsible, but many of those downloading *Asteroids Deluxe* from Xbox Live or any of the umpteen back-listed *Mario* titles to their Wii are from the Atari, NES and N64 generations, and they've often families of their own. While they might happily decapitate zombies and watch the resulting resplendent streams of blood by themselves, they are also reaching back to their childhoods for kid-friendly titles, bringing a whole new audience to the back catalogue. Low price points and ease of availability, too, are crucial. In early 2008, Nintendo announced ten million Virtual Console downloads; given that the lowest-priced of these up to that point cost the equivalent of just $5, this was both a bargain for gamers and a significant chunk of income for Nintendo, with nearly no development or distribution costs. And once again, it underscored the powerful role Nintendo's playability-first ethos has had in its long-term success.

Backlists haven't always been so easily available. Console gamers had been made to wait until the PlayStation era, when the CD-ROM-based format allowed publishers to batch up arcade-based compilations. PC gamers had long been satiated, in part, with classic compilations on cassette, floppy disk and CD-ROMs throughout the 1980s and 90s (Microsoft's precursor to Xbox Live Arcade, Microsoft Arcade, arrived on a 1.44MB floppy format in 1993) – but they were severely deprived of official console ports.

Even for console owners, though, the experience of playing *Super Mario Bros.* in the era of the GameCube could only be achieved by hunting down both a NES and a compatible game cartridge. As such, console-based retro-gaming became pretty much the preserve of collectors or anyone who hadn't gotten around to throwing their old stuff away. PC users wanting that same experience, however, have always had the option to operate in the controversial area of console emulation. Software that mimics the functionality of a given console's hardware and then plays virtual copies of the games on it, emulators are widely available online, are easily set up and are frequently unofficial – and are therefore in danger of attracting publishers' and console manufacturers' wrath for breach of copyright. There's no little irony in the fact that the current generation of consoles use emulators to play their predecessors' backlists; and that emulation has helped its most vociferous critic, Nintendo, to bounce back to success.

The Wii's Virtual Console lets you revisit classics like the colourful *Fatal Fury* without having to haul your NeoGeo up from the basement.

be fixed with recycled parts from other, potentially defective machines (it wasn't unknown for recipients of faulty machines to have to make multiple returns). On the upside, Microsoft acknowledged the scale of the issue with a repair budget of over one billion dollars; but as increasing insider details leaked out about a 2005 launch strategy that had focused on beating Sony to the market at the expense of quality testing, many owners felt like they'd been taken for a ride.

While those affected were indeed vocal on blogs, fansites and the company's customer complaints' hotlines, Microsoft's console still managed to do enough to keep attracting newcomers. By the beginning of 2008, it had sold just under 18 million units, just a few million short of its predecessor's total lifetime sales, and it was widely regarded as having a superior library of games to its true rival, the PS3. Apart from its buggy launch, Microsoft's first-to-market strategy couldn't be called anything but a success.

Enter the PS3

If Microsoft thought it had it bad in the press stakes, the weight of expectation on the PlayStation 3 initially proved to be something of a millstone for Sony. Unveiled to the public at the 2005 E3, things looked promising, as the technical specs – not least the inclusion of Sony's Blu-ray technology – were outstanding. But they also had the whiff of brinkmanship: coming just months before the Xbox 360 launched, the announcement was accompanied only by movie previews and some distinctly non-functional prototype consoles.

Still, it got the media sufficiently onside for them to express strong disappointment at Sony's admittance, in early 2006, that the projected March launch might have to be pushed back due to problems mass-producing the Blu-ray drives (insiders intimated that a lack of development tools for game coders was also at fault); in fact, not only did Sony delay the global launch until November that year, it then waited until September to announce that this would in fact only apply to the US and Japan and that it would be launching with just fifty percent of the previous forecast of four million units – with the rest of the world having to wait until at least March 2007. All the while, criticism of the projected high price of $600 ($200 more than the Xbox 360) was met with comments such as those from Ken Kutaragi, head of Sony Computer Entertainment, that this was "probably too cheap" and that Sony wanted "to get consumers to think to themselves, 'I will work more hours to buy one.'" While he

The PS3's glossy exterior hides a Blu-ray disc player and integral Wi-Fi, and is apparently future-proof.

was certainly right about the price not meeting the $800-and-upwards manufacturing cost, the press smelled unprecedented arrogance.

Despite Sony ultimately doing the right thing by ensuring its hardware was as market-ready as possible, the original postponement came just as Nintendo announced that it was ahead of schedule, sending a clear message about the reliability of its machine (it went on to debut three months ahead of the PS3). In the event, Sony couldn't even meet its downwardly revised launch figures. Add to that a muted gaming media reception and subsequent press coverage that included the PS3 as one of the top technical cock-ups of 2006, and the biggest PR disaster the industry had ever seen.

Meanwhile, with the build-cost outstripping the shelf price, Sony was posting an annual operating loss of $2 billion by March 2007 (when, perhaps coincidentally, Kutaragi announced his retirement). But the PS3's woes weren't fated to do to Sony what the original Xbox's had done to Microsoft. A combination of price cuts, re-specified models and reduced hardware costs saw such a remarkable turnaround in fortunes that Sony actually turned in a profit by the end of that year.

Under the Blu-ray bonnet

Initially, the most appreciative reviews of the PS3 came from the non-gaming press, which was telling: Sony weren't just competing in the gaming arena, they were taking on home-entertainment systems as well. Not only did the PS3 have a Blu-ray drive, it supported Dolby Digital sound and its built-in Wi-Fi meant it could stream multimedia files from computers onto an HDTV. Furthermore, its use of USB slots for data transfer and back-ups – including game saves – meant that for the first time Sony wasn't insisting on using proprietary hardware (they even went so far as

to allow users to install their own hard drives).

Owners of the wireless PSP suddenly had new functionality for their handheld too, working as it does as a more sophisticated remote control than the Bluetooth-enabled Sixaxis controller. Looking for all the world like a wireless DualShock 2, the motion-sensing capabilities of the Sixaxis provoked criticism for being announced some eight months after the Wiis, as well as for lacking the rumble technology of its Xbox 360 rival. Sony made amends, however, releasing the DualShock 3 in Japan in 2007, and the US and Europe the following year.

Looking to the future, the PS3 has the potential for far larger games than its rivals thanks to the sheer size of Blu-ray discs (which start at 50GB and only get bigger); while in the other direction Sony have tackled backwards compatibility in different ways. Early PS3s catered to nostalgia through the inclusion of the Emotion Engine chip, which allowed the PS3 to emulate PS2 and the original PlayStation hardware and so play their CD-ROMs and DVDs; but the chip fell victim to cost-cutting measures and disappeared early on. In its stead, Sony went down the route trodden by Microsoft and Nintendo by offering downloadable emulations of older (initially just PlayStation) games through the new PlayStation Network. This itself also offers a unified portal for mostly free, online multiplayer gaming (exceptions such as MMORPGs are fee-based), plus it has the now-standard voice and video chat, a messaging service and a web browser.

The biggest online innovation, in the battle for gamer loyalty with Nintendo and Microsoft, was to be the introduction of PlayStation Home, a social-networking site á la *Second Life*, in which gamers' avatars interact in a 3D world (still in beta at the time of writing). Like Microsoft, Sony is transforming our notions about what a games console should be.

SOMETHING ROTTEN IN THE STATE OF GAMES

Given that many videogames only hit the press for perceived contravention of standards of decency, it wouldn't be surprising if outraged parents' groups considered all games to be in bad taste. It's a considerably more complicated picture than that of course, which is exactly why censorship has its role to play, and games such as *Manhunt* (see p.33) and *Bully* (see p.252), while dividing opinion, justify their existence through their gameplay. Cultural differences can also be extremely divisive – witness the Japanese shockers *Biko 3* and *Battle Raper*, games that owe their existence to a *hentai* tradition with no counterpart in the West. And while blatantly offensive fringe titles like the racist *Ethnic Cleansing* are pathetically obvious, the truly jaw-dropping moments come when developers and publishers seem to have suffered a collective blind spot as to exactly what they were saying about themselves through their game. The following are a few such moments.

Start with the questionable theme of soccer hooliganism (note the blood on the grass), throw in poor execution and you end up with the failed strategy game that was *Hooligans: Storm Over Europe*.

America's 10 Most Wanted
PC, PS2; System 3; 2004

America's 10 Most Wanted wasn't the first game to capitalize on George W.'s war on terror, but it was the first – and to date, last – published and promoted game that trivialized killing living people (Bush's list of Al Qaeda members). Given the strong feelings engendered by 9/11 and the war in Afghanistan at the time, many didn't know what to make of a game that shamelessly piggybacked on the "with us or against us" language in the name of entertainment; luckily, the dire gameplay meant reviewers could concentrate on discussing poor mechanics rather than divisive politics.

BMXXX
PS2, GC, Xbox; Acclaim; 2002

Acclaim must have been scratching its head as to how to recover from its vaunted association with BMX champion Dave Mirra going down the pan after he refused to endorse the proposed *Dave Mirra BMXXX*. Their solution: take out his name and re-frame the gameplay to be about topless women performing extreme-cycling stunts. Acclaim salvaged attention alright, but from the wrong quarters, with many stores refusing to stock the game; while the press just saw a distinctly average game. It sold poorly, and Dave Mirra still sued them for damaging his image.

Custer's Revenge
Atari 2600; Mystique; 1983

One of the more outrageous titles to slip past Atari's quality-control checks in the early 1980s, *Custer's Revenge* was most definitely not based in history. The nub of the game was thus: an aroused, and thankfully highly pixellated General Custer must avoid a hail of arrows as he makes his way across the screen to a naked Native American maiden tied to a cactus. Needless to say, this mightily offended the general public, not to mention women's rights outfits, rape-victim support groups and Native American organizations. Mystique closed down a year later.

JFK Reloaded
PC; Traffic Games; 2002

It takes some chutzpah – or a warped understanding of what comprises good timing – to take a game that posits the player as JFK's assassin and launch it on the anniversary of his death. While Traffic's director desperately claimed the game would bring "history to life and stimulate a younger generation of players to take an interest in this fascinating episode of American history," their website told a different story: "When you're ready … KILL JFK and win up to $100,000."

Hooligans: Storm Over Europe
PC; DarkXabre Games, Sold Out; 2002

Having searched two years for a publisher willing to take the PR hit for a game about the very real problem of European soccer violence, DarkXabre strove hard to market their game as a darkly humorous strategy game. But reviewers found little comedy in the poor AI, not to mention the concept of leading a gang of stereotyped soccer thugs through a football season rife with extreme violence, drug and alcohol abuse, and looting.

Postal
PC, Mac; Running With Scissors; 1997

Great shoot-'em-ups provide compelling reasons to go around blasting other lifeforms – such as an absorbing narrative or basic survival. Not so *Postal*. A pre-Columbine public felt mostly turned off, not least for the game's numbing repetition. A post-9/11 world was then treated to *Postal 2* (2003), which threw *GTA's* knowing humour into sharp relief by adding urination, STDs, homophobia and racism (specifically against Middle Eastern folk) into the mix. Even then, it somehow contrived to be dull.

Super Columbine Massacre RPG!
PC; Danny Ledonne; 2005

Like much of the game itself, it's unknown how much irony is behind the exclamation mark in the title. But out of all the games referenced here, *SCMRPG!* was taken seriously enough to have been controversially shortlisted (and then just as controversially dropped) as a finalist in indie-gaming's annual Slamdance awards. Ledonne's justification for the game – a peculiar collage of digital mediums that follows the killers on the day of the massacre, and may or may not be a critique of aspects of US society – is that it helped him move away from a similar path as it "implores introspection".

It launched on the anniversary of JFK's assassination, but there was never going to be a right time to release this bad-taste shooting game where you take the role of an assassin.

Nintendo's Revolution: the Wii

The announcement in April 2006 that Nintendo's long anticipated Revolution console was actually going to be called Wii caused an outbreak of puerile humour across the English-speaking world, and seemed to diminish whatever the company's aims were for its new console. Even if the name "revolution" was more enticing to Westerners, it was always going to be problematic internationally and would need to be abbreviated for ease of use. So Nintendo resolved the issue before it became one, taking the opportunity to emphasize

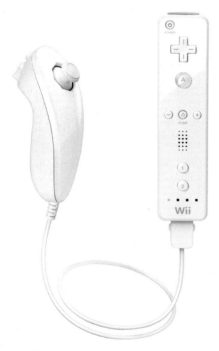

Revolutionizing game controllers, the Wii remote – here without its nonslip safety jacket – and accompanying nunchuk were designed to appeal to nongamers.

the "everyone" nature of the new console, garnering a massive amount of press and lowering expectations at the same time. Now something not to be taken quite so seriously as a revolution, the Wii was launched in November 2006, two days after the PS3, but in a completely different cultural space; in Europe, the PS3's delay meant the Wii launched three months ahead of Sony. From the outset it looked as though Nintendo was going to lose the latest console war, as it had done with the GameCube. No one quite understood that it had chosen to fight a different battle – one it had begun with the DS two years earlier.

In keeping with its name, the design of the console summed up the everyman philosophy: it was small, it was white, it was nondescript; it didn't say "fun and games" like the purple GameCube, or come across as a hi-tech piece of audiovisual equipment. It was less powerful than the Xbox 360 or PS3 and didn't even support HD, but was there room for another powerhouse in the living room anyway? As Miyamoto put it: "Too many powerful consoles can't coexist. It's like having only ferocious dinosaurs. They might fight and hasten their own extinction". So Nintendo was putting a different beast out there, to take on a less aggressive but ultimately far greater opponent, namely the general public's lack of interest in videogames. As with the DS, the Wii was meant to attract those who were otherwise put off games by their reputation for violence, or assumed that all gamers were teenage boys doing fast, incomprehensible stuff with their fingers and thumbs. So the non-confrontational design ethic of the console followed through to the controller, styled to evoke the familiarity of the TV remote. Just as revolutionary was the console's price, exactly half that of the PS3; Sony and Microsoft were both relying on the established financial model of releasing a console at a high launch price and discounting it a

Wii Sports
Wii; Nintendo; 2006

Five sports in one game, some of them – bowling, especially – using the controller more realistically than others. There's nothing resembling a single-player career mode, but plenty of training options to work through before you gather friends and family for a surprisingly fun evening's entertainment.

WarioWare: Smooth Moves
Wii; Nintendo, Intelligent Systems; 2007

Evolved from 2003's *WarioWare Inc* for the Game Boy Advance, and including bits from Nintendo classics of yesteryear, this collection of over 200 stupendously silly, superfast minigames works brilliantly with the Wii Remote. As with most minigames, it's better played with others.

Rayman Raving Rabbids
Wii; Ubisoft; 2006

Michel Ancel's limbless platform star returns for a collection of absurd minigames, tenuously wrapped round a story. Gorgeous animations and horrifically cute characters make even the slightly random games worth playing (single-player too), as Rayman is forced into performing for the evil rabbids' amusement.

Take the mopheads bowling in the Wii's flagship game, which shipped with the console in Europe and became Japan's top-selling title.

year or two in, as more games became available, to pull in a less dedicated market. Even at this price, the Wii may have been underpowered, but it wasn't outdated, featuring inbuilt WiFi (unlike the Xbox 360), and a downloadable Internet channel that would allow it to team up with the BBC in providing UK gamers with the still relatively new streaming TV on demand service, BBC iPlayer. And whereas the remote may have looked simple, it worked with a sensor placed on the TV to detect motion, a system that could easily have been disastrous in practice, but in fact performed incredibly well.

The Wii was naturally designed for more than the latest multiplatform port, but as usual, Nintendo had to lead the way with the software. From the start, the console shipped with the game that had the broadest possible appeal, *Wii Sports*, which also acted as a kind of trainer for the new controller; what's more Nintendo made the game's technology freely available to other developers. The definitive Wii game, *Wii Sports*, was 2007's top-seller in Japan, where it wasn't bundled with the console. Commercials for it were ubiquitous, demonstrating celebrities and ordinary people of all ages playing, and it would have been hard not to get the message, sandwiched as it was around prime-time TV shows, aimed unerringly at the mainstream audience. There was some less positive media coverage too, for instance controllers flying out of people's hands and smashing through TV screens, resulting in the replacement of some 3 million wrist straps; other coverage had people either suffering from sports-type injuries, or using the game for physical rehab; but the biggest story of all was the fact that there just weren't enough consoles to go around.

While working on growing a new audience, Nintendo couldn't afford to forget its traditional fanbase, so the Wii provided straightforward backwards compatibility with GameCube discs, plus, even better, a growing library of downloadable online games from long-dead systems, by means of the online Virtual Console. This brought the likes of *Donkey Kong* to younger gamers for the first time, and presumably put a lot of pirates and hackers out of business in the process. Software from third parties was predictably slow off the mark, perhaps because they half-expected the Wii to fail, with only the likes of Ubisoft and EA coming up with the goods at first. The real problem, though, for everyone involved, wasn't the games: the Wii's components were not being manufactured quickly enough to supply the astonishing level of demand for the console. Even though the production rate had almost doubled, it still wasn't enough, and the usually slow summer, which allows hardware companies to stockpile for the holiday shopping season, wasn't slow at all. These crippling shortages make it all the more incredible that the number of Wiis in the UK had outstripped Xbox 360s by the end of 2007, even though the latter had been around a year longer. And this was before the release of *Wii Fit*, with its pressure-sensitive balance board, a frighteningly media-friendly exercise game for all the family, which would see even further widespread acceptance of gaming in an obesity-obsessed climate.

The Wii's astronomical degree of success gave everyone in the industry pause for thought. Microsoft hurriedly rolled out a new, cheaper Xbox Arcade to replace its Core System, offering a bundle of family-friendly Xbox Live Arcade games and no hard drive for the 2007 holiday season, which somehow missed the point of the Wii. It's quite possible that the majority of Wii-owners remain hardcore gamers, for whom the Wii is often a second system. In order for Nintendo's plan of a genuinely expanded market of videogamers to happen, though – rather than just a Wii-obsessed fad – the players of *Wii Sports* will need to become players of *Rayman Raving Rabbids*, perhaps moving onto *Super Mario Galaxy*, first of all. It then remains to be seen whether they'll progress to playing games on the Xbox 360 or PS3, and if so, exactly what sort of games they will be.

The Canon

The Canon

Animal Crossing: Wild World

DS; Nintendo; 2005

Weeds have taken over your carefully planted garden; cockroaches scuttle across your birch flooring; there's a stack of mail you haven't opened; you've missed countless neighbours' birthdays – in fact you've not seen another soul for weeks. No, you haven't been spending too much time playing videogames, but too little in *Animal Crossing: Wild World*. Because when you're not tending to this weird, offbeat version of village life, it carries on without you.

In this reworking of the GameCube title, the protagonist is you – or rather your cute little humanoid avatar, who is responsible for the development and upkeep of the "town" you've named as your own. Which makes it sound like a seriously strategic sim game – it's not. For a start, the other inhabitants are talking animals, and you spend much of your time interacting with them: stopping for a chat, visiting their homes, sending and receiving mail, sharing gossip and exchanging advice. And each of your neighbours has his or her own little phrases and in-jokes, even a special nickname just for you. All of which sounds too twee for words, so it's just as well that most conversations are funny, absurd and usually both, even turning snappy if someone's in a bad mood.

You'll get complaints if you're not keeping up with the civic weeding and flower-watering, so there's loads of gardening to do, for which you'll need tools and seeds from Tom Nook's store, one of those shops that sells everything from writing paper to pianos. He's got you under his thumb, that raccoon, thanks to a crippling mortgage on the little hutch you call home, so

Head to the café at 8pm on a Saturday night for the weekly gig by K.K. Slider, the offbeat character with the acoustic guitar and the wet nose. Requests are welcome!

you need to start earning bells by working for Nook and selling stuff – to him, naturally – including fruit you've shaken out of trees and shells you find on the beach, putting some away in a savings account at the post office when you can afford to.

In this consumerist society appearance is everything, so naturally there's a clothes store, where you can buy ready-to-wear or design your own outfits. And in a nod to ethical living, the town hall provides a recycling bin, where you can pick up or donate unwanted items. Before long your house will be crammed with useless junk you've bought, found or been given. A serious clearout would seem to be in order, but the Happy Room Academy judges you on your choice of the right wallpaper with the right carpet, furniture and ornaments – whether train sets, hifi or rubber plants – and minimalism incurs as much disapproval as clutter.

Other recreational activities include fishing, digging for fossils and catching insects, thereby filling the empty aquariums and display cases in the town museum. While you're there, pop downstairs to the coffee bar, or up to the observatory for a spot of star-gazing, something to do at night when most places are closed. When it's daytime, a quick burst of play can stretch into hours of gentle, addictive entertainment, even though there are no monsters to kill and nothing much to win unless you count fishing contests. Keeping an eye on the noticeboard is the best way to discover one-off events, but unless you're going to play every day you may have to turn the clock back occasionally. Should you ever start to get bored in your own environment, it's easy to explore friends' villages via WiFi – each is different – or stop playing for a month or so and let the changing seasons transform the town. Everyone will pretend not to recognize you when you return, though they'll soon remind you exactly how long it's been since your last visit, welcoming you with that familiar, oddball charm that says there's no place like home.

Baldur's Gate II: Shadows of Amn

PC, Mac; BioWare, Interplay; 2000

Now around a decade old, the original *Baldur's Gate* was the videogame that single-handedly revived the traditional, in-depth RPG on the PC, a fact evidenced by global sales of over two million copies. The game effortlessly bridged the gap between an *Advanced Dungeons and Dragons* purist's dream (almost every *AD&D* die-throw and complicated formula was catered to and could be watched unravelling on screen) and outright fun. (And if your D&D-ing wasn't that advanced, you could just let it run these rules in the background without worrying a jot about understanding them.) *Baldur's Gate* also set many of the conventions for single-player team-based gaming that *Neverwinter Nights* and *Dungeon Siege* would profit from soon afterwards. Having set the bar so high for themselves, and with these pretenders to the throne hot on their heels, it was going to be tough for BioWare to satiate the fans clamouring for a sequel.

Baldur's Gate II, however, took the bull by the horns and went for an even trickier task: translating the second-generation *AD&D* rules onto screen. (As with the older game, if you didn't already know what that meant, you were just thankful you didn't have to.) They also threw in a few extra character classes and further pushed the envelope in terms of playability – which was good news whoever you were. Its release to great acclaim in 2000 was a watershed moment, simultaneously turning heads for the sheer depth of its plot and the vastness of its geographical setting (both batons that *The Elder Scrolls* have since picked up; see p.78) whilst marking the last and most glorious breath of the isometric viewpoint in PC gaming – a convention that had been around since the 1980s in titles such as the pixillated classic *Knight Lore*. It's a look that still has the power to beguile beyond simply appealing to your sense of nostalgia. Within *Baldur's Gate II*, the essentially two-dimensional graphics reveal an astonishing attention to detail as you move across the Amn region, between streets and shops, to ruined castles, charming grottoes and abandoned mines – all energized with their own unique atmospheric

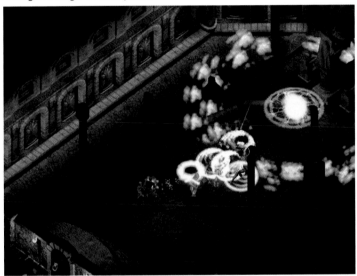

The isometric viewpoint is perfect for devising your party's strategy – and watching the results.

soundtracks (the conversational hubbub in taverns is a particularly nice touch).

In keeping with the swords-and-sorcery literature from which the game takes its inspiration, certain creatures tend to inhabit specific locales; kobolds are particularly fond of the aforementioned mines, whilst travelling at night through the Wood of Sharp Teeth is likely to elicit a hostile reception from the native werewolves. It follows, of course, that you shouldn't expect the Sea of Swords to be the place for a spot of afternoon boating.

This level of detail is part of a much, much larger picture, however. Like the Middle-Earth stories that this D&D world draws upon, "epic" only scratches the surface of what to expect from the quest-driven main plot and countless subplots (you're looking at a couple of hundred hours of gameplay). Surviving everything Amn can throw at you depends on your choice of companions, whom you enlist as you progress along your travels, and ensuring that they are well equipped (a trip to the nearest supplies store can sort this out, providing you have the means). Making sure that they share a good range of skills – magical, combat and stealth abilities – is a good start; likewise that they get on and that you don't ask them to act against their consciences (otherwise you'll hear grumblings). Once you have achieved these minor miracles of personnel management, the world of Baldur's Gate is yours to explore – taking into account, that is, the small matter of the fate of gods and nations that seems to have been thrust upon you.

And if that's what stokes your roleplaying fire, then you can expand the geographical world with the *Throne of Bhaal* expansion pack. It may not add to the main plot, but it'll certainly eat into the time you would otherwise spend developing your character in the real world.

Battlefield 2

PC; Digital Illusions CE, EA; 2005

The history of multiplayer team-based shooters is littered with the bodies of good, great and middling games. Whilst *Battlefield 2*'s precursors, *Battlefield 1942* and *Battlefield Vietnam*, were previously responsible for many of those bodies, *Battlefield 2*'s appearance in the field meant they joined their victims. Up to that point, they had

Tribes 2

PC, Mac; Dynamix, Sierra; 2001

Before the actually-quite-good *Tribes: Vengeance* finished off the series, many believed that *T2*, as it was fondly known, represented the future of strategic FPS multiplayer battling. It was certainly the first such game to incorporate indoor and outdoor arenas within the same maps: it featured customizable classes; and it improved upon the original's vehicles. But it was also plagued by tech issues – as manifested by the need to download a patch to fix up the game's very patching utility.

Unreal Tournament 3

PC, PS2, Xbox 360; Epic Games, Midway Games; 2007

It's not often that a game can be likened to a musical style, as it may be to a film, but when the music in question is as hardcore as techno and the game is as old school as *Unreal Tournament*, you get some idea of just what to expect from this single and multiplayer extravaganza: brashly colourful visuals, insistent action and a concept boiled down to its bare bones. If that all sounds too much, don't worry, the game's cheerful overindulgence in big weapons, beefy psychopaths and nonstop cursing will win you over with its ludicrousness.

been the kings of open warfare, a kind of *Medal of Honor* meets *Tribes* (as opposed to the more tactically nuanced franchises such as *Ghost Recon* or *Team Fortress*) that threw troops, vehicles, ships and aircraft onto the battlefield and let players choose their method of warfare. *Battlefield 2*, however, brought a new level of maturity and strategy to the chaos of the digital battleground.

That's not to say the usurper has no sense of playfulness. If anything, positing the near future as a place where China, the US and a newly formed Middle Eastern Coalition are at war and then making their epic battles so immensely entertaining takes a determined cheerfulness – but then the ability to endlessly respawn after being fragged certainly takes the sting out of death's tail.

DICE took a singular approach to making this work. First, they slimmed down the game modes to just Conquest, in which players must capture – and retain – multiple flags spread across vast maps. Then they decided that while some games thrive on a variety of game types, *Battlefield 2* would flesh out the one mode so comprehensively that there's no need for anything further. The maps alone are huge, featuring vastly different terrains that invite all kinds of strategies for the plethora of troop-types, vehicles, planes and helicopters at players' disposal.

For a more comprehensive game, also read more grown-up: despite the propensity for bigger explosions and the breakneck speed of battle, this is a game that rewards teamwork. Individual players pick one of the seven classes (from Assault to Medics, Mechanics and Special Forces) and choose a team to join – but they can only rise to become squad commanders if more deserving than others. The game tracks and

The *Battlefield 2* game takes very contemporary-looking warfare into the near future in the most sophisticated episode so far.

ranks a whole host of player stats, and such activities as giving squad members first-aid or showing good leadership skills earn ribbons and medals that feed back into your rank, all the way from PFC to General. It's akin to social networking, reinforcing both a sense of camaraderie and competition – something that's further underlined by the maps, which scale up or down in size according to whether there are 16, 32 or 64 players, completely changing the dynamics of battle and communication.

Pulling the previously retrospective *Battlefield* takes on warfare straight into the twenty-first century, *BF2* certainly invokes a frisson of forbidden excitement: whilst the scenarios for each war ground are fictional, they bear close resemblance to global troop activities in recent history. But recognition that the game's true worth is in its gameplay, rather than its setting, came from the modding community. No sooner was it released than a raft of total conversions appeared, with EA's full blessing, taking the setting back to World War II (not least the excellent *Forgotten Hope 2*) – tacit acknowledgement, perhaps, that in the world of videogames, it's still everybody's favourite war.

BioShock

Xbox 360, PC; 2K Games; 2007

Students of literature, hold onto your hats. As unlikely as it may seem, this near-perfect FPS takes its cues directly from some pretty heavyweight authors: Poe, Orwell, Verne and Philip K. Dick, to name but a few. Even Old Testament references are thrown in for good measure, alongside a few narrative-perspective tricks as originated by Henry James and Joseph Conrad. But no one influence is more in evidence than that of Ayn Rand, author of *Atlas Shrugged* and the founder of Objectivist philosophy, which she described as "the concept of man as a heroic being, with his own happiness as the moral purpose of his life, with productive achievement as his noblest activity, and reason as his only absolute". It's a frame of reference that informs absolutely everything about *BioShock*.

Even so, *BioShock* exists within its own fully formed and self-contained universe: Rapture, a massive submarine metropolis on the Atlantic floor. Created in the late 1940s by one Andrew Ryan (Ayn Rand, indeed) as an Eden for souls wishing to throw off the yokes of religion and State to build a society based on individualism, it was to be a Disneyland for the ego (and Ryan does bear more than a passing resemblance to Walt). But paradise lost, not found, is the cornerstone of *BioShock*. The emergence of an intellectual elite, which allowed genetic experimentation on children in the name of furthering humanity (echoes of Nazi experimentation are firmly underlined here), and the rise of a criminal underclass lead ultimately to internecine warfare and the breakdown of society.

Which is the point at which the player enters the scene as sole survivor of a mid-ocean plane crash, washed up at the surface entrance to Rapture and apparently suffering from post-traumatic memory loss. The first of many narrative sleights of hand, this is swiftly followed by the establishment of the game's narrative device, with the plot unfolding via a series of radio messages and discovered memos – significantly, you very rarely get to meet the protagonists attempting to steer you in conflicting directions. It's a mechanism that both builds tension and slots in well with the game's exploration of free-will within the inherently contradictory set-up of a linear shooter.

In a city in acute decay, its population massacred and the survivors crazed junkies (splicers) out to kill you, sometimes the choices are clear. But the most significant moral dilemma arrives in the form of ADAM and EVE, the steroid-like substances developed from the stem-cell research. As well as the splicers roaming the city there are the Little Sisters, the genetically engineered children who exist solely to manufacture ADAM within their bodies

Rapture: this underwater metropolis is perhaps the most chillingly atmospheric setting for a game yet.

– and to harvest it from the corpses of the splicers and their victims. As such, they are Jack's source of his own genetic upgrading: by harvesting the girls himself, and thus ending their lives, he receives a large boost of ADAM; by releasing them instead, a far smaller amount is granted, with the reward being a beautifully engineered moment of emotion for the player. Trouble is, the benefits of ADAM (the ability to electrocute or throw fireballs at your enemies, for example) can be key to surviving Rapture, and they hold an obvious appeal beyond the more conventional, albeit upgradeable, weaponry at Jack's disposal – especially when used in combination with it.

As well as flaunting its more serious influences, embedded within *BioShock* are the genetic codes of *System Shock 2* (see p.75), *Deus Ex* (see p.74) and the *Fallout* series (see p.81). Like them, *BioShock* is a distinct evolutionary step for storytelling in games, which is a wonderful irony, given that you spend most of your time wondering whether you can believe the stories you're being told.

Black and White

PC; Lionhead Studios, EA; 2001

Imagine a fairy-tale archipelago of blue seas and sandy beaches, lush lowlands, fields in which livestock graze, with highlands and mountains in the background. Then imagine being able to swoop

An animal avatar needs close management to prevent it eating any potential worshippers.

around the place and find it dotted with villages worshipping whichever local deity is demanding their attention. Now put yourself in the position of that deity, and you have the essence of 2001's *Black and White*, arguably the game that propelled Peter Molyneux (see p.247) into the really big time (he was awarded an OBE in 2004). While his 2005 sequel introduced more structure, the original remains more appealing for its delightfully open-ended strategic and roleplaying elements. It's also beautifully rendered, captivating to play and very, very funny. Which is just as well, as there's an immense amount to get to grips with.

You begin the game without any followers, the goal being to become deified by villagers. This is achieved through supernatural deeds – and the more people believe in you, the more you are capable of. Once the mere mortals are on board, there's the pressing matter of slugging it out with rival deities.

All this is done through a two-pronged approach, but with the premise that no action is right or wrong – it simply has a knock-on effect on how events turn out. That said, the physical manifestations of your conflicting conscience (a devil who sounds like Danny DeVito and an angel who doesn't) will try to swing you one way or the other.

The first of your two prongs is the "hand-of-god", a cursor that manipulates the environment, moving objects about and even throwing them around – there's nothing more likely to inspire villagers' belief in the supernatural than being lifted up by unseen forces and chucked into the sea. Likewise, spells can create food supplies for grateful farmers, while arbitrary fire from the heavens will also impress. Once convinced, worshippers will pay their respects at a local temple: the more followers you have, the more your sphere of influence extends across the land and the more your godly powers increase. Then it's on to the next village for increasingly tougher challenges and even more power.

The second – and more entertaining – approach is to train up a giant anthropomorphic creature (such as a cow, ape or tiger) as your earthly avatar to continue impressing people in one village while you're off converting another. This is where the game really comes into its own, with the animal's superb AI. Just like a puppy, it's curious, gets hungry and needs to answer the call of nature: if you don't train it to do things in a way (and in places) you see fit, it'll get bored or hungry, or both, at which point villagers and livestock might get munched, or trees uprooted and hurled around. Administer several hand-of-god slaps and it will learn that it's done wrong; to encourage repeat behaviour, tickle it instead (the tactile equivalent of doggie chocs).

Vast, beguiling and humorous, *Black and White* offers an immersive world where opposing gods fight using giant cows as weapons, where errant avatars cause chaos until disciplined, and where a few headstrong mortals will stubbornly refuse to believe in you until you pick them up and give them a good shaking.

Fable

PC, Mac, Xbox; Lionhead Studios, Microsoft Game Studios (PC & Xbox), Feral Interactive, Robosoft Interactive (Mac); 2004

Peter Molyneux had grand ambitions for his RPG: its working title was *Project Ego*, with free will and moral choice at its core. His aim was the ultimate sandbox, in which gamers would continuously mould their character through actions, rather than predefined sets of attributes. But such lofty ideals don't find their best expression when the consequences of moral choice are so literal and colourful. Playing as evilly or in as saintly a manner as possible certainly leads to some interesting narrative; the nuanced, greyer areas in between, however, see good and evil simply counterbalancing each other, and the point of the sandbox is lost.

Broken Sword: Shadow of the Templars

PC, Mac, PS; Revolution Software, Virgin Interactive/Sony; 1996

The Parisian café scene marks the start of both George's story and one of the most successful adventure game series ever.

You'd be forgiven for thinking that it was Dan Brown who popularized religious conspiracy theories, but Charles Cecil and his company Revolution Software had done it seven years earlier with the first *Broken Sword* game, despite its age still the cream of the adventure game crop. Subtitled *Circle of Blood* for the US market, its original name was restored for a re-release on the Game Boy Advance in 2002. There have been three subsequent games in the series so far, inevitably produced in 3D the last couple of times, a shift that doesn't automatically mean a better gameplay experience; in fact, the fourth episode includes an additional point-and-click interface for purists.

Despite its contemporary setting, the game has a determinedly old-fashioned Saturday-morning serial feel: bravery in the face of danger, sneaking around, a bit of fighting, plenty of eavesdropping, and a will-they, won't-they romance between naïve American tourist George Stobbart and glamorous Parisian photographer Nico. Things start with a bang as George narrowly avoids being blown to pieces in an explosion at a Parisian café, a scenario complete with a dead body and a mysterious clown fleeing the vicinity. Caught up in events a wiser man would run from, he's soon travelling to an Irish village, a mansion in Spain and a historic site in Syria, all the while trailed by a killer in fancy dress, to uncover a web of intrigue that began with the disbandment of the Knights Templar in the fourteenth century. Each location is painstakingly rendered, changing in between visits – especially in the case of Paris, Nico's home and the hub of the game – to provide a vividly real world for the stylized animated characters to inhabit.

No surprise from a developer who's a firm advocate of games learning from the older and more successful medium of film, *Broken Sword*'s cinematic influences are striking. Cut scenes show events unfolding of which the characters are unaware, lending a tension that's enhanced by composer Barrington Pheloung's sympathetic soundtrack, while the dark themes of conspiracy, murder and world domination are pricked by Indiana Jones-style humour, not least in the ironic commentary of the unlikely hero. It's this liveliness that prevents a game where so much depends on dialogue – a lot of it expository, too – from becoming boring, the relationship between the characters and their personalities investing a complex historical plot with spark and relevance. Fortunately, extensive knowledge of medieval religious orders isn't required, though you'll certainly be better informed by the time you reach the climactic finale.

Though scrolling can be a little jerky and character movement sometimes teeth-grindingly slow, the script keeps you hooked from the very first scene; from then on the narrative is checked only by your own actions or inactions. George always knows exactly what he's meant to achieve; it's how he does it that's the trick, and while almost every puzzle is logical in the extreme, its solution isn't always obvious. Perhaps best of all, in this speech-based adventure every laugh is intentional: foreign accents and all, the acting is just as classy as the script.

Burnout Revenge

PS2, Xbox, Xbox 360; Criterion Games, EA; 2005

The original *Burnout* of 2002 was born into a racing-game world that had grown old before its time. Serious sims like *Gran Turismo*,

Broken Sword 2: The Smoking Mirror

PC, PS; Revolution Software, Virgin Interactive/Sony; 1997

Set six months after the first episode, *The Smoking Mirror* features a few familiar characters but takes the action to another continent, allowing the skilled background artists to paint the imposing temples and detailed carvings of the ancient Maya in Central America, in a plot involving a cult devoted to a bloodthirsty god.

Broken Sword: The Sleeping Dragon

PC, PS2, Xbox; Revolution Software, THQ; 2003

After six years the series is reborn in 3D, with a simultaneous console and PC release. George and Nico look splendid as they trot the equally splendid-looking globe, chasing a conspiracy from the Congo to Glastonbury. The game suffers from an awkward control system, however.

Broken Sword: The Angel of Death

PC; Revolution Software, THQ; 2006 (released in the US as *Secrets of the Ark*, 2007)

Marks a return to point-and-click gameplay – in a 3D world – with the emphasis on infuriating puzzles rather than action events. Our hero's roped into a convoluted plot centred on that ever-popular biblical artefact, the Ark of the Covenant.

Project Gotham Racing (see p.159) and the *Colin McRae* and *TOCA* series abounded; even the granddaddy of console-based racers, *Ridge Racer* (see p.30) had lost its *joie de vivre*, while *Need For Speed* had simply lost its way. For the first time since *Demolition Derby* (1995), here was an arcade-style game that appealed to humanity's hitherto unrewarded primal urge to race pell-mell through the streets, highways and freeways of a heavily trafficked city and to cause jaw-dropping mayhem with multiple-vehicle pile-ups. Skip forward several excellent instalments to *Burnout Revenge*, wherein everything was turned up to eleven in the enjoyment stakes. While its predecessors had gamers smiling knowingly at reckless abandonment, *Revenge* leaves them grinning, and quite possibly drooling, like village idiots at its sheer lunacy. Subtlety, then, is not a concept obviously associated with *Revenge*; but it's by no means a simpleton's game, with a sophisticated level structure and some impressive programming under its hood.

Adrenaline is what it's all about. The graphics engine, for example, shifts things along at sixty frames per second (bear in mind that movies usually move at around 24 FPS), giving the impression of playing *Wipeout* on four wheels, but with oncoming traffic. Usually punishable activities such as near misses, tailgating and playing chicken with oil tankers are rewarded with boosting power, a necessity to win races and useful in providing the extra oomph to eliminate rivals by sideswiping them into

Rewarding reckless racing with dramatic takedowns, *Burnout* is not a game for Sunday drivers.

immovable objects or shunting them into other vehicles – so-called "Takedowns", which come with gratifyingly instant replays. Most impressive of all are "Vertical Takedowns", wherein judicious use of boosting power and strategically placed ramps can see players sail right over their rivals and then take out the leader by landing on its roof. Players whose cars fall victim to the blisteringly fast pace and end up crashing still have a chance to take out pursuing rivals, thanks to an aftertouch system that allows them to influence the trajectory of their hurtling wreck. The game's in-menu indie, dance and punk soundtrack, meanwhile, offers no respite from the lunk-headedness of it all.

Of the various race modes available – and all have reckless driving as their *raison d'être* – the one that confirms *Revenge*'s position as racing's *Jackass* is the Crash mode. Not in fact a race at all, the proposition is thus: take a given road junction or traffic situation (preferably one with as much potential for destruction as possible); point the player's car at it; then catapult them towards it, letting the player control direction only; then sit back and watch the destruction. The more vehicles taken out, the closer the player gets to being able to use the "Crashbreaker", a detonation that jettisons the player's crashed car skywards – thereby allowing aftertouch to be applied to take out any traffic previously missed.

As one of the most pick-up-and-playable driving titles ever created, there's no best time to serve up *Revenge*. Its successor, *Burnout Paradise* (2008) was excellent, but its enticingly open-world environment frustrated many for its lack of save points. More criminally, it ditched the moronic thrills of the Crash mode, ultimately missing the point of the game's existence.

Call of Duty 4: Modern Warfare

PC, Mac, Xbox, Wii, Xbox 360, PS3; Infinity Ward, Aspyr, Activision; 2007

Medal of Honor (see p.71) has much to answer for. It was almost single-handedly responsible for World War II becoming one of the most popular settings for the FPS genre, the *Allied Assault* (2002, on the PC) and *Finest Hour* (also 2002, for consoles) episodes representing the pinnacle of cinematic shoot-'em-ups, taking Private Ryan's Normandy beach-landing experience and transferring it straight to the gaming screen. Then came the *Call of Duty* franchise, initially developed by Infinity Ward, which successfully outclassed all subsequent *MoH* games. But unwilling to let things go stale, they bravely, and briefly, refrained from working on the series after the second instalment, handing the reins over to Treyarch instead, who had in their ranks several former *Medal of Honor* developers. *Call of Duty 3* was subsequently hugely successful, and many believed that

Treyarch had nailed the genre. But they weren't counting on Infinity Ward's next project: taking the franchise into the next combat arena with *Call of Duty 4: Modern Warfare*. It didn't do anything radically different (beautifully refined visuals aside), but it did make everyone realize that all the series needed was a breath of fresh air to remain king of the wartime hill.

From the outset, the depth of intensity is key to the single-player experience, with the game's high production values performing the remarkable trick of making you forget that this is actually an on-the-rails shooter. Set during a fictional contemporary war in the Middle East and Russia, whose roots aren't too far removed from today's political crises, you play from the perspective of a US Marine and two British SAS soldiers. Swapping between these perspectives as the story progresses through its short but exhausting single-player experience (lasting around seven hours at the regular difficulty setting), you get to rappel from helicopters, bolt from doorway to doorway in war-ravaged cities so as to avoid fire, and inch your way through the undergrowth in forests as you attempt to stealthily approach the enemy. If you

In both multiplayer and single-player modes, the action doesn't let up long enough for you to stop and admire the incredibly detailed environments.

had time to, you'd probably marvel at the beautiful (and destructible) environments – the detail in the vegetation (see picture above), as well as ambient effects like water reflections, would be seductive were it not for the reason you're there. The likelihood is that you won't, though: with the sound of incoming shells, the panicked shouts of the enemy and your comrades in the chaos, various pieces of scenery exploding and grenades landing at your feet, your main priority is going to be finding safety before poking your head out to take a pot shot at the enemy. The AI-controlled soldiers will be doing the same: you'll see the enemy making some realistic group AI decisions, such as a mass fall back when defending unsuccessfully, rather than making the classic videogaming AI error of stubbornly holding their ground until dead. Likewise, your own squad members are just as likely to give you covering fire and smoke grenades when you move up into the danger zone as they are to make the decision to lead the charge themselves. Whack the difficulty level up to Veteran mode and you're in suicide alley.

Once you've been satisfyingly traumatized by the single-player story, the online mode offers up to eighteen players the chance to answer the call-up together. Various character classes, which can level-up via experience points, a decent clutch of modes, vehicles to utilize and even the ability to call in airstrikes make for a multiplayer experience that demands intelligent teamwork. And the usual concerns about a drop in graphical quality from the solo game can be dismissed: the multiplayer version is every bit as intense as the Story mode. Much like the real wars it's based on, it's as if George W. had never declared "Mission Accomplished".

Command & Conquer

PC; Westwood, Virgin Interactive; 1995

The origins of the RTS genre aren't exactly murky, but they are the cause of debate amongst RTS fans. As far back as 1989, *Herzog Zwei* on the Mega Drive (Genesis) showed signs that developers were beginning to think in RTS frames of reference, offering the ability to command multiple individual units in real time to attack and defend bases. A bigger defining moment was Westwood's *Dune II* (1993), for its use of resource gathering, structural development trees and opposing forces with customized weaponry. Blizzard's *Warcraft: Orcs and Humans* (1994) evolved things by adding in multiplayer options. But it was *Dune II*'s development team that hit the nail on the head with their next title, *Command & Conquer*, which was, as developer Brett Sperry remembers, "the net result of the *Dune II* wishlist."

The first instalment of the franchise that would go on to sell 25 million units between 1995 and 2007 (when it was batched up with

Medal of Honor: Allied Assault
PC, Mac; EA, 2015 Inc; 2002

Medal of Honor: Frontline
PS2, Xbox, GC,
EA, 2015 Inc; 2002

Once king of the World War II FPS, the *Medal of Honor* series has become tired of late. Their finest hours were the same set-piece battle that these two titles share – that of the D-day beach-landings. These were among the first times that you began to believe that gaming could rise above B-movie pretensions. Unfortunately, the games peak fairly early on, with later levels set in sniper-infested bombed-out towns with the most insanely difficult gameplay.

Age of Empires
PC, Mac; Microsoft, Ensemble Studios; 1997

In equal parts god-sim and RTS, *Age of Empires* was as much an educational tool as a game, with players guided through the Egyptian, Greek, Babylonian and Yamato civilizations through the Stone, Tool, Bronze and Iron ages. It's a surprisingly hypnotic experience: perhaps it's the soothing background music; or the enjoyment of watching your subjects go about their daily business from on high. But let your attention slip and it's goodnight civilization, as your delicately laid-out nation is ravaged by an altogether more military-minded country.

Battlezone
PC; Activision; 1998

A far cry from Atari's 1980 dual-joystick and periscope-equipped arcade cabinet in implementation, Activision's later adaptation captured the original's spirit and then added extra zest. Not only were the graphics state-of-the-art 3D, but added to the shooting action was a kind of first- and third-person *Command & Conquer*-style of gameplay in which resource gathering and commanding forces were equally as vital as getting your cross-hairs over the right target. Moreover, you got to control a whole host of vehicles manually.

its whopping twelve sequels and various add-ons as the twelfth-anniversary *C&C Saga*) wasn't just about revolutionary gameplay, effectively setting the basic rules for RTS games thereafter; it was also a massive shot in the arm for PC gaming – exactly what it needed in the face of the PlayStation's rising star. (Despite being ported to several consoles, it suffered on these for having the classic mouse-and-keyboard control system at its heart – something console handsets of the day adapted to poorly.) Furthermore, despite the growing trend for graphics-intensive, resource-hungry PC games, playing *C&C* was so far within reach of the average home computer that its original pressings didn't even need Windows 95, being run instead through DOS. The most futuristic bit of kit needed was a CD-ROM drive.

Around fifteen years on, *C&C* remains an object lesson in generating exhilaration through judicious detail. The astute use of inter-level cut scenes – which seemed cheesy at the time but now, in our post-9/11 world of Bin Laden video scoops, cable news bias and satellite uplinks, feels disturbingly insightful – propels the plot forward at a terrific rate, giving depth to the conflict being played out by the Global Defense Initiative and the Brotherhood of Nod across the world. Then, segueing neatly into the battlefields, the pace of conflict ebbs and flows according to the missions, which strike a balance between handholding and setting the player free. Even the basic viewpoint and character animations, comprising nothing more sophisticated than a bunch of 2D pixels moving a little jerkily across an unrotatable landscape, retain the power to charm thanks to being coupled to some effective audio components – moments such as a commando shouting "Got a present for ya!" after sticking a C4 charge to an enemy SAM site, and a nonstop in-game techno soundtrack, pretty much sum up *C&C*'s pace and cheerfully gung-ho take on war.

It would require days to list the titles that wouldn't exist without *Comand & Conquer* and to calculate its popularity. Suffice to say that when Electronic Arts released it as a free download to promote the *Saga* compilation, they received so many online hits that they had to take it offline, passing the weight of traffic to third-party FTP sites. A present for ya indeed.

Company of Heroes

PC; Relic, THQ; 2006

Company of Heroes developer Relic has a reputation for greatness and innovation in the RTS world, responsible as they were for the epic fantasy-cum-sci-fi RTS *Warhammer 40,000* in 2004, and the pioneering *Homeworld* (see p.37) in 1999. So it was with reservations that gamers received the news that their next project would be set in World War II, a setting done to death over the years, and done, for the most part, blandly. It didn't help, either, that the game's publisher would be THQ, a company better known for its World Wrestling Federation games than anything cerebral. Yet both outfits broke the mould with *Company of Heroes*, a game that includes everything that's great about the genre and then shows you how it can be even better than you thought: the intensive gameplay, visceral, fully 3D graphics and ambient audio effects combine to leave you feeling as though you've just stepped out of an IMAX screening of *Saving Private Ryan*.

Using a historic setting is one thing – in this case following the progress of the US Army's Able and Dog companies from their D-day landings through to the decisive battles that gained the Allies a foothold in France – but the depth of realism here extends to bringing the classic RTS conventions right down to earth. There's no truck with the notion of harvesting a generic resource à la Tiberium, for example. Instead, you must capture the enemy's limited fuel and ammunition dumps for yourself, and take strategic points in order to call

CoH immerses you in the sights and sounds of wartime chaos as you direct troops in the Allied attacks on Normandy.

Myth II: Soulblighter
PC, Mac; Bungie Studios; 1998

In between *Marathon* and *Halo*, Bungie left the FPS field to develop one of the more tactically nuanced RTS games of the 1990s. Rejecting resource-gathering outright, gameplay focuses instead on the use of terrain and troop formations, which counted as highly advanced thinking a decade before *Company of Heroes*. But the medieval-horror atmosphere sucked you in just as much – weather and ambient effects like rolling fog, lightning, wandering wildlife, falling leaves, destructible landscapes and a rotatable and zoomable viewpoint also prefigured *CoH*'s attention to detail. The AI, however, can't touch it.

up reserves from behind the front lines; and you need to keep your supply lines open for these to be of any use to you in the first place. Even if you're not used to thinking beyond the rock-scissors-paper tactics of most RTS games you'll soon be thinking in ways that would make generals Eisenhower and Bradley proud, outflanking Panzers with your less-powerful Shermans to punch holes in their rear armour, placing heavy field guns in elevated cover to create deadly killzones and marshalling your Rangers to cut off retreating enemies in ruthless pincer movements. If things go well, units accrue tactical awareness, but they'll also lose morale if casualties mount up.

As with any decent RTS, you can move around the map at will, but what's not de rigueur is the fact that the scenery will change as you do. You might leave a group of Rangers quietly holing up in an abandoned house to establish a base of fire, then have to return in haste to evacuate them as it starts to collapse under the strain of mortar fire; muddy craters appear as shells fall; and fences and walls collapse as tanks roll relentlessly through them. The sense of apocalyptic destruction couldn't be more acute as you move around each of the fifteen levels' maps, with the sounds of battle growing and fading as you scramble from flashpoint to flashpoint.

Whilst aimed squarely at a non-hardcore audience, *CoH* is still a tough slog. Bertrand Russell's observation that "War does not determine who is right – only who is left" wouldn't normally be called up in reference to a videogame, but it encapsulates perfectly the sense of nihilistic exhaustion engendered by the field-by-field and street-by-street progress through Normandy's countryside and cities that *CoH* is all about.

Deus Ex

PC, Mac; Ion Storm, Eidos Interactive, Aspyr; 2000

Those who have been paying the slightest bit of attention to current affairs over the last few years will recognize how prescient *Deus Ex* was in 2000. Raising its central themes at the dinner table – bioweapons, nanotechnology, war on terror, the return of fascism, an unaccountable secret service – will no longer get you labelled as a nutter. There are nods to the loopier side of conspiracy theorizing for sure, including the Illuminati and Majestic 12, and these provide entertainment in and of themselves until you realize that this pre-9/11 game's rendering of the New York skyline leaves out the Twin Towers – an omission justified by the developers as being the result of a terrorist attack prior to the game's setting. (Interestingly, the data for the towers is actually included in the game's code, but remains unused due to the Unreal graphical engine's texture-memory limitations.) Intentionally and otherwise, *Deus Ex* handles some pretty dark materials.

Most obviously and deliberately, however, it pays homage to such futuristic dystopias as *Blade Runner*, *Logan's Run* and *The Matrix* (lead character J.C. Denton owes a huge sartorial debt to Neo in particular), with the long reach of *System Shock 2* (see p.75) also in evidence. In this particular vision of the 2050s, the world is a dark, grubby place, with civilization on the brink of collapse and its population at the mercy of the Grey Death, a plague against which there is just one defence – the Ambrosia vaccination. Ambrosia's availability, however, is limited to an elite, including the heads of FEMA and UNATCO (United Nations Anti-Terrorist Coalition), the militarized organizations that control its distribution (in further deference to false-flag conspiracists, Ambrosia's manufacturer also turns out to be the Grey Death's producer). Faced with no democratic alternative, opponents to this policy have taken up arms to appropriate Ambrosia for the masses – for which the state designates them terrorists. Step forward J.C. as the UNATCO nanotech-enhanced agent charged with objectives that increasingly have more to do with the erosion of civil rights than crime.

Which is significant, as *Deus Ex*'s mechanics are based on choice, allowing players to use their moral compass to steer aspects of the plot – and while it predates *BioShock* by the best part of a decade, it's still a neat counterpoint to the latter (see p.62). As J.C. becomes ever more immersed in the personal and governmental politics of those around him – civilians, enemies and allies alike – the more his actions and words forge his own moral maze. Perhaps significantly, it's never made clear what J.C.'s initials stand for, and not for nothing are Icarus and Daedalus referenced in a story involving hyper-ambition and superhuman abilities.

Wherein lies the second-most important aspect of *Deus Ex*: the ability to upgrade the self through nanotechnology. It's an addictive

System Shock 2
PC; Irrational Games, Looking Glass Studios; 1999

Although *Deus Ex* is the superior title, it wouldn't exist without *System Shock 2*. Marrying the FPS to the RPG genre and throwing in emergent gameplay, *System Shock 2* showed that all-out action is a perfect foil for more balanced storytelling elements. A naval spaceship's experimental journey has gone drastically wrong, and the player must work their way through it to survive. It's closer to Danny Boyle's *Sunshine* horror than Kubrick's *2001* musings, with successive clues as to what has happened uncovering a grislier and more sinister picture, cranking up the tension until you're a bundle of nerves.

and very necessary survival tool, but its ramifications – that the more non-human one becomes, the more inhuman it is possible to be – are made clear early on in the form of a cyborg who has lost all the redeeming features of its original humanity. In a neat inversion of the original deus ex machina, God – or the agent of free will, in this case Man – has become machine.

Director Warren Spector (see p.254) never explicitly stated that there were existential conundrums he wanted to explore, as Ken Levine did with *BioShock*, but scattered references throughout to Asimov, G.K. Chesterton and even *Richard III* indicate they were playing on his mind. And more power to *Deus Ex* for it: in 2000, its plot seemed lifted from the pages of a graphic novel: nearly ten years on, it looks like it was ringing alarm bells. Next step: bionic CIA agents.

Devil May Cry 3: Dante's Awakening

PS2, PC; Capcom; 2005 (Special Edition, 2006)

What to make of a game that's all about stylish gun- and swordplay? It's an uncomfortably hot theme in the current political climate, but this is no *Manhunt 2*; the violence may be "casual", in fact it prides itself on being so, but there's no evidence of the "sadism" or "callousness of tone" mentioned in the BBFC's report on that game. Violence in *Devil May Cry* would be better described as exhilaratingly acrobatic, the massacre of swarms of nasty demonic creatures by a silver-haired, swashbuckling chap with a pretentious name. Dante has devil blood in him, but he's won the DNA lottery on that score, with all the superhuman powers but none of the hideous looks: a perfectly muscled specimen with a rockstar attitude, he's exactly the kind of protagonist that Jaffe's team rejected when creating *God of War* (see p.93).

The original *Devil May Cry* in 2001, which as legend tells it began development as a *Resident Evil* game (funnily enough, the same studio was later responsible for *Resident Evil 4*), was a revelation for its fast and fluid animation, over-the-top violence and atmospheric 3D environments. *DMC2* made for a disappointing follow-up, but *DMC3*, a prequel to the first game, raised the series to a new high point. The heavy metal and gothic imagery, hell and demonspawn, the towering, tumbledown architecture and moody lighting are all still present and correct, but with better music, better graphics and better overall flow. The script's overdramatic, throwaway lines are delivered with suitable arrogance, but anyone old enough to play this game should be taking the coolness factor with a pinch of salt anyway; still, as rogue demon hunters go, better to be Dante than Wesley.

Behind the style there is a story, broken up into bite-sized cut scenes that top and tail the intensive missions – they feel like prizes you've earned and indeed you can view them at leisure when you've unlocked them. But all in all the game is less about the eternal good–evil struggle between Dante and twin brother Vergil and more about the fighting. An adrenaline rush from start to finish, it's endlessly entertaining, the melee weapon and gun combos much easier to accomplish than their magnificent results would suggest. It's a long way from a fighting sim but that doesn't mean it doesn't ask for a good amount of strategy, both in the actual battles and when choosing which upgrades and special attacks to buy. Boss enemies follow a mythical pick-and-mix theme, including Cerberus and Beowulf, for example; beat them and you get to play with their weapons afterwards. Defeating enemies is only part of

Devil May Cry 4
PS3, Xbox 360; Capcom; 2008
DMC goes multiplatform, to the dismay of the 12,000-odd PlayStation fans who petitioned Capcom to keep the game a Sony exclusive. Longserving Dante (mostly) hands over to new boy Nero (pictured below on the right), brandishing a new weapon in the Devil Bringer, which shakes the game up as much as the next-gen looks and huge, beautifully detailed environments (so big, you need to install the game on the PS3's hard drive to reduce loading time).

winning, though: to seriously bulge your purse it has to be done in style, as judged by the number and variety of attacks as well as avoiding getting hit.

DMC3 is not an easy game, even in its *Special Edition* released to compensate for the insane difficulty of the original, where Normal was based on the Japanese Hard mode unlocked by a first playthrough. Hardcore fans may feel it's been tamed too far, despite extra playability as Vergil, but it's still a game that's designed for the skills of the practised gamer, one who thinks of *Street Fighter* on hearing Dante's battle cries. Taken on its own, high-powered terms, it's a demonstration of how to make a short-attention-span action game while luxuriating in the balletic moves of combat and gun battle in the same way as *The Matrix* or *Kill Bill Vol. 1*. Film buffs often sneer at these, but you suspect that deep inside they're thinking "How cool is that!"

Elder Scrolls IV: Oblivion

PC, Xbox 360, PS3; Bethesda Softworks, 2K Games; 2006

On its release in 2006, *Oblivion* was widely feted as the best role-playing game ever, which, whilst no mean feat, wasn't entirely unanticipated. The *Elder Scrolls* series has always thought big, and this episode – a whopping four years in development – is the most all-encompassing release yet, with its unprecedented depth and open-endedness of gameplay and enormous, beautifully rendered environments bulldozing even its harshest critics into begrudging praise. Yet more impressive is that in an era when the worth of a "next-gen" title is often measured by how much its online and multiplayer capabilities will carry it beyond the single-player plot, *Oblivion* achieves greatness whilst remaining a defiantly solo and offline experience, save for its downloadable expansion packs.

It's the holistic approach to roleplaying that sustains *Oblivion*'s momentum. To begin with, Bethesda created an astonishingly varied world encompassing scraggy mountains, lush pasture, coastal scenery and human settlements, from cities to lone hovels. They then populated it with around 1500 NPCs, each with their own agenda and personality (voice actors include Patrick Stewart and Terence Stamp); and an array of flora and fauna that is just as much a part of the gameplay as the people – flowers and herbs are there for utilizing in potions and lotions, whilst hunting down the frolicking deer will provide you with a decent supply of food (which is also pretty much how the prowling bears and wolves view you). Welcome to Cyrodiil, capital province of Tamriel, a pseudo-medieval swords 'n' sorcery world where spectacular sunsets and misty dawns (plus the occasional downpour) form the backdrop to an epic tale of intertwined loyalties, heroic achievements and dastardly deeds.

The story begins with you witnessing the assassination of Tamriel's emperor and then being entrusted with tracking down his successor. From then on, things are completely up to you, from picking your character's attributes (a process that hits the right mark between addressing hardcore RPG fans and easing newcomers into things) to choosing which strands of the plot you want to follow up on or skills you want to develop. So open-ended is the game, for example, that it's perfectly possible to become a top-notch mage without opening up the main story at all, thanks to the numerous subplots that take on lives of their own. You can gain influence in society by joining factions such as the fighters' or thieves' guilds, or purchase houses and even make business investments. This go-anywhere, do-anything approach extends to having multiple solutions to even the most minor of issues. Take being able to enter every single location in the game, even if it's ostensibly off-limits. Budding trespassers need only pick

Gorgeous as the environment looks, a suit of armour is never a wasted investment.

the lock of a closed shop, or, if their skills aren't yet up to that, they can try to pickpocket the key from the building's owner. Failing that, they could just mug them or, in some instances, persuade them to hand over the key; they might even cast a spell that unlocks the door – and so on.

Paralleling this freedom is the way *Oblivion* dispenses with the notion of morality, replacing it instead with Cyrodiil's legal system so that your deeds and misdemeanours (or those committed in public, at any rate) become the yardsticks by which NPCs judge you. On the surface you may be an upstanding member of the mages' guild, but in reality you might also be part of the murderous assassins' brotherhood. It's that level of depth that encapsulates *Oblivion* so well – scratch the surface and you'll end up seeing a lot more than you bargained for.

Fahrenheit (Indigo Prophecy)

PC, PS2, Xbox; Quantic Dream, Atari; 2005

David Cage, founder of Quantic Dream, thinks about interactive storytelling a lot. The manual for *Fahrenheit* (released as *Indigo Prophecy* in North America), for example, includes an impassioned plea for videogames to reach for the emotional depths of books, films and music. His premise – that this can be done in ways that don't involve pure adrenaline stimulation and still appeal to hardcore and non-gamers alike – effectively goes against how much of the gaming industry thinks, and *Fahrenheit*'s concept was greeted as vain ambition by many. And while *Fahrenheit* can't lay claim to reinventing the wheel, it's a significant step forwards in generating an emotional interactive narrative.

The opening scene gets straight to the nub of things by asking: what would you do if you found yourself in a position with no understanding of how you reached it? Especially when that involves waking from a trance in the restroom of a NYC diner to find a dead body at your feet and a knife, dripping with blood, in your hands. The player knows only what that character, Lucas Kane (pictured, left, at three different points in the game), believes: that whilst he was physically responsible, it was an unconscious act carried out as though possessed. At one level we identify with Lucas as frightened and panicked, and understand that he doesn't want be discovered; but our moral framework has been completely redefined. Does Lucas try to hide the body? Should he try to clear up the tell-tale bloodstains as well? Should he simply try to leave the restroom and risk the body's detection? Each choice has consequences for the plot.

Cage's chief line of gamer-engagement is to quite literally offer alternative perspectives. At one level, this involves choosing from multiple camera angles throughout the game, allowing a degree of directorial input. More significantly, it's through playing the action out alternately from the (third-person) viewpoints of a host of people, forcing the player to make choices as one character that will affect them later on as another. Most commonly these are in the roles of Lucas, on his increasingly desperate quest to uncover the reason for his actions before getting caught; and the two police officers assigned to catching him, Carla Valenti and Tyler Miles, adding a curious layer of foreknowledge that touches on the question of true freedom in gaming. Furthermore, these are highly complex, well-developed characters, with relationships and backgrounds that the player is required to engage with. Real-time events and common-sense prevail as they would in reality too: a ringing phone, if not picked up soon enough, will take a message. If Lucas takes medicine to calm his nerves (his state of mind is measured, as are all the characters', by a stress barometer), then following it up with an otherwise relaxing vodka can prove fatal.

Ultimately, *Fahrenheit* feels like the videogaming equivalent of a great indie flick: it takes the risks that the big studios won't and ends up teaching them new tricks. This hasn't been sufficient to realize Cage's dream of widening the appeal of gaming; but as a masterclass in stimulating and suspenseful storytelling, it stands tall in videogaming's recent history.

Fallout

PC, Mac; Black Isle Studios, Interplay; 1997

It's a rare videogame that lingers in the imagination as long as Black Isle's RPG *Fallout*, a masterclass in single-player storytelling that evokes a sense of immersion more usually associated with a favourite film or novel. Perhaps that's because its vision of a post-apocalyptic future, in which the world has effectively bombed itself back into the Stone Age, engages its audience as a more realistic proposition than any swords and sorcery theme could; or that it offers the player realistic choices within a semi-recognizable society; and that its influences are just as rooted in serious literary narrative as they are in popular cinema. All this is true to certain degrees, but *Fallout*'s greatest achievement is its implementation of the concept of free will in a game, attaching significance to almost everything that can be done. Like the *Elder Scrolls* series (see p.78), *Fallout*'s world can be explored and its characters interacted with in almost any order and manner the player chooses. But unlike *Elder Scrolls*, the results of conversations and actions cannot be easily undone, permanently changing the course of the game and thereby forcing the player to constantly re-orient their "what if" compass. No wonder, then, that over ten years on from its original release – and despite being a resolutely turn-based affair without recourse to the graphical flourishes of today's titles – it is frequently cited as one of the most re-playable games ever coded, for which it continues to receive expansions and additions from the modding community.

But *Fallout* was very nearly a game that wasn't, thanks, during its development, to Interplay's acquisition of the rights to the use of *AD&D* rules (at that time, *Fallout* was based on Steve Jackson's rival, less popular "Generic Universal RolePlaying System" rules; it was later converted to its own "Strength Perception Endurance Charisma Intelligence Agility Luck", or SPECIAL, rules). Effectively downgraded

Pulp fiction-style design elements permeate the game, from loading screen to manual.

to a B-list project thereafter, Black Isle took advantage of Interplay's relative disinterest to craft one of the most nuanced titles of any genre (the irony being that they laid the groundwork for the success of *Baldur's Gate* – see p.58 – the very title that bumped them from pole position in the first place).

The attention to detail they invested in the game yielded a richly detailed, irradiated landscape populated by ciphers from cult TV shows: *Flash Gordon*, *Doctor Strangelove*, *Mad Max* and Interplay's C64 game *Wasteland* are all referenced either literally or figuratively – and most importantly, relevantly. But *Fallout* finds its closest cousins in Russell Hoban's cult novel *Ridley Walker* and Walter Miller's classic *A Canticle for Leibowitz*, for their mutual understanding that more has been forgotten about the world's past than will ever be remembered. It also celebrates humanity's related ability to interpret new significance from the surviving shards of the past – often ending up with interpretations that are far removed from their original meanings. It's also disturbingly knowing about mankind's fascination with cyclical self-destruction, which the masterful scene-setting footage underlines by owing more to the Cold War era than to contemporary politics.

Which is to make *Fallout* sound heavy handed, whereas it's actually an engaging juxtaposition of dark brooding and sardonic wit, liberally referencing pulp fiction and steam-punk imagery as much as its heavy-weight sci-fi origins (at one point, even the TARDIS makes an appearance). Indeed, much like the period its visuals are so clearly influenced by – witness the Vault Boy cartoon figure – *Fallout* realizes it is dealing with dark matters but that the path to redemption lies in being determinedly, not to say insanely, optimistic.

Final Fantasy VII

PS; Square, Sony; 1997

It brought the Japanese roleplaying genre onto mainstream Western consoles; it was the ammunition Sony needed to make the PlayStation a success in Japan; it boasted cinematic sequences the likes of which had never been seen; it legitimized games as a popular art form; it was the fastest-selling game ever – just a few of the feats attributed to this PlayStation RPG from 1997. Truth or hype, one thing that's

---

Planescape: Torment
PC; Black Isle Studios, Interplay; 1999

Having made *Fallout 2* in 1998 – effectively more of the same, but bigger – Black Isle moved on to transferring AD&D's *Planescape* setting to the PC. The result: the videogame equivalent of the Necronomicon. It embraces Kafka-esque notions, seventeenth-century English slang and a floating skull with an acerbic wit. This was the first known implementation of consensus reality in a videogame, virtually no combat, and some very, very long conversations. But whilst the dialogue options were myriad, they had the effect of making the plot feel far more on rails than intended, whilst simultaneously requiring close attention: definitely not a game to be played after a beer or two.

undeniable is the still fierce devotion of its millions of fans, which the 2006 computer-generated movie sequel, *Final Fantasy VII: Advent Children*, and spinoff titles have done nothing to quench.

In many ways, the game simply marks the culmination of *Final Fantasy I* to *VI*, at a point before technology began to route the series in a subtly different direction. Whether it stands up these days to the minimum fifty hours of play is debatable, but watching just the cut scenes as an *Advent Children* DVD extra shows that its power to affect hasn't weakened with time, even if the intervening years have seen several of its gaming conceits – such as annoyingly frequent random encounters – undergo drastic change. Indeed, it's still regularly voted number one in polls for the best RPG and sometimes even the best videogame of all time.

It's the characterization that earns much of the praise: Cloud Strife, the shy and unwilling hero, one corner of a love triangle with feisty childhood pal Tifa and ethereal flower-seller Aeris. At a time when computer-generated characters and voice acting simply weren't good enough to express much in the way of humanity – and took up too much CD space, besides – these squat, child-like 3D characters function as emotional shorthand: with their spiky hairdos, puppy eyes, huge boots and gigantic weapons, they allow us to take more seriously the complicated science-versus-nature storyline. Perhaps even more relevant now than then, it starts as a rebel plot to disrupt Shinra Corporation's attempts to harness the world's life energy, developing into

First seen on the game's packaging, Cloud Strife and his massive sword would become an iconic image of the game.

an epic battle to save the earth from the destruction wielded by Cloud's nemesis, Sephiroth. Against the backdrop of this gorgeously rendered post-industrial fantasy world, smaller-scale themes of betrayal, sacrifice, memory and the search for identity are played out through adeptly translated scripts, complete with naturalistic pauses and interruptions.

Dotted throughout the game are the side-quests and arcade-style minigames that provide many of the lighter moments, top amongst them snowboarding and chocobo racing. Indeed, if you spend some time breeding different versions of these chickens-on-steroids, you can ride them into otherwise inaccessible areas to uncover secret items. Mostly, though, you'll be fighting your way across the vast world of Gaia, using an "active turn-based battle system" that relies on strategy rather than swift button pressing. The plot is more than just a frame on which to hang the combat and subsequent levelling up, however: fans reminisce about the times they were moved to tears, and somehow the game really does manage to involve, to surprise, and even shock the player. From its mood-setting, memorable orchestral score to its iconic characters, its well-executed script to its absorbing gameplay, *Final Fantasy VII* is huge, ambitious and continually challenging; and it all works exactly how it's supposed to, which in videogames is as rare as chocobos' teeth.

Final Fantasy XII

PS2; Square Enix; 2006

Final Fantasy VII was the game that introduced phoenix downs and mithril vests to millions of PlayStation owners, but *Final Fantasy XII* is the one to finally smudge that line between east and west. The numbers I to XII signify no more than the passing of time, really – it's not a sequential series, each game a variation and development of a collection of common themes. The music and design are universally superb, but the games can have a decidedly different feel, featuring cutely deformed characters or pouting, snub-nosed teens, with integral trading card games, even an online multiplayer world. With *FFXII*, though, the series sets out in a new direction while preserving long-held values such as a script that doesn't shy away from long words. It also offers a cinematic story where the characters are just fantastic

---

Crisis Core: Final Fantasy VII
PSP; Square Enix; 2008

Where *Dirge of Cerberus*, the 2006 action-shooter sequel featuring Vincent Valentine, was a crushing disappointment, *Crisis Core* proved to be worth the almost interminable wait – released nearly four years from Square's announcement, the US waited a further six months after the game had pumped up PSP sales in Japan. A prequel this time, it focuses on the story of another minor character, Zack, and his cohorts (including Cloud) based in Nibelheim. All that development time has made for breathtaking looks, as well as an RPG mechanic adapted to better suit the handheld system. It manages to pack in plenty of emotional punch all the same, as well as a somewhat bewildering levelling up system, as it moves inexorably to the ending all too familiar to veterans of *FFVII*.

The soaring skylines of Archades can be viewed in all their glory from the deck of an airship.

enough to be believable, reinforced by some emotionally resonant voice acting. That it all works so well is largely due to the richly detailed setting, the thoroughly imagined recurring world of Ivalice, where the small crossroads nation of Dalmasca is under occupation by the technologically superior Archadian empire, which is in turn at war with Rozarria. In Ivalice, like many a space opera, weird and wonderful creatures live alongside "humes"; from moogle salespeople to scaly baangas and graceful, rabbit-eared vieras, each race has its own quirks and abilities. Meanwhile, airships are the most glamorous way to travel between the nations, from the Arabic-styled Dalmascan capital, Rabanastre, to the soaring skyline of Archades, across the various deserts, steppes and coastlines in between.

Pickpocket Vaan from Rabanastre's slums is the main character, but this is really the story of a progressively interwoven cast of characters. In this war-torn world of high-level politics and betrayal, people often aren't who they appear to be. They are all, though, from rebel princess Ashe to sardonic sky pirate Balthier and his viera companion Fran,

Vaan's childhood pal Penelo, and disgraced Dalmascan knight Basch, plus various NPCs, determined to rid Dalmasca of its occupiers and to unite Ivalice under one ruler once more. Once they've joined the party, the main characters can be switched in and out, even in battle, which, for the first time, is seamlessly integrated into field exploration – there's no special command screen, no random encounters, nothing to break the flow. But instead of transforming completely into a real-time action game, it uses the Gambit system, which rewards strategic players rather than those with the fastest thumbs. Essentially prioritized instructions given to characters, Gambits keep up the battle speed and momentum, the effect something like an updated *Baldur's Gate*: it's fine to sit back and let the characters do their stuff but possible at any time to step in and take over manually.

Which makes it sound easier than it is, because building and maintaining a balanced party takes some work. Starting characters have attributes (higher hit points, or magick resistance, for example) that align them to certain roles, but otherwise they're blank slates, ready to be developed via a sort of chequerboard device whose squares are gradually uncovered to reveal abilities – magicks, technicks, weapons, armour, etc – that can be bought with licence points earned in battle. A varied party will have characters opening up different parts of the licence board, giving a satisfyingly visual sense of direction and progress. Buying, upgrading and equipping items and spells is made easy too, with a well-designed interface removing much of the hassle while leaving the fun bits.

The game's directors and art director had previously worked on other Square titles, and the seeds of many of these innovations can be spotted in *Final Fantasy Tactics* (1997; set in a world called Ivalice), *Vagrant Story* (2000; also set in Ivalice, and with seamless fighting and uncannily similar battle chains), and *Final Fantasy Tactics Advance* (2003; Ivalice again, with attendant bangaa, viera, clans and judges), which seems fitting for a game that, twenty years after the first *Final Fantasy,* shows just how far the series has developed. One of only a handful of titles to have received a full score from Japan's notoriously picky *Famitsu* magazine, *FFXII* is welcoming to newcomers as well as old-timers, providing scores of utterly absorbing hours of main story plus side quests, which those who are tired of more traditional fantasy RPGs will never want to end.

Final Fantasy XII: Revenant Wings
DS; Square Enix; 2007

The main series may be still with Sony, but Nintendo gets its fair share of *Final Fantasy* exclusives these days, including this worthwhile sequel to *FFXII*. Taking place a year after that game, main characters Vaan and Penelo, now captain and navigator of an airship, are depicted in the deformed cutesy character style absent from their original outing. The gameplay is entirely different too, though with an unmistakable *Final Fantasy* slant; officially a real-time strategy game, for hardcore *FF* fans it could be described as somewhere between a *Tactics* game and an RPG. Hardcore military strategists need not apply.

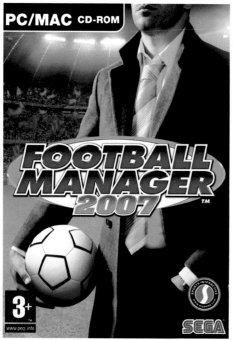

A tantalizingly anonymous cover image to say that it's you, the player, who's really the manager in question.

PC/MAC CD-ROM

FOOTBALL MANAGER 2007™

3+
www.pegi.info

SEGA

Football Manager 2007

PC, Mac, Xbox 360, PSP; Sports Interactive, Sega; 2006

There's more than one name for the beautiful game. *Worldwide Soccer Manager*, for instance, is called *Football Manager* in the UK, and was known, not so long ago, as *Championship Manager*. Designed by bedroom coders Paul and Oliver Collyer for the Amiga and Atari ST, *Champ Man* came out pretty much every year from 1992 until 2004, when the brothers split from their publisher, taking their code to Sega and leaving Eidos with the best-known name in sports management sims, but no developer to actually make the game. *Football Manager 5*, then, had to demonstrate that it and not *Championship Manager 5* was the true successor to *Championship Manager 03/04*. Each year since there's been a top-of-the-table scrap between the two (Eidos's game developed internally by Beautiful Game Studios), armed with scores of new features, not to mention expansion onto various consoles including, in *FM*'s case, the PSP.

Needless to say, the console versions offer a slightly different experience to the original PC/Mac game, due mostly to the lack of a mouse and, depending on the size of your TV, potentially eye-straining text. Even on a PC, though, when graphics and sound have become so integral a part of the gaming experience, it seems perverse that a game offering a top-down pitch view and no sound to speak of is as sophisticated as this one.

A love of football is the one essential requirement, since this is roleplaying in its purest sense, donning the sheepskin mantle of Ron Manager to take on every aspect of the day-to-day running of a football club: negotiating player contracts, scanning physio reports, managing not only a squad of players, but perhaps a youth team, a number of scouts, the club board and – one of the most crucial players in the game today – the media.

When it comes to choosing or building a team from dozens of leagues around the world, there's a distinct advantage to picking the one you support; knowing a squad's strengths and weaknesses certainly helps speed things up at the start. Not that this is a game for anyone with a short attention span, involving as it does screen after screen of statistics and data, initially worrisome but before long utterly engrossing. It's this astonishing level of detail that makes the game so deep and rewarding, whether it's comparing potential transfer targets to existing players, perfecting a training regime for the left back, deciding how best to utilize your scouts' specialities, building a relationship with a feeder club, or picking the in-game tactics for the team and each individual player, right down to length of throw-in. Beginners can safely ignore much of this until they're familiar with the basics, which shouldn't take long.

The matches themselves somehow recreate the feeling of listening to a radio broadcast, the game's one concession to sound – the roar of the crowd – ever present in the background, as commentary-style messages flash up in support of the numbered dots moving about the screen. Saving matches allows them to be viewed and analysed at a later date.

As in life, talking a good game can make the difference, and a manager can inspire or criticize individual players both on the pitch – the assistant coach will report on the impact of any team talk, whether gentle encouragement or boot-hurling rage – and in the press. All of which affects the performance of the team and manager. At the end of the day, though, winning on the pitch might not be enough; if a manager's financial performance isn't up to scratch, the board may be inclined to let him go; conversely, bigger and better jobs might beckon, perhaps even abroad. And the outer world is a constant presence, with news reports and emails filling the screen between matches.

With games like *FM* sucking hours out of the day, it's no wonder British manager Harry Rednapp mourned the scarcity of young, home-grown footballers in *The Sun*: "Now I rarely see a kickabout in the park. All I see are the dazzling lights of bedroom windows from the glare of TVs and computers. It seems football cannot compete with an Xbox." What he failed to mention is the corresponding growth of a generation who, with their in-depth knowledge of tactics, wage budgets and work permits, no doubt feel they could do a better job as manager.

For a statistics-laden game, *Out of the Park Baseball* has some remarkably colourful, engaging screens.

Football Manager Live
PC, Mac; Sports Interactive, Sega; 2008

This is an online fantasy football game where you buy and sell real-life players to build your own team and play matches against your friends, winning points in a complex reward system. It's a game that – unlike the original – is designed to be enjoyed without having to devote great swathes of time to it. As Oliver Collyer, its creator, explained: "We've had these divorce case situations where *FM* has been cited – this is to fix it and get people together…"

Out of the Park Baseball 2007
PC (US only); Sports Interactive; 2006

Sports Interactive took over the highly successful franchise from Markus Heinsohn's Out of the Park Developments with the 2006 edition, but it's with this subsequent entry that the team got properly into their stride. Enviable experience with *FM* and no small amount of player testing have resulted in its regaining – perhaps even superseding – its former status as the best ever baseball management sim.

Elite

Amiga, NES, PC; David Braben and Ian Bell, Acornsoft, Firebird; 1984

Up until Braben's and Bell's clarion call to intelligent gaming, the level of interaction in single-player, real-time graphical games was limited to shooting space invaders or gobbling up dots. The longer the game went on, the more you noticed that the only thing that really changed was the score. Influenced enormously by the pen-and-paper sci-fi RPG *Traveller*, movies like *2001: A Space Odyssey*, and most obviously by Thatcher-endorsed Reaganomics, *Elite* changed this forever. Set in a 3D (wire-frame) multiple-galaxy depiction of space, players could trade commodities across space and within different socio-economic systems, fight pirates or become marauders themselves – all to earn enough credits to upgrade their ships and equipment in a quest to earn the ultimate "Elite" status. It proved so in step with the times that it sold almost 150,000 units for its original platform, the BBC Micro – which was also, not coincidentally, the number of BBC Micros in the world at that time.

Freespace 2

PC; Volition; Interplay; 1999

In the geeky world of PC simulators, declaring the best space sim of all time is akin to slapping a target on your chest and then going for a walk across a shooting range. It would be entirely possible to write a book dedicated solely to debating the merits of each title in an area that the PC, especially, has done so well ever since *Elite* (see box) showed us what the power of RAM and imagination could conspire to create. Nascent coders reared on that classic grew to develop their own ideas for the genre, and thus the 1990s and early 2000s were packed with a slew of titles that took advantage of increasingly powerful hardware and new online opportunities to break down the physical barriers previously restricting the virtual version of mankind's final frontier.

TV and film franchises, naturally, have been massively influential. Legions of fans flock to the steady stream of *Star Wars* and *Star Trek* sims, such as the excellent *X-Wing Alliance* from 1999. There were innovative, oft-ignored gems, including the *Privateer* games, spin offs from the much-loved *Wing Commander* series; and a few that wandered around the shop in terms of quality, such as the *X* series (not to mention the notoriously flawed *Battlecruiser 3000AD*). Microsoft were so eager to break into the club they even released three space sims – *Allegiance*, *Starlancer* and *Freelancer* – within a few years of each other. But the truly great hurrahs of this now relatively quiet genre belong to *Independence War 2* (see box opposite) and *Freespace 2*, the latter of which wins out for remaining more of a game and less of a hardcore simulation – in *Freespace 2*, looks and fun matter more than the actual physics of space flight.

Or rather, as in *Half-Life 2*, the physics are deftly woven into the grand narrative, visual and aural backdrop that takes its cue from any number of Hollywood and TV sci-fi favourites. Old alliances, rebel forces and hostile aliens plotting revenge from the furthest reaches of space are just a few elements of the epic, branching single-player plot (relatively unusual for a game of this ilk at this time) that pitches the player as a member of a vast interstellar navy and a mere pawn in a huge war – though one with the power to affect its outcome. (It was a nice touch too, in 1999, to play out much of the plot in-game, without relying heavily on between-mission cut scenes.)

Freespaces 2's universe may be violent, but it's beautiful and it's beguiling. Planets and nebulae give a dreamy sense of a vast galactic expanse, but they're not simply eye candy – the energy fields surrounding them create static interference that affects your ship's equipment. And then there are the seventy or so ship types, from small fighters to monster-sized cruisers and destroyers that lumber majestically and bristle with the kind of heavy weaponry that would make even the Death Star turn tail.

In fact, thanks to Volition releasing the open-source code in 2002 – a huge reason for the game's enduring popularity – you really can get stuck in and mod in a *Star Wars* theme. Indeed, Hard Light Productions' adaptation of *Freespace 2* to the *Babylon 5* universe, *The Babylon Project*, as well as their *Beyond the Red Line*, which takes it into the *Battlestar Galactica* arena, both continue to ensure that this decade-old game inspires well after the peak of its genre.

Gears of War

Xbox 360; Epic Games, Microsoft Studios; 2006

Hailed as the first fully next-generation title on the Xbox 360 for the way it completely utilized the machine's capabilities in rendering sound and movement, expectations were huge for this title in 2006 – not least because the game's lead designer, Cliff Bleszinski (aka CliffyB), had been incredibly savvy about generating and then maintaining game journos' interest in the title throughout its development. That, and the saturation marketing it enjoyed on its release, meant that this was an A-list title fanboys were salivating to get hold of. But a warning to gamers who are more in touch with their *Nintendogs* sensibilities than their inner *Turok*: *Gears of War* will scare you. Not because the gameplay is nerve-jangling, but because it's the antithesis of all that is cute and fluffy, pumped, instead, full of macho attitude, where even the weaponry feels like it's on steroids. That CliffyB drew his inspiration from a game of paintball might inspire guffaws, but if he hadn't pointed this out in the manual it would be very easy to believe it was put together by a bunch of body-building gun fanatics.

Independence War (released as I-War in the UK)

PC; Particle Systems, Infogrames; 1997

Clearly not ones to shirk a challenge, Particle Systems' first space sim had lofty intentions. Not for them the lightning fast cut and thrust of dogfighting in small craft: this was about putting a medium-class dreadnought through its wartime paces. And it succeeded; no other title before it had made you feel you were directing the crew from Kirk's captain's chair, or messing around with some highly sophisticated engine-management systems on Scotty's behalf. But it's far more simulation than shooter and as such can be as unforgiving as, presumably, real-life space flight, with all the effects that inertia and lack of friction entail coming into play: heaving to, or docking, for example, is very likely to end up damaging your ship.

This impression is only reinforced by the deliberately simplistic action-movie plot and limited dialogue. You play as Marcus Fenix, an outlandishly muscular member of a small squad of similarly square-jawed soldiers charged with the destruction of the Locust Horde, an alien species that manifests itself variously as lizard-like humanoids; grossly enormous insectoids known as Corpsers; and Beserkers, who look and act for all the world as though they're in Lord Sauron's employ. The Horde have a penchant for tunnelling their way around

Larger-than-life high-definition monsters add to *Gears of War*'s all-out action-movie feel.

and are thus able to surface in unexpected places; the only way Marcus and his team can destroy them is to confront them at source, underground. No surprises, then, that this is going to be one massive firefight, and even in single-player mode the action can reach the frantic intensity of *Unreal Tournament* (see p.269), also developed by Epic Games.

It's also at these times that you really appreciate the most significant gameplay element on offer here, that of being able to use any solid surface in your surrounding environment for cover, whether crouching down behind a vehicle and firing blindly over the top, or leaning around a corner to take a carefully aimed shot at the enemy – tactics that gain immensely from being shown from the third-person viewpoint. What it quickly becomes about too, though, is breaking that cover, and you soon learn to string together moves that help Marcus dodge the bullets. He might choose to roll out from the low-lying wall he was behind or launch over it; then, crouching low, run to the next piece of cover before performing a perfect reload to gain a limited damage-bonus for the next burst of fire.

The abiding impression of a full-on grunt-fest is, however, a massive sleight of hand by the developers, for behind the big bangs lies a great amount of subtlety. The incredibly intuitive implementation of the cover system, for instance – one button and a push of the thumbstick suffices for all the options – finally moved the shoot-'em-up genre beyond the idea that you could avoid taking hits by simply strafing and circling your target. It's also worth taking time out between the action scenes to listen to the audio effects and admire the lush graphics. This might be a world populated by monosyllabic beef cakes and grunting aliens, but in their high-definition detail they look like works of art.

God of War

PS2; SCEA, Sony; 2005

Right from its unforgettable opening, *God of War* exudes darkness. As the protagonist plunges endlessly from the summit of Mount Olympus in a bid to end ten years of madness, time stops abruptly and we shift back three weeks, straight into a shipboard battle and the start of a satisfyingly long journey through Kratos's past. Like the Homeric

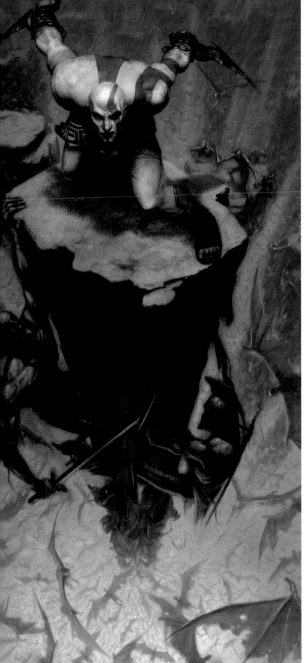

myths that inspired the plotline, this is no simplistic good versus evil fable but a tale of violence, terror, revenge and insanity – nothing less than you'd expect from an epic tragedy set in classical Greece. Kratos is a puppet played by the gods, a tormented antihero – desperate, amoral and filled with rage. Blood flows freely as he battles to save Athens from the titular Ares, in return for which he has been promised relief from his nightmares, at least according to the anonymous narrator, voiced by Linda Hunt.

A muscular, scarlet-painted Spartan warrior, Kratos is the antithesis of Japanese action adventure heroes in looks, if not in the speed of his reflexes. He's a super-powered brute who can cause destruction at the press of a few buttons with his twin Blades of Chaos – functioning at both close and long range, meaning there's no need to swap out weapons – or else simply by picking enemies up and casting them down. This glamorized cinematic violence, performed by means of responsive controls, contextualized attacks and rapid action finishing moves, is the mainstay of the game, a joyful blast of violent mayhem. Victims of Kratos's fury are largely mythological monsters, so magnificently visualized as to bring a tear to Ray Harryhausen's eye, at least until they're dispatched in clouds of blood. It's no coincidence that the lead animator, Cory Barlog, went on to become the director of the sequel. Every now and then, though, a never-ending stream of monsters makes it clear something other than slashing needs to happen, perhaps cutting off their entrance route? Just one example of the puzzles embedded seamlessly into the action.

Athens and around constitutes a vast playing field, with no loading time to speak of; nor is there any unnecessary padding: every corridor takes you somewhere you need to go. The scenery is stunning and darkly threatening, the shifting (computer-controlled) camera opening up new vistas of places you will somehow need to get to, panning across a backdrop brimming with activity and

Raging Kratos in all his towering glory dramatically prepares to do battle.

detail, whether it's the monsters you'll have to fight or the casualties they've already left behind. In one scene, a Titan can be glimpsed moving past through the gaps between buildings of burning Athens. A Wagnerian score is adeptly orchestrated to match the mood, choral themes for the rain-lashed seas, a tense drumbeat above the crackling of flames in war-torn Athens.

God of War hasn't won its awards for educating the masses in Greek mythology, but rather for its utterly perfect execution, a lesson to wannabe designers in storytelling and action. Despite influences from the Japanese classics of the genre, it remains uniquely Western in its approach and viewpoint, directed by the notoriously outspoken David Jaffe (see p.232), then of Sony's Santa Monica Studio. Unsurprisingly one of the highest budget titles of that year, it's a spectacular, grand opera of a game on an epic scale. Truly the stuff of legends.

GoldenEye 007

N64; Rare, Nintendo; 1997

On its release in August 1997, all odds were stacked against *GoldenEye 007*. It was nine months too late to feature in the N64's launch lineup, and came almost two years after the movie on which it was based. What's more, it was a console first-person shooter at a time when *Quake* was king, and no one believed you could play this kind of game without a keyboard and mouse. Expectations were not high, but the game sold nonetheless. And it continued to sell for another three or four more years, more than 8 million copies in all. At first it's hard to see what could have taken so long – licensed games tend to be some of the fastest churned out, with little time needed on script or character development. In this case, though, there's no doubt that every extra minute taken by the small, inexperienced team at Rare, led by Martin Hollis, was well spent, their innovation, perfectionism and sheer creativity delivering one of the most compelling games on the N64.

It wouldn't win any prizes today for its graphics: Pierce Brosnan's Bond (see image overleaf) and Sean Bean's rogue former agent Alec Trevelyan are instantly recognizable, albeit in a cardboard-cutout kind of way, and while environments are inevitably blocky and bland,

God of War II
PS2; SCEA, Sony; 2007

A splendid sequel and a high point in pre-PS3 gaming. Kratos is now a god, which means an even more extensive, fantastic battleground and loads more altercations with Greek mythological figures, even a Pegasus ride. The script puts less emphasis on our morally dubious hero's personal tale, but that doesn't prevent the gameplay from being just as thrilling, if not more so, than the first time round.

God of War: Chains of Olympus
PSP; Ready At Dawn, Sony; 2008

In squeezing the franchise onto a pocket-sized system, developer Ready At Dawn had a challenge on its hands to deliver anything approaching the original *God of War* experience. Although clearly reduced in length and scope, it's actually a thoroughly exciting pre-god Kratos adventure, and as reminiscent of its PS2 antecedents as could have been hoped, featuring glorious graphics and an almost identical control system.

this is due to technical restrictions rather than anything else – just look at the menu screens to see how much attention was lavished on the game's visual design. There's no voice acting either. As for the plot, it mostly follows the movie, with 007 on the trail of a secret helicopter and the GoldenEye missile in a string of exotic locations between Russia and Egypt, performing some jaw-dropping stunts along the way and variously aided and hindered by a cast of lovely foreign ladies. Where the plots do diverge, it's where designers have taken time to elaborate on the terrain – the levels were designed independently of the gameplay, so some detailed areas ended up with absolutely no function, providing a genuine sense of space where the choice of a route is actually meaningful.

There are nine main levels, split into twenty sub-missions, and each must be completed before moving on – a design Hollis borrowed from *Mario 64*, which the team got to play during production. It's by no means a straightforward shoot-everything-in-sight slog; stealth and restraint are required, as well as choosing the correct weapon or gadget for the job, for example using the sniper rifle to take out security cameras and guards. Despite their looks, the guards feel remarkably realistic in their movement and reactions, this prominent enemy AI forcing the player to adopt a strategic approach – silent head shots are always a good bet. Gratifyingly, enemies die in myriad dramatic ways, inspired by John Woo's style of cinematic violence, a novelty in 1997 but later developed and popularized by the likes of *Max Payne* (p.136). Punctuated by the gunfire, a magnificent score dominates the game, its mood and tempo switching to suit the action.

Best of all, at a time when you otherwise needed an expensive multitap adaptor or a LAN to play games with more than one other person, *GoldenEye 007* offers a full split-screen four-person multiplayer deathmatch, with dozens of Bond characters to choose from across a number of arenas. It was probably the best console multiplayer shooter until *Timesplitters* (created by ex-Rare *GoldenEye* team members David Doak and Steve Ellis). Although it's been variously touted to appear on Wii Virtual Console or Xbox Live (now that Rare is part of Microsoft), you can't help but fear that it might disappoint on a next-

Despite showing its age in terms of graphics, *GoldenEye 007* is still the best Bond game to date.

gen console. One of a very few great movie-licence games, *GoldenEye 007* is even more rare amongst a now sizeable breed of Bond games, and it's probably still true to say that nobody does it better.

Gran Turismo 5 Prologue: Spec II

PS3; Polyphony Digital, Sony; 2008

Kazunori Yamauchi's first PlayStation title for the West, *Motor Toon Grand Prix* (1994), may have been a driving game, but it wasn't exactly a calling card for his next title. Despite the fact that it featured some interesting track design, which hinted at Yamauchi's potential, it was strictly for fun – being not so different in terms of aims to relative contemporary heavyweights such as *Ridge Racer*. In 1997, however, his *Gran Turismo* changed the way console driving games were thought of.

Subtitled *The Real Driving Simulator,* this new game took the genre into previously unknown territory with its sheer level of realism:

This 2008 iteration of Gran Turismo *continued to raise the bar in terms of realism, as seen in this incredibly photo-realistic shot.*

its beautiful graphics (especially the then-stunning replay mode); its endless body tweaks and engine upgrades; the vast library of real-life cars; and the ultimate driving companion, an achingly hip, licenced soundtrack. Unlike *RR*, however, it made you work for the privileges. The career mode wouldn't let you start until you'd passed a licence test, and even then, embarking on a racing profession was severely hampered by your finances – you had to hunt down a secondhand hot rod and build things up from there. Despite the lack of a damage model it was as real as virtual driving could get. The critical and public acclaim was instant: not only did the genre

DiRT (Colin McRae: DiRT)
PC, PS3, Xbox 360; Codemasters; 2007

Bearing the name of the man many admired as a quiet-spoken offroad-driving hero, Codemasters' first next-gen rally outing pays him suitable homage. Graphically gorgeous, the gameplay bridges the gap between simulation and arcade, broadening its appeal beyond the more rally-focused McRae titles up to this point. A variety of racing disciplines, modes and wonderful damage modelling help build the attraction – though the fun in getting mud-splattered would have had an even broader audience with an online component.

F1 Challenge 1999–2002 (F1 Career Challenge)
PC; ISI, EA; 2003

Console gamers who happen to be Ferrari or Williams fans may remember EA's detailed *F1 Career Challenge* as the best F1 sim on their platforms back in 2003, but PC gamers have always known that their version, *F1 Challenge 1999–2002*, despite its age, is still the daddy. Supported extensively down the years by the modding community, its attention to microscopic detail and unprecedented AI was already impressive: so while *rFactor* (Image Space; 2005) may have been the later kid on the block, it couldn't compete against mods from the likes of Ralph Hummerich, or the retro *F1 '74 '75*.

Forza 2
Xbox 360; Turn 10 Studios, Microsoft; 2006

One of the most sophisticated driving simulators on any console, *Forza* puts clear water between itself and the likes of *Project Gotham Racing*'s stylishness or titles in the arcade market. It also has the most customizable learning curve on offer – which makes it far friendlier than *Gran Turismo*, a game that is otherwise its closest rival and to which it so clearly owes its existence.

The Xbox 360's answer to *Gran Turismo*, *Forza 2* is a classic racing game in its own right, complete with iconic makes of car.

have new purpose and vision, the PlayStation had a new A-list starlet that was to push sales of the platform itself.

While lesser mortals might have paused to rest on the laurels of such acclaim, Yamauchi has instead focused successively, and obsessively, on making each new generation of hardware capture the essence of driving – to the extent that he claims not to refer to rival games such as *Forza 2* (see opposite), concentrating instead on the real-world motoring industry. While this attempt at emulation is still manifested in some traditional videogaming ways – different cars, varied tracks and more detail with each new release (*GT3 A Spec* even saw the introduction of oil changes) – the boundaries between the automobile industry and *Gran Turismo* have blurred. This has been most evident in the way the game's regionalization has tailored the in-game race events and automobile manufacturers to reflect those found in Japan, Europe and the US markets. This has ultimately given the non-local manufacturers an exotic appeal, introducing a host of (predominantly male) US and UK gamers, for example, to the driving delights of Nissan's Skyline models. So successful has this aspect of the GT series been that in 2007, the US's *Motor Trend* magazine named Yamauchi as one of the top fifty most inspirational people for motoring enthusiasts – ahead of Ferrari's CEO and even Jay Leno. Car manufacturers aren't averse to gifting him vehicles in recognition of his services to the industry, either.

All this is an indication of how seriously to take Yamauchi's series of games, and what it can do to change traditional concepts of driving games. Whilst *GT5 Prologue: Spec II* itself is something of a stop-gap release, it's what it hints at for *GT5* proper (unavailable at the time of writing) and his titles thereafter that matters. Alongside the much-requested damage modelling, the promised online modes will be the next big steps. They are to include the ability to form car clubs and racing teams, and watch real-time in-game TV footage. Yet just as each release starts to sound like the complete package, Yamauchi himself is at pains to point out that reaching the perfect simulator is an ongoing affair. Until he reaches his goal, we can all look forward to enjoying the product of his obsessive efforts.

Sega Rally Championship
Arcade, Saturn, PC; AM3, AM5, Sega; 1995

This hit for Sega (which first appeared in arcades in 1995) featured the ability to drive real cars – albeit just two, with a third unlockable one – on simulated driving surfaces that included gravel and mud. This was as near to rally driving as was possible when sitting inside the arcade cabinet's cockpit. When ported to the Saturn, however, the game's arcade roots were clearly on show. But in a pre-*Colin McRae* world, *SRC* showed how rally should be depicted – a debt that developers such as Codemasters were the first to acknowledge.

Grand Theft Auto: Vice City

PC, PS2, Xbox; Rockstar; 2002

Grand Theft Auto is the series, according to moral watchdogs, that encourages the inner thug. It's the game that puts a baseball bat in your hands and encourages you to mug grannies; the game that hides an Uzi behind an oil drum and then shows you how to organize a drive-by shooting. This is supposedly the game that corrupts the minds of all who play and is responsible for the swathes of desensitized couch potatoes who would be out carjacking and pimping if they could only be bothered to leave the sofa.

There's no getting away from it: jacking cars and running with mobsters is what *GTA* has been about since its first incarnation on the PC in 1997. What has changed, though, is that whereas it

Exploring the streets of Vice City, whether by motorbike, car or on foot, can be a thrill in itself.

once was not, it is today an example of excellent game design and narrative development. *GTA* began its life with substandard graphics and average gameplay, but some savvy marketing provoked high-profile pundits to hold it up as a sign of the impending downfall of society (an outraged *Daily Mail* called it an "evil game"). You can't buy publicity like that, and the growing clamour soon drowned out the fact that the game itself had received a lukewarm critical reception. Such a phenomenal profile for the game had been created that from the time of its 1998 PlayStation release, it was to spend two years solid in the UK charts.

Though videogame vets found little radical or shocking about what *GTA* offered, the concept of a gaming area so big that you were given a sheet map to navigate had novelty, as did the ability to joyride in pretty much any vehicle that took your fancy. What felt really fresh, however, was the humour with which it was implemented. This was violent comedy along the lines of *The Simpsons'* "Itchy and Scratchy Show". This loopiness masked shortcomings that both expansion pack *GTA London* (1998) and sequel-proper *GTA 2* (1999) failed to address.

It wasn't until late 2001 that the series made a significant leap forward, when *GTA III* did everything its predecessors had done but this time so much better and brasher. Out went old-school 2D; in came a fully explorable 3D world on an unprecedented scale for a console. ("The evil returns in three dimensions!" was the *Mail's* response.) It was goodbye to a soundtrack of pastiches and hello to a stonking selection of real-life in-car tunes (albeit selected with tongue placed firmly in cheek). And here was an immersive, tightly scripted plot that referenced *The Godfather*, *Goodfellas* and *Scarface* and drove the gamer to unlock content.

It's a formula the developers have pursued with *GTA III's* successors. With each release, everything has screamed "bigger" – grander production values, more intricate plotting, more movie references, further famous voice actors (such as the unmistakable Samuel L. Jackson) and increasingly vast, living cities. *Grand Theft Auto: San Andreas*, for example, features no fewer than three cities plus all the farmland, desert and mountains that lie between them. Each new incarnation has been peopled by an increasingly diverse population – it's not been just about cars for quite some time. Yes, you can jack one and cruise the city's neighbourhoods, but you can also clamber

Grand Theft Auto IV
PS3, Xbox 360; Rockstar; 2008

The most anticipated episode ever in the series, *GTA IV* does for the PS3 and Xbox 360 generation what *GTA III* did for the PS2 and Xbox one: it sets a very high standard but leaves you feeling that it could get even better. Rather than being a leap forward, its features come across as the developed nuances of those of old. The cell-phone calling system, for example, is still just a logical extension of the call-boxes of the first *GTA*; the TV stations an update on the in-car radio; and there are even a few tantalizingly withheld delights (the lack of planes, for starters). Its online multiplayer capability is a more significant addition. It's a new arena for the game, and whilst its GTA Race mode is anarchic, hilarious fun, other modes have a lot to learn. *GTA IV* certainly flies the flag for the franchise, but here's to the game's successor fulfilling its potential.

LOCK UP YOUR DAUGHTERS

How a game with old-school graphics, average gameplay and luke-warm critical acclaim managed to evolve into a multiplatform, plati-num-selling juggernaut for the new millennium has much to do with the adage that it ain't what you do, it's the way that you do it; and the way *Grand Theft Auto* has done it has always been on a grand scale. For starters, *GTA*'s original development studio, DMA, hired consummate UK publicist Max Clifford to make sure that the media was highly aware of just how violent and amoral the original game must surely be. And sure enough the publicity snowballed. Then again, gameplay elements that included being rewarded for running down multiple pedestrians within a fixed time, or taking out an entire group of Hare Krishna monks in one hit, were always going to be sure-fire bait.

aboard a helicopter, climb to a few hundred feet and watch the sun behind the skyscrapers as you fly through partial cloud cover. It's touches like this which make fans wax lyrical about Rockstar and the level of detail the developer employs when rendering new environments, each landscape clearly modelled on reality. Liberty City (which first appeared in 3D in *GTA III*) relates closely to New York; Vice City to Miami; and San Andreas's three cities are based on LA, San Francisco and Las Vegas. *GTA IV* marking the series' debut on the latest generation of hardware, fittingly returned to Liberty City. What is particularly interesting is that they are similar, but not identical, to their real counterparts, reinforcing the point that these games are satires.

San Andreas marked the appearance of minor RPG elements – from developing skill sets to deciding on your appearance, from clothing to physical shape (Elvis-like proportions were possible if you ate burgers non-stop from the fast-food joints in town), but *GTA IV* ditched the frankly gimmicky concept in favour of a return to *Vice City*'s focus on story. Regardless of *GTA IV*'s massive success (within a week of release, sales revenue had topped $500 million), it was *Vice City* that really nailed the series' *raison d'être*: this wasn't a game under the influence of pop culture, it was an outright homage to it. Late-twentieth-century mobster films (reflected in the voice acting of Ray Liotta), TV cop shows (not least *Miami Vice*) and music and fashions formerly thought of as uncool were all rolled into a joyous neon tribute to the Rockstar boys' 1980s childhoods. *GTA IV*'s successor now faces the daunting challenge that *Vice City* surmounted so triumphantly: of taking the first, already excellent next-gen game of the series and more fully fleshing out its well-loved genius.

Grim Fandango

PC; LucasArts, Activision; 1998

Mixing equal parts film noir, Mexican folklore, Mayan and Aztec art, and drop-deadpan humour, *Grim Fandango*'s blend of all the best elements of 1980s and 1990s adventure gaming still feels fresh today.

Grim Fandango's quirky, stylized look blends film noir with Aztec and Mayan architecture, probably for the first time.

Its graphics have stayed smooth, its puzzles remain fiendish, and its dialogue, which Philip Marlowe wouldn't be ashamed of, is still a benchmark for aspiring script writers. No surprise, then, to find that this was the work of Tim Schafer, whose superb *Psychonauts* (see p.162) and *Day of the Tentacle* are very close relations.

The setting is the Land of the Dead, where, in Aztec folklore, the souls of the recently departed must travel for four years to reach the Ninth Plane, their final resting place. As Manny Calavera, an employee of the Department of Death issued with a standard Grim Reaper outfit and scythe, your job is to visit the Land of the Living, pick up these souls (known as "reaping"), and then sell them a travel package to get them to the Ninth Plane in as quick a manner as possible. This is paid for in what are effectively moral credits – the better the person has been in life, the more they can afford, the ultimate prize being a ticket for the No. 9 Express, cutting the four-year journey down to a matter of days. And it's handy for Manny if they can afford the luxury options, as he gets commission on each deal sold – which he needs, big time, because he's tied into working for the Department (and thus never leaving the Land of the Dead) until he has repaid the sizeable debt he owes them.

Trouble is, all his clients are moral paupers: the best package he's managed to sell so far is a walking stick with a compass built into it. Even when he gets his big break – collecting a saintly but sexy dame – her account is empty. Department corruption is clearly afoot, but, although he's smitten with her and does his best to find her some kind of tour package, he has to let her go across the Land, alone and on foot. This is the cue for the start of a journey to find out who she really was and who's behind the corruption.

At the time, LucasArts' decision to replace the once traditional 2D point-and-click interface of the early 1990s with smoothly rendered 3D environments (though viewpoints are fixed) seemed cutting edge, though today it feels a little awkward. In traditional adventure style, however, Manny can pick up and carry around a number of objects, all of which you can try out on the surrounding environment: if it's a good idea, you'll soon see it work; if it's not, you'll receive a witty, if slightly concerned, remark from Manny on its inappropriateness.

For film buffs there are references galore. At one point, *Casablanca*-style, Manny ends up running a bar, hoping every night that the girl he thought he'd lost forever will walk through the door (his staff are fed up with him going on about it). In another, the entire underground resistance movement to the Department of Death is revealed, in the spirit of Woody Allen's *Bananas*, to consist of just two members.

Sparkling wit, intensely lateral problem-solving and some truly lovely attention to detail made this a must for all adventure fans in 1998. Nearly ten years into the new millennium, it's testament to expert craftsmanship never losing its shine.

Guitar Hero II

PS2, Xbox 360; Harmonix Music Systems, RedOctane; 2006

At last a rhythm/music game that's about live performances of rocking music, with no keyboards, DJs, rappers or dance moves in sight. Just you and your band, on stage in a small, underground club to start with, your adoring fans screaming out for more, as you hold the sustain on the last note of the night, then smash your Gibson SG to splinters at the close of the show. OK, you're actually alone in your living room, holding a shrunken plastic guitar with several large coloured buttons on its neck. But with this toy instrument slung across your body you'll feel like a bona fide rock star, whether or not you know a G from an A or a plectrum from a toothpick.

As guitars go, it's pretty easy to pick up and play, but putting in the rehearsal time is still well worth the effort, if only to avoid the squawk

Taking it to eleven: master the single notes as they appear on the central fretboard and you're ready for some simple chords.

and thunk of each duff note as the fretwork conveyor belt rolls off the bottom of the screen. In a great addition to the first game, *Guitar Hero II* recognizes that practice makes perfect with an incredibly deep and rewarding training mode. Songs are broken down into manageable sections which you can gradually build up into an entire track minus distracting vocals, each section playable as many times as you like at a pace to suit you: uncomplicated choruses at regular speed, perhaps, but the solo more slowly until it's familiar enough to take on tour.

Out on stage, the toil proves worthwhile, as you watch your funky caricature band rack up the points, but perform poorly and the botched notes start to draw boos from the crowd, until eventually the band gets thrown off stage. It's not just the glory and adulation that keeps you coming back, or even the chance to unlock new guitars and characters, but the fact that career mode is the only way to lengthen your playlist with all-important new songs. Most tracks are hard rock (both classics and originals), with some Nirvana, Police and The Kinks thrown in for the golden oldies, plus more to download via Xbox Live.

HIT ME WITH YOUR RHYTHM STICK

From about 1998 to 2000, the PlayStation experienced a flurry of rhythm games, some with weird and wonderful controllers (*Beatmania*), some just demanding fast fingerwork (*Bust A Groove*), progressing with the PS2 into cooler, more grown-up music games like *FreQuency*. These days, with the exception of *Guitar Hero III*, which has erupted with varying success on all three main consoles, the so-called rhythm action genre has proved to be particularly at home on the DS, whose touch screen is perfect for tapping out beats. For more on music games and pseudo-instruments, see p.278.

Vib-Ribbon
PS; NanaOn-Sha, Sony; 2000

Unreleased in the US (though rumoured to be coming to PlayStation Network), *Vib-Ribbon* is a uniquely lo-fi game. You control a scribble of a white rabbit as she jumps over a ribbon of obstacles on a black screen – blocks, squiggles and suchlike created by the music – and either evolves into a princess or dissolves into a frog, depending on how well you play. Ingeniously, the program runs from the system's RAM, so the disc can be removed and replaced with your own CDs, which makes for a uniquely personalized experience.

PaRappa the Rapper
PS; Sony; 1997

Kickstarting an entirely new genre, *PaRappa* (pictured in his hallmark hat) came as a breath of fresh air. The eponymous paper-thin dog undergoes seemingly mundane trials – learning to drive, cooking burgers – in a quest to be worthy of his dream flower girl, Sunny Funny. This involves

following the instructions of a Master Rapper in each of six scenarios, copying and freestyling for a better rating. The re-release on PSP (2007) looks and sounds as cool as it ever did, but it's also just as short as it was back then.

Elite Beat Agents
DS; iNiS, Nintendo; 2006

A Westernized remake of the acclaimed *Osu! Tatakae! Ouendan!* but with Cher, Madonna and the Village People instead of catchy J-pop/rock. Like their Japanese forebears, the trio of men in black are called on for cheerleading support by various folks in trouble, whose stories appear on the top screen. From the TV weatherwoman who predicts sunshine so as not to spoil her son's picnic, to the treasure-hunting ship's captain who can't find any treasure, whether their problems are resolved depends on how accurately you tap decreasing circles in time to the music – not as easy as it sounds, but with enough practice you might eventually save the world.

If you happen to have a friend who's also a rock fan, it's worth getting that extra guitar, since each song has two tracks, allowing two players to riff alongside each other cooperatively on lead and bass or rhythm, as well as in competition.

From the name-dropping anecdotes of the tutorial to the set lists scrawled on dog-eared schoolbooks, the game achieves a purity of purpose and theme, while not taking itself too seriously. Indeed, fans of one of the world's best rock acts will be glad to see that although the dials no longer go up to eleven as they did in the first game, there's still an excellent Tap track to unlock in *Tonight I'm Gonna Rock You Tonight*.

Half-Life 2

PC, Xbox, PS2, Xbox 360, PS3; Valve, Vivendi Interactive; 2004

When a review declares that a videogame is so good that "the excuse that 'it's just a game' won't cut it anymore", you'd probably think it over the top. When the aforesaid comment comes from the well-respected and hard-to-impress *Edge* magazine's (see p.279) summary of *Half-Life 2*, however, you sit up and pay attention. Of course, even hardened critics are susceptible to overstatement, but measure up *Half-Life 2*'s astounding achievements against its predecessor's already massive contribution to the FPS genre and you get where *Edge* is coming from. Like its progenitor, this instalment reached greatness not by instigating any new gaming concepts but by instead taking existing ones to the next level. It does so with seamless storytelling, intelligent level design and characters that provoke a real emotional response. And this, combined with its graphical, audio and narrative detail, redefines what it means to feel involved in a game.

The plot follows the progress of *Half-Life*'s original hero, Gordon Freeman, through the alien-infested industrial wastelands, polluted coastlines and ruined cityscapes of a sick, dying Earth, and it pulls you along relentlessly with a sense of paranoia and urgency that the seamless FPS view never lets up on (there are no cut scenes or loading screens). This adroitly reinforces the sense of being Freeman rather than merely playing as him, a feeling underscored by the excellent AI and character modelling of the game's NPCs (fans will be particularly pleased to see that Barney is back). You can enlist these NPCs to help fight your cause; their voice acting and facial movement in particular are exceptional. The physical dynamics of your environment are the icing on the cake, however: one moment sunlight is streaming peacefully through the cracks of a wall as you prepare to make a break from shelter; next, you're running across open ground, feeling it shake as gunfire rains down on you, while burning cars are tossed into the

Crysis
PC; Crytec, EA; 2007

With *Far Cry* (Ubisoft, 2004), Crytec propelled themselves into the ranks occupied by id and Valve for being one of the PC's top FPS developers, and *Crysis*, whilst similarly offering nothing radically new, extends that justification. By swapping the latter's *Lost*-style plot of abandoned World War II genetic experiments on a Pacific island for *Predator*-style shenanigans on an island off the coast of China, *Crysis* continued to build on the imaginations of those who went before it. But this time it was smarter, bigger, better looking and therefore, for the time, boasted whopping technical specs.

Doom III
PC, Mac, Xbox; id Software, Vicarious Visions, Aspyr Media, Activision; 2004

When *Doom III* was announced, many were sceptical, given that John Romero's own effort to further the FPS genre – *Daiaktana* – was an abject failure. Kudos to original id member Adrian Carmack, then, that despite his original opposition to the game, *Doom III* deservedly kicked the brand back into life. This time, whilst it didn't lead the way in gameplay, it did show the world how atmospheric lighting and sound effects can be just as scary as the monsters themselves.

Portal
PC, Xbox 360, PS3; Valve, Vivendi; 2007

Available as part of *The Orange Box*, many reviewers chose to focus on this new addition to the *Half-Life 2* universe rather than retread old ground. Part first-person puzzler, part action game, the player is the latest disposable subject to be put through Aperture Science's nonchalantly murderous test chambers by the increasingly deranged GlaDos computer. But *Portal* is also very funny: "Frankly, this chamber was a mistake. If we were you, we would quit now." Most, however, regard such warnings as reason enough to want more of *Portal*'s delightful insanity.

Team Fortress 2
PC, Xbox 360, PS3; Valve, Vivendi; 2007

This is one of the other goodies to be found in *The Orange Box*, alongside *Portal*, but is also downloadable via Steam. *Team Fortress 2* joyously runs with the original's concept – of two opposing teams, "Reliable Excavation Demolition" (RED) and "Builders League United" (BLU), hammering it out with nine playable classes. The cartoon-like animation – not least the comic facial expressions that show off the Source engine behind *Half-Life 2* – and artwork combine to make this particular multiplayer experience a hoot.

Quake II
PC, Mac, N64, Playstation; id Software, Hammerhead, Activision; 1997

This was the last true originator in a relatively unsophisticated genre at the time. And it should be noted that *Quake II* is not for the faint-hearted. The plot sees you play a space marine set down on the planet of the Strogg, a race intent on destroying Earth. You are charged with clearing the base of every cybernetic creature; but story doesn't count for much in *Quake II* and your goal can be stripped down to one directive: kill the bastards. It may have set the standard in 1997, but *Half-Life* was just around the corner.

air by shells; then, as you hunker down into cover with any squad members you have who survived, you hear the ominous drone of an approaching alien craft. There is no let up – everything you go through, everything you see, is an intense, visceral experience. Even the puzzle elements, which *Half-Life* games set the benchmark for in the FPS genre, can take on an aggressive edge. The gravity gun, for example, is ostensibly used to manipulate objects remotely to overcome physical hurdles, such as building a makeshift bridge over radioactive water – but it can also be used to hurl the same objects at your enemies.

Like its gameplay, the series itself has the feel of an unstoppable juggernaut. The original blockbuster garnered the kind of mainstream recognition normally the preserve of Hollywood, with sales of around eight million units. This instalment alone took around five years to produce, so Valve decided to release a series of episodes that furthered the plot in smaller steps – prosaically named *Episodes One* and *Two* – rather than making fans wait another half-decade for a single, bigger hit. All three were made available in Valve's 2007 bumper compilation *The Orange Box*, which also includes *Portal* and *Team Fortress 2* (see opposite). This simultaneously represented an extraordinary act of generosity and savvy marketing on Vivendi's behalf, as well as a greatly extended adrenaline boost that manages to be both bloody big and bloody clever.

A rare sighting of Gordon Freeman – normally you're looking through his eyes – accompanied by Alyx Vance.

Halo 3

Xbox 360; Bungie Software, Microsoft Game Studios; 2007

Two-player co-op mode has one person play as Master Chief (left), the other as the Arbiter (right).

Its launch was the gaming event of 2007. But also, the release of *Halo 3* revealed just how far videogames have permeated the mainstream. With more press attention and marketing spend than most movies, it earned more in its first 24 hours than either the highest-grossing movie of the year (*Spider-Man 3*), or the last in the *Harry Potter* series, rising to a total of $300 million in the first week. Even Japan, famously resistant to the FPS genre, joined in, with sales of the Xbox 360 tripling as a result. More than a million people played the game online on the first day, with countless others shut out by system glitches. Add to this scores of licensed products, from novelizations and comics to keyrings and belt buckles, and it's not altogether surprising to hear Microsoft bigwigs mention the game in the same breath as Word and Excel. Nor that when developer Bungie split with the company, they left the rights to *Halo* behind. Of course, none of this could have happened if the game had been dodgy. Thankfully, like its forerunners, it's the consummate example of its particular strand of FPS: not as intellectually demanding as *Half-Life*, not as emotionally gripping as *BioShock*, but within its parameters perfectly judged in every respect.

Halo 2 ended on a cliffhanger (thanks to the developers running out of time) and that's where this game starts, with Master Chief, last of the genetically enhanced SPARTAN warriors, crash-landing on Earth in his bid to prevent the destruction of the universe. In many ways it's a straightforward continuation of the previous game, with its gloriously familiar but deeply alien 26th-century world and a history riven with confusing betrayals and alliances. Outside the story, there's the same unobtrusive interface, with no inventory or map screen, just the elegant simplicity of the HUD. Master Chief hasn't learned yet to carry more than two weapons plus grenades, with the exception of

"MY OTHER CAR IS A WARTHOG"

Halo has become a cultural phenomenon, spreading far beyond videogaming's own borders. Even the most successful adult-oriented titles, unlike say *Mario* or *Pokémon*, rarely see quite so much in the way of merchandising and exploitation of a so-called intellectual property (or IP). By far the most common route for a successful FPS or action game to enter popular mainstream culture is via a film franchise, but *Halo* has struggled to make this transition, in spite of having a director and producer (Peter Jackson) lined up. When you consider how much more profitable *Halo* the game is than *Halo* the movie, with its astronomical budgets and lower retail price, could ever be, it seems distinctly possible that it may never get to the cinema screen. Footage from *Halo* games themselves, though, has reached plenty of smaller screens via the relatively new artform of machinima (see p.268), for which *Halo 3* in all its HD glory has proved to be an unmatched resource. Microsoft, instead of outlawing this unapproved use of their property, has in fact embraced it, no doubt seeing it as a free brand-building exercise.

In terms of merchandizing, as well the usual T-shirts, hats, posters and action figures, there are *Halo* licence plate holders, party cups, and at least three types of pen available on the Bungie website. While these might show off your love of the game, they won't feed your thirst for *Halo* knowledge; this is where novelizations, comics and graphic novels come in, expanding the game universe into areas that haven't been, and usually won't be, addressed by a game script. For instance, the first *Halo* novel, *The Fall of Reach* – written in just seven weeks by Microsoft employee and sci-fi novelist Eric Nylund – is a prequel showing how the SPARTANs came into being; it's been followed by *First Strike*, *The Flood* and *Ghosts of Onyx* by the same author. More recently, the novel *Contact Harvest* was penned by one of the writers of *Halo 3*, Bungie's Joseph Staten, and like the game, headed straight into the bestseller lists, in this case number 3 in the *New York Times*.

Of course *Halo* is just the most prominent of a huge range of novelizations and comics of videogames: *Resident Evil* novels have been based on the games and on the films based on the games. In the case of *World of Warcraft*, the world has been built up to a level that the players will never be able to experience. The *Halo* universe, too, has spawned comics, and a graphic novel including work by the esteemed artist Moebius, proving that the translation of game properties across media boundaries is nothing to be ashamed of. What's more, since it's unlikely anyone but gamers would read spinoff books, the success of these titles challenges the widespread theory that people who play videogames don't read.

"equipment", such as new single-use items like the bubble shield. Also still in place are the invisible checkpoints and absence of loading time (but for starting screens), meaning that transitions between areas barely register as transitions at all.

It's been said that all of *Halo* could fit into one level of *Halo 2*; *Halo 3* is on another scale entirely. The terrain, whether rocky escarpment, snowy forest or jungly swamp, stretches into the distance, and it's possible to spend ages running around on foot or driving a Warthog or Scorpion, while your companions fire at the alien Covenant ships swooping overhead. The endless landscapes aren't as flashily next-gen as in more recent games, but they're otherwise flawless, with nothing to break the spell of a thoroughly absorbing atmosphere. The game also has a yet to be surpassed rhythm, consistently swapping between quiet exploration and intense firefights. Getting lost, like falling off cliffs or not figuring out how to destroy the huge Scarab machines, is something the developers have anticipated, with the sort of testing normally reserved for blockbuster movie endings or laboratory guinea pigs. Keep an eye and ear out for your troops or the annoying Guilty Spark, whose subtle clues and nudges help to keep the action astonishingly fluid and continuous. The AI has always been a particular strength of *Halo*, right from the first game when you were amazed to hear Covenant grunts talking about you as you sneaked up on them. Now their actions are even less predictable, and with up to thirty characters on screen at once, there's frequently something going on, whether you're in the midst of it or not. All of which makes for a thrillingly immersive experience – even in the single-player campaign, you're made to feel like a part of a bigger team.

Alien vehicles and weapons are there for the taking, once their Covenant owners have been dealt with.

Naturally the multiplayer options are superb, with a cooperative mode (split-screen or online) that now features optional competitive scoring, plus the benefit of being able to take on tougher difficulties with the Arbiter at the Chief's back. As successor to the game that single-handedly made Xbox Live, *Halo 3*'s online play was greedily anticipated and proved worth the wait for those who didn't get in on the public beta. Even if multiplayer holds no appeal, there are still online perks, such as being able to view other players' movie clips (your own gameplay is also recorded, ready for editing your best and worst bits) so you can see how the pros did it. Best of all, perhaps, is The Forge, which provides the chance to unleash all that creativity (and stupidity) on a customizable environment; as with so much of *Halo*, it's been hijacked for all sorts of purposes, including creating bizarre artworks. Which in some ways sums up a game that feels somehow like it belongs to the players, a unique achievement for an intellectual property owned by one of the world's biggest multinationals.

Hidden and Dangerous

PC; Talonsoft, Take 2; 1999

The huge advances in the graphics capabilities and processing powers of PCs across the 1990s were only infrequently accompanied by an equivalent gearing up in developers' imaginations, serving mostly to prettify existing ideas rather than push the boundaries of what games could be. So when the new kid on the genre-block arrived in the form of the squad-based tactical shooter (see p.37), taking full advantage of the move from pixels to polygons and faster processing speeds, there was considerable excitement. Yet the nascent genre was typified by flawed gems, populated by titles that were either alienating to casual gamers by being too complicated, such as *Tom Clancy's Rainbow Six*, which required you to have the planning skills of an SAS veteran; to ones like *Spec Ops 2*, which erred on the side of action (and buggy programming) rather than thinking. Step forward *Hidden and Dangerous*, an object exercise in how to lead non-hardcore strategy gamers to drink at the tactical well.

One of the PC's best-looking games in 1999 and subsequently tarted up for a 2002 re-release.

Its secret ingredient is atmosphere – shovel-loads of it. Even today the *Rainbow Six* series can come over as decidedly po-faced, whereas *H&D* relishes its theatrics, from the over-the-top orchestral score that could have been lifted straight from a World War II drama to its delightfully motley crew of Allied commandos at your disposal: all of which is introduced by a British voice the likes of which hasn't been heard since John Mills and Sylvia Sims finally got their drop of the cold stuff in *Alex*. The fact that the action takes place behind occupied lines and involves carrying out acts of sabotage, rescuing POWs and making hard-as-nails raids on V2 sites adds a certain frisson to the whole affair, but while you may well be planting one on Jerry in the name of the fight against fascism, all told *H&D* is as much about having fun whilst doing it.

THE TOM CLANCY LEGACY

The Tom Clancy name is usually associated, in videogaming, with blockbuster hits, but it wasn't always so. The company responsible for this success, Red Storm Entertainment (co-founded by Clancy in 1996), didn't get off to an auspicious start: its first steps – *Politika* (1997), *Dominant Species* (1998) and *ruthless.com* (1998) – either underacheived as games or stepped too far outside of the Clancy universe. But these were staging posts along the road to *Rainbow Six* (1998), a defining moment in both areas. Like his books, the game was both highly technical (it was originally intended to simulate a day in the life of the FBI's Hostage Rescue Team) and a hugely entertaining flight of fancy. The PC hit was subsequently ported to consoles, spreading the word to gamers on all platforms and attracting the interest of Ubisoft, whose subsequent ownership of Red Storm helped roll out the brand. Each of the series – covering counter-terrorist ops (*Rainbow Six*; see below), squad-based field manoeuvres (*Ghost Recon*; see below) and espionage (*Splinter Cell*; see p.139) – has become glitzier and less hardcore with each incarnation, something the later *Vegas*-themed editions of *Rainbow Six* explicitly acknowledged. Indeed, if there's one criticism that can be laid at their door, it's that the gritty realism of the first titles now has a distinct CSI-styled sheen. Their commercial success, however, is staggering, prompting Ubisoft to buy out Clancy's royalties in all games and related merchandise for a multi-million dollar sum in 2008, possibly in anticipation of huge sales of the then-forthcoming *EndWar* and *H.A.W.X.*

Tom Clancy's Ghost Recon
PC, Mac, Xbox, PS2, GC; Ubisoft, Red Storm Entertainment; 2001

The world had already been treated to *Metal Gear Solid*, but no one had attempted a stealth game based in the great outdoors before. The wind whistles, the grass rustles and the undergrowth crackles as you take your heavily camouflaged squads through enemy territory in Eastern European countryside and cityscapes. In this environment he slightest mistake means you're a man down.

Tom Clancy's Rainbow Six: Vegas
PC, PS3, Xbox 360; Ubisoft; 2006

The game that helped breathe life into close-quarters-battle sims in 1998 has been throwing out sequels ever since. *Vegas* – the first *Rainbow Six* incarnation for the PS3 et al generation, pictured left – illustrates the fact. An excellent game in its own right, it was just the latest evolution and was soon trumped by *Vegas 2* – and so on. That the *Rainbow Six* universe was in need of freshening up was tacitly acknowledged by Ubisoft's next Clancy ventures *EndWar* and *H.A.W.X.*

Which is apposite, as the first thing that strikes you about *Hidden and Dangerous* is how easy it is to pick up and play. It positively waltzes you through the intuitive set-up screens: choose a squad from a larger pool of individuals, each of whom has certain strengths and weaknesses, and equip them appropriately according to the briefing received from HQ. Then things kick off properly, introducing you to your squad in the flesh, as it were, and their highly immersive world. Back in 1999, this was one of the best-looking games on the PC. Around a decade on, things still look pretty good thanks to Take 2 sprucing things up in 2002, when they improved the graphics, upped the resolution levels significantly, and offered the game and its expansion packs as a free download as part of their publicity for *Hidden and Dangerous 2* – itself a fine game but one that backtracked on being friendly to non-hardcore gamers.

The opening scene of the first campaign (of which there are six in the main game) sets the tone perfectly: four commandos parachuted into Piemonte, Italy, must make their way through a mountain valley to rescue a downed RAF crew. From the vantage of the squad's point man, you spot the emerging figure of a German soldier patrolling the only bridge across the river. Bringing the squad to a halt, you assume control of the team's sniper, crawling forward to a better vantage point to ascertain whether the sound of a shot ringing out is worth the risk of alerting guards on the opposite bank, or whether it's possible to simply evade the danger; or if the danger can be eliminated silently by ordering the stealthiest member of the squad to get up close to execute a brutal slash of their commando knife to the guard's throat. The rain is beating incessantly, thunder is rumbling, the suspense is palpable and the first shot hasn't even been fired. It's not all about unreleased tension either; in one gloriously gung-ho mission, the squad must make a dash across an open airfield to jump on board a waiting aircraft whilst enemy troops and firepower pour in from all sides, leaving your heavy machine gunner with some serious backside covering to do.

Whereas Tom Clancy games (see opposite) gain their nervous energy by being based on contemporary, unresolved conflicts and terrorism, it seems fitting that a war that we already know the result of should inspire, in *Hidden and Dangerous*, a game that feels comfortable and nostalgic. It could be that Sandhurst voiceover in the briefings; it might be that those soldiers named Private Henry William "Big Willy" Slim and Lieutenant Sir Thomas "Lord Mule" Wolly could only have existed in a bygone era. Either way, *H&D* leaves you feeling as though those Brits got through World War II thanks to large doses of stiff upper lip and that, my goodness young man, that's exactly what the youth of today could do with.

Hitman: Blood Money

PC, Xbox, Xbox 360, PS2; Eidos; 2006

In Italy, the birthplace of opera and a country with a penchant for subtlety of expression, it's not uncommon to hear victims of assassinations and Mafia hits described as having suffered a *bella morte* ("beautiful death"). In a gaming world where violence and death are not just accepted but often a *raison d'être*, it seems odd that 2000's *Hitman: Codename 47* debut on the PC should have drawn such criticism for its clinical approach to being an agent of death. The 2002 sequel *Hitman: Silent Assassin*, however, appeared as though it was going to tap directly into a more human, bittersweet acceptance of *bella morte*. The story begins in Sicily and involves a Mafia kidnapping and your semi-anonymous protagonist's vengeful retribution. This opening level manages to pull off a sense of menace more normally associated with being in the presence of Don Corleone. It was a shame, then, that the atmosphere changed as the plot developed into more of an assassin's grand tour of the globe than a fateful vendetta. The third instalment, *Hitman: Contracts* (2004) did nothing to build on the ambience, as it lacked a developing story (each level was a standalone mission).

For a true sense of a tangled web being woven, however, skip straight to *Hitman: Blood Money* where the philosophy of Frederick Forsyth's "Jackal" – that professional murder is intellectual artistry – is married to an accomplished narrative approach that's not afraid to reference even classical song, in the form of Schubert. Use of the latter's haunting *Ave Maria* gives proceedings just the right amount of gravitas from the outset (it's a piece 20th Century Fox also thought fitting to use in their film adaptation of the game).

While the premise of the game is to carry out a series of contract hits without getting caught, it's actually perfectly possible to play

Killer7
GC, PS2; Grasshopper Manufacture, Capcom; 2005

It split reviewers down the middle on its release because it felt, to many, that this wasn't really a game as much as a psychedelic assault on the senses. The cel-shaded anime graphics, the topic of mental disorder (the gamer plays through the seven viewpoints of an assassin's multiple-personality disorder), the beautification of violence as a kind of social commentary, and a mind-scratching soundtrack were beyond the frame of reference for many. Others recognized that *Killer7* pushes the boundaries of what games can be, and for that, as well as its highly artistic intentions, it's to be commended.

the game as a shoot-'em-up (you can play from both first- and third-person perspectives) as opposed to a stealth game: but you'd be missing the point if you did. In fact, it's a game that gives far more back the higher you set the realism levels. It's not uncommon to walk away undetected from a successful hit feeling that you've just engineered the most devious, heartless and purest of deaths, simply because creating your masterpiece required so much skill, patience and planning.

The protagonist, Agent 47, has many means of disposal at his command, and it's usually the least direct ones that are the most interesting (and tricky) to employ. Equipped with your choice of weapons and a map of an open-plan environment that you can move around at will, you might poison someone's food, inject them directly or simply shoot them: but you'll need to figure out how to do all of it without being spotted. On a grander scale, and most satisfying of all, you can organize your hits by proxy. In one particularly finely judged level, you have the opportunity to substitute a replica pistol being used in an opera house production with a real, loaded one. This then ends up as the weapon that kills your mark, an actor in the production; once the murder has been realized, you can engineer a chandelier to fall onto the unsuspecting second mark, who has come to inspect the body. Or you could lie in wait for the actor in his dressing room and silently garrotte him; or disguise yourself as various members of the opera house staff and infiltrate the place unrecognized and unremarked. Far more so than in *Hitman*'s previous incarnations, this version boasts gameplay with options.

Agent 47's world is still one that courts controversy, though. The publicity campaign ads pictured a woman in lingerie lying

Thief: The Dark Project
PC; Looking Glass Studios, Eidos Interactive; 1998

Before Agent 47 had fully matured and whilst Solid Snake (see p.138) was still neutralizing FOXHOUND, master-thief Garrett was helping pioneer the so-called "stealth-'em-up". Breaking the mould of the first-person-shooter, he commits larceny in a series of manor houses, haunted mines and assorted pseudo-medieval setting with the aim of absolute secrecy. Staying in the shadows, treading softly, listening out for patrolling guards and peeking around corners took Garrett to some very dark places indeed.

Played as a third-person stealth game or first-person shooter, the goal is the same: make the hit without getting caught – and there's more to it than just concealing your gun behind your back!

elegantly posed on a bed, apparently asleep, but with a bullet hole in her forehead. The caption read: "Beautifully executed". *Bella morte* indeed.

Ico

PS2; Team Ico, Sony; 2001

It's not often a videogame can be called charming. Cute (or tacky) perhaps, but genuinely endearing is not something many games even aim for, let alone achieve, and when they do they're usually from the Nintendo stable. *Ico*, however, was a welcome exception from Sony, based on an invented, elegantly simple fairytale and invoking a sense of wonder at its ethereal audio and visual qualities – an impression that remains with you long after you've stopped playing.

The back story is suitably wispy but to the point. In an unspecified time (although the Japanese and European medieval ages appear to have been a huge influence on its looks), in an unidentified country and village, once every generation a boy is born with horns growing from his head. The boy is traditionally reviled as the source of all bad fortune, and on his twelfth birthday is taken by the villagers to an enormous, forbidding castle, empty of occupants and full of cavernous rooms, where he is shackled into a tomb and left to the mercy of fate. Except that this time, after the adults have departed, the tomb cracks

Ico leads ghost-like Yorda through the castle: a simple concept and a wonderful gaming experience.

open, and Ico, the boy, tumbles out. Knocked unconscious by this, he dreams of a figure trapped somewhere within the castle; on his subsequent recovery, which is where you pick up the reins of this third-person puzzler, it's up to you to set off and rescue this ghost-like waif of a girl, Yorda (there's not much else to do, after all). Once you've rescued her, which should be within five minutes given the game's well-balanced level of difficulty, you need to guide them to escape. This is where the unusual gameplay really starts to kick in, for Yorda is pretty much powerless to do anything unless Ico makes it possible for her to achieve it.

This isn't complicated and frequently means, rather sweetly, holding her hand to lead her around the castle, or calling to her to come over to you; which is about all you get in terms of dialogue. In fact, as far as sound goes full stop, it's a beautifully pared-back, ambient affair, with only sparsely interspersed instrumental flourishes.

As for physical prowess, running and walking are pretty much all Yorda has to offer. Unlike the precocious athlete that Ico turns out to be, she cannot jump to get to hard-to-reach ledges nor dangle precariously off bits of stonework. No: it's Ico's job to make sure she can do everything as daintily as possible, so cue lots of lever-pushing and crate-pulling puzzles to get all the necessary pieces into place for her. Simple as this may sound, there's a fair amount of deduction needed.

It's not just puzzles that Yorda needs help with either: the castle does, after all, seem to have some kind of life within it. It's more a case of the undead than the living, however – black, wraithlike humanoid and arachnid figures who materialize from nebulous black holes that appear and disappear in the ground, which they keep trying to drag Yorda into. Ico, armed at the beginning with nothing but a stick (and later an infinitely more useful sword and mace), must whack them until they disappear into thin air. As the game progresses, there's even the ultimate fairytale nasty to contend with: an evil queen.

The focus on such refreshingly simple gameplay and purity of concept, complemented by the kind of artistic integrity on display, turned out to be something of a statement of intent for Team Ico (the Sony development team), for in 2005 they gave us the equally stunning *Shadow of the Colossus* (see p.174). Interestingly, the former,

Jet Set Radio Future
Xbox; Smilebit, Sega; 2002

Sega's demise as a hardware manufacturer enabled Microsoft to snap up many a previous Dreamcast software exclusive, and their desire to see the DC classic *Jet Set Radio* (*Jet Grind Radio* in the US) bolster up the Xbox was justifiable. Like *Ico* and *Shadow of the Colossus* (see p.174), the lines between gaming and art are fuzzy – though the setting couldn't be more different. The near-future city of Tokyo-to is a battleground for rebel gangs and the authorities. It's down to you – an inline-skating graffiti artist – to spraypaint the city in your colours, if you can stay alive long enough. Beautifully designed in Manga style, the sequel to the Dreamcast's coolest, most compulsive and original game became compatible with the Xbox 360 in 2007.

whilst receiving many industry and media awards and nominations, sold relatively poorly, but the success of the latter prompted Sony to re-release *Ico* in Europe in 2006 – an act virtually unheard of in the videogaming industry, especially for a piece of software that was five years old. But then *Ico* is anything but straightforward. Or to put it another way, *Ico* is a textbook example of how to get an understatement to make a huge impression.

IL-2 Sturmovik 1946

PC; 1C, Ubisoft; 2006

There was a period in the late 1990s when it seemed as though you couldn't move for combat-oriented flight sims on the PC, with even Jane's putting their name to a couple of EA's releases. Different combat arenas were covered to varying degrees of verisimilitude – such as Korea (the now defunct Rowan's *Mig Alley*), the Gulf (MicroProse's *Falcon 4*) and Israel (Jane's *Israeli Air Force*). And then there were those like MicroProse, who decided that focusing on light fighter aircraft wasn't really where simulations were at and went the whole hog with *B-17 Flying Fortress: The Mighty Eighth* (see p.120). But even with these World War II titles, it took until the new millennium for anyone to nail a truly great simulation set during that war.

It wasn't in a geographical arena that most expected either. Microsoft were already battling over the Pacific and Europe with their *Combat Flight Simulator* series, whilst Rowan fought their own *Battle of Britain* just as the aforementioned *B-17* was rumbling high above mainland Europe. Then, just when it looked like World War II was being fought on every border, *IL-2 Sturmovik* took you on a seat-of-your-pants flight over the Eastern Front. It was territory long overdue coverage, especially given combat flight sims' traditional focus on historical accuracy: there had been huge importance attached to this extra front opening up when the pact between Russia and Germany collapsed. Diverting tens of thousands of German troops away from fighting the other Allies and helping turn the tide of the war in Europe, it was a time of enormous sacrifice for Mother Russia. It's fitting, then, that this game was given life by a Russian developer, and in such a hugely atmospheric and educational way.

B-17 Flying Fortress: The Mighty Eighth
PC; Wayward Design, MicroProse; 2000

Just like the bomber that this simulation is based upon, *B-17 Flying Fortress* is an absolute behemoth. Set during the USAF massed bombing raids of Axis-occupied Europe during World War II, it encompasses virtually every aspect of executing and defending bombing runs, whether as pilot of an individual plane or as squadron commander. To its credit, the game's holistic approach never stops it from being relatively easy to get to grips with.

Propeller heads wept with joy on news of its 2001 release. Suddenly they had access to pieces of previously inaccessible aviation history, from the eponymous tank-busting IL-2 Sturmovik to the Yak, across unfamiliar terrains that included the Crimea, Stalingrad and Kiev. Expansion packs over the years posited further fronts, including the Russo-Finnish Continuation War of 1941–44 (*Forgotten Battles*, 2003) and Pearl Harbor (*Pacific Fighters*, 2004), and brought the number of flyable aircraft to a staggering 300 or so by 2006, when Ubisoft packaged the half-dozen episodes together as *IL-2 Sturmovik 1946* (so named because the last expansion saw an imagined continuation of the Russo-German front into that year). Like the attention paid to the geographical and historical specifics, the in-flight details are astounding: whilst elements such as contrails, gun convergence and wind buffeting have long been present in flight sims, dynamic extras like ice forming on the wings (and the need to take the airflow over them into account) make *IL-2* as much a flight school as a game. Novice pilots, however, can take heart from the fact that all the difficulty elements are customizable. That flexibility extends to how the game plays, too, offering historical linear campaigns, single missions (that present a variety of scenarios), randomized missions and the ability to build them yourself.

It's testament to the superiority of *IL-2* that its 2001 build needed only to receive expansions to shoot down newer competition – including the release date of its successor, *Storm of War: Battle of Britain*, which, under the weight of considerable expectations, kept shifting further into the future as *IL-2* continued to patrol.

Incredibly detailed in-flight graphics add to the veracity of the gameplay.

Legend of Zelda: Ocarina of Time

N64; Nintendo; 1998

Acclaimed by fans and the games industry alike as probably the best game ever made, millions of words have been written – and continue to be written – about this cartridge-based game that's ten years old and counting. True, it's been reissued a couple of times, most recently as a Wii Virtual Console download, but in the budding art form of videogames, *Ocarina of Time* is the *Citizen Kane*: everyone's heard of it, most have played (at least some of) it, and although it can't help but look its age, it remains as playable and as modern in its design as anything on the shelves today.

Fusing RPG and action/platform elements to create its own subgenre, the *Legend of Zelda* series had long established a name for innovation, but it's this fifth instalment that first stepped into the 3D territory already conquered by stable-mate Mario (see p.240). The game was hugely delayed, coming out five years after *Link's Awakening* and, even worse, around two years after the release of the console it was supposed to help sell. At a time when *Half-Life* was astonishing PC gamers with its immersive, futuristic world, and *Tomb Raider III* had PlayStation fans grunting at Lara's latest exploits, it was Shigeru Miyamoto's latest masterpiece for the N64 that topped the games charts, its holiday sales beating even those of the hit movie *A Bug's Life*.

Anyone who's ever played a *Legend of Zelda* game knows the story: Link, a lowly forest boy, is charged with saving the world (and the eponymous princess) from an evil wizard king. Like all the best stories, though, it's the telling that counts, and here the player is made to feel genuinely involved, partly through Link's own blankness as a character, as well as the openness of the gameworld.

N64-era Link and the iconic Triforce, recognized across the gaming world as the series' symbol.

Places are reached via the broad, grassy expanse of Hyrule Field, first on foot, later on horseback, with Link's steed Epona one of many recurring characters from earlier games – and in subsequent ones. Wandering around Hyrule, whether to fulfil a quest, visit shops, take part in minigames or simply explore, it feels like a real world, where Link engages with the other inhabitants, visiting defined areas that are home to races as distinct as the rock-eating, pot-bellied Gorons and slender, aquatic Zoras. It's impossible to forget the main quest, though, thanks to Link's attendant fairy Navi's persistent "Hey!!! Listen!"

The rest of the game takes place in labyrinthine dungeons designed around the series' trademark puzzles and featuring familiar monsters such as skulltula spiders, nutty deku scrubs and bat-like keese. Each dungeon, whether it's in the forest or the belly of a giant fish, is masterfully designed so that getting lost is a distinct possibility but getting stuck is (almost always) out of the question, and shortcuts facilitate quick returns to the site of each final boss fight. Fighting uses a targeting system that's rarely been bettered, the N64 controller in perfect sync with the game in an intuitive, contextual system (which is just as easy to use with the GameCube controller). Choose items to map to the buttons from the inventory screens, which keep a score of progress in key plot items, too.

These include the songs that Link learns to play on his ocarina, a player-controlled effect that can change night to day, bring rain, summon Epona, and a lot more. It's this kind of deep player involvement that makes the game so emotionally gripping, together with the deliberately affecting storyline. Using the common *Zelda* device of dual worlds, Link is also played as an adult in a world ruled by Ganondorf, the very scenario he tries to prevent seven years earlier. It's a dark mirror of the world of boy Link where, for example, the watery domain of the Zoras is an icy cavern.

Thankfully there was only a two-year wait for the sequel, *Majora's Mask*, a great game in its own right, as is the cel-shaded *The Wind Waker* on GameCube, whereas the Wii's uniquely controlled *The Twilight Princess* offers an improved all-round experience in many ways. Still, there's a thrill to be had in exploring and learning this vast and astonishingly beautiful world for the first time, which is unlikely to be surpassed.

Legend of Zelda: Phantom Hourglass

DS; Nintendo; 2007

Link is no stranger to the Game Boy, but this is the first time he's graced the DS, and so all the more gratifying that *Phantom Hourglass* is both an original game and one destined to be a classic. Diehard Zelda fans should be satisfied by its well-judged mix of innovation and familiarity, but it's also the perfect entry point for a gamer who's never been anywhere near the land of Hyrule. After the GameCube's *Legend of Zelda: The Wind Waker* made less of an impact than expected, Nintendo decided to go all out for a more realistic-looking game in *Twilight Princess* (see below), believing that *Wind Waker's* cel-shaded design had led gamers (in the US particularly) to see it as too cartoony and childish. As a sequel to that game, featuring the same style of artwork, *Phantom Hourglass* uses this perception to its advantage, showing it has the same universal appeal as the DS itself. Producer Eiji Aonuma, accustomed to working closely with Shigeru Miyamoto, has propelled the game in a slightly different direction, making it less emotionally gruelling, and on nothing like as epic a scale as many previous Zeldas, in either theme or length – as suits the nature of the system.

How it looks and how it plays are so thoroughly integrated, it's impossible to discuss one without the other. Much like *Twilight Princess*, the game feels shiny and new – not so much through its stunningly designed setting, lovely though it is, but thanks to its unique control system. Using the stylus exclusively makes for a whole new way to play, and even if old hands have used the boomerang to hit switches hundreds of times before, they've never done it quite like this. The usual dungeons, here with a top-down isometric viewpoint, intersperse the exploratory gameplay, set in the sea-based overworld of *Wind Waker*, with Link travelling from island to island in a boat in his quest to find and rescue feisty pirate Tetra.

Negotiating routes on the sea means drawing them with the stylus, the joy of sailing coming in thankfully smaller bursts than in

The dramatic appearance created by cel-shading Link was a bold step for Nintendo, perhaps better received the second time around.

Wind Waker. The stylus is also used to write on the map, especially useful in dungeons for scribbling notes about locations of keys, entrances and exits, and often forming the basis of puzzles, which are, as usual, the crux of the dungeoneering. Blowing in the mic to put out candles, occasionally shouting out, and plotting routes for the boomerang are all excellent fun and the last also incredibly useful, since it means you can accurately send the weapon around corners out of sight. The other slice of DS joy is in the game's use of the upper map screen. It's integral to the gameplay, for instance when used to avoid the patrolling phantom guards in the Temple of the Ocean King, a dungeon revisited time and again, where Link relies on stealth in combination with the phantom hourglass (an item that prevents the evil atmosphere from killing him). There are plenty of monsters to fight, too, the stylus used to slash or spin attack, and since aiming isn't a problem, it's generally not too tricky, even the bosses, although they do demand the usual lateral thinking.

Charming both visually and in its humorous script, not to mention the expressiveness of huge-eyed Link, it's an altogether shorter and easier game than might be expected of a *Zelda* instalment, albeit with a multiplayer battle game included. So, now Nintendo has succeeded in bringing the series to a new audience, where next for *Zelda*? Will it continue down the less hardcore route or split into two subseries? If, as seems likely, it proves to be a long wait till the next new game, there's still a lengthy backlist, much of which is thoroughly deserving of a replay.

THE LEGENDARY LIST

1987 *The Legend of Zelda* – NES, also GBA 2004
1988 *Zelda II: The Adventure of Link*
– NES, also GBA 2004, Virtual Console 2007
1992 *The Legend of Zelda: A Link to the Past*
– SNES, also GBA 2002, Virtual Console 2007
1993 *The Legend of Zelda: Link's Awakening*
– GB, also GBC 1998
1998 *The Legend of Zelda: Ocarina of Time*
– N64, also GC 2003, Virtual Console 2007
2000 *The Legend of Zelda: Majora's Mask* – N64
2001 *The Legend of Zelda: Oracle of Ages* – GBC
2001 *The Legend of Zelda: Oracle of Seasons* – GBC
2003 *The Legend of Zelda: The Wind Waker* – GC
2004 *The Legend of Zelda: Four Swords Adventures* – GC
2004 *The Legend of Zelda: The Minish Cap* – GBA
2006 *The Legend of Zelda: Twilight Princess*
– GC, also Wii 2006
2007 *The Legend of Zelda: Phantom Hourglass* – DS

The Legend of Zelda: A Link to the Past

A bestseller on the SNES and again on the GBA, the third, still eminently playable *Zelda* game, is a 2D gaming classic, featuring an expansive world strewn with side quests, begging to be explored. There are several small firsts for the series, such as heart pieces to collect to make a heart container, and one very crucial big one – the trademark trope of turning the world on its head.

The Legend of Zelda: Twilight Princess

As stunning as a non-HD Hyrule can be, with a darker edge to it than any *Zelda* since *Majora's Mask*, and the same haunting (if still synthesized) musical themes. After a slow start, this epic game comes into its own, Link switching between the normal world and the world of twilight, where he transforms into a wolf, aided by mischievous sidekick Midna. Using the Wii remote for swordfights is a novelty, but it works brilliantly for the bow or slingshot.

Lego Star Wars II: The Original Trilogy

Xbox 360, Xbox, PS2, PC, PSP, DS; TT Games, LucasArts; 2006

This is a videogame that recreates a trilogy of movies, representing live action by means of plastic bricks, which are themselves recreated using computer imagery – trying to deconstruct *Lego Star Wars II* is more trouble than it's worth. Simpler to get your head around is the fact that this ingenious combination of middle-aged but eternally popular fantasy sci-fi films and toy building blocks adds up to a superbly entertaining, unmistakeably twenty-first-century experience.

Seeing the screen crawl begin with its accompanying fanfare provides a genuine nostalgic thrill; inevitably, a good proportion of the fun comes from taking part in some of the best-loved movies of all time (mostly why this game is superior to the first, based on the *Star Wars* prequels), entering those familiar scenes, from impressive space vistas with swooping TIE fighters to the misty swamps of Dagobah, from the bumpy asteroid field to the jungletops of Yavin's fourth moon, all of it built from virtual Lego bricks. The characters are brick constructed, too, but with expressive faces drawn on their smoothly moulded heads, as they interact in scenes that are instantly recognizable, spiced up with plenty of (visual) jokes, for instance Han throwing Chewbacca a bone to get him into the garbage chute. Faithfulness to the source material doesn't make it a great game in itself, but the story's accompanied by fast and furious action, battles galore, and more than a few puzzles – block-moving, building equipment with piles of Lego bricks, plus swapping playable characters in and out so that Artoo, say, can open a computer-operated

Princess Leia's familiar hairdo, seen here in situ, can also be applied to other characters.

lock. Everything's achievable in the single-player game, but it's even better fun with two playing cooperatively.

The developers have been given some licence to mess with the sacred canon, but there's nothing to really outrage fans; even seeing Han sporting Leia's hairdo, huge shades and a moustache can't disguise the fact that this is a game that can take its place proudly in the Star Wars universe. The absence of dialogue is a blessing, allowing the plot to unravel through

Pilot AT-STs around Tatooine: all the familiar vehicles and creatures are present and correct.

action and cut scenes, expressed through the characters' hilariously expressive faces and the noises they make. Occasionally, there are more direct ways to get the point across – Darth Vader's climactic speech to Luke in *The Empire Strikes Back* has him whip out a family snapshot.

Gory violence has no place in *Star Wars*, but there's plenty of fighting all the same: battling X-wings in the Millennium Falcon, taking out dozens of storm troopers with a trusty blaster, and of course a lightsaber duel with Darth Vader. Death in this game means never having to go back to the start; instead, there's an eerie shriek and a bloodless cascade of component pieces, and if you're quick you can snatch them up again once you've respawned. Each death reduces the total number of studs collected, but even at zero you can still continue indefinitely, a device that makes even the trickier parts – though none of it's really that tricky – refreshingly unfrustrating. The goal is to finish each chapter with a perfect True Jedi score, having collected up all the possible studs, and since everything's made out of impermanent building blocks, this involves destruction as well as construction, shooting anything and everything, even building stuff just to blast it back into bricks and studs. Studs are currency to be spent on different characters to take back into the chapters when you've cleared Story mode, whether to replay it at ultra fast speed, or in Free Play, where you can explore at leisure, investigating areas only accessible to certain characters.

Designed with children in mind, *Lego Star Wars II* is one of those things – like early Pixar movies or Philip Pullman novels – that appeal just as much to adults, something that's unfortunately not that common in games. Even rarer is to come across a game of a film that more than lives up to its promise, giving you the opportunity to be part of – and to play around with – one of the most popular movie series of all time.

Lumines

PSP; Q Entertainment, Ubisoft; 2005

Sometimes, explaining what happens in a game – especially a puzzle one – is no explanation at all. Take *Tetris*, a game comprising falling, differently shaped blocks that must be rotated and interlocked to avoid the board filling up. Whilst a strictly accurate description, what is more difficult to convey is its hypnotic, addictive qualities and the jitterbug mindset resulting from the hundreds of calculations you make as the blocks descend. It also ignores the fact that despite its beautiful simplicity – now as taken for granted as noughts and crosses (tic-tac-toe) – there was a time before it existed.

And so it is with *Lumines*. At its simplest, *Lumines* is a *Tetris*-like game in which all the falling, rotatable blocks are squares comprising four smaller units. These quarters may be any of four different colours; and the aim is to match up four quarters (or more) of the same colour to create a single block of green, red, orange and so on. This disappears (adding points to the running score), and as it does, the remaining coloured blocks around it redistribute themselves downwards into the now empty spaces. So far, so so – on paper at least.

What takes *Lumines* beyond that basic premise is creator Tetsuya Mizuguchi's contention that "Playing a game and performing music are structurally similar; they both entail a call-and-response style of repetition." While his earlier *Rez* (see p.169) was a literal interpretation of this, with the player required to anticipate musical beats with button presses, here the gently pulsating dance tracks don't so much dictate your actions as influence your thought processes – a kind of *Tetris*-meets-chill-out DJ mix set against a constantly shifting background of neon-inspired light shows. The result is surprisingly calming and charming: in place of the bug-eyed, twitchy *Tetris* addicts of the 1980s and 90s, *Lumines* players are more likely to be smiling as though they've dropped a mild E and had a few puffs on the bong; whilst non-players in close proximity to the PSP have been known to tap their toes and bob their heads in time to its soundtrack. And they've done it for extended periods, too; what should ostensibly be a time-killer can last hours in the right hands. As such, it's perhaps better defined as a sensory, almost abstract experience than a game per se – in a similar vein to *Everyday Shooter* (see p.170) – and one that's far greater than the sum of its parts.

Like an insanely catchy tune heard for the first time, the evolutionary step from *Tetris* to *Lumines* seems so obvious that it's something of a mystery as to how no one had discovered it before. But only Mizuguchi could have had the vision for a game to transcend gameplay and to fulfil, to a much greater extent, his ultimate aim for *Rez*: "to impart the sensation of synaesthesia."

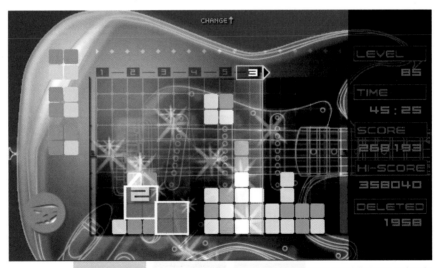

Hypnotic gameplay, vibrantly themed screens and chilled-out sounds make for a distinctly twenty-first-century puzzle game.

Madden NFL 2004

PS2, Xbox, GC, PC, GBA; EA Tiburon, Budcat, EA; 2003

Turned out annually since the early 1990s, EA's juggernaut *Madden NFL* series has gathered such pace that it's now rather like any mass-produced expensive wine – a quality product that's become so ubiquitous it practically sells itself, regardless of variations in quality. That's not to say EA rests on its NFL laurels. Far from it: over the years there have been occasional bold, sweeping changes to the body of the gameplay, as well as more frequent subtle differences that suit some palates more than others. But the latest release isn't by default the most creative, no matter how much better-looking it may be than previous incarnations, and so far the series has

developed in an unsensational manner on the latest next-gen hardware. In this respect, EA finds itself between a rock and a hard place: to a greater or lesser degree, aesthetics are the larger part of what it has to play with, as to reinvent the wheel would defeat the point of *Madden* (not to mention alienating the fanbase); but a game that asks players to effectively re-purchase it every twelve months obviously needs to justify itself.

It's ultimately an arbitrary decision, but from a historical perspective, *Madden NFL 2004* can be considered the last great vintage title for the series so far. Having had the chance

A creative peak for the long-running series in terms of gameplay, the 2004 edition also provides an incredible amount of onscreen detail.

to bed down on the PS2 and Xbox consoles from the 2001 edition onwards, and broached online play in *Madden 2003*, *Madden NFL 2004* is its highest evolutionary peak thus far in terms of changing its gameplay – perhaps because up to that point the creativity bar was still being significantly raised by 2K's excellent online-enabled *ESPN NFL 2K* and Microsoft's *NFL Fever* series. (It was a situation EA ended abruptly that very year by hoovering up the sole licensing rights to all current NFL leagues, teams and players, killing the competition stone dead as well as, some felt, EA's own competitive hunger. 2K resurrected its title as the so-so *All-Pro Football 2K8* in 2007, featuring a fictional league and signing up retired AFL and WFL stars – including O.J. Simpson.)

EA Sports' familiar mantra – "If it's in the game, it's in the game" – has increasingly held true over the years, but the level of detail added to the 2004 edition remains especially impressive (and unlike the later PS3 and Xbox 360 versions, this version still has Madden himself on commentary duty). The AI, upped significantly from *Madden 2003*, is particularly apparent in the defensive comeback play – always something of a thorn in the series' side – whilst the Playmaker ability allows players to add innumerable tweaks to an already extensive but refreshingly team-specific playbook: the animation here is so subtle that it's best appreciated through the slow-motion replays. The crowd boos bad calls and poor home performances, whilst off the pitch, the stalwart Franchise mode includes a training season, a preseason mode, and an ownership mode that allows you to regulate everything down to the price of hotdogs and beer at your home stadium – as well as fun stuff like hiring and firing the coaching staff. If that doesn't do enough to satisfy the fans, you can spit the dummy and relocate the team, that most American of sporting traditions.

A few years have passed and a new generation of consoles has since appeared, but so far EA has only built out from *Madden NFL 2004*'s achievements rather than take any meaningful steps beyond it. When that does happen it may well be after 2009, when its NFL rights expire, and the playing field is levelled once again – but in the meantime, let yourself be steamrollered by the *Madden* powerhouse.

NFL 2K2
PS2, Xbox, DC; Visual Concepts, Sega; 2001

Historically important for splitting the *Madden* market, the decision to make *NFL 2K2* multiplatform was both Sega's response to EA refusing to put *Madden* onto the Dreamcast and an arcade specialist's take on an how to do an in-depth sports game. It wasn't the statistical monster that *Madden* was, but *NFL 2K2* did for football what Jerry Rice and Brett Favre were doing for NFL itself. In short, it looked superb and it played blindingly. Realistic graphics and commentary that actually reflected the game in question (even today an issue in sports games), playing at speeds about twice that of real football, and quarterbacks who could turn on a dime, all made for a *Madden-2K2* match with real grunt.

Mario Kart DS

DS; Nintendo; 2005

Born on the SNES in 1992, a new version of *Mario Kart* has turned up on every subsequent Nintendo system, but it wasn't until the DS release of 2005 that it felt like every box had been thoroughly checked. Here, in the tiniest of packages, is a culmination – and celebration – of all that history: 32 tracks, half of them original, half revamped favourites, an arsenal of powerups traditional and new-fangled, plus the usual Nintendo cast of characters (Mario, Princess Peach, Donkey Kong, Yoshi et al), together making for hours and hours of addictive gameplay.

It may seem like you've seen it all before, and of course you have, in the three earlier versions, not to mention dozens of imitators over the years, some worthwhile (see box), others less so (anyone

KARTING CRED

Mario Kart can be seen as the granddaddy of all racing games with combat characteristics, even the futuristic *WipEout* or dark, horrific *Twisted Metal* (see p.233), but plenty of games have opted for sticking more closely to the original theme, featuring karts or similar cartoon-style vehicles and backdrops, rather than aiming for realism. Dozens of franchises and characters have taken to the tracks, from Mickey Mouse to the Muppets, Banjo Kazooie to Bomberman, making it difficult to spot the decent games amid the dross. Following is our leaderboard of non-traditional vehicular combat games.

CTR: Crash Team Racing
PS; Naughty Dog, Sony; 1999

One of the Sony mascot's earlier appearances, before he made one too many games and became a tired old has-been. It's a clear homage to *Mario Kart*, but the *Crash* characters and locations are brilliantly executed and it's still laps ahead of much of the pack (see picture on right).

Wacky Races
DC; Infogrames, Sega; 2000

Convincingly like watching a Hanna-Barbera cartoon, though the kooky drivers' home-made vehicles aren't as easy to race as you'd think. Cheating and taunting are rife, thankfully.

Jak X Combat Racing
PS2; Naughty Dog, Sony; 2005

A refreshingly speedy racer featuring the tall one from *Jak & Daxter*, with heaps of variety, sumptuous settings and both split-screen and online multiplayer options.

remember *South Park Rally*?), but in typical Nintendo style *Mario Kart DS* continues to plough its own furrow, as though the competition didn't exist. In kart racing, it's only the race itself that matters: there's no collision damage to admire or worry about, not much variation in lighting or weather conditions; figure out the power slide and you've got all the driving techniques you need. Tracks cover the usual range of themes – from beaches with tempting watery shortcuts to icefields with rolling snowballs to dodge, from heavy-going chocolate canyons to Bowser's broad-paved, lava-pitted castle, and the infamous final Rainbow Road – half of them need to be unlocked by winning Cup competitions in Grand Prix mode.

While the 50cc races aren't too much of a challenge, the pace picks up considerably with 100cc and 150cc, when skill and timing start to mean something. Boxes containing random power-ups are strewn across the tracks at intervals, providing boosts and weapons such as shells you can fire to overturn karts, floating heads that splatter ink over your opponent's screen, a bullet to carry you speedily and safely along the track, overtaking everyone in your path, or the stars that provide a rainbow speed boost while giving you immunity – it's worth hanging onto these items until the time is right. The DS system comes into its own here, the map on its touch screen useful for locating the shortcuts and pitfalls ahead, but just as importantly the position of the other drivers, so you can pinpoint the exact moment to launch a backwards attack or dodge one. It also lets you know when you can ease your thumb off and cruise gently over the finish line.

Luigi takes to the air…

Don't get too comfy though, as the next step is to move on to real-life opponents; they may be less clever but they're no more predictable than the AI you'll meet in single-player Grand Prix, Battle or Versus modes. In a generous gesture, up to eight players can compete using just the one game card, though only the game's owner gets to choose their character. Even better, as the first game to take advantage of the Nintendo Wi-Fi network, *Mario Kart DS* allows you hook up to the Internet to race friends or to be matched with players all over the world. One big addition to the already addictive gameplay and another of the endless reasons to keep coming back to a game that's packed with layers of options, plus tons of unlockable stuff. Small but perfectly formed, this is one adrenaline-fuelled thumb-busting blast of joy from starting flag to finish line.

A Salarian bartender, one of the alien inhabitants of *Mass Effect*'s universe.

Mass Effect

Xbox 360, PC; BioWare, Demiurge, Microsoft, EA; 2007

Most fans of BioWare's excellent RPG *Star Wars: Knights of the Old Republic* (see p.225) would happily acknowledge it as superior to its sequel, *KOTOR: The Sith Lords*, developed by Obsidian. More controversial, however, is the question of whether BioWare's next big project, *Mass Effect*, is better than the hallowed *Star Wars* game. The answer is a delicately balanced "yes", despite, as Jedi purists are wont to point out, *Mass Effect*'s universe being so clearly based on an amalgam of ideas pinched from their own, alongside those of *Star Trek*, *Battlestar Galactica*, *Babylon 5* and *Stargate* – to wit, a plot involving the crisis of consciousness in man (and alien) and machine and the inherent conflicts of interest in their coexistence. But *Mass Effect* is still very much its own creature, and those who can't get beyond their so-near-yet-so-far feelings would do well to remember that BioWare deliberately passed over *The Sith Lords* to develop instead this piece of flattery by imitation – and that it slots neatly into any of those frameworks in all but name.

It's true that players of *KOTOR* will recognize many of the mechanics at play here, from team selection to some familiar character-building and level architecture: but BioWare has paid close attention to the evolution in technology and digital storytelling since. At this level, *Mass Effect* is best contrasted with open-ended RPGs like *Fallout* (see p.81): where these continue to offer a huge variety of consistently branching scenarios within a relatively small geographical area, *Mass Effect* uses the power of the DVD (and the ever-expanding hard drive, in the PC's case) to work out an incredibly tight main narrative across visitable galaxies, star systems and planets. Within that framework, elements can turn out in several ways – and there are myriad strands, some beneficial, others merely diversionary – but the main thrust remains firmly controlled.

The biggest step up, however, is in the way *Mass Effect* unabashedly drives you to new levels of emotional engagement with that story and its protagonists. From the

There are plenty of different planets to explore, some of them less hospitable than others.

outset, it encourages you to identify with the appropriately named lead, Commander Shepard, by allowing full customization of his/her appearance. And where *KOTOR* saw a light flirtation between its characters, BioWare have boldly plumped for a sophisticated dialogue model that allows for tonal variation and can ultimately lead Shepard into the complications of emotional and physical relationships (for which the game was briefly and inaccurately maligned in sections of the US press: the sex scenes are no more explicit nor frequent than any found in *Lost*, a former accuser admitted). It's not just about specific words, either: *Mass Effect*, alongside *Uncharted: Drake's Fortune*, matches them to some of the subtlest facial expressions and characterful voice acting in games since *Half-Life 2*.

Greater realism has also been achieved (as seen in the illustration above) in the adrenal stakes, with real-time combat that tips a nod to *Gears of War* for its tactical run, duck and cover approach, a wink to *Ratchet and Clank* for its fluid weapons- and powers-selection system, and a tip of the hat to *System Shock 2* for its customizable armoury. And for a game that places such emphasis on dialogue, there are a *lot* of weapons to back up your words with – each has its own overheating point and level of stability and responds just as well to close attention as any personal relationship does – but this level of detail is just one of the finishing touches in fleshing out BioWare's new gaming world. BioWare may not officially have the Force, but it has certainly gone boldly where no other RPG has been before.

Max Payne

PC, Mac, Xbox, PS2, GBA; Remedy Entertainment/Rockstar, Gathering of Developers/Rockstar/MacSoft; 2001

Before there was high-definition, there was *Max Payne*, a game whose graphics demanded such tremendous processing power that it prompted waggish reviewers to remark on the "Payne" of not having a PC that was up to the job. The later Xbox and PS2 versions were actually pretty much picture perfect, but the glorious cinematics were only part of a bigger package, with Finnish developer Remedy's stated intention being to take storytelling in games to new heights through reference to both written and film media. It's not unusual for videogames to do this, of course, but its execution in *Max Payne* is so spot-on that it's a tribute to the designers that influences as diverse as film director John Woo, Norse mythology and pulp detective novels can all be thrown into the mix with the game still managing to be most determinedly its own, coherent whole.

Taking heavy fire in a set that could be straight out of a John Woo movie, only bullet time can save Payne now…

The linear levels play out as chapters, each preceded by scene-setting graphic-novel storyboards voiced over with dialogue that pokes fun at the film-noir world that Max inhabits ("The wind was tearing at my face like sand paper and razor blades"). It simultaneously pays the genre respect with some real corkers ("You play, you pay, you bastard"); the great voice acting always gets the balance right. Incidentally, Max's face is modelled on that of Sam Lake, writer of the game's script and dialogue, so in many ways you're getting the story straight from the horse's mouth.

Something of a roller-coaster ride, the twelve or so hours of gameplay you get are relentless, racking up one of the highest ever bodycounts for a game this length. Things kick off with Max, an NYPD cop, returning from work to find his wife and daughter murdered in his apartment, unleashing a *Deathwish*-esque persona in Max. His pursuit of revenge complicates matters, however, as he soon ends up getting framed for murder and being pursued by the police, the Mafia and Russian mobsters involved in a Nordic death cult, all the while trying to unravel the conspiracy that was ultimately responsible for his wife's death. That's quite a bit to take in, and this being Lake's noir-ish take on the graphic novel, what other option does Max have but to shoot his way to a solution?

Max, it transpires, is a lethal weapon. Given just a relatively simple automatic he can cause carnage, but his portable arsenal soon opens up to encompass the usual videogame array of shotguns, grenades and Uzis, but the freshness of its execution comes right off the back of *The Matrix* and *Hard Boiled*, as Remedy have nabbed wholesale their concepts of temporal distortion and applied it liberally to the combat system here. Dubbed "bullet time", the world around Max is reduced to a slow-motion blur as he remains able to perform actions in real time, giving him a distinct advantage over the opposition. Not surprisingly, this is when the game becomes most like a movie: mobsters copping bullets fly backwards gracefully, bullets lazily snake their way towards Max, allowing him to dive out of their way, freeing him to take on multiple enemies without (as much) fear of being outgunned. Even the audio is stretched out.

There have been plans to transfer this movie-influenced story onto celluloid for a while now, but it remains to be seen as to whether 20th Century Fox will end up with a *Deathwish*-type cult series for the twenty-first century or whether it will follow the trail of so many game-to-movie franchises and end up as a miserable failure. But it's debatable as to whether that really matters, so comprehensively does Remedy round off the story in its two episodes; you get the feeling Max thinks it's all over anyway. As the man says: "The final gunshot was an exclamation mark to everything that had led up to this point. I released my finger from the trigger. And then it was all over."

Max Payne 2: The Fall of Max Payne
PC, PS2, Xbox; Remedy Entertainment, Rockstar; 2003

Picking up exactly where the first story ends, the plot may be longer and more convoluted than its predecessor, but as far as gameplay goes it's more of the same, and so feels like a missed opportunity. The best thing about it, however, is that there's yet more pearls of Payne wisdom.

Metal Gear Solid 4: Guns of the Patriots

PS3; Kojima Productions, Konami; 2008

You have to hand it to *MGS*'s Solid Snake: he's tough. And not just for putting up with that name (actually a reference to Snake Plissken, played by Kurt Russell in the 1981 movie *Escape from New York*). Since 1987's *Metal Gear*, he's been a member of the elite FOXHOUND group; been betrayed by its leader, Big Boss; discovered that Big Boss was his genetic father; and killed the subsequent leader of FOXHOUND, his cloned brother Liquid Snake. To cap it all off, Liquid's personality has now been transmitted into the person of long-time adversary Revolver Ocelot, resulting in new villain, Liquid Ocelot. Snake, meanwhile, assigned to assassinate Ocelot, is suffering from severe premature ageing. But if this semi-Oedipal internecine killing seems confusing on paper, that's to detract from Kojima's digital story-telling genius. Where he led the way in bringing cinematics to the PlayStation with *Metal Gear Solid*, he has now rounded off his and Solid Snake's involvement with the series with an indulgent, massively compelling directorial flourish.

Metal Gear Solid 4 is set five years after *MGS2* (which Solid Snake was last seen halfway through; *MGS3* meanwhile, concentrated on the adventures of a young Big Boss, aka Naked Snake). The world is now a very different place to when Snake last saw any action.

Grizzled and gaunt he may be, but Solid Snake's still got what it takes.

It's a bleak (though perhaps not entirely unimaginable) vision Kojima has for our future, where armed conflict in the Middle East is constant. It's an age where warfare is to the twenty-first century's economy what oil was to the twentieth's, with nation states rendered meaningless and the fighting being run by private military corporations, who combat local militias with swathes of nano-enhanced foot soldiers (a nice counterpoint to Snake's freshly engendered human frailty).

It's against this oppressive backdrop that Snake now operates, so it's no surprise to see that Kojima decided to add Psyche and Stress gauges to the Stamina gauge of previous titles. He's also working in a more open-world environment than before, with more than one way to accomplish each task, the ultimate goal being to reach Liquid Ocelot, the supremo of the PMCs. It's an interesting premise, as Snake is ostensibly a neutral party to the militias: theoretically sharing the same enemy, he even begins the game in a resistance member's garb. But in a warzone trust needs to be earned, and there's a delicate balance between deserving their support and taking it for granted, at which point allies may turn into foes.

In keeping with the greater freedom afforded by the new environment, there's an increased repertoire of moves to take open battlefield conditions into account, such as being able to fire weapons from any stance. There are also some new close-quarters battle tactics – sneaking through the detritus of battle or engaging in running battles are now both valuable options (the latter unthinkable in previous *MGS* games). Snake's equipment has been upgraded, too: even the iconic eyepatch has incorporated thermal and night vision, as well as a zoom lens.

Although clearly the result of considerable effort, the execution of it all is so fluid and beautifully depicted that both Snake and Kojima can bow out in style. It remains to be seen whether the legacy of their extraordinary – in the truest sense of the word – adventures can be matched by others.

Splinter Cell: Chaos Theory
PC, PS2, Xbox, GC, DS; Ubisoft Montréal & Annecy; 2005

You have to feel sorry for Ubisoft. Their stealth series is not only the best in the Tom Clancy range – and one of the top two espionage series on the market full stop – it has a more intuitive control system than *MGS* and is packed full of the kind of spy gadgets that would make James Bond go green. Unfortunately, Solid Snake's world has always been more epic than Sam Fisher's. The plus side for Sam's world is that it is a far more realistic place with far more specifics to interact with. Last in the series for the PS2 and Xbox, *Chaos Theory* piles on yet more detail visually, in the AI, and most perfectly in the co-op and multiplayer modes. Next-gen titles continued to improve the game, but this remains a *Splinter Cell* benchmark.

Syphon Filter: Logan's Shadow
PSP; SCEA, Sony; 2007

Always playing third fiddle to *MGS* and *Splinter Cell*, *Syphon Filter*'s Gabe Logan and Lian Xing have always felt closer to the popcorn spirit of 1980s–90s-era James Bond than anything vaguely gritty. *Logan's Shadow* doesn't do much to counter this, but like its predecessor *Dark Mirror* it does demonstrate the PSP's ability to handle near-console-level gameplay, graphics and storylines. Underwater spear-gun battles, tense gunfights and an improved control system are incentive enough to invite Gabe along to the party with Snake and Fisher.

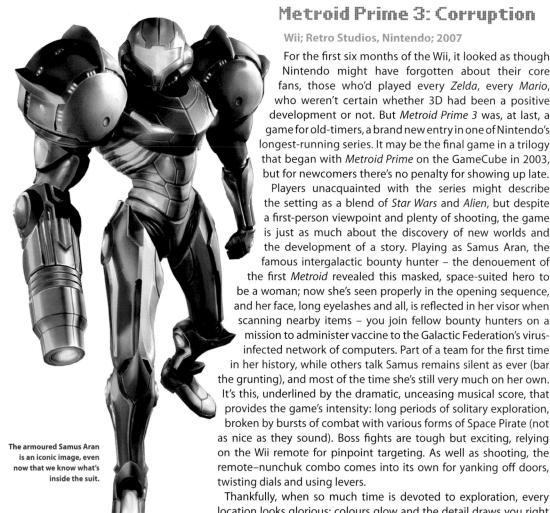

The armoured Samus Aran is an iconic image, even now that we know what's inside the suit.

Metroid Prime 3: Corruption

Wii; Retro Studios, Nintendo; 2007

For the first six months of the Wii, it looked as though Nintendo might have forgotten about their core fans, those who'd played every *Zelda*, every *Mario*, who weren't certain whether 3D had been a positive development or not. But *Metroid Prime 3* was, at last, a game for old-timers, a brand new entry in one of Nintendo's longest-running series. It may be the final game in a trilogy that began with *Metroid Prime* on the GameCube in 2003, but for newcomers there's no penalty for showing up late.

Players unacquainted with the series might describe the setting as a blend of *Star Wars* and *Alien*, but despite a first-person viewpoint and plenty of shooting, the game is just as much about the discovery of new worlds and the development of a story. Playing as Samus Aran, the famous intergalactic bounty hunter – the denouement of the first *Metroid* revealed this masked, space-suited hero to be a woman; now she's seen properly in the opening sequence, and her face, long eyelashes and all, is reflected in her visor when scanning nearby items – you join fellow bounty hunters on a mission to administer vaccine to the Galactic Federation's virus-infected network of computers. Part of a team for the first time in her history, while others talk Samus remains silent as ever (bar the grunting), and most of the time she's still very much on her own. It's this, underlined by the dramatic, unceasing musical score, that provides the game's intensity: long periods of solitary exploration, broken by bursts of combat with various forms of Space Pirate (not as nice as they sound). Boss fights are tough but exciting, relying on the Wii remote for pinpoint targeting. As well as shooting, the remote–nunchuk combo comes into its own for yanking off doors, twisting dials and using levers.

Thankfully, when so much time is devoted to exploration, every location looks glorious: colours glow and the detail draws you right into the strange, atmospheric worlds Samus visits. The three very different planets are alien all right, and rather than bland, repetitive corridors, feel like real spaces to negotiate, and gradually get to know your way around; the 3D map system takes some getting used to, well designed as it is, and in the end, it can be easier to map the place in your head. Then, the satisfaction of figuring out a puzzle, the excitement of progressing through and ultimately defeating a level and its secrets, often by returning more than once, is unbeatable. All the while, Samus gathers information through her scan visor, which seems fussy to use at first, but becomes invaluable for clues on how to solve puzzles, as well as data on the past and present, characters and world history. Her own development is strictly in-game, with new abilities and suit improvements available at frequent intervals. One talent she has from the start is the morph ball, whereby she and her suit roll up into a sphere that can be propelled up pipes and along tubes – a bizarre but fun alternative means of getting from A to B. And an ability that's been unchanged through the series, however much it's evolved from its original 2D roots. Thoroughly absorbing, the final game in the Prime series but the first for the Wii is a defiantly single-player experience that revels in its sense of solitude, a game that demands you take your time, and where every minute is a pleasure worth savouring.

MORE MAYHEM... MORE METROIDS

1986 *Metroid* – NES

1991 *Metroid II: Return of Samus* – GB

1994 *Super Metroid* – SNES

2002 *Metroid Prime* – GC

2002 *Metroid Fusion* – GBA

2004 *Metroid Prime 2: Echoes* – GC

2004 *Metroid: Zero Mission* – GBA

2005 *Metroid Prime Pinball* – DS

2006 *Metroid Prime: Hunters* – DS

Monkey Island 2: LeChuck's Revenge

Amiga, PC, Mac; LucasArts; 1991

Over a decade before Captain Jack Sparrow brandished a sword in *Pirates of the Caribbean: Curse of the Black Pearl*, wannabe pirate Guybrush Threepwood was trading sword-fighting insults in *The Secret of Monkey Island*, a laugh-out-loud graphical adventure game published by Lucasfilm's games studio. Not the first of its type, it was still an outstanding example of the kind of game that has no levels, where you could (mostly) take your time, you couldn't really die, and at which you could only lose by getting stuck. They don't make them like that anymore.

Its sequel in 1991, after which creative genius Ron Gilbert (along with Dave Grossman and Tim Schafer) moved on to other things, is the highlight of the series and may just be the greatest adventure game of all time. Its inventiveness is apparent from the first scene,

The Secret of Monkey Island
Amiga, PC, Mac; LucasArts; 1990

Guybrush's first, unforgettable outing, introducing Elaine, the Voodoo Lady, Herman Toothrot, Stan and Ghost Pirate LeChuck, plus of course the sword-fighting insults that would return in subsequent games. Still playable thanks to ScummVM (see box), though minus the old-school anti-copy measure of a Dial-A-Pirate wheel, where matching up pirate faces provided the answers you needed to type into the game. As much fun as you can have without an E-ride ticket and a pint o' grog.

The Curse of Monkey Island
PC; LucasArts; 1997

The intervening years saw the series gain a stylish, animated-movie look, the inevitable voice acting, plus ship-to-ship combat, all stirred together with oldie but goodie jokes and puzzles as Guybrush bravely attempts to rescue Elaine, who's been turned by LeChuck into a gold statue. As envisaged by Ron Gilbert, the third game would wrap up the trilogy (and let us in on the secret), but since he left LucasArts after *LeChuck's Revenge*, this isn't it.

Escape from Monkey Island
PC, Mac, PS2; LucasArts; 2000

Escape features a veteran cast and locations, plus a script heavily woven with references to past events, but enjoyable for all that. Guybrush's main quest is to find the ingredients of the Ultimate Insult, a curse that will destroy pirate souls. LeChuck returns once more from his watery grave to wreak havoc, assisted by the more mundane Ozzie Mandrill, an Australian property developer bent on turning the Tri-Island Area into a vanilla tourist trap – a target for some heavy satire on consumerism.

Dem bones ... as the ending gets closer, the unorthodox *Monkey Island 2* takes a bizarre turn.

which has Guybrush and love interest Elaine Marley dangling from ropes; all but the last section of the game is then played out in flashback as Guybrush explains to Elaine exactly how he ended up there. Equally imaginative in plot and script, featuring challenging, off-the-wall puzzles and deconstructivist self-referential jokes, the game satirizes itself as successfully as it does almost everything else. What's more, it does all of this gloriously in only 256 colours and two dimensions, and while the music by Michael Land sounds similarly dated in a technical sense, the tunes themselves are likely to stay with you forever.

Complicated though the story may be, the gameplay is simplicity itself: clicking the mouse on one of a list of actions and an item gets Guybrush to interact with his inventory and whatever's on screen. Which isn't to say it's necessarily

SCUMMVM: ADVENTURES IN HACKING

While working at Lucasfilm Games, Ron Gilbert, realizing how long it was going to take to write code for the game he wanted to make, developed with colleague Aric Wilmunder a scripting engine that speeded up the programming considerably, thereby allowing him to focus on the all-important design and content of the game. Known as SCUMM (Scripting Creation Utility for Maniac Mansion), its use didn't end with the eponymous B-movie horror spoof game; rather, it was continually developed and rewritten, forming the backbone of LucasArts' graphic adventures right up until Gilbert left in 1992. It's commemorated by, among other things, the name of Mêlée Island's infamous pirates' bar in *The Secret of Monkey Island*.

Technically, it works by interpreting a game's data files, which makes porting games to different systems a simple matter of converting the engine but still using the same original data files. Like many an interesting, past-its-date computer program, it's been taken up by a group of developers who've gone on to create ScummVM, a freely available virtual engine that allows a huge number of graphic adventure games (not just Scumm ones) to be played on various modern-day systems, from Macs to the PSP to mobile phones. An enormous project, which in the community spirit of most hacker sites encourages other developers to take it further, it's constantly expanding to cover new systems. Although it's perhaps not something for the technophobe to attempt, especially on handheld systems, since it requires installing software that the manufacturer never intended.

Original data files are necessary to play most of the games, available from original game disks or CDs, which can be picked up on sites like eBay. One game that's available for free, though, is Revolution Software's *Beneath a Steel Sky*, a cyberpunk-style adventure with artwork by *Watchmen* artist Dave Gibbons. Charles Cecil was so impressed by ScummVM that he decided to donate the source code to the project and this old favourite from 1993 has been so successful that there's rumoured to be a sequel in the works.

The ScummVM site (scummvm.org) provides downloads plus reams of information, including a list of compatible games.

obvious how to go about solving some of the joke-based puzzles: put the banana on the metronome to hypnotize the piano-playing monkey, then you'll be able to pick him up, put him in your bag, and later use him as a wrench … As well as the often ridiculous puzzles and quests (the nauseating ingredients for a voodoo doll, for example), there's some hilarious dialogue, minigames aplenty, plus a smattering of *Carry On*-style cross-dressing, all set on a vividly realized Caribbean archipelago made up of Scabb, Phatt, Booty and Dinky islands.

In-jokes and references abound, most obviously to the first *Monkey Island* game, and to the Pirates of the Caribbean ride at Disney World (there's a dog called Walt, who holds the keys to Guybrush's jail cell, if he could just tempt him to come a little closer). Film fans will spot a lot of references, too, particularly to *Raiders of the Lost Ark* and the original *Star Wars* trilogy. Still, what goes around comes around: on seeing a trailer for Disney's *Pirates of the Caribbean: Dead Man's Chest*, Ron Gilbert at first thought he was looking at his own undead übervillain LeChuck's wriggling beard, saying "let's be honest, if I'd thought of the squid tentacles for a beard, I would have done that."

NBA Street V3

PS2, Xbox, GC; EA; 2005

The introduction of 3D graphics and CD-ROMs in the 1990s was something of a mixed blessing to sports sims on consoles, the genre's primary platform. They certainly brought a new level of realism along, enabling superior visuals, enhanced audio and deeper gameplay through the sheer volume of player stats they contained alone. But this in turn set unrealistic expectations that all sports would find their best expression in lifelike simulations, rather than embracing the surreal edge that videogames can bring to them. Soccer and NFL did indeed hit the realism mark early on in the form of, respectively, *Pro Evolution Soccer* (see p.157) and the *Madden* and *NFL 2K* series (see p.26); but titles such as EA's own *NBA Live* and Sony's *Total NBA* only flattered to deceive, a tendency that continues today even in the *NBA 2K* series, which came closer than any to achieving the holy grail in its 2K2 edition. But no matter how shiny the floor, no matter how squeaky the players' sneakers or smooth the commentary, there is yet to be a basketball title that captures the essence of the five-on-five game, perhaps not least because of the ferocious demands the pace of a match makes on the AI.

Whilst purists might baulk at choosing a three-on-three street game over one that allows them to play a season as their favourite real-life team, the reality is that EA's *NBA Street* series, which debuted

V3 nailed the series' gameplay in terms of depth and its intuitive controls, as well as being immensely cool to look at.

in 2001 on the PS2, was the first game to accurately reflect a quality in basketball that others had thus far missed: fun. The spiritual successor to Midway's long-running *NBA Jam* arcade series, on the surface it had little to do with the pro game, insofar as the outrageously entertaining dunks, slams and tricks were more the stuff of vintage Harlem Globe Trotters clowning than classic Chicago Bulls offence. But unlike *NBA Jam*, EA's title didn't trivialize the action by setting ballers quite literally on fire when they were on a hot streak, with its realistic animations and settings instead rendering the over-the-top premises as feasible. And as such it was that rare sports game that appealed to both sporting fans and pure gamers. (EA Big took this as their cue to apply the *Street* format to their NFL franchise, which they did with qualified success; their attempt at doing the same for FIFA, however, was regrettable.)

Two editions down the line, EA had, in *V3*, nailed the *NBA Street* format to the point that its next incarnation, *NBA Street Homecourt* (Xbox 360 and PS3), left much to be desired, looking simply like a case of the emperor's new graphical clothes. Not only are *V3*'s visuals already at photorealistic levels and include full player customization; and not only does its career mode offer an experience akin to the franchise modes more usually found in EA's in-depth sims, even encompassing players' morale levels; but the biggest gameplay tweak of all, its new trick-stick system, means that the high volume of acrobatics at your disposal can be executed fluidly and intuitively at the flick of the thumb and press of a button.

It's a simple enough mechanic on the surface, but it's one that's served EA well in their *Tiger Woods PGA* series, and subsequently found even smoother expression in *skate* (see p.184). It may well be that developers had been looking for their balling grail in the wrong place: the secret to cracking the full basketball experience may already have been in their very own hands(et).

Ninja Gaiden Sigma

PS3; TeamNINJA, Tecmo/Eidos Interactive; 2007

Acknowledged as one of the toughest, most unforgiving games ever published, the *Ninja Gaiden* Xbox game of 2004 made the surprising leap to Sony's next-gen console for a third and final

Though the levels given over to the improbably proportioned Rachel have their own unique appeal, she lacks the acrobaticism of Ryu.

iteration, before spreading the love further with a DS game and then heading back to Microsoft for a console sequel. More than likely the motivation was financial, but it's nicer to think that the developers wanted to let the Xbox boo-boys have a go at this extraordinary game. After all, when TeamNINJA, headed by the resolutely individualistic Tomonobu Itagaki, adopted the name of the original NES trilogy (1989–1991) to make a new action-adventure title, it would be a Microsoft exclusive, at a time when other Japanese developers were sticking with the relative safety of Nintendo and Sony. Fans already will have played either *Ninja Gaiden* (2004) or the expanded reissue *Ninja Gaiden Black* (2005) on the original Xbox; anyone else should consider opting for the high-definition PS3 version of the classic.

Apart from the title, the only connection with old NES platformers is the name of the protagonist, Ryu Hayabusa, super ninja of the Dragon Ninja Clan and later (in game time) a *Dead Or Alive* contestant. His story is a mythic tale of vengeance set in Japan and the mysteriously secluded Vigoor Empire, where armed with the Dragon Blade, he is charged with recovering the evil Dark Dragon Blade stolen from the protection of his clan. Story isn't really its strong suit, though, and it's best seen as a kind of beat-'em-up grown into fully fledged action adventure. Tomonobu Itagaki has been quoted as saying that "a game should be beautiful, first and foremost, because it's a visual medium", and it's a theory his team have upheld, making the game stunning in its new high-def version. All of which is really just a backdrop to the typically fast, fluid and relentlessly exciting action. Ryu is a graceful acrobat with the astonishing skills of a classic movie ninja, here replicated by simply holding down X while running up a wall, say, or across water. The childish thrill of performing such incredible feats effortlessly via the control pad never goes away. Rather less graceful – or perhaps simply less polished – is the fiend hunter Rachel, as S&M-clad, improbably proportioned *DoA*-style blonde, who in this version has some individual story chapters of her own. What she doesn't have is the Dragon Sword, or the benefit of some of Ryu's other superior weapons, such as the twin katanas, also new to this version. Their enemies, as might be guessed, are not just common or garden ninja, samurai or monks, but far worse creatures.

And yes, it is fiendishly difficult, despite an increased number of save points and shops where you can stock up on health potions before boss fights. The first boss is tough enough, with his screen-wide health bar, and it just gets worse from then on. It feels like you're fighting for your life, spinning round to clear rooms of spawning enemies, sprays of blood clouding the air and pooling on the ground. There's no getting away with endless button bashing: you need to use special weapon techniques, and Ninpo magic, but the most crucial tactic is to avoid being hit, which means making the most of the space around Ryu, dodging, rolling and setting up special attacks, a finger constantly on the block button.

Resist the temptation to give up: there is an easy difficulty but like the hard ones it has to be earned, in this case by dying a few times, after which you will be repeatedly shamed when playing at Ninja Dog level, but let's face it, Mission mode was already out of the question. And if this is the only way to get through the game, then so be it; it's worth the indignity for the gorgeous settings, the engrossing gameplay and the chance to experience a thoroughly rewarding game that defines the word hardcore.

Nintendogs

DS; Nintendo; 2005

An adorable, ageless puppy you can play with, then put away as soon as you get bored – what more could anyone want in a pet? Nintendo's strategy for getting their DS system into the hands of people outside the traditional gaming market couldn't have been led by a more appealing game (or one with a better name) – the three simultaneously released versions of *Nintendogs* sold a quarter-million copies in their first week in the US. But amongst these new dog-owners must have been at least a few hardcore gamers, who perhaps bought the game for someone else but then found their heartstrings irresistibly tugged by these tumbling balls of fluffy cuteness, which rapidly become just as attached to you as you to do them.

The most difficult part of *Nintendogs* can be choosing one of the plethora of pooches on offer to take home with you in the first place.

Choosing one of the eighteen initially available pups to adopt in the first place, it might seem like all you'll be doing is admiring the programmer's animal modelling skills; but pick a dog with a temperament you think you're going to get on with, because this is a partnership and the personality of your dog really does affect how it reacts to you and therefore what kind of experience you're going to have. However beautifully drawn and animated these creatures, what's astonishing is how realistically they behave, so much so that you can almost forget you're poking at an LCD screen with a plastic stylus, absorbed as you are in tickling your puppy's tummy till she glows, wriggling with delight. And this is basically how you build a relationship with a dog in the virtual (or real) world: by playing with her, looking after her basic needs, and, of course, training her. At first the aim is simply to get her to come when you call her name into the microphone, but soon you'll be teaching her to do tricks using commands she'll eventually recognize, so long as they're spoken clearly enough. (This is insanely irritating for anyone else in earshot, and the one thing that prevents the game being the perfect commuting time killer.)

If you want to get on in this game your connection with your pup is crucial, partly determining how well she performs in the obedience, agility and disc-catching competitions that you need to win to earn cash for food, toys, collars and hats, maybe even a doggie companion or two, or a freshly decorated apartment. Despite the efforts of a couple of cheesy announcers, there's a genuine sense of drama as you put your puppy through her paces in public. The whole thing is eerily lifelike – when a strange mutt keeps running off with your Frisbee while you're practising for the disc competition in the park, you half wonder if it's going to follow you home. At times, your pup may be too tired or disobedient to work with any more, so you'll be forced to put her away for a while. This isn't a bad thing: just as in real life, looking after a dog can get pretty repetitive, however easy and intuitive the controls. In the final judging, though, for making the most of the unique capabilities of the DS, as well as taking the company another step towards its ambition to expand the definition of videogames, *Nintendogs* wins best in show.

Oddworld: Stranger's Wrath

Xbox; Oddworld Inhabitants, EA; 2005

In early 2005, *Oddworld: Stranger's Wrath* was released, just four months after the sales-record-breaking *Halo 2*. Both games are first-person shooters; both offer extensive worlds to explore, broken up into missions; both are fantastic works of fiction. In one the player takes the role of a faceless, superhuman military hero of the future; in the other, it's a species-indeterminate bounty hunter in an Old West-flavoured Oddworld. And of course one enjoyed fewer marketing

Oddworld's bounty store is a typically detailed and atmospheric Wild West environment.

dollars and a fraction of the sales of the other.

The kind of success that calls for same-again sequels has so far eluded Oddworld Inhabitants, the studio set up by Lorne Lanning and Sherry McKenna in 1994, and it's got a rather messy relationship history to show for it. Not only has the vaunted Oddworld quintology come to a halt with *Stranger's Wrath*, but also potentially Oddworld itself, after the company publicly announced it had ceased making games. Each episode has aimed higher technically, taking advantage of new hardware, but without losing its dedication to quality, and

Oddworld's last shout, if that's what it turns out to be, marks a suitably high point to end on.

Abe, the hero of *Abe's Oddysee*, *Abe's Exxodus* and in large part *Munch's Oddysee*, who freed his fellow Mudokons from slavery (and worse) at Rupture Farms, is absent, but Lanning's wildly creative dystopia continues. Inhabited by several races of varying ugliness, it's a place where fast food is addictive, advertising is rife, and corporations bleed the land dry for the sake of a buck. It's these themes, partly, but also the attention spent on character development and the offbeat and occasionally scatological humour that distinguish *Oddworld*; plus, it's the epitome of story and gameplay designed to work as one. Abandoing with Abe the platform puzzler genre, it's still largely a third-person action game, as well as an FPS; what's unusual is that the viewpoint isn't pre-ordained for particular scenarios but can be changed at any time by the press of a button.

Shooter it may be, but don't assume that means guns; Stranger, a towering, stetson-hatted fellow with Clint Eastwood's swagger and a laconic gravel drawl (provided by Lanning himself), uses a home-made double-barrelled crossbow armed with live ammo. That's "live" in the sense of chattering and wriggling, there being nine basic types of ballistic beasts; the main way of loading up is to shoot the critters as you find them – except for readily available Zappflies, equivalent to an infinite-ammo handgun. Which ammo to use, or whether indeed to go into third-person melee combat to fulfil a mission, depends on your chosen strategy. Blasting everything with heavy-duty explosive Boombats is one option, but a subtler, stealth-oriented approach, perhaps using spidery Bolamites or stinky Stunkz, may neutralize outlaw minions, if not their bosses, long enough to be taken alive. And live bounty pays more moolah than dead.

It's in the third-person action portion that Oddworld gets to shine, with Stranger travelling from town to town, taking whatever missions are offered by the local bounty office to save the moolah needed for his "little operation", a story that comes to the fore as the game progresses. The minor platform elements – climbing ropes, jumping – show the world at its sumptuous best, but the most exhilaration is to be had from thundering on all fours through vast expanses of rocky desert at an astounding 55mph. In this beautifully stylized, utterly absorbing world, the smallest of details, like the sign outside a town store showing "new items available", reveal a creative integrity that's rare, especially when combined with a sharp political edge. With cut scenes that wouldn't look out of place on the big screen, it's not surprising to learn that Lanning and company are working on various properties for both movies and games. It might not be the end of the Oddworld after all.

Okami

PS2, Wii; Clover Studio/Ready At Dawn, Capcom; 2006

Okami is a game like no other, steeped in centuries of Japanese myth and art. The creation of Hideki Kamiya, director of *Viewtiful Joe* and the first *Devil May Cry*, it was the penultimate product of Capcom's ill-fated Clover Studio. Like most games, the opening shouldn't be seen as an indication of gameplay to follow; while it's an interesting and stylish preamble, it's also extremely long – hang in there, though, for the story of the wolf named Shiranui, who aided the warrior Nagi in defeating eight-headed Orochi and saving the Nipponese village of Kamiki. Gameplay proper begins a hundred years later, when Shiranui's statue comes to life as an avatar of Amaterasu, the Shinto sun goddess, a white wolf who must rid the world of the dark corrupting evil that's arisen once again.

Utterly beautiful, and with the design awards to back up a serious claim as videogames' highest artistic achievement, it shies away from photographic realism, representing the world in the style of a Japanese ink and watercolour painting. In some ways a traditional *Zelda*-esque exploration game, it's this vision and the integrity with which it's

Along the way, Amaterasu meets various folk, each uniquely drawn, as seen in this character artwork.

employed – in music, story, menu screens – that make the game into something far more than the action adventure tag implies, as Amaterasu heads off on her quest, meeting characters across a world of villages, towns, fields and dungeons, clearing the land of its shadowy taint along the way. Deity though she is, Ammy is wolflike in most things – she can run, jump, smash things, dig things up and carry them in her mouth, but she can't speak. Her wisecracking bug companion, named Issun (after a Japanese fairytale character), does that for her, acting as a mouthpiece for the wordless wolf in a sort of Jiminy Cricket role, explaining and giving instructions, as well as piercing oversolemn moments with a joke.

Lovely though it is, the artistic style isn't just about looks: it's also an integral part of the gameplay. One of Ammy's godlike powers comes in the form of a brush that's dragged across the screen to create various real-world effects, from slicing rocks or monsters in two with a slash, to restoring light by drawing a sun, or curing unhealthy trees so that they flower – there are more than a dozen gods' powers to be granted. Transformation can be achieved at any time with a touch of the button: the colourful scene changes to a flat monochrome inkbrush on parchment, waiting for the slash, bomb, freeze pattern … The possibilities of the Celestial Brush aren't unlimited, but options grow more varied as further techniques become available. Even quite early in the game, it's extraordinary to watch the cherry blossom explode over bare branches, and flowers blooming to rapidly carpet the once-diseased land.

These brush techniques are used for fighting too, in conjunction with the wolf's weapons, when Ammy is surrounded by a swirling red mist of kanji that seals her in the battle arena (though random battles can often be avoided – a boon in such a long game). The controls are wonderfully responsive – it feels somehow different to controlling a bipedal character – important not just for fighting, but for other staple action elements, such as platform-jumping, and the stacks of stuff to collect. Ammy's various powers increase in a suitably idiosyncratic

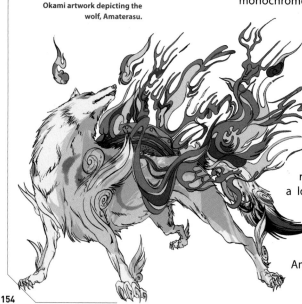

Okami artwork depicting the wolf, Amaterasu.

way, through praise orbs earned from fulfilling godly tasks and strengthening others' belief. In what other game could a character level up by feeding wild animals? As well as providing points, they reward you by frolicking around with little lovehearts over their heads. Very cute, but the game never turns saccharine, with these elements balanced by the often dark storyline.

Despite the awards and universal acclaim, *Okami*'s sales were disappointing in all territories, so it was all the more surprising when Capcom responded to fans' demands by porting the game to the Wii. As the West's interest in Japanese culture shows no sign of diminishing, though, this quirky work of art seems destined to be a cult classic, always available in some form or another, continuing to provide an incomparably joyful, not to say divine, gaming experience.

Prince of Persia: The Sands of Time

PC, Xbox, PS2, GC, GBA; Ubisoft Montréal; 2003

When videogame developers turn to remaking a classic, they tend to genuinely revisit its essence, and so face few of the criticisms that their movie counterparts do for relying on updated technology to mask, often unsuccessfully, a lack of creativity. When the game in question, however, has been away for a decade, and contemporary equipment offers a genuine chance to radically revisit things, gamers can afford to get *really* excited. In 1999, therefore, expectations were high for *Prince of Persia 3D* on the PC (released as *Prince of Persia: Arabian Nights* on the Dreamcast in 2000). And it was a decent game, but it was also a victim of its predecessor's success, 1989's 2D *Prince of Persia* having been so deservedly popular that it was ported to every home platform conceivable, including the humble Amstrad CPC. Players wanting the originality that Jordan Mechner's first adventure-platformer had in such abundance found that the Prince had been away too long: upstart Lara Croft had not just moved in, she had given the genre an extreme makeover and raised people's expectations.

It was to take another four years, a different publisher and developer, as well as Mechner's re-involvement with the script, to produce a sequel that did justice to both his original and the new world videogaming order of 3D, with *Prince of Persia: The Sands of Time*. Taking its narrative

Assassin's Creed
Xbox 360, PS3, PC; Ubisoft Montréal; 2007

Hugely anticipated for its stunning graphics alone, Ubisoft's other series about a man with an aptitude for jumping off stupidly high structures is decidedly more po-faced than *Prince of Persia: SoT*, despite being kind of *Grand Theft Auto* set in the Third Crusade. Altair the assassin has the terrain of four fully explorable cities – Jerusalem, Acre, Damascus and Masyaf – at his disposal for plotting the deaths of a number of key Assassin Brotherhood enemies. Unlike the *Hitman* series (see p.116), however, the murders themselves become repetitive – but for unparalleled execution of atmosphere, look no further than the impressive graphics and audio allow you to.

and visual cues from sources as diverse as *A Thousand and One Nights* and Disney's *Aladdin* (which in turn paid subtle tribute to the original game), the story, set in ancient Persia and involving a beautiful princess and an army of evil undead, is an unabashed old-fashioned blast, feeling for all the world like the plot of a Ray Harryhausen film – only considerably more complicated. It's also an astonishing synthesis of sprightly gameplay, visuals and brain-teasers that remains utterly faithful to its 2D origins whilst meshing ingenious level design and an intuitive combat system into something original. Take the Prince's beautifully animated athletics: not only are they crucial to exploring and solving the puzzle-based levels, they're also essential to his survival in a fight. Thus the moves that allow him to avoid a deadly buzzsaw, or run up a wall to activate an otherwise unreachable switch on high, are the same guiding principles that enable him to leapfrog an undead (but deadly) opponent or backflip his way out of a sword's reach. So intuitive is the transition from platform exploration to combat that it takes a while to realize that the same mechanics are producing very different results.

Then there's the Prince's hugely handy ability to manipulate time, a seamlessly integrated concept in terms of both plot – especially towards the finale – and action. A tightly controlled system, it allows the player to rewind their actions at any time, effectively giving the player the chance not just to revive the Prince after dying but to examine the course of action that got him into that situation in the first place – and then do it differently ("That's not how it happened," the Prince politely informs you after each such occasion, firmly underlining the point that a game is still a predetermined narrative).

Red Orb Entertainment, developers of the ill-starred *Prince of Persia 3D*, must have wished they had the very same ability.

The Prince caught in a typically acrobatic wall-walking leap.

Pro Evolution Soccer 6

DS, Xbox 360, PS2, PSP, PC; Konami; 2006

The *Pro Evolution Soccer* series (titled *Winning Eleven* in the US) has long been the cause of anguished debate among videogaming journalists. Constantly playing second fiddle to EA's juggernaut *FIFA* series (see p.231) in terms of sales, budget and official licences, it has also lacked, to most people's chagrin, in presentation. And yet of the two, *Pro Evolution* continually wins the cognoscenti's hearts because it effortlessly understands the beautiful game's soul in a way that *FIFA* simply doesn't want to. It's like the difference between Pele and

The beautiful game at its finest: impressive animation usually without the distraction of famous faces.

FIFA 08

PS2, PS3, PSP, Wii, DS, Xbox 360, PC; EA Canada; 2007

Another year, another *FIFA* title that struggles to convince that its embarrassment of official licences and brand endorsements means it's the real deal on the field. *FIFA 08* is not really any different from any of its predecessors nor will it be, in all likelihood, to those that follow, but allow yourself to be swept up by the ultra-slick presentation and you'll be convinced you're watching Sky Sports. Of course, whether you think that's proper football or not is another matter.

Beckham: one is content to let his skills speak for themselves while the other's are viewed through the prism of glamour.

Pro Evo 6 is true to its pedigree, and as such it's still the game of choice for seasoned pros – if the uninitiated have the difficulty setting on anything other than easy, they're going to find it very, very hard to score goals, let alone win matches. (Konami really rubs things in: the next level up, but leagues apart in terms of skill, is referred to as "amateur".) Gameplay modes are as expected: jump into one-off matches at a club or international level; or engage in more depth by taking teams through national or regional league and cup campaigns. But for a sustained mental as well as sporting challenge, go for the real meat of the game – the Master League.

Whilst there are a few scaleable difficulty settings in this mode, however they're set it's both the most daunting and hence rewarding aspect of *Pro Evo*, bringing total football, videogame style, to the screen. Taking control of an amateur club in the lower half of a two-division league, you're as much coach as manager and player, responsible for everything from the formation and positions players adopt to the mentality individuals bring to each

You can almost hear the crowd singing about the dodgy keeper; low-angle views offer a superb behind-goal perspective.

game (such as the level of defensive or attacking play, who they mark and so on). Judicious regulation of the squad between games is also required: whilst players can suffer from varying degrees of injury, age over the seasons and tire if they're not rested, they also gain experience (and so increase their skills) the more they play. During the transfer window, you can set the negotiation terms for obtaining new players, reserving or selling older ones, or loan them either way. That's a lot to take care of, and that's not even talking about being on the pitch – which is, hopefully, where your carefully made strategic decisions will pay dividends.

Matches themselves, whilst falling far short of the graphical beauty of *FIFA*, still reach a level of verisimilitude not obtained by their rival. The animation, for starters, is beautiful: the ball deflects realistically off players; stars such as Ronaldo, Saha and Henry all have remarkably different gaits as they jink through into the box; whilst less naturally skilled players tend to make it look more like the hard work it actually is, with many misplaced pass and shots flying well over the bar (and appropriately, only highly skilled players can pull off fancier moves such as scissor kicks). Goal differences are usually small, a win will be the result of tactical nouse as much as teams' physical prowess, and half time always comes at the wrong moment – it's like being out on the grass (or terraces) yourself. Younger, prawn-sandwich versions may have appeared since, and on an alarmingly *FIFA*-style annual basis, but *Pro Evo 6* is the veteran Roy Keane of soccer games.

Project Gotham Racing 3

Xbox 360; Bizarre Creations, Microsoft; 2005

PGR3 is the assured and beautifully produced game its forerunners had been promising, and the sweet spot before Bizarre Creations went all out with the bells and whistles for *PGR4*. Originally designed as *Metropolis Street Racer* for the Dreamcast in early 2001, reincarnated later that year as *Project Gotham Racing* for the Xbox launch, it was genuinely innovative, refusing to fit neatly into any narrow racing game category. If its realistic city streets and system of awarding Kudos points for bravado driving seem overfamiliar today, it's only because they've successfully become part of the racing game vernacular.

Cool cars are available from the outset; there's no need to go secondhand.

Even if you've played earlier versions, there's still plenty to enjoy here; fewer tracks, it's true, but in the best locations, namely London, New York, Tokyo and Las Vegas, as well as the infamous Nürburgring Formula 1 racetrack in Germany – not exactly a city, but with a similar number of courses winding through lush green mountainsides. Every location is gorgeously detailed, whether you're racing the palm-lined boulevards of Las Vegas past Caesars Palace and the Bellagio, weaving around the monuments of Whitehall and the Mall, through the underpasses of Tokyo, or alongside City Hall Park in lower Manhattan. Of the various ways to take in the scenery as it whizzes by, most exciting is the cockpit-style Dash view, which puts you literally in the driving seat of your chosen car, complete with accurately modelled steering wheel and radio and authentically smeared windscreen. The cars are cool without exception; for the non-petrolhead, there's no shame in driving a more forgiving D-class Honda until you can afford (and have the skill to master) the finicky Ferrari F50 GT.

There's no stinginess when it comes to awards either: you get trophies for winning races, badges for racecraft skills and career achievements, which unlock new tracks, while you're also earning credits to buy new cars. But it's the Kudos points won by flashy driving at high speed that give you real bragging rights, as well as more credits and secret Concept cars to unlock; not to mention the priceless thrill as the Kudos meter ticks up and then chimes to say you've kept the points (collide with anything before they've been banked, and they'll tick away just as quickly as they totted up).

One of the first Xbox 360 games with a significant online offering, *PGR3* sports an Online Career mode alongside the single-player version, in which you can race against matched opponents via Xbox Live, as well as watch replays of races on so-called Gotham TV. This doesn't sound particularly interesting compared to real-life motorsport, but then again, you can also do clever stuff like race the ghost of any top-ten player worldwide. You won't beat them, but you might be able to learn a trick or two for Tokyo's fittingly named Crazy Turns track. Xbox Live is where you'll also find extra content for the game, such as extra challenges, more than twenty new cars to buy and a few free ones.

No racer would be complete without music, and here you've got a wide CD collection ranging from classical to alternative rock, hip-hop to industrial, via bhangra, plus the option to plug in an MP3 player, though as in life, fiddling around changing CDs instead of watching the road is never a good idea. It's not just the photorealism and smooth performance of *PGR3* that delight, though, but the fact that it offers so many options, and an abundance of achievements and rewards which are flexible enough for novices to set their own level, while maintaining – especially online – the challenge that keeps the hardcore coming back for more.

Racing in familiar but strangely traffic-free city centres is a thrilling experience when you normally traverse them by subway.

Psychonauts

Xbox, PS2, PC; Double Fine Productions, Majesco/THQ; 2005

When Tim Schafer, abundantly talented creator of *Day of the Tentacle* and *Grim Fandango* (see p.103), announced his new development studio and a game to go with it, expectations were high. They were more than met by the award-winning *Psychonauts*, a hugely inventive, mindbending ride of a game, which excelled in every department except for sales. What's awkwardly known as a character action adventure, it takes the customary ingredients of the genre formerly known as 3D platformer and whips them up into a game that's original, stylish, entertaining and ridiculously immersive.

You play as Razputin, the type of know-it-all kid that gets right up your nose (at least until you get to know him), who has run away *from* the circus to join a summer camp for junior psychics at Whispering Rock. With a setup that's more reminiscent of Louis Sacher's novel *Holes* than any game, with its oddball kids thrust together, a family curse and even some strange-looking lizards, this is nonetheless a distinctly original universe. Or rather two of them, as Raz gets to explore both the real world of the summer camp, and the one that exists inside people's heads.

Whispering Rock begs to be discovered: an expansive sprawl of interlinked areas with serpentine tracks heading up hills, across streams, down to a beach, through woods that cloak experimental apparatus; what's more, there are countless nooks and crannies outside the main

Raz in thoughtful mood: the *Psychonauts* character designs are without exception quirky and expressive.

areas, plus posts and boulders to climb, cables to tightrope-walk, and not just for the sake of admiring the surroundings, either. The rewards for persistent exploration are collectible Psi cards and the game's currency, arrowheads, which allow you to purchase gear and access new powers that open up the surroundings even further. The various kinds of collectibles seem bewilderingly numerous until you realize they all add up to the same thing: earning ranks to gain new abilities. Wandering around, you'll also encounter the other kids, with a chance to eavesdrop and perhaps befriend them.

However much you love the great outdoors, at least as much time is spent in the mental worlds of the other characters, accessed via Agent Nein's Brain Tumbler contraption. While the camp has a skewed Disney feel, each of the mind-worlds is individually themed and uniquely visualized down to the lighting and music, whether it's Nein's Cubist-inventor shooting level, Milla's funky psychedelic disco party (where you get to bounce around on a levitational bubble of thoughts) or Raz's own dark and scary forest. The attention paid to these exhaustively detailed worlds runs through the entire game: Raz's abilities are awarded as merit badges stuck onto his omnipresent backpack, hints are scrawled in a journal, figments (transparent floating sketches) collected appear in a scrapbook.

Beneath the surface of the usually brightly lit camp life runs a dark and sinister plot, but this – like the weird and wonderful characters, the collecting of things, the training in psychic abilities – is another element that's seamlessly meshed into the whole. There are levels, but they don't feel like levels, only characters, events and chapters filling the short time Raz has at camp before getting picked up by his parents. Neither does the script disappoint, with its witty and wicked characterization of both kids and teachers. They're funny, yes, but in a game that's about what goes on in the mind, there's more to it than laughs and you'll be drawn into wanting to know what happens next. Can Raz discover what's happening to the kids' brains? Will he notice or care that Lili, the coolest kid, has got a crush on him? Will he get to unlock all of the sepia Viewmaster memories of the teachers, sequestered in trunks along the way? And how does that janitor manage to be in three places at once? Take this exhilarating mind trip of an adventure and find out for yourself.

Ratchet & Clank Future: Tools of Destruction

PS3; Insomniac Games, Sony; 2007

Platforming action-adventure double acts are nothing new. Banjo carried Kazooie in his backpack in 1998, and then in 2001 Daxter helped out Jak, before Ratchet and Clank made their first intergalactic appearance in 2002. Heroes frequently have a useful – and sometimes playable – sidekick, but Ratchet and Clank have a valid claim to being the most popular pairing, with regular annual outings exclusive to Sony. That their first PS3 adventure is a classic is mainly due to the polished gleam evident in every element of the game – although the cuteness of the long-eared Lombax and his robot companion can't be dismissed; and neither can their big guns.

As is usual for the sci-fi themed *R&C*, the game spans around a dozen planets, each harbouring several quests; innumerable crates and scenery to smash for bolts (currency and levelling up), ammo

Racing through Metropolis on a sci-fi motorbike isn't quite as much fun for Clank (left) as it is for Ratchet (right), apparently.

and raritarium (currency for upgrading weapons); plentiful enemies to destroy (for more bolts); and a gorgeous environment to explore. Painted in intensely saturated colours, with beautiful lighting and water effects, each planet is a novel environment, ranging from the huge panoramas of the towering sky Metropolis on Kerwan, as breathlessly fast-paced as an opening level should be, to the long-deserted Lombax city on Fastoon, with its disused mines and underwater tunnels. Ratchet gets about these areas by running and jumping, of course, but also by using ziplines, special jump pads and grinding rails, plus a number of cool tools and devices, such as the Robo-Wings, which allow flying using the Sixaxis controller, the Swingshot, gravity boots and the Gelanator, which shoots out jelly cubes to use as stepping stones or climbing blocks. Most are useful; some are also ingeniously funny. Take the Groovitron, which chucks a disco mirrorball at enemies causing all within range to dance in sync, while you slaughter them like some kind of cartoon Scarface. Then, of course, there are the weapons.

Shooting things has rarely been this much fun, partly due to its ease – there's a lock-on strafe mode as well as regular third-person – but mostly the almost infinite variety of effects gained by using different weapons and devices; even when Ratchet's collected the whole arsenal, each has multiple upgrades to purchase. With an eventual three screens full of weapons and devices to choose from, a battle can involve lots of switching in and out for the perfect, flashiest means of attack, but this is smoothly handled by holding down the triangle button and picking from a wheel of choices while the gameplay is paused. Clank, meanwhile, stars in his own sections of the game, where he uses the abilities lent to him by the Zonis, glowing-eyed robotic creatures that only Clank can see and hear. As if that weren't enough variety, there are ball-rolling maze minigames, arena fights, interludes with pirate dancing games, and three space-based shooting levels.

If this reads something like a checklist, it's because there's so much to do in this game, all of it honed to perfection. *Tools* isn't trying to reinvent the series, just do it better and in HD, shown off by the fluid gameplay, which is bookended by story-progressing cut scenes. As well as rescuing the galaxy, the plot uncovers what happened to the Lombax race, of which Ratchet is the sole surviving member

Jak & Daxter: The Precursor Legacy
PS2; Naughty Dog, Sony; 2001

The PS2's first platform action-adventure game, featuring bouffant-haired Jak, furry Daxter and an expansive, continuous 3D world, which is still luscious-looking to wander around in today. In trying to appeal to everyone, though, it ends up feeling a little less edgy than Naughty Dog's previous work on *Crash Bandicoot*.

Daxter
PSP; Ready At Dawn, Sony; 2006

The ottsel goes solo, armed with an electric flyswatter and a bug spray, in one of the PSP's smoothest platform games. As well as regular levels, dream scenarios have Daxter star in minigames themed after films like *The Matrix* and *The Lord of the Rings*.

– though not for long if the Tachyon emperor has his way. Moments of dramatic tension, laugh-out-loud humour, believable characters and great scripting make it easy to forget you're not in some Pixar-created world, a self-professed aim of the developer. And just like a Pixar movie, it's not too hard (a more challenging difficulty level is unlockable), a fact that some critics have bemoaned, but perhaps it's because the game is designed above all to be inclusive, not only in its range of gameplay elements, but also in the range of people who'll be able to enjoy playing it.

Resident Evil 4
GC, PS2, Wii; Capcom; 2005

Despite a clunky interface, annoying paradigms and sometimes-laughable dialogue, there's always been something special about *Resident Evil*. Limitations that might have seen off a lesser game have become affectionately regarded quirks, and no amount of petty criticism has been able to stop its superhuman onward march – with the occasional stumble – to become one of the longest-running game franchises, appearing on every platform since the PlayStation, not to mention spawning a movie trilogy (see p.266). And it's a special something no other game had achieved before – it scares you. The plot may be a cliché these days, but in 1996 it was a first for a console game: a frantic battle to escape the zombie hordes created by evil scientists as a biological weapon – hence the game's Japanese title, *Biohazard*.

Its worldwide success was to influence dozens of subsequent games, the real progenitor – after a couple of false starts – of the survival horror genre (see p.229). Many of the series' idiosyncrasies have turned into staple genre motifs: the

The hordes of *Resident Evil 4* are faster than your average zombie, as Leon quickly finds out.

THE EVIL GOES ON... AND ON...

1996 *Resident Evil* – PS
1997 *Resident Evil Director's Cut* – PS
1998 *Resident Evil 2* – PS
2000 *Resident Evil 3: Nemesis* – PS
2000 *Resident Evil Code: Veronica* – DC
2000 *Resident Evil: Survivor* (light gun game) – PS
2001 *Resident Evil Code: Veronica X* (port of the DC game) – PS2
2001 *Resident Evil Gaiden* – GBC
2002 *Resident Evil Survivor 2: Code Veronica* – PS2
2003 *Resident Evil Zero* (prequel) – GC
2003 *Resident Evil: Dead Aim* (light gun game) – PS2
2004 *Resident Evil Outbreak* (online enabled) – PS2
2005 *Resident Evil Outbreak File 2* – PS2
2006 *Resident Evil: Deadly Silence* (remake of the first game) – DS
2007 *Resident Evil: Umbrella Chronicles* (shooting game) – Wii

Like Leon, Ada returns from a previous canon game, this time with the addition of a playable side quest.

infrequent typewriters where you can save your game; the "files" you discover which allow you to piece together the backstory in dribs and drabs; the animated "You Are Dead" screen, dripping with blood; protagonist as rookie police officer, special ops soldier or innocent searching for a lost relative. And all of them are present and correct in the series' crowning glory, *Resident Evil 4*.

Released initially on the GameCube in 2005, *Resident Evil 4* was nonetheless a major step forward for the series. Dispensing with the tank-like character movement of earlier games – how many depends on whether you count remakes, prequels, side stories such as *Code Veronica* and light gun games, a long list further complicated by Capcom's exclusivity deals with Sony and then Nintendo – it builds on *Code Veronica*'s real-time polygonal backgrounds of five years earlier. It's only with *RE4*, though, that you get the full benefit, with the camera following the character instead of locked into set viewpoints. For all its FPS look and feel, you still can't move and shoot at the same time, but this succeeds in racking up the tension in the face of advancing enemies, just as it always has done.

From the outset, *Resident Evil* has offered more than one playable

Resident Evil: Deadly Silence

DS; Capcom; 2006

At this size it's not quite such an easy scare, but still just as frustrating to be stuck in a corner, unable to see what you're attacking. Accompanying the original game is a revamped version that utilizes the DS controls in the form of stylus-based attacks and blowing into the microphone.

Resident Evil: Umbrella Chronicles

Wii; Capcom; 2007

Capcom's answer to Sega's *House of the Dead*, this marks a step upward from the PlayStation shooting games (plus there's no need for any special peripheral, the Wii remote does the trick). Basically it's a nastily atmospheric, on-the-rails shooter through the *Resident Evil* canon, starting with the abbreviated events of *Resident Evil Zero*.

This zombie's weakest points are helpfully picked out; the rest is up to you.

character, with different plot paths, but although *RE4* includes an unlockable side game with Ada, you play the main game as Leon Kennedy, one of the series' original stalwarts. Umbrella Corporation, source of the T-Virus and the enemy of all rightminded people, has been shut down by the government, and Leon's been dispatched to a Spanish-speaking village in central Europe to look for the President's missing daughter. This chillingly atmospheric setting is far from the Spencer Mansion, and in another break with the past, the enemies aren't even zombies but something altogether faster and harder to kill, lumbering peasants brandishing pitchforks, grenades and chainsaws, their raucous growls backed by an incessant, tension-building drumbeat. Fighting – or rather, slaughtering everything that crosses your path – is the real thrust of the game, and using the laser sights on the shotgun you can appreciate just how good the AI is: shoot a villager in the foot and he'll limp, in the stomach and he'll flip backwards, just don't expect too many headshot kills.

Purists can now go back to the series' earliest days with *Resident Evil Deadly Silence* for the DS. Make sure you switch the blood to red and plug in the headphones, then succumb to a blast of nostalgic zombie-slashing that'll make you marvel all the more at how far the series has advanced without losing its familiar, gory heart.

Rez

DC, PS2, Xbox 360; United Game Artists; Sega, Microsoft; 1999

Does Tetsuya Mizuguchi dream of electric sheep? He certainly seems driven to find the spots where minds and machines meld. *Lumines* (see p.128) – successor to *Rez* by several years – takes the path of hard-wiring binary logistics into your mind: *Rez*, meanwhile, does the opposite, taking geometric certainties and evolving them into organic shapes through a synthesis of sound, vision and touch. It should be no surprise then, that as an undergraduate, Mizuguchi studied Kandinsky, the abstract artist who famously said that "Colour is the keyboard, the eyes are the harmonies, the soul is the piano with many strings. The artist is the hand that plays, touching one key or another, to cause vibrations in the soul." Ravers worldwide probably understand where he was coming from.

Famously influenced by Kandinsky's work, Rez's mindblowing effects are a synchronization of colour, sound and light.

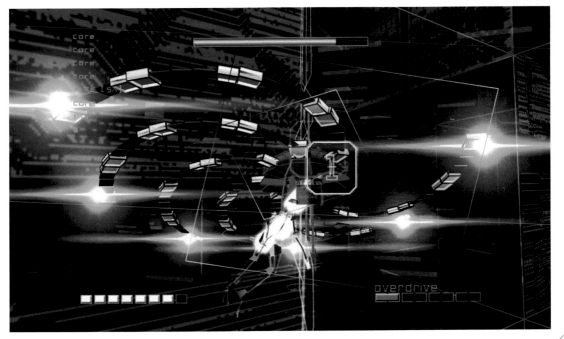

Everyday Shooter
PS3 via PlayStation Network;
Queasy Games, Sony; 2007

Winner of a clutch of awards at the 2007 Game Developers Conference, the influence of *Rez*, *Lumines* and *Geometry Wars* is writ large on this excellent indie title – though it's arguably a better, more humane title than *Geometry Wars*. Sensory overload combined with simplicity itself, the twin-stick control system combines with an acoustic-guitar soundtrack to come close to Mizuguchi's classics in inducing a feeling of having ingested an illegal substance.

Part *The Fantastic Voyage* (in which doctors are miniaturized in order to perform highly brain invasive surgery on a patient) and part *Tron* (about a man who is downloaded into a malevolent computer; see also p.272), *Rez* is another take on people being inserted into things they really shouldn't be (still, better than vice versa). The premise here revolves around Project K (a tip of the hat to Kandinsky), an artificially intelligent computer network that keeps the world in order. Unfortunately, while its core can handle all the data it needs to, it can't get its head around the sentience that this entails. An existential breakdown ensues, taking it off-line and threatening the stability of the globe: someone needs to literally dive into the system and bring the AI back online. As the briefing states, "you were the first person we thought of".

Often described as an on-the-rails shooter for its control system – which comprises moving across the screen from left to right and back again, locking onto targets, and firing at them – *Rez*'s journey to Eden is in fact, appropriately, more about evolution than destruction. Passing through abstractly depicted environments, from internal computer components to various world locations, the avatar must neutralize the different anti-hacking devices bearing down on them (viruses, firewalls and the like), depicted in various organic forms such as fish. At the outset, these are basic, black-

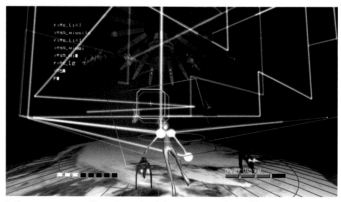

As the game progresses, the avatar evolves into an ever more advanced form.

and-white wire-frame affairs, but as the rhythm and pace increase, the imagery starts to glow with colour and life, increasingly filling out with pulsating, living detail. The same goes for the avatar, who evolves from vaguely human form into something like the shape-shifting Terminator in *T2* (and also devolves according to the damage taken from missing a virus; the last form taken before the player's existence is snuffed out is a rather endearing ball of primal electricity).

Likewise, the trance soundtrack is built upon with the sound effects of every button press, lock-on and explosion, which, combined with the ever-evolving graphics and the rhythmic pulsing of the vibration in the controller, conspires to make you feel as though you're creating one big remix. Indeed, gamers have noted that *Rez*'s soundtrack, when played separately, lacks the engagement of this unpredictable interactive experience. Mizuguchi himself acknowledges that the synchronization of sound, light and colour in Rez is akin to being at a rave; and having once demoed the game at a club, on a huge screen and through the club's sound system, the word he used to best describe his emotional state was: "high".

Rome: Total War

PC; Sega; 2004

It's been remarked that Vice President Dick Cheney's undue influence across the entire policy of the United States government stemmed from his ability to preside from on high by reaching down to the lowest level. Some might call this megalomania; others might say it is the latest manifestation of man's empire-building mindset as played out across history. That humanity has always played games reflecting this – from chess to *Risk* – shows we recognize this to be a basic instinct. Which is where *Rome: Total War* steps in. Think of anything George W.'s administration has been accused of and this historically accurate title shows that there's nothing new under the sun: from political cronyism to dubious alliances and treacherous volte faces, pecuniary issues and military over-ambition, it's all here. Welcome to Rome, 272 BC.

Renaissance Italy gave us the terms Machiavellian and nepotism. These, however, were just new names for centuries-old tactics in a

Geometry Wars: Retro Evolved
Xbox 360, PC; Bizarre Creations, Microsoft; 2005

With the original being a hidden minigame in *Project Gotham Racing 2* and the sequel a five-buck download from Xbox Live, Microsoft were hardly promoting the game that hardcore retro-gamers couldn't get enough of. Like *Asteroids*, *Defender* and *Space Invaders* it keeps things simple: one level, three lives and a limited number of smart bombs to score as many points as possible by shooting down geometrically shaped enemies. It's even set to just a single looped techno beat. But in glorious high-definition it looks like something Jean Michel Jarre might have thrown together for his famously extravagant sound-and-light concerts – awesome.

When thousands of soldiers are gathered on screen at once, it's impossible not to be awed by the epic scale of the game.

country driven and riven by family politics. Set in the sparring city states of pre-Christian Italy, Rome's narrative is woven through the history of three such provincial Roman dynasties – the houses of Julii, Scipii and Brutii, one of which the player must become – who vie to be top dog in an expansionist waiting game that plays out over a quarter of a millennium. With the ultimate aim of taking the eternal city in a coup, acts of espionage, betrayal and assassination are every bit as justified as trade agreements, pacts and declarations of war. A fine balance of forceful conquest and diplomatic acquisition of territories is key.

So, too, is the judicious appointment of family members, who possess all too human traits, into key positions of government or generalship. Some you wouldn't trust to run a gelati stand; others will be masterful at screwing the last taxable denari from it; yet others will find a way to embezzle its accounts. Hands-on management, then, is especially important: the game does offer across-the-board AI-management, but it's far better to rummage around in the detail, Cheney style – checking the finances, directing building policies and the like – than risk an inept governor, civil unrest and invasion. In the meantime, new family members are born, some pass away and others join – if you give your blessing to marriage proposals – while you continue to field military and diplomatic requests from the senate. Directed from the turn-based topographical campaign map, this is admin at its grandest level – and it's surprisingly hypnotic watching the results of each decision roll in at the end of each turn.

Which is not the case on the battlefield, where the real-time 3D battles couldn't get more epic or adrenaline pumped, with thousands of soldiers rendered on screen with an excellent variety of animations. A crucible for budding tacticians, the game places an acute emphasis on skilled troop deployment and direction across a variety of terrains: while your generals play a large part in rallying troops' morale, allowing a Carthaginian troop of elephants to outflank and then squish your archers tends to induce a rout rather than confidence in your strategic skills. You come, you see, and you really do need to conquer.

Caesar III
PC, Mac; Impression Software, Sierra Studios; 1998

An addictive, real-time exercise in city construction and population management, *Caesar III* showed just why, plots and betrayals aside, imperial laurels were never designed to be rested upon. *Caesar IV* may have taken it from an isometric perspective to 3D, while the interim *Pharoah* and *Zeus* games changed the setting, but this was the title that really demonstrated how a few wrong steps can have you tumbling from the career path of becoming a mighty emperor.

Shadow of the Colossus

PS2; Team Ico, Sony; 2005

"When people say this [Shadow of the Colossus] is 'art', I am honoured ... But I would like to have a broader audience ... this is definitely not an art."

Fumito Ueda, Lead Designer, Team Ico

The scale of the colossi in this misty, washed-out world, echoes the enormity of Wanda's task.

Ueda may not be keen to align his work with the potentially alienating concept of "art", but the fact remains that his gaming career has been singularly focused on making games that push our understanding of the parameters of this form of digital entertainment. Whether that's art or not is a much bigger question, but his previous work as animator on the Saturn's *Enemy Zero* (1997) – which, like its predecessors, the *D* series, was significant for its take on narrative perspective – was clearly a formative experience. *Ico* (see p.118), his next title, was a distinct next step along that road. But it was *Shadow of the Colossus* that established how games can be about more than just playing.

Shadow of the Colossus inhabits a similar pseudo-medieval world to that of *Ico*, with both bathed permanently in desaturated light. But where *Ico* could be described as a platform-puzzler that plays with the philosophy of narrative, *Shadow of the Colossus* is a metaphysical exploration of the purpose of gaming, no less.

Despite its epic narrative sweep, involving themes of eternal (and unattainable) companionship, the fulfilling of one's destiny, and some grandiose scriptural references, the game finds its most striking expression in that most traditional of videogame elements – the boss fight. Here, there are just sixteen instances, with no other form of combat in between. In the stead of action is a narrative that begins with the character Wanda arriving on horseback at a bridge that leads from his world to a forbidden one, where lies a ruined temple. He crosses, dismounts and unslings the baggage he has been carrying – it's the body of his beloved Mono. He lays it at the temple's altar; the disembodied voice of Dormin offers him the chance of resurrection if he takes on the task of destroying the sixteen idols lining the temple's hallways, itself accomplished by killing sixteen colossi found throughout the land. Dormin is a clear reference to the Bible's Nimrod (idolater and builder of the disastrous Tower of Babel), but whatever his background, Dormin's offer comes with the warning that the price may be far higher, which would make most people think twice about the undertaking. But the point of *Shadow of the Colossus* is that we make choices based on emotions rather than logic. Indeed, many of the colossi are passive creatures that need goading into anger if the player is to stand any chance of getting a fight.

The game's epic structure is echoed in its vast, uninhabited wasteland of mountains, deserts and ruins, which present Wanda and his companion steed Agro with a literal and metaphorical landscape to explore. The story's cyclical nature is reflected in its setting too, for with every colossus defeated – in marathon, problem-solving battles – Wanda returns to the temple to begin his hunt anew and repeat history.

Despite Sony's motto of "Live in your world. Play in ours", Ueda makes it very clear, through *Shadow of the Colossus*, that videogaming is capable of straddling both those worlds by significantly engaging the player's emotions. Whether the realms of imagination that he crafts are to be defined as "art" or simply originality, is really down to the interpretation of the individual player.

Sid Meier's Civilization IV

PC, Mac; Firaxis, 2K Games; 2005

In existence since the mid-1990s, *Civilization* is the title that persuaded parents that there was a benevolent side to gaming. Never mind that little Greg was getting by on two hours' sleep a night, at least he wasn't shooting people – or if he was, it was only with muskets… Despite the evolution of its interface – now prettier to look at, easier to use and with myriad options for different styles of play – *Civ*'s addictive qualities remain undiluted, and it's still the gripping, satisfying challenge it always was.

Before Sims were going about their daily business buying furniture and taking out the garbage, citizens in *Civ* were doing far more important work: constructing cities, inventing technologies, developing the arts, spying on their neighbours, trading and going to war. Taking the whole of history as its source, *Civ* is inevitably long and complex, and each individual game is a unique experience. Starting with a few unpromising bits of terrain on which to found a city in 4000 BC, the goal is to become the first civilization – there are eighteen to pick from, from Incan to Indian – either to reach Alpha Centauri, resisting self-destruction and assimilation by other nations, or to conquer the rest of the world by means of war, domination, cultural or diplomatic victory, the last of which can only be accorded by the United Nations. This is anything but a straightforward race through time, though, each

From an unpromising patch of terrain, you're soon looking at a landscape covered with all the trappings of early civilization.

game is so minutely complex that it can take hours just to reach the Industrial Age. Since it's based on such a detailed premise of cause and effect, it's not a game you can dive into first time without a tutorial or instruction book; then, later, looking things up in the Civilopedia, reading advisors' tips, plus the optional hints that appear each time there's a choice to invest or divert resources into a new technology, system of government or religion. But it hardly matters, as this isn't a game to be rushed: patience, thoughtfulness and strategic planning are system requirements. Those with a shorter attention span might want to check out *Civilization Revolution*, an adaptation for consoles.

Building wonders like the pyramids has a beneficial effect on your budding civilization.

SERIOUS GAMEPLAYING

It doesn't take a genius to figure out that you can learn something from *Civilization*. However, Bitcasters and 2K Games took the idea to its logical conclusion, with a mod entitled *HistoriCanada: The New World*, which was donated to 100,000 Canadian high school students in 2007. Already known for providing reams of historical background information, *Civ* was the perfect vehicle for enlivening one of the least interactive of school subjects. In the UK, too, there's work going on, particularly through Learning & Teaching Scotland's Consolarium project, whose founder Derek Robertson has been evaluating the use of videogaming in teaching. One of his experiments involved children aged 9 and 10 playing *Dr Kawashima's More Brain Training* for fifteen minutes before maths classes; not only did the children improve in speed and accuracy, but they were found to be more focused and more enthusiastic about the subject than children in the control group. To teachers unfamiliar with videogames the idea of combining them with learning might seem heretical, but as tomorrow's teachers are also likely to be gamers, using videogames to keep students involved and interested could become a far more common practice.

It wasn't difficult for the brain training game to keep the kids' attention as, with any commercial release, it was designed to do just that. Rather less fun for the player is the appropriation of games for sending didactic messages. What better way to persuade young men, a notoriously hard to reach section of the population, of the perils of drinking and driving than by advertising on billboards in *Project Gotham Racing 4* on Xbox Live? That's what the Scottish government concluded, anyway. Drunk driving is a popular issue: appropriate to the age of many gamers and uncontroversial as a message, it's also been picked up by students at the University of Calgary, who liaised with the police to make a game that simulates driving while intoxicated.

The US Army has been using games as training simulations for years. The official, free PC game, *America's Army* (also available as an Xbox 360 spin-off) has become one of its biggest recruitment tools, featuring training, full missions and a focus on teamwork. Unlikely to be played on the same computer, *PeaceMaker* (pictured below) is an award-winning diplomacy sim where you can play as either Israeli or Palestinian premier. It's available in Arabic, English or Hebrew language versions, and is packed with real news footage. A bit worthy? Perhaps, but that's the main challenge to be overcome by any serious or educational game.

Whereas the anti-drunk driving message has yet to yield results, studies by the likes of Munich University and the British School of Motoring have shown that players of racing games are more likely to take risks when driving in real life. Similar points have been made about drivers who listen to certain types of music, however, and a game of slow and careful highway driving seems almost as ridiculous as banning car radios. Organizations such as Games for Change (part of the Serious Games Initiative) work with the public sector and games companies to help promote a positive social message in games, but for an educational game to really succeed, it has to be worth playing in the first place. Gamers can recognize propaganda as well as anyone else can.

Time not reading or checking statistics on various menus and panels is spent on the main map, a startlingly colourful gridded expanse of sea and varying land types, transformed one by one from dark, featureless squares by scouts and explorers. Over time you'll see one-square cities guarded by spearsmen develop into vast, hi-tech affairs with the attendant problems of pollution and overpopulation, a sumptuous world accompanied by appropriate sound effects and music, from the crashing of waves, the roar of a disgruntled populace or the chink of chisel on stone to the rousing *Lion King*-style opening theme.

The computer has always been a formidable opponent in itself but there are now various multiplayer options, including hot-seating on a single computer and playing by email, as well as full online multiplayer. In line with the endlessly varied nature of the core game, there are customizations, downloads and mods galore, thanks to 2K Games' provision of software development kits on its website. Officially published add-ons (*Civilization IV: Warlords*, 2006, and *Civilization IV: Beyond the Sword*, 2007) have brought more civilizations, more leaders, wonders and whatnot, plus the long-omitted option that seems an inevitable sign of the times: an Advance Start game beginning in the modern day.

Time passes by uncannily quickly in *Civ*, whether it's several hundred game years or many hours at the screen – perhaps the time to get from spears to nuclear weapons, from horses to spacecraft. Veteran players know that while you're so engrossed attending to your virtual world, you're entirely likely to miss something going on in the real world, to which end the developers have seen fit to include an alarm function.

Silent Hill 2

PS2, Xbox; Konami; 2001

What other game could open with a scene in a filthy, disused public toilet, the protagonist talking to his reflection in a mirror? With *Silent Hill* for the PlayStation in 2000, Konami took horror games to a place they'd never been before, providing a psychologically disturbing gaming experience quite unlike anything else. *Silent Hill 2* takes the themes of its predecessor and channels them deeper, creating an even more atmospheric and genuinely frightening game, focused unflinchingly on the dark heart of human nightmares.

The setting is the same as before: a more or less abandoned, out-of-season lakeside resort town, grimy and dilapidated, and that's just the foggy overworld of Silent Hill, which cloaks a far darker side. The inhabitants are new, however, chief among them James Sunderland, who's driven here after receiving a letter from his wife Mary, who died three years earlier from an unnamed disease, asking to meet him at their "special place".

Mostly the game consists of playing through the action in the third person, as James strives to resolve the mystery of Mary's letter, but layered under this is the curious history of Silent Hill itself. Time spent chasing clues and solving puzzles, referring to dog-eared maps on which clues and dead ends are marked in red pen, is interspersed

The themes of *Silent Hill* are reflected in the physical representation of light (often torchlight) and darkness.

with brief, sudden combat – the town is literally crawling with monsters. Whether bashing these abominations with a stick or firing a handgun, James' rather awkward animations demonstrate that he's no STARS team member, but just a regular guy in a very bad place. He can't even run that fast, panting for breath when he comes to a standstill.

Visually, the world of Silent Hill is overlaid with a grainy filter that makes everything a little less clean-looking, more surreal and dreamlike, the colour palette shying away from anything remotely bright or sunny. Interiors such as the apartment building are gloomy places, illuminated by faint daylight through grimy windows or the brighter light of your torch – a second reason why the game's best played in the dark. However dingy it gets, the staple genre pickups of health drinks and bullets are hard to miss, thanks to James turning his head to look at anything of interest.

Silent Hill's uniquely eerie atmosphere can be attributed just as much to its use of sound (designed by Akira Yamaoka, who has also been overall producer of the series since *Silent Hill 3*). It's a heart-stopping moment the first time the radio leaps into its urgent buzzing crackle at the proximity of a monster invisible through the mist. Unexpected noises have you wondering whether you really did hear another set of footsteps alongside James's; that's before you hear the grating, jarring vocalizations of the monster itself. Only distantly related to the common-or-garden zombie, they're hideously deformed beings with human-like features, shuffling or dragging themselves along. Distorted forms such as the Pyramid-headed entity echo our fears and night horrors – similarity to the work of Francis Bacon is no coincidence. Despite all this, there's something familiar and comfortable enough about this small town to keep the player there without going insane.

However gory the combat, there's not much trigger-happy joy to be found here, the violence verging on an almost realistic awfulness, and it's this sense of defeated heroism that helps define the game, along with the mature storyline, rife with love, sex and death, plus the subconscious workings of the mind. Core to the plot is the question of Mary's death; characters from the hospital and grotesquely faceless, sexily clad nurses offer clues, but the script teases and toys with the player as it does James. Take for example the Maria character, who has the same features and voice as his dead wife, but her own distinctive personality.

Of the mass of games that can be tagged survival horror, *Silent Hill 2* stands as the antithesis of games of the *Resident Evil* school. Like the latter, it boasts an expanding game universe, through *Silent Hill 3, 4* and *5, Silent Hill Origins* and a CG movie. But while Raccoon City resembles a familiar world overrun by man-created terror, Silent Hill is an altogether different kind of town, a darker place of alternate reality, where evil plays with the minds of all who visit.

The Movies

PC, Mac; Lionhead Studios, Activision (PC), Robosoft Technologies, Feral Interactive (Mac); 2005

Whilst the premise is movie-making from the ground up – build a studio; fill it with staff; make and edit films; then hope for a blockbuster – Molyneux is cross-fertilizing his own sandbox dreams with those of Will Wright here. The myriad roles that the Sim-like avatars inhabit range from directors and lighting controllers to scriptwriters, whilst personality-wise, a happy twenty-something romantic lead can easily turn into an tantrum-prone alcoholic forty-something if not properly cared for. A PA, plastic-surgery and rehab can work wonders! The post-production editing of the resultant films, like all things Lionhead, is a thing of detailed beauty.

The Sims

PC, Mac; Maxis, Aspyr Media, EA; 2000

It's hard to imagine a world before *The Sims*, so ubiquitous is the series. It's yet harder to think that the best-selling gaming franchise of all time – within a mere two years it had outstripped *Myst*'s sales and has, to date, sold well over 70 million units – was nearly rejected by Maxis, despite it being the brainchild of their co-founder Will Wright (see p.258), already the creator of cash cow *SimCity*. In fact, it took EA's buyout of the company, with an accompanying change of vision, to pull Maxis back from a decision that would have been videogaming's equivalent of turning down the first *Harry Potter* novel. In fairness to them, Wright's original proposal probably seemed a tad boring in comparison with the sweeping ambition of building a city – at that stage, his digital dolls' house simply comprised the ability to set up a few walled spaces and insert a bunch of AI-controlled characters into it, with nothing for them to interact with except a toilet. All credit to EA, then, for understanding his vision of capturing the psychological intricacies of everyday human life in a virtual glass house.

Things start off deceptively simply. Select a family group to

Backpacking Sims, wearing his 'n' hers shorts, take a vacation in Japan in the *FreeTime* expansion.

guide through life, created either from scratch (personalities included) or chosen from ready-made ones; the former need to be matched to a suitable home, which needs equipping and furnishing; the latter come ready housed. Thereafter, however, chaos has the potential to reign, as from here on in the game is about attending to their desires and needs, whether that means putting up a relaxing picture on the living room wall or installing a multigym so they can work out. Everything the gamer chooses to do, or neglects to consider, has consequences that play out in the Sims' words (conveyed to the player in the distinctive and endearing Simlish language) and actions: not letting them sleep or eat, or making them clean up all day without anything more interesting to do, will result in severely depressed, insubordinate Sims. Social interaction plays a huge part in their happiness, too, and they can be married off if they spend enough time flirting with the right person (though rejection is also a sad possibility) while, as in real life, jobs earn the cash to support their lifestyles. And Wright's original interactive object, the toilet, is still integral to their lives, though the screen tastefully fuzzes the focus on the screen at the appropriate moment.

The fact that so many gamers, casual and hardcore, took their human *pokémon* to heart (its popularity supported a whopping seven expansion packs) can be explained partly by the fact that the game offers a playful take on the layers of our communal accountability – if Sims neglected to clean out their pet hamster's cage, for example, the rodent's resultant and often fatal virus would spread throughout the Sim community (although in a case of inverted responsibility, Maxis later downgraded the virus

THE SIMS: THE LEGACY

Once they had been unleashed into the PC and Mac worlds, the demand for Sims on other platforms, and in expanded arenas, rocketed, and the following are the episodes and expansion packs released in quick succession to satiate gamers' appetite for Sims in their lives right up to *The Sims 3*. Note that the first console titles were very different from the versions on PC and Mac, hence their separation below.

The Sims (2000; PC, Mac; expanded with *Livin' Large, House Party, Hot Date, Vacation, Unleashed, Superstar, Makin' Magic*)

The Sims (2003 console version; PS2, Xbox, GC)

The Sims Online (2002; PC)

The Sims: Bustin' Out (2003; PS2, Xbox, GC, GBA,)

The Urbz: Sims In The City (2004; PS2, Xbox, GC, GBA, DS)

The Sims 2 (2004; PC, Mac, PS2, Xbox, GC, DS, GBA; PC/Mac-only expansions were *University, Nightlife, Open for Business, Seasons, Bon Voyage, FreeTime, Apartment Life*)

The Sims 2: Pets (2006; PC, Mac, PS2, GC, PSP, GBA, DS)

The Sims 2: Castaway (2007; Wii, PS2, PSP, DS)

MySims (2007; PC, Wii, DS)

The Sims Life Stories (2007; PC, Mac)

The Sims Pet Stories (2007; PC, Mac)

MySims (2007; Wii, DS)

The Sims Castaway Stories (2008; PC, Mac)

MySims: Kingdom (2008; Wii, DS)

The Sims 3 (due 2008/9; PC)

MySims: Party (due 2009; Wii, DS).

to a cold after complaints that the game came with no instructions as to how to care for hamsters). But the runaway success of the original game on the PC and Mac was ultimately testament to the enjoyment afforded from playing in an eternal sandpit with no narrative, goals or win conditions (an environment the console versions closed down slightly), something gamers were encouraged to engage with by customizing the game, from creating new skins for their Sims to modifying the interface. The reaction from the gaming community to this in particular was overwhelming and became the biggest point of reference for Wright in his next magnum opus, the evolutionary – in many senses – *Spore*.

skate.

Xbox 360, PS3; EA; 2007

skate is cool, and *skate* knows it. It could so easily have overplayed its hand by being called *Sk8*. But instead it has an understated lack of a capital letter and a full stop, to emphasize that it gives you *all* you need in a skateboarding game, period – but without shouting about it. Even the menu screen exudes class, with EA Black Box rejecting the latest skate-punk thrashings in favour of the eminently more dude-like *Green Onions* from Booker T and the MGs. And the in-game playlist reads like a muso's guide to the classic acts of hip-hop, punk,

Pulling off this kind of trick is less hardcore than it looks, thanks to *skate*'s Flickit control system.

thrash and funk: there can't be too many games where Black Flag, Bowie and Gang Starr coexist.

But *skate* isn't exclusive and positively welcomes you to its club. Unlike the *Tony Hawk* series (see box), which has become an increasingly hardcore gaming experience since its inception, *skate* takes its rival's convention of pulling off board tricks with ever-more convoluted sequential button presses and d-pad manipulations, looks at it, and then dumps it for good. In its place comes the intuitive Flickit system, which uses the controller's dual analog sticks alone: one stick to control upper body movement; the other to determine leg and foot position. This redaction is profound, for where real-life skaters will instantly identify with the system, non-skaters are being taught how to work the board rather than how to play a videogame about skating. To pop an ollie, for example, think in terms of how it would work in real life; pull the skater back on the board; then flick the stick forward to throw their weight to its nose. Further flicking of the levers makes basic fliptricks, grinds and manuals a breeze, with more subtle and complex manipulation implementing more advanced tricks accordingly. The net feeling of an organic simulation, rather than a videogame, is further underlined by the most convincing animation ever seen in a skating game – not least some sickeningly painful bails and sacks – and beautifully tactile surfaces (skating across cobblestones and grass are fundamentally different experiences to asphalt, as any skater knows).

But simulation or otherwise, *skate* still knows that going street is primarily about having fun, so whilst the Career mode sets up the competitive aspects of the sport, gamers can pursue this completely at their leisure, opting instead to spend some quality time freestyling around the city and suburbs of San Vanelona. A open-plan amalgam of San Francisco, Vancouver and Barcelona, its communal parks, storm drains, shopping malls and handy subway system offer a wealth of opportunities for throwing together lines – some obvious, some not – and to pick up tutorials from a raft of legendary concrete carvers, from Danny Way to Chris Haslam.

As with attitude, image is all important, and skaters can be customized physically and sartorially, with a plethora of branded clothing, decks, trucks and wheels. The attention you really want to draw with your freshly kitted-out newbie, however, is that of a

Tony Hawk's Pro Skater 3
PC, PS2, Xbox, GC, PS, GBA, GBC, N64; Neversoft, Activision; 2001

It may not have discovered an open world environment by this instalment, but *Pro Skater 3* underlined why the *Tony Hawk's* series had ruled the skating roost for so long and why it would continue to do so until *skate*. The first in the series to be developed specifically for next-gen hardware took advantage of the fact, offering players eight large levels in locations ranging from Tokyo to Rio. Players also got the opportunity to customize their skaters, and then put them through their beautifully animated tricks book. The series continues to produce quality titles, but it hasn't perfected itself any further since.

sponsor, and clothes alone can't do that. Magazine coverage, however, can: check out the in-game map, locate a skating photo journalist, complete the trick they set, and as your pics and film footage are published, your profile increases along with your attractiveness to sponsors. It's about the most artificial aspect of *skate* – there can't be too many skaters who build a pro career so easily – but it does introduce the neat video-editing feature that allows you to record your best lines and post them online.

Built by skaters for skaters, *skate*, whether going vert or street, goofy or regular, is a sidewalk surfers' dream – even down to banning fruit booters from San Valenona…

SoulCalibur II

Xbox, PS2, GC; Namco, EA/Nintendo; 2003

Not all female fighters have bouncy boobs. Some do, of course, but for every buxom, barely dressed Ivy, there's an athletic-looking Talim, both of them moving with equal grace and speed – such is the delicately balanced diversity that makes *SoulCalibur II* a superb fighting game. If *Dead or Alive* is about the physics and *Virtua Fighter* (see p.208) is about the technique, then *SoulCalibur*'s about the balance: of the fighters' abilities, but also of players' abilities, so that while veterans can study its myriad subtleties, newcomers aren't excluded from performing sweetly devastating, flowing moves, without needing millisecond-perfect timing.

Gravity-defying Taki is a series regular, appearing in every game from the original *Soul Edge* to *SoulCalibur IV*.

The first *Soul* arcade game, *Soul Edge*, was ported to PlayStation as *Soul Blade* in 1996; but for its follow-up, Namco realized they needed to go elsewhere for their graphics to shine, and so *SoulCalibur* was a 128-bit Dreamcast exclusive, a supremely confident game that's rightly rated among the best fighting games of all time. *SoulCalibur II* isn't drastically different from its forerunner – sporting nicer graphics, some gameplay additions and a few more characters – but it is drastically more accessible, Namco opting for the other extreme and producing versions for Xbox, PS2 and GameCube. (Note that each has a different guest character: the Xbox has Spawn from the Todd McFarlane comic, the PS2 has *Tekken*'s Heihachi, and Link features in the GameCube version.)

These new characters join the old for a roster that encompasses the frighteningly freaky (Voldo, with his blade-hands) and the tormented (azure-eyed Nightmare, possessed by his Soul Edge sword), as well as the classically Greek (Sophitia and her sister Cassandra), an undead pirate (Cervantes, also Ivy's father) and a brawny Golem serving the god of war (Astaroth). Each has a particular weapon and attendant fighting style, from Ivy's chain-link whip sword to Maxi's nunchaku, with another eleven weapons to unlock. Each also has some connection with the weapon (the evil Soul Edge) at the centre of a good-vs-evil story.

Unusually, the game is set in the late sixteenth century, a time of privateers and the beginning of world exploration, as represented by stages in ancient Egyptian ruins, European cathedrals, mountain castles in Japan, and Caribbean pirate cave hideaways. Incredibly detailed 3D backgrounds, while not exactly interactive, always offer an edge to chuck opponents off, particularly satisfying when it's into the water. What's more, this being weapon rather than hand-to-hand combat brings range into the equation, allowing for an adjusting scale that really makes the environments shine while showing off some beautiful animation and light effects – spinning blades glinting in the light and so forth. Incidentally, the language is best switched to Japanese; even if you don't understand the words, it avoids any off-putting and awkward anglicizations.

SoulCalibur II uses a more complex combat system than stablemate *Tekken*, but the horizontal, vertical and kick attacks feel smooth and responsive. It can be deceptively easy to start mastering combos, so that character animations flow into each other in a nonstop balletic dance. Lose concentration for a couple of seconds, though, and a nine-tenths full health bar is nine-tenths empty. Winning takes anticipation, guarding and precision counter attacks, especially at higher difficulty levels. As well as the usual modes (excluding online), single players are treated to the RPG-style Weapon Master, which sees your character progress around a map, with new missions opening up – fighting in quicksand, making 20 hits against the clock, for example – accompanied by a bit of story along the way. You are also offered the

Katana-wielding samurai Mitsurugi is another *SoulCalibur* staple, his history tied up with that of his native Japan.

chance to earn gold for buying extra weapons and costumes for each character. All of which adds up to plenty of game to get stuck into. So while *SoulCalibur 3* and *4* fulfil the narrator's claim that "…this tale of souls and swords is told eternally", if truth be known, it's largely a case of polishing something that's already all but perfect.

Street Fighter Anniversary Collection

PS2, Xbox; Capcom; 2004

If ever a game was designed to remind nostalgic, misty-eyed lads of their lost youth, this is it. Celebrating fifteen years of *Street Fighter*, the *Anniversary Collection* is a port of the arcade game of the same name – a hybrid of the five *Street Fighter II* games released between 1991 and 1994 – alongside the final episode in the *Street Fighter III* series from 1999. It's not quite capable of shifting time back to the sticky-floored, smoky arcades of the early nineties, but it does an admirable job in allowing you to replay all of your favourite fighting moves backed by an inimitable soundtrack, as Ryu, Ken et al "hadouken!" and "shoryuken!" each other into submission in two glorious dimensions.

Ken performing his legendary *hadouken* move.

The *Street Fighter* series is a web of prequels, sequels and incremental tweakings. Four years after the original *Street Fighter*, the reworked and improved *Street Fighter II* became a smash hit in arcades, shopping malls and motorway service stations worldwide. Building on this phenomenal success was the prequel *Street Fighter Alpha*, which soon had its own sequels (and its own compilation, see below), followed by *Street Fighter III*, a shorter-lived trilogy from 1997–99, a time when the arcade had begun its creeping decline. Back in the day, only Midway's *Mortal Kombat*, with its headline-grabbing gory finishing moves, challenged *Street Fighter's* 2D credentials, and there was a scramble to exploit the popularity of both games in other media. Of the comic books, TV series and two movies based on *Street Fighter*, one of the better examples is the anime included (in dubbed and edited form) on this disc, though of course it doesn't have Kylie Minogue in it.

Successfully transferred onto home consoles, the series has proliferated on a dozen systems, although naturally the hardcore would sooner play with six buttons and a joystick. In the same way that *Resident Evil* (see p.112) has been made and remade in numerous forms, Capcom has thoroughly exploited the *SF* brand, even trying to emulate the arcade experience with Quarter Mode in the Xbox Live Arcade game of 2007. Meanwhile, the various ports to handheld systems feel even more distant from the arcade but have nonetheless delivered pretty decent gaming.

The most passionate devotees are loath to sacrifice the purity of their favourite *SFII* incarnation, however much fun it is to pit opponents from the different versions against each other, but for the rest of us, *Anniversary Edition* offers the best of all gaudily coloured worlds in one. It's *Street Fighter III* that's perhaps the better game on the disc, heresy though it may be to say it, with its superfast animations, hip-hop soundtrack and game-changing parrying moves.

Never easy to master with its three kicks and three punches, as opposed to *Tekken*'s simpler four-button system, *SF* is all about building up combos and special moves. A dozen and more characters, including every boss – the code to unlock secret boss Akuma is handily provided – are present and correct, from the founding fighters Ryu and Ken, to kickmeister Chun Li, and later challengers such as Brit Chammy and Mexican T. Hawk, at venues all over the world. Training and learning to counter opponents' special moves is just as crucial as performing your own, but even on the lower difficulty and speed settings, the CPU remains a seriously tough opponent. Single-player gaming provides only half the fun, and while going online is unlikely to make the going any easier for novices, finding a friend at the same level makes for a perfect match.

It's anyone's guess how *Street Fighter* will develop as it approaches its third decade – it's already tackled 3D with the competent *Ex* series, and at a time when hyper-realism is often seen as the holy grail, its 2D gameplay has been remarkably durable. So far the core gameplay has been adorned by a glossier look and feel, as in the downloadable *Super Street Fighter II Turbo HD Remix* and the stunning-looking next-gen *SF4*. Perhaps there is a significant leap forward yet to come, but for the moment, looking back is way more fun.

Super Mario 64

N64; Nintendo; 1996

Not many games have been credited with reinventing a genre, but *Super Mario 64* deserves the accolade. The N64's killer launch title, it fulfilled Nintendo's goal of providing a game with enough appeal to sell its new system, while invoking the usual jaw-dropping amazement at the genius of its designers, in particular Shigeru Miyamoto (see p.245). However revolutionary it was, though, you wouldn't expect still to be playing and indeed marvelling at it some ten years – and several generations of console – down the line, or that so many of its innovations would remain essential components of games today. The world's first platformer in 3D, *Super Mario 64* rendered the term an awkward fit for every title in the genre since.

The most familiar figure in videogames, still wearing the cap and gloves that defined his earliest appearance (see p.11).

For anyone who hasn't played this piece of gaming history, the plot goes like this: an Italian plumber is invited to tea by a princess, turning up to find her imprisoned in her castle by Bowser, a nasty, bespiked turtle-dragon creature. Bowser has stolen the power stars that protected the castle, thereby allowing all sorts of villains to take up residence, and only Mario can rescue the princess by – and this is the important bit – finding the missing stars, which open up doors in the castle, eventually leading to Bowser and the princess. A device seen in countless subsequent games, the castle forms a central base that lets you run around and practise moves, then enter levels by having Mario jump through paintings on the walls.

The world reached through those star-marked doors is huge: fifteen multilayered levels that check off the usual themes of underwater, lava, snow, desert, all designed with an inventiveness that comes from having no blueprint to follow. These brightly coloured cartoon-style environments may look unsophisticated in comparison with today's games, but in terms of gameplay they stand up just fine. It's all about exploration, rather than following a route from A to B, using the camera controls to look around for where you might go – another first for this game, and if the camera's sometimes frustratingly imperfect, at least there's an excuse for it here. Musically, too, there's plenty to enjoy, with changing themes defining even tiny areas, such as the lullaby that plays while you tiptoe around the snoozing piranha plant monsters.

As for Mario himself, this rotund, moustachioed plumber in overalls has a sophisticated range of moves, making full use of the N64 controller that was designed in tandem with the game (although the Wii Virtual Console version plays fine using the Classic or GameCube controller): he can run fast or creep slowly, he can crawl, strafe, perform various jumps and somersaults, punch things and slam onto them, swim two different strokes, and by picking up various hats gain temporary powers like flying. All these skills come into play as each level boasts five further quests-cum-courses that award you additional stars after you've defeated the boss, gradually ramping up the challenge from easy races to some immensely tricky jumping courses. However, only a certain number of stars are needed to progress along the main path, so you can return to old levels to have another go whenever you like. Whether you rush to the end or collect every last star (best download a walkthrough), the game manages to remain challenging while allowing you time to plan and take on each level at your own pace. What's more, the invisible cleverness of the design constantly delights, for instance when you mess up a jump, but end up landing someplace with lines of coins plus a shortcut back again.

Mario's subsequent platform outings, such as *Super Mario Sunshine* for the GameCube and especially the superlative *Super Mario Galaxy* on the Wii (see p.192), aren't to be sneezed at, but new control system or not, they're still following a blueprint established here. Other games may offer better-looking environments, fancier weapons and sexier characters, but for inventiveness and pure, challenging gameplay, *Super Mario 64* has yet to be surpassed.

Super Mario 64 DS
DS; Nintendo; 2004

Apart from *Madden NFL*, probably the biggest title released at the DS launch, and the one designed to bring traditional Nintendo gamers on board. It's a rerun of the original but with some crucial differences, namely a trio of characters to play as, more stars to find, and a whole host of wacky minigames. The biggest difference, though, is that there's no equivalent to the N64's responsive analog controller, making Mario more clumsy than usual, whether controlled via the digital d-pad, or the inventive new touch-screen system.

The original adventure revised and augmented, to take advantage of the handheld's dual screens.

Super Mario Galaxy

Wii; Nintendo; 2007

A landmark game for fans and Nintendo alike, the Wii's first 3D Mario adventure was an opportunity to show that the console was capable of providing hardcore gamers with their fix. It had a lot of history to live up to, especially after the underwhelming *Super Mario Sunshine*, but Nintendo achieved the seemingly impossible, producing not only an engrossing and thoroughly entertaining Mario title, but one that reaches levels of originality few can match.

For a start they chose a setting that allowed for infinite variety and downright wackiness in its level design. From the germ of Miyamoto's idea of a spherical gameplay area developed a system of galaxies containing planets of all shapes and sizes, from tiny discs with a single objective like flipping floor-switch tiles, to larger areas with more traditional-style levels, such as the Honeyhive ones. You can clearly see other planets in the galaxy from the planet you're on – even if the way there isn't yet clear. Needless to say, the art is sumptuous: a brightly colourful universe, gleaming in the starlight, and accompanied for the first time by a full orchestral score of new and classic Mario tunes.

The first proper planet Mario visits from the hub, where he runs around to the other side and down becomes up, brings the first laugh-out-loud OMG moment of many; there are endless surprises in this game, each new level setting the brain whirring into action as it anticipates the challenge ahead. Especially on the spherical planets, the gravity effect can be dizzying, but acclimatization is remarkably quick, thanks to the excellent camera – player control, when available, is rarely needed. Following a well signposted route through each level – though, as ever, diversions can be rewarding – it's hard to get lost, which lends the pacy feel of a 2D Mario game, a linearity that's comforting for aficionados of old-school platformers.

Mostly the game is still traditional Mario: collecting stars, coins, 1-Ups and now Star Bits. Typically for games under Miyamoto's purview, the design of the world and means of player control go hand in hand, and so the Wii remote has given rise to new gameplay elements, including pointing at the screen to pick up Star Bits; and spinning, which is Mario's main form of attack, produced by shaking the remote sideways. This gives a quite different feel to the gameplay, at its most dramatic when you spin Mario into a Launch Star and whoosh through the dark universe to another location. As is traditional, Mario picks up various costumes for extra temporary powers: Bee Mario is a sight to behold, and flying quite easy to control in comparison with Spring Mario, where he's stuffed in a giant spring, or the motion-sensor controlled Manta-ray ride along a bouncy, perilously narrow water track. Learning how to do the trickier stuff is part of the challenge though, and the game provides excellent training through its graduated difficulty level, always reminding you how much you've achieved and giving incentive to keep trying again when Mario dies. Figuring out what to do next is straightforward, thanks to visible clues like shadows or the bees practising jump-stomps close by a stomp-activated button. Boss fights require more persistence, but when they seem too tough, it's sometimes due to overlooking a more obvious solution.

Super Mario Galaxy released Mario into a varied and explosive universe of strange planets and space travel.

For Mario veterans, it's a reasonably long game, with plenty of replay potential after Bowser's finally beaten. What's surprising is that it simultaneously makes a decent stab at accommodating the Wii's brief to expand the gaming audience – mainly through the inventive Co-Star mode, where one player has the remote plus nunchuk (and so control of Mario), while a second player can use another remote to pick up Star Bits, point at things and freeze certain enemies. Its most obvious use is for a novice to help the main gamer, but it's perhaps more fun when the stronger player takes the supporting role, guiding a child, nongaming friend or partner through the boards. What's more, with little narrative to worry about – Princess Peach is captured by Bowser again – they can join or leave at any point. A more interesting story, if just as tangential to the game, is the affecting tale of how Rosalina and her Lumas came to be on the comet, told through storybook screens.

Inevitably, *Super Mario Galaxy* draws comparison with *Super Mario 64* (see p.190), to which it's been nominated (by Nintendo, no less) as the true, spiritual successor. That game revolutionized the genre with 3D; this one has taken things even further down the physics avenue. However, it really doesn't matter whether players are aware of its legacy or recognize the brilliance of its design. It's simply pure delight to play, evoking joy, laughter, awe, and a genuine sense of triumph on obtaining each star. Amidst all the huffing and puffing about videogame violence, *Super Mario Galaxy* is a potent reminder of what games are all about.

Super Smash Bros. Brawl

Wii; Game Arts, Nintendo; 2008

Super Smash Bros. Melee was the GameCube's bestselling title, so excitement about its Wii successor was only to be expected. Far from being secretive about it, Nintendo fuelled the fervour with a development website which, over a period of months, revealed to fans exactly what they'd be getting – from controller layouts to music samples and, later on, descriptions of secret stages. And it paid off: when the game was eventually released, it became the fastest-selling title in the history of Nintendo of America, shifting more than two copies per second in its first week. Reviews didn't really matter; it was simply a game that every Nintendo fan had to own, a celebration of the company and its past catalogue in the shape of a multiplayer beat-'em-up.

While most fighting games court realism as a matter of course, becoming ever more technical and anatomically perfectionist, *Super Smash Bros.* is a refreshingly silly antidote, fast and furious multiplayer action taking the place of chess-like move and countermove (and despite the Teen rating, there's no realistic violence on show). As it looks, so it plays, with each character sporting just half a dozen attacks, plus jumping, throwing and shielding. There's no lexicon of intricate moves to get to grips with; in fact you don't need to memorize anything at all. Which isn't to say it's simple or boring, as some characters, such as Captain Olimar and his Pikmin, have quite complex options. And then plenty of other effects are available via dozens of pickups, some being familiar platform items, but others, such as Poké Balls and Assist Trophies, bringing extra characters into play. The aim, as before, is to raise your opponents'

Sonic's appearance as a playable character in Nintendo's flagship game would once have been unimaginable.

damage percentage high enough that a smash will send them flying, while an unseen audience cheers your performance.

All the regular fighting modes are present, from Training to single-player Classic, plus Event matches, but this is really just the start of the gameplay options. Packed into the one disc (the Wii's first dual-layered, precipitating the return of thousands of consoles to Nintendo for cleaning) is a full single-player adventure game called *The Subspace Emissary*, also playable co-operatively. It might have been there on *Melee*, but Miyamoto persuaded director Masahiro Sakurai (of Hal Laboratory) to concentrate on multiplayer at the time. Here at last, with the aid of a huge one-off development team, he gets to do both, stacking a decent platformer on top of the unbeatable multiplayer game, which itself offers endless possibilities for both offline and online play, customizable to the nth degree.

Pokémon bring even more variety to the megamix of Nintendo characters.

In terms of characters, it's a who's who of Nintendo past and present: along with the stalwarts from *Mario* and *Zelda* games, plus Samus Aran and Kirby, there are reinvigorated old-timers like *Kid Icarus*'s Pit, while secret characters to unlock include the graphic Mr Game & Watch; also making a much anticipated appearance are Snake (Hideo Kojima originally wanted his *Metal Gear Solid* character in *Melee*) and Sonic. All the characters are in 3D, some for the first time – and with more or less detail applied, to make them consistent – though the action itself is all on a 2D plane. Just as broad in range is the music, provided by everyone who's ever composed music for a Nintendo game, it seems, with the storming theme music by *Final Fantasy*'s Nobuo Uematsu, and tracks from the musicians responsible for *Animal Crossing*, *Devil May Cry*, *Chrono Trigger* and *Kingdom Hearts*, as well as the usual *Zelda* and *Mario* tunes. The stages too are based on iconic settings and invariably interactive, ranging from the shifting platforms of *Donkey Kong* to minigame interludes in the Wario levels. Playing on a big TV is advisable – even in single-player mode, relatively few matches are one-on-one for long, and at times it's hard to spot your character amongst the hordes of enemies and allies onscreen at once.

A nostalgic treat, *Super Smash Bros. Brawl* is like a big tin of Quality Street at Christmas – everyone has their favourite and just thinking about it brings a warm and fuzzy feeling. So much content has been crammed in: from creating a diorama of the trophies you've won, playing minigames to win more coins, applying virtual stickers in your book, playing demo levels of classic NES and SNES titles (immodestly named "Masterpieces"), taking screenshots and recording gameplay to share with friends, to designing your own stages, and even a list of all Nintendo's games for every platform. It's a completist's dream, offering enough reasons to replay that it's hard to get the game out of your system. And the nostalgia factor even reaches to the deliberately retro control scheme, in that of several control options, it's actually best suited to the old GameCube controller, harking back to a time before motion sensors and *Wii Sports* defined the Nintendo experience. A gift for old-school gamers, Sakurai said his team designed it as though it would be the last in the series, but it's perhaps confirmation that even though there are two very distinct strands to Nintendo games, it's not giving up on the hardcore quite yet.

Tekken's Brazilian beauty Christie Monteiro is a relatively recent addition to the roster and the game's first female capoeira practitioner.

Tekken 5

PS2; Namco; 2005

Alongside the more hardcore *Street Fighter* and *Virtua Fighter*, *Tekken* deserves a place on the winners' podium of arcade fighting games. Having made its debut in arcades in 1994, a year later *Tekken* ("Iron Fist") was only the second beat-em-up to appear on the PlayStation; since then it's been consistently battling it out against the competition, in both arcades and the living room – or more specifically on the PlayStation, due to an all but exclusive relationship with Sony. Every subsequent arcade instalment has been ported flawlessly to Sony's consoles but the pinnacle of the series has to be *Tekken 5*, which restored credibility after the disappointing *Tekken 4*, a game everyone would rather forget, including Namco, it seems: *Tekken 5*'s History mode features full arcade versions of *Tekken* to *Tekken 3*. Four games in one, then, enough to satisfy its intensely devoted following and to demonstrate what, as Namco immodestly claims as "A decade of dominance".

That loyalty is partly down to its persistent, if convoluted storyline, focused on and around the Mishima Zaitbatsu company, sponsor of the competitions that have brought together the stories of around thirty combatants all in all. Disregarding the weak adventure game extra *Devil Within*, the gameplay isn't itself the vehicle for storytelling; events are all told in intro or end sequences, in snippets of dialogue before and after fights, and in manga-style painted scenes within each character's individual Story mode. The diverse bunch of entrants into the "King of Iron Fist Tournament 5" includes all the regular

As well as traditional martial arts, many
Tekken characters have the ability to
unleash supernatural attacks.

Tekken Tag Tournament
PS2; Namco; 2000

One of the PS2's launch titles, *Tag Tournament*'s a side dish to the main menu but it shouldn't be overlooked. For a start, it far outshone the arcade original, taking the series in the visual direction of *Tekken 5*. And unlike some fighting games, it encourages experimentation, since you need two fighters to work as a complementary team, switching them in and out – even mid-move – at the touch of a shoulder button. Naturally it's great for two players, with the option of pairing up or playing in opposition, but includes a one-on-one mode for *Tekken* traditionalists, plus an unlockable bowling minigame for the more sedate.

stalwarts – glamorous white-haired assassin Nina Williams, King the jaguar-hooded wrestler, ninja Yoshimitsu with his robotic arm and iconic sword, various members of the Mishima family, cursed by the Devil gene – to choose from or to fight against. The characters' backstory gives their motivation for entering the contest: it might be to inflict revenge or to prove a point to another character, providing the emotional impetus that helps make this more than just another technical one-on-one display fight, even when playing against the AI (there's no online option out of the box, although it's available as a downloadable update to the PS3's *Tekken 5: Dark Resurrection*).

The characters' energetic moves mean fighting is a satisfyingly visceral experience even without any blood: the force exerted is palpable through the controller. Alongside their individual motivations, there are more styles of combat here than in any other game, based on genuine martial arts in many cases; the clues are in the characters, especially in earlier versions, where Marshall Law is obviously modelled on Bruce Lee, Lei Wuhong on Jackie Chan. But there's a huge variety here, including Panda and Kuma, that broadens the game's appeal beyond the hardcore. That said, random button mashing doesn't work for long, although some stunning manoeuvres can be pulled off without mastering anything too complicated. Controlled uniquely by a system where each limb is pegged to a button, being competent at *Tekken* isn't the same as being good, achieved via hours and hours of practice, of studying opponents' moves and learning a decently sized roster of kicks, punches and combos – with well over a hundred per character, there's enough choice to offer an edge of unpredictability even playing against the same character. Just as graphical improvements have led to better detailed characters, the game long ago left behind real-life venues like Monument Valley, to opt for more detailed, expansive settings.

Tekken inhabits a special place in the lineup of fighting games. Compared to *Virtua Fighter*, it's cartoonishly vulgar; it's the polar opposite of *Street Fighter*'s purist 2D stylings; doesn't compete with the buttery smooth responsiveness of *SoulCalibur* (with which it's crossed over, superhero-style); offers far fewer bouncy boobs than *Dead or Alive*, and not a single *Mortal Kombat* evisceration; but it's got a distinctive character and masses of attitude, engaging the heart as well as the brain and fingers.

TimeSplitters 2

PS2, Xbox, GC; Eidos, Free Radical Design; 2002

Perhaps it's the way your handheld weapon bobs cutely around in front of you as you move. Perhaps it's the stylized retro settings, or the understated cartoon-style animation, or the soundtrack that sits just so with the action. But for an FPS, *TimeSplitters 2* is downright endearing and decidedly goofy – not exactly qualities one expects in a world of *Halos* and *Half-Lifes*. And no matter how frantic the action, it's such a smoothly rendered experience in terms of graphics, movement and pace that its adrenaline buzz often transitions, unlikely as it may seem, into zen-like equilibrium.

This isn't so surprising, given its pedigree, which stretches all the way back through the N64's *Perfect Dark* (see p.251) to *GoldenEye* (see p.95), both of which are referenced in its looks and level architecture – the opening one being a recreation of *GoldenEye*'s Siberian dam, for example. But it's far more than a rehash of past glories, and

In the frantic experience that is *TimeSplitters 2*, the selection of weapons available changes in line with the era of the setting.

the ex-Rare founders of Free Radical had already announced their intentions for console-only shooters with the original *TimeSplitters* in 2001. But that version was a PS2 launch title, and whilst an excellent multiplayer game, it fell short in single-player mode, which some felt was the result of the rush to meet the PS2's deadline. There were a couple of notable firsts, though: as a launch title, it was one of the first PS2 shooters to put the new Dualshock 2's two analog sticks to full use, allowing console gamers the freedom of in-game vision more traditionally afforded to mouse-and-keyboard PC users; and it included a map editor, something previously lacking from console shooters.

Enemies, as well as player characters, differ wildly in each level, from the chassis bot pictured here to Aztec high priests.

TimeSplitters 2 doesn't try to fix previous accusations of lacking a narrative, though: the Story mode, involving hunting down the eponymous evil Timesplitters through different eras in human history, is still just a peg to hang the beautifully designed levels on, from the Wild West of the 1890s to the gangster city of Chicago in 1930. What we get instead – and the level designs are integral to this – is a Free Radical master class in reward-based gaming: a gamer's game that entices with seemingly endless modes and unlockable levels, and a profile-tracker that records a host of eccentric stats that only a hardcore nut would think of (average speed, melons burst, UFOs spotted...). From micro to macro level, everything the player can do is given purpose, with more interesting challenges and more complex levels the higher the difficulty rating. Go through the Aztec Ruins level on medium, and then replay it on hard, for example, and entirely new ways of navigating the map open up. Add in the Challenge, Arcade and the reprised Mapmaker modes, and it represents a significant amount of variation (and replay value) on just the one theme.

The game continues its predecessor's excellent split-screen options too, which even today shows just how much multiplayer fun it's possible to have offline – though in keeping with the rewards system, how much of it you can access depends on your achievements in single-player mode. The two-player co-op mode is already present in Story mode, and four multiplayer levels (including the amusingly titled Capture the Bag) are available from the start, but to get the really juicy versions like Thief or Gladiator, as well as extra characters and levels, putting in the hours solo counts.

The original game's lack of blood was often cited as a disincentive to seasoned gamers, but it's testament to Free Radical's determined pinning down of videogame mechanics (and fun) that its absence in *TimeSplitters 2* wasn't even remarked upon on release. Once a Nintendo developer, always a Nintendo developer.

Tomb Raider: Legend

GC, PC, PS2, PSP, Xbox, Xbox 360; Crystal Dynamics, Eidos Interactive; 2006

In 2006, Lara Croft, star of the *Tomb Raider* series, turned ten years of age. This was a sobering moment for the generation of gamers who thought of the original game, starring the young, pneumatic pistol-packing ambassador of videogame cool, as cutting-edge entertainment. Sure, Croft had maintained her hyper-real physique

Even swimming through underwater tunnels is done with grace and style by Ms Croft, though, with regard to gameplay, this is one of the harder skills to acquire.

across each incarnation, but the years had not been as kind to the franchise itself. Having had such a flying start (especially with regard to the first PlayStation version of the game) it was always going to be hard to keep the momentum going, but an increasing slackness in quality control and growing paucity of imagination certainly hadn't helped her – or what she got up to – get any more interesting. Each subsequent release saw a tailing off of the sense of wonder that had been so well evoked in the first episode.

So it was with relief that fans greeted 2006's *Legend*, which turned out to be the quality follow-up they had been waiting for since 1996. Publisher Eidos achieved this by both looking back to what made *Tomb Raider* great in the first place whilst simultaneously replacing the original, and once-great, Core Design development team with fresh blood in the form of Crystal Dynamics. It was a bit like leaving everybody's favourite veteran football players off the team sheet – a shame, given their past glories, but their more recent efforts had been very tired indeed.

Crystal Dynamics' fresh eyes certainly spruced things up. Everything is so well executed that the last, unavoidably inherited vestiges of all that went wrong in the wilderness years – such as product placement, here involving a couple of clunky scenes that see Croft riding a Ducati motorcycle – stand out by a mile in comparison. But these problems are few and far between; the abiding impression of *Legend* is one of rekindled passion. A true sense of adventurous exploration has returned; there are exotic locations and puzzle solving that taxes the brain without inducing a migraine – much of it revolving around the pull-this-push-that school of problem solving.

The attention to detail really convinces too, producing a wonderfully immersive atmosphere. The third-person perspective, for example, shows off Lara's highly realistic animation as she dodges deadly traps, somersaults between cliff ledges and swan-dives into sparkling waterfall plunge pools. Graphics and ambient sound combine so well that you can almost feel the humidity in the Bolivian jungle or the breeze of a Tokyo rooftop at night. It's nearly enough to make you forget how much of a straightforward 3D action platformer this is, with extraneous features so pared back that even its intuitive combat system has been relegated to the background – aside from the boss fights, most of Lara's dangerous exploits involve dodging the whirling

Many *Tomb Raider* cut scenes are clearly created to generate a surge of pre-gameplay excitement amongst Lara's male audience. And those shorts, dear me…

blades of yet another temple trap, rather than bullets or the teeth of a nasty beast.

The plot – concerning Lara's search for an old friend she thought dead – continues the series' tradition of revealing past elements of Ms Croft's life. But that's not really why fans love *Tomb Raider* so much. It's really about unlocking the inner Indiana Jones; about feeling nostalgic for the first game (or even that game's clear influences, the first *Prince of Persia* titles) without having to squint at now-dated 32-bit polygons; and for some it might well be about putting a well-endowed, shorts-and-singlet-wearing heroine through her acrobatic paces. Pick your preference; what matters is that *Legend* brought *Tomb Raider* back to its roots with style and grace even before the 2007 *Anniversary* edition reaffirmed she was back to stay. It was a very happy birthday party.

Uncharted: Drake's Fortune

PS3; Naughty Dog, Sony; 2007

Featuring a running, jumping, shooting treasure hunter, *Uncharted* was never going to escape comparison with *Tomb Raider*, but to see it as a gender-switch imitation misjudges the depth and creativity behind one of the PS3's early must-have games. Naughty Dog, no stranger to making games for a new Sony console, manages to reference both *Crash Bandicoot* and *Jak & Daxter* (note the Ottsel-brand wetsuits) in this gorgeous-looking, tautly structured action adventure. Influenced by the same pulp serials of the 1930s that inspired *Raiders of the Lost Ark*, it's set in the present day and stars a timelessly rugged hero in scruffy jeans and T-shirt who makes Lara Croft look like a cardboard cutout. Calling it a platformer's not too far off the mark, but it's evolved into something the developers call "traversal", which neatly sums up the breadth of the setting as well as the actions performed by Nathan Drake. A self-proclaimed descendant of Sir Francis, in search of his ancestor's fabled lost treasure, Nate looks like a composite of various movie stars (Sean Bean and Dylan McDermott amongst them, though he's also thought to be modelled on one of the development team).

The traversing takes place in Central and South America and begs the question: how many shades of green are there in the rainforest? Most of them can be seen here, in a setting that's the antithesis of more popular grey-brown utilitarian environments, lush and bursting with natural life – burgeoning greenery, toucans flying overhead – photorealism with a stylized cartoonish sheen. Enhancing this are some spectacular technical effects, for instance the light (especially the long shadows of late afternoon), and the masses of water everywhere, from calm blue ocean to rushing rivers and splashy, flooded buildings; the architecture, whether colonial cloisters or ruined Incan temples, shows off crumbling, tactile textures. This

Nate can take on his attackers hand to hand when they're too close for a gunfight.

close attention to detail extends even to collectibles – Drake could be picking up identical Spanish coins, but instead he's uncovering a silver idol, or gold cup studded with jade.

Of course the environment's not just eye candy – and interaction is on an equally heightened level, with Drake leaping precariously from ledge to ledge, or swinging from vines or chains. Often finding

DOWN IN THE UNCANNY VALLEY

The Uncanny Valley is a term coined nearly forty years ago by Japanese robot designer Masahiro Mori, to describe a stage in our response to robots as they reach increasing levels of realism. Simply put, when robots look like robots, any human-like behaviour makes them feel more familiar (think of the affection felt for R2-D2); at the other end of the spectrum, when they look almost totally human, we're repelled by them. In this context any non-human aspect is greatly magnified and provokes feelings of serious discomfort, a kind of self-defence against being tricked. In a movie setting, when CGI characters enter the Valley, it wrecks the audience's suspension of disbelief, causing an instant disconnect with the story. It's a theory often used to explain why the movie *Final Fantasy: The Spirits Within* wasn't more successful.

The concept applies just as much to videogames, and *Uncharted* exemplifies many of the issues facing developers. Naughty Dog chose, for example, to hand-draw all the character model textures rather than using photographic images, presumably because they didn't want them to look too real. They're still real enough to distract you from the story occasionally, however, for a bit of inspection and reality-criticism, in a way that games free of detailed human representation don't.

Of course, the scope of player–character interaction also affects what's acceptable to us. In Drake's case, he's well developed through speech and actions, as well as facial expressions, plus the engrossing story gives you a real incentive to want to stay immersed. Funnily enough, it's not that we need to actually believe a character's real; it's sufficient that we're comfortable suspending disbelief without feeling stupid about it. In contrast to the challenge facing Drake's animators, it's much easier for a figure seen in the distance to look perfectly real. The cannon fodder baddies are a perfect example: not nearly as developed as Drake is, they seem just as lifelike because all they have to do is shoot and die, both of which they do incredibly convincingly.

a route across vertiginous drops is the puzzle itself, and the game's forgiving attitude to jumps and generous checkpointing give licence to experiment. Aside from jumping, the other main gameplay element is shooting. Duck, cover and snipe is the only way to survive, and so each combat scene is strewn with masonry, trees and other obstacles, with Drake able to roll from one to the next. Despite the game's large arsenal, he can only carry two guns at once, an example of the simple, never distracting interface. Enemy AI is outstanding; there are dozens of them in each scenario and they'll gradually surround Drake unless he moves or dispatches them quickly – sometimes a bit of melee fist action is the best bet. It's pretty tough, but even when you have to replay a battle, you're working towards one of the game's rewards, a 1000-point Achievement-style cache divided between combat and treasure-finding, which unlocks extras.

Not every character is detailed to the same degree, but core cast members like the cigar-chewing Sully and feisty filmmaker Elena are incredibly lifelike, their movements derived from motion-capturing real actors as they performed the excellently scripted dialogue, making their gestures, like their speech, exceptionally realistic, and cut scenes really quite gripping. Drake's own behaviour, though inevitably repetitious, also feels natural – he wobbles on a ledge,

Uncharted's lush tropical setting, with its jungle sound effects, is never less than wholly evocative.

mutters "oh shit!" in a gunfight. In fact, sound contributes greatly to the overall effect; whether it's the swelling orchestral score, eerie panpipe music or individual sound effects, everything's perfectly attuned to the action on screen.

Limited loading times between chapters increase the sense of a flowing, filmlike structure, and while the game is relatively short it's always action-packed, with quiet moments of exploration interspersed by gunfights, or events like an edge-of-your-seat jungle Jeep chase, with Drake shooting at pursuers. For a traditionally problematic genre, where so many things could easily have felt misplaced or hit the wrong note, it's great to know that, like the riproaring Saturday morning serials it emulates, Drake's adventure is to be continued.

Virtua Fighter 5

Xbox 360, PS3; AM2, Sega; 2007

High-definition technology has polished *Virtua Fighter 5* to a glossy perfection, more vividly sumptuous than anything in real life. And like a valuable work of art, it's been protected from the vagaries of fashion and allowed to mature into a perfectly preserved piece of gaming history, still accompanied by the digitized electro-rock that typifies games of a certain era. Jump-starting the 3D fighting genre with Yu Suzuki's original masterpiece, *Virtua Fighter* cabinets have dominated arcades since 1993, but although the character models are unmistakably 3D, the gameplay is in the same two dimensions as ever. What's more, the style of fighting – less flamboyant than the performances seen in the *Tekken*, *Mortal Kombat* or *Dead or Alive* series – doesn't involve such dramatic animations that you can pretend it's genuinely 3D. So this is what Sega's AM2 development team calls "the impression of realism". Beautifully lit, flawless, traditionally styled characters, duking it out in the usual gallery of

Goh takes on Eileen, at the less realistic end of the impression of realism scale.

indoor and outdoor venues, including vast glittering arenas and misty mountain settings, as lush and awe-inspiring as you'd expect. Apart from some breakable fences, though, the environment isn't as integral to the gameplay as it is in, say, *Dead or Alive*; here it's looks that count. Concentrating on what it isn't, though, misses the point of *VF5*.

This is a grown-up game, one of strategy and restraint, of punishing accuracy, and intricate techniques – like the martial arts it depicts. Spending time learning the moves provides a sense of achievement akin to learning a new language. Newcomers might well be put off by the speed necessary to enact anything but the simplest move; it's no coincidence that veteran players talk in terms of frame numbers. It's worth persevering, though. The Dojo mode allows practice of the quick thinking needed to take advantage of an opponent's weakness, providing Command Training to run through the basic moves, as well as more complex manoeuvres (avoiding throws, defending while rising, plus combos for each character). It's not just for beginners, either, as experienced players can work up their speed with Command Time Attack or further hone skills with Free training.

Arcade mode, on the other hand, simulates the traditional experience of playing gradually tougher opponents versus the AI. Should it feel like yours is the billionth clone of Jacky, never fear, there's ample customization to make a character your own, ranging from hairdos to items of clothing to makeup or even coloured contacts. Winning these special items or the money to buy them forms an essential part of the Quest mode that takes you, the player, on a virtual tour of Sega arcades, fighting other virtual players to rise through the 28 ranks in special tournaments. All of which is about as good as a single-player fighting game gets and unless you've got plenty of pals to invite round, as good as the PS3 version gets, winning it the accolade of being first PS3 game to top the Japanese gaming charts. It wasn't until the Xbox 360 version that *VF5* finally managed to get online, a non-negotiable requirement for any serious modern fighting game. Unfortunately, you can't take your ring name or other data with you when battling others online.

As with most fighting games, there's a backstory of revenge and manipulation, giving each of the regular 17 characters a reason to fight, from posterboy Akira (a tough one to master) to ninja Kage-Maru (easier for novices), and including, as is traditional, a couple of new faces: Mexican wrestler El Blaze and cute Eileen, whose style is monkey kung fu. Each fighting style can be checked out via VF.TV, which runs nonstop exhibition matches or, more fun, replays of your own bouts or those of other successful players via the online leaderboards – get to see how the professional players do it.

Faced with the challenge of bringing in next-gen players while also satisfying a committed and demanding fan base, Sega succeeded in style. Any more tinkering with the formula would be unnecessary and unwelcome, muddying the purity of the game – like asking for McDonald's ketchup in a fancy Japanese sushi restaurant.

Virtua Tennis 3

PC, PS3, PSP, Xbox 360; Sega AM3, Sumo Digital, Sega; 2007

When *Virtua Tennis* first stepped onto the court on the Dreamcast in 2000, it proceeded to ace the competition. Several contenders subsequently rose through the rankings to compete for the champion's spot – notably 2K Sport's *Top Spin* (2003) and Namco's *Smash Court Tennis* series – but the player with the greatest stamina and consistency remains Sega's. It may have dropped a set or two to the pretenders in its time, but it's never lost a match (though sadly for Wii owners, it's barred from competing with *Wii Sports*).

Like Pistol Pete Sampras, however, it has suffered criticism for being something of an automaton, relentlessly serving up the same shots with each edition. But what Sega has realized is that the key to retaining the top spot lies in maintaining the gameplan of the first edition: namely, the ability to play equally well from all areas of the court and so appeal just as much to tennis fans as to gamers. The fact that it has always been developed first and foremost for the arcade cabinet is doubtless a factor in this; its roots plainly show in the simple and highly effective three-button control mechanism that determines the execution of topspin, slice and lob shots.

With *Virtua Tennis 3*, however, it's the finer points of the game that have changed, most notably in the World Tour career mode. Anyone who's ever swung a racket and felt the satisfaction of the ball hitting the strings – and the resultant exhilaration of perfect shot placement – will want to get stuck right into this basic RPG-like mode in which you create a customized player (male or female), establish a global base for them, and then attempt to take them from being seeded 300th to the top of the game through a twenty-year period. All this encompasses a training academy, a professional coach, friendly games and competitive events. As for opponents, you get to lock rackets with players as diverse as Federer, Hewitt, Davenport and Hingis (there's a total of twenty in-game real-life players). The skills-levelling aspects also reflect the truisms of the sport: that the more you practise, the better you become. And just like in the real world, sooner or later, you find your optimum operating level and realize that the next step up is a *very* big one indeed. Games won without much effort when ranked 300th are tournaments away from Fererro's strong forehand and Sharapova's powerful hitting later on in the game. Players in need of quicker fixes can always opt for the

The combination of long shadows, bright light and great sound effects makes for a convincing recreation of the lawn tennis experience.

Exhibition or Tournament modes, or indulge in multiplayer doubles, where the easy control system takes *VT* into party-game territory. Xbox 360 gamers won't even need to invite friends around for this, thanks to the inclusion of an online mode.

The minigames for which the series is so well known still feature, though their inclusion within an otherwise serious-minded game can jar a little, especially when they involve collecting pieces of fruit whilst dodging giant tennis balls – which is either Sega referencing *Super Monkey Ball* (see p.31) or something they came up with after getting sunstroke on court.

In the run-up to the 2006 US Open, American Express launched a spoof Roddick-versus-*Pong* ad in which the man's big serves were easily returned by his relentlessly robotic opponent. It was a mark of how far games had come as reference points in popular sporting culture: *Virtua Tennis*, however, represents how far videogames have come in reflecting that sporting culture back the other way.

We Love Katamari

PS2; Namco; 2005

When games cost as much to produce as movies, releasing something as innovative as *Katamari Damacy* (Namco, 2004) is seen as highly risky, but it can sometimes pay off, as it did in the case of this modestly priced, quirky little title, which was swiftly revamped into a sequel (published by EA in Europe, 2006). Gaining a few extra features but leaving the original's surreal humour and wacky design intact, *We Love Katamari* celebrates the unexpected success of a highly stylized game that consists of rolling a sticky ball around to pick up everyday items.

Self-referential in the extreme, its *raison d'être* in game as well as out is the popularity of the original: nowadays everyone loves katamari (most commonly translated as "clumps") and the game's fans are pleading with the unfathomably huge King of All Cosmos to demonstrate more cleverness and sort out their problems for them. That's the plot, such as it is, and it's the fans' requests together with the King's own whims that provide the player's goals. As before, he enlists the miniature Prince to do the honours by rolling the ball – controlled via the two analog sticks – to collect inanimate objects and living creatures alike. As the clump grows it can pick up progressively bigger items, the scene switching scale every so often to provide the consistent perspective of a small fish in a vast sea of stuff, eventually forming a katamari sufficiently big to be placed into the cosmos as a star. Ultimately, everything's eligible to be rolled up, from the tiniest pin to the sun.

The stylized world the Prince rolls around is packed with seemingly random items, often laid out in neat lines, and there's a bit of a strategy to choosing a route: starting in a living room and collecting the tokens under a coffee table, perhaps, then onto batteries and pieces of sushi, rolling out through a gap in the railings into the yard before the katamari's too big to do so, and eventually into a street of altogether larger targets. Whatever the item, it's obsessively detailed with a specific measurement and sound effect as it's rolled up, down to the miaow of a cat, or the shriek of a person blithely out shopping. Rolling a ball around is by necessity repetitive, but there are just enough themed levels to keep things interesting, such as an underwater level or a rose garden, a sumo wrestler rolling up food, or the challenge of rolling a flaming ball until it's big enough to light a pile of logs without letting the fire go out. It's also possible to change things around by swapping the Prince out for one of his cousins (some of whom are pictured here in their wildly different outfits), or donning one of the presents – most often hats or similar articles – both of which are rolled up like everything else.

Impressive physics mean picking up a chopstick, say, causes the katamari to limp along slowly and lopsidedly until the load is more balanced, and there's a real sense of gravity and increasing momentum while navigating obstacles. This endless rolling is done to the rhythm of a genre-busting soundtrack, featuring J-pop, techno, jazz and swinging crooner tunes amongst others, all as hummably memorable as each other.

From the musical "speech" of the King to the psychedelic, nonsensical storyline and cries of the Pythonesque cartoon-style fans, a unique design is coupled with unapologetic self-referential

20cm8mm
1m
LOOK OUT!
Milk Jug
2

Beautiful Katamari **transports you to a mouse-eye view of the material world reminiscent, at times, of the environment found in the classic *Micro Machines* game.**

Me and My Katamari
PSP; Namco; 2006

This is a downscaled version that came hard on the heels of *We Love Katamari*, with the Prince creating islands rather than planets. Despite the less intuitive digital controls and loading times, it's still the only way to carry your katamari with you.

Beautiful Katamari
Xbox 360; Namco; 2007

Microsoft wins the battle for next-gen high-def exclusive here, with downloadable content, twice as many cousins, and online multiplayer gaming through Xbox Live. It's not quite the revelation it once was, though.

absurdity. One of the tasks requires letting an old man see what the game's about before buying it for his grandson, since he knows "Videogames can be bad for you". If the Prince then fails to produce a large enough katamari, the King will be immensely disappointed; too slow in a speed level and he'll complain about his sleepy life; fail to get anywhere near the goal and he'll fire lasers from his eyes down at the Prince, who runs desperately along the bottom of the black screen.

If the amount of dedicated fan sites is anything to go by – anything from earmuff knitting patterns to rolled-up Da Vincis is out there – the Prince has many more katamari yet to roll. Somewhat ironically for a game with such originality at its core, it's become the subject of a series of repeat outings.

THE HIGH COST OF ORIGINALITY

For every *Katamari Damacy* that makes it into stores, there are hundreds of formulaic World War II shooters, copycat sports sims and movie tie-ins. But originality carries a hefty price when a new PS3 game costs $10–15 million to produce, three times the average cost of a PS2 game, an increase that's largely down to the extra work involved in creating high-definition graphics. Considering that the retail price of games hasn't increased much over the years, you can see why the estimated at $100 million *Grand Theft Auto IV* has been one of very few titles to justify a large-scale, mass media advertising campaign. Marketing obviously influences sales figures, but the prevailing retail system of pre-ordering means that games without a sufficient pre-launch buzz may not get much shelf space; and by the time word of mouth gets around, it can be too late.

When production costs are so steep and the number of next-gen consoles in homes still relatively low, publishers are understandably shy of taking risks. Even Keita Takahashi's *Katamari* proposal was rejected at first, but then it went on to sell enough to result in a handful of sequels. Seen by many as a depressing trend, sequelitis is almost unavoidable for publishers with shareholders to please – there's no safer bet than a follow-up to a successful game. Having said that, taking risks with new ideas is still infinitely easier for the bigger publishers with their own development studios than it is for a small independent company, which has to invest in actually producing a game to the stage where it can be touted around publishers, knowing there's a chance that no one will bite.

In the last year or so, there have been several major publisher mergers, and the swallowing up of many successful independents, improving publishers' control of production costs and giving them ownership of valuable intellectual property. Innovation and creativity are often said to flourish best in small teams, though, and in Japan a number of producers have quit the big companies to form breakaway independent studios. Independent game production isn't quite as celebrated or influential as independent filmmaking, though events and organizations such as the Independent Games Festival are thrusting it into the limelight. There's still the overriding problem that the way the industry works makes it difficult for games that are original or innovative to get financed. But things are starting to change, especially with the opening up of alternative distribution channels, such as the Internet, PlayStation Network, Xbox Live and Wii Ware, which provide the opportunity to reach a massive audience for games that are small in size, but not necessarily in scope.

LocoRoco
PSP; SCEJ, Sony; 2006

An ingeniously novel (and utterly charming) platform game for a new platform, *LocoRoco* showed Sony can still rival Nintendo in innovative handheld gameplay. Each of the forty levels is a shortlived, 2D side-scrolling delight, as you use the shoulder buttons to tilt the ground in order to propel your cute little LocoRoco across the gorgeously designed environments, gradually picking up more members to add to the growing katamari, all the while avoiding enemies. When the going gets tough, you can split them up again to stream individually through a narrow gap, then call them back into a whole – you'll hear them chatter and scream in excitement when not singing along to the soundtrack.

World of Warcraft

PC, Mac; Blizzard Entertainment; 2004

By no means the first massively multiplayer online roleplaying game, and certainly not the last, *World of Warcraft* has been surely the most successful in the West. With ten million plus subscribers, a real-world Azeroth would be the world's 82nd most populous country, beating the likes of Hungary, Sweden and Bolivia. It probably takes up more newspaper column inches worldwide, too, for reasons as diverse as the study of players' leadership techniques, an award-winning episode of *South Park*, a *World of Warcraft* credit card, or the controversial practice of gold farming in China. Thoroughly absorbed into the mainstream, it's a social as well as a gaming phenomenon – and signals just how small the industrialized world has become in the Internet age.

Designing an expansive world, not to mention the systems that make it work for millions of players across the globe, is an unfathomable undertaking, the result of years of initial development and a commitment to maintain it for years to come. Blizzard gave itself a head start by using the setting of its existing *Warcraft* games, so right from the start

Day or night, you can count on finding a fight somewhere in Azeroth.

players were entering a complete world with all the history and conflict necessary for exciting adventures. To succeed, though, it needed players with a computer and online connection plus the ability to pay a monthly subscription, and it had to keep them gripped enough to continue playing beyond the free trial period. All these boxes were unequivocally checked. Thanks to a clear interface, learning the ropes is easy, but the gameplay grows ever more complex and customizable as characters level up. What's more, progression is fast and the next reward, item, skill or spell tantalizingly in view, just out of reach. No wonder it's addictive.

For a fantasy setting, *WoW* has a quaintly old-fashioned look, rejecting muddy realism in favour of radiant environments and stylized,

iconic character design. Creating a character involves choosing from a limited number of highly differentiated races (and classes), from the eccentric little gnomes to the imposing, horned Tauren. For the early levels based in the character's racial home territory, it's easy to feel like a clone, but as quests take characters further abroad, they become better defined through choosing a talent path. But even if playing a similar character to thousands of other Night Elf Hunters, say, doing the same quests, both heroic and incredibly mundane, the game can be a radically different experience, depending on individual players' inclinations. *WoW* is equally accommodating to those in search of a social network (parties and bigger organizations are always recruiting new members, see picture above), a solitary playpen (it doesn't discriminate against loners, who can level up just as fast), a competitive arena (get the best loot and beat everyone else in Player vs Player realms), or a stage on which to practise creative roleplaying (RP servers forbid discussion out of character). Whatever a player's preferences – and a combination of all these is perfectly possible – the excitement and unpredictability of exploring a world filled with other players makes for an experience like no other, while tackling a dungeon cooperatively in a group is an adventure no offline RPG can provide.

Central to the experience is the culture that's emerged in *WoW*, with an initially impenetrable language founded on the ease of quick keyboard entry, and an etiquette and a set of rules for living and questing in a massively multiplayer environment. Blizzard naturally organized much of this, but it's constantly changing and adapting to conform to players' needs. The shared-world community is expanded and built on by an outstanding amount of material outside of the game itself, with the official site hosting not just FAQs but fan art, fiction, and discussion forums for each realm and class. This extra content has continued to expand alongside the game itself, in spite of predictions of decline, moving forward with expansions like *The Burning Crusade* and *Wrath of the Lich King*, which bring new races, higher levels, better items and virgin continents to keep the old-timers playing. When the crash does come, it's likely to be devastating (on *WoW*'s starting up, another MMORPG reportedly lost a third of its subscribers). Whether it will be replaced by another subscription-based online game is debatable, because for anyone who's played and been welcomed into the *World of Warcraft*, anything else would need to be very special to compete with this game that's not so much defined a genre but popularized a whole new way of playing games.

Zack & Wiki: Quest for Barbaros' Treasure

Wii; Capcom; 2007

In some ways, this game's working title, "Project Treasure Island Z", might have been more fitting, because this isn't the derivative platform adventure game it sounds like, but an intensely brain-challenging puzzle game in the tradition of old-style point-and-click graphic adventures. Capcom's winning formula is based in essence on *Monkey Island*, smothered in a glorious anime cartoon style, with the witty script and most of the story removed. What defines it more than anything, though, is that instead of a mouse, it uses a motion-sensing controller.

The kid with the toothy grin and the big hat (that's Zack), and his flying golden monkey accomplice (Wiki) may not be characters you'll feel much connection with emotionally, but after forty-odd hours, they'll either feel like part of the family or you'll be playing with the sound turned off (perhaps both). A chocolate-chomping apprentice pirate, Zack's task is to put together scattered pieces of the infamous pirate Barbaros, who's promised his ship in return. To find them Zack and Wiki have to beat stages of varying size and complexity, grouped on a treasure map in various themed areas, such as jungle or ice. On entering a new stage, the camera zooms around the convoluted level to focus on the treasure-chest prize, *Mario 64*-style, giving a chance to admire the consistently lovely artwork, as well as try to map out the maze-like challenge ahead. As detailed and meticulously planned as a *Mario* or *Zelda* game (from which it borrows some treasure-finding animation styles, sound included), even the "Sea Rabbits hideout", Zack's base, is fun, with pirate bunnies handing out hints and tips and offering to go treasure hunting (for a price), plus a library of books recording every item, creature and enemy you've come across.

The anime-styled characters Zack (right) and Wiki (left) look out from the ship's deck.

Never actually impossible, the game definitely has its tricky moments, with a lot of trial and error involved. Each stage is essentially a complex puzzle of things to pick up and place, move and manipulate. All this employs the Wii remote as a clamp, or an umbrella (to turn winches and keys, to lift up pots and plug up holes); it can even be played like a flute. Its most critical use, though, is to shake Wiki, who conveniently turns into a bell, resulting in an "itemization" effect that transforms live creatures into objects, and vice versa. This is the key to many of the puzzles, and can affect even boss monsters at the end of a series of stages.

Part of the reason the game can be difficult is that mistakes aren't readily forgiven: slip up in many places, and Zack dies – in some gratifyingly amusing death scenes – which forces a restart or the use of a Platinum Ticket (bought from Granny at ever-rising prices); you can also buy hints in a similar way. Redoing a level isn't too bad, though, since what takes the time is figuring out the puzzle in the first place. In fact, there are few time restraints, useful as many solutions require thoughtful observation, as well as lateral thinking.

Despite the cartoon appearance, it's a game younger kids will find difficult, although up to three extra players can join in to a lesser degree, using their remote as a pointer to make suggestions – which can seriously clutter the screen and make moving around pretty confusing. Still, it's a valuable option in that it's an easy way for non-gamers to become involved. One of the first games to really push the Wii remote envelope, since it's not a platformer, it rewards brains rather than dextrous jumps and spins. Rewards are actually given in the form of points at each bit of the puzzle, as well as Capcom-style performance comments, though instead of the "Stylish!" or "Brutal!" of other games, you'll be congratulated by seeing "Smart!" plastered across the screen.

The Players

The Players

Videogames culture has a long way to go before its designers, directors and producers are household names. In an industry as young as this one, though, a famous name is usually justified by some genuinely game-defining work – even the invention of an entire genre. As well as individuals, certain firms, both publishers and developers, have had an equally significant impact on the industry – challenging standards and expectations on the business side as well as creatively. Naturally the list of these industry players is as long as a piece of string, and forever changing, so we've had to choose just a handful to write about here, omitting many who have played just as important a role. Here, then, are some of those real-world players (and a few of their most significant character creations) without whom games wouldn't be what they are today.

Activision (Activision Blizzard)

Developer and publisher, 1979–

French media giant Vivendi's acquisition of Activision, and the marriage of it to Blizzard in 2007 – with the divisional name of Activision Blizzard – were both decisions informed by good business sense. On the one hand, there finally existed a rival to Electronic Arts in depth and breadth, with a host of worldwide development studios producing triple-A titles that ranged from Blizzard's own *World of Warcraft* (see p.216) and StarCraft to Activision's *Call of Duty* (see p.32) and *Guitar Hero* (see p.104) franchises. On the other hand, and despite the associated irony of creating a conglomerate, they had an eye fixed firmly on being associated with the history of independent gaming development.

Founded in 1979 by David Crane, Larry Kaplan, Alan Miller and Bob Whitehead, Activision was created as the world's first third-party game developer and publisher and was the result of the so-called Gang of Four's dissatisfaction with former employer Atari. At that point, they calculated, their work was responsible for over fifty percent of their former employer's multi-million-dollar income and yet were refused even an in-game credit, let alone any kind of royalty ("You are no more important to Atari than the person on the assembly line who puts the cartridges in the box" is how Atari's then-president put it, according to Crane). They weren't alone in this dissatisfaction – the first known videogame Easter Egg (Atari's *Adventure*, in which developer Warren Robinett secreted his name) appeared the same year. But putting aside such in-game rebellion, the Gang of Four were the first to actively pursue the concept of developer-as-author. Their initial success, which included 1982's genre-defining *Pitfall!*, was outstanding, encouraging the establishment of other independent developers such as Electronic Arts (see p.230).

Pitfall!

Atari 2600, Atari 5200, Atari 8-bit, Colecovision, C64, Intellivision; Activision; 1982

Without *Pitfall!*, there would be no *Prince of Persia*. Without *Prince of Persia*, there would be no *Tomb Raider*. Without Lara Croft, mainstream acceptance of videogaming would be about ten years behind where it is today. So, here you guide Pitfall Harry through a jungle littered with hazards: jump over quicksand and swing on vines over tar pits whilst avoiding rolling logs and scorpions. As far as gamers were concerned, designer David Crane need never do another day's work to justify his existence.

By 1983, with sales of over $60 million, the company had found the financial muscle to start buying up other, smaller outfits. But the videogame crash of 1984 was to take its toll on Activision as much as everyone else, with its fresh purchases leaving the company rather less financially secure than imagined.

The resultant fallout was bad for Activision but wasn't to the detriment of gaming as a whole. Kaplan, for one, returned to Atari; Miller and Whitehead left to form Accolade, pretty much going back to Activision's original fight-the-system roots; whilst others would leave to form Acclaim. A merger with Infocom in the following years was partly responsible for continuing reduced returns, and disagreements with a new CEO encouraged Crane to jump ship in 1988, when he co-formed Absolute Entertainment. The CEO then changed the company's name to Mediagenic, an attempt to broaden their product palette to encompass business-solutions software. This, and a subsequent relocation, proved so misguided that the company had to file for bankruptcy in 1992 – at which point saviour Bobby Kotick stepped into the breach.

The company soon returned its focus to games and games alone, with 1994's *Return to Zork* sign-posting a complete reversal of fortunes for Kotick's Activision. A slew of great, bestselling titles followed, among them the *Quake* (see p.37) and *Mechwarrior* series, as well as one-off hits like *Interstate '76* (1997). Their success buoyed up a new raft of independent acquisitions, this time successful, which included Raven, Neversoft, Infinity Ward, Treyarch and Bizarre Creations, meaning the Activision name, once synonymous with the golden age of 1980s videogaming, was again at the forefront of games publishing. In 2002, *Fortune* magazine ranked Kotick among the fifty richest people under forty years of age; and by mid-2007, even before Vivendi's purchase, the company was quoted as receiving nearly $20 million more sales income than EA.

Like EA, however, this massive profit may have come at a human cost, with the fallout from the EA Spouse affair (see p.231) extending to the vast holding company that Activision had effectively become. This took the form of a class action filed against it in

2006 over disputed large amounts of unpaid overtime worked by employees. The case was still to be resolved at the time of writing, but whatever the outcome, the days of Activision playing David to the industry's Goliath have certainly gone.

BioWare

Developer, 1995–

Perhaps it's something to do with being founded by three medical doctors with (presumably) good bedside manners, but BioWare's RPGs, its staple area of development, have always been amongst the genre's more human titles. Even its first game, the action-oriented mech-based *Shattered Steel* (1996), had elements that were to feature strongly in BioWare releases thereafter. These included a strong narrative, considered dialogue and a real sense of belonging within its imaginary world; this was achieved through unprecedented levels of detail.

But RPGs were what had kept Canadians Ray Muzyka, Greg Zeschuk, and Augustine Yip going through medical school, and it was to these that they turned their hands in 1995 with the formation of BioWare. Even before *Shattered Steel* was finished, they were hard at work developing the little-known *Battle: Infinity*, whose driving force, the real-time Infinity Engine, so impressed Interplay that the publisher quickly handed them their recently acquired AD&D rights in order to produce *Baldur's Gate* (see p.58).

By this time, Yip had returned to medicine, but *Baldur's Gate* put BioWare firmly on the PC's RPG map, with the game and its sequel enjoying widespread acclaim. Not only that, but the Infinity Engine was picked up and put to good use by third-party developers on bestselling titles such as *Planescape: Torment* (see p.83) and the *Icewind Dale* saga. BioWare's subsequent *Neverwinter Nights* series (published in 2002 by Atari, after the demise of Interplay), was also a big critical hit, though where *Baldur's Gate* had distinguished itself from the pack in both gameplay and visuals, *Neverwinter* initially suffered for its rather lacklustre single-player campaign and for looking rather similar to Microsoft's contemporary *Dungeon Siege*. The former issue, at least, was resolved in part by shipping the game with its editing tools, allowing the modding community to swiftly plug the gaps, while the multiplayer aspect positively flirted with being an MMORPG.

A brief change of focus in 2000 had seen the release of the cross-platform beat-'em-up-cum-third-person-shooter *MDK*, which made a few waves for the sheer speed of its gameplay, but it was the switch in tactics to developing RPGs on consoles that got gamers really excited. Whereas Japanese games in this genre had a long history of being developed for this platform (see p.23), the PC's dominance of Western-style RPGs was widely regarded as having skewed expectations of what they should comprise, and consoles were traditionally seen as the less capable platform. Between them, Bethesda's *Elder Scrolls III: Morrowind* (precursor to *Oblivion*, see p.78) and BioWare's *Star Wars: Knights of the Old Republic* (see overleaf) proved doubters wrong. But while Bethesda made real a long-hoped-for open-world environment completely of its own making, BioWare probably had the more difficult task of creating a persuasive *Star Wars* environment. But succeed it did with one of the best-received *Star Wars* titles to grace any platform, a game that also laid the groundwork for a style of play that would reappear in the first episode of the *Mass Effect* trilogy (see p.134). But *Mass Effect* wasn't the first title since *Shattered Steel* to be set in a proprietary BioWare universe. In between, the oriental-themed *Jade Empire* (2005) had been published, but it was *Mass Effect* that was the first to create its own sense of the epic. The thread common to them all, however, is the developer's

Jedi and Sith do battle in the Old Republic: the iconic lightsaber has to be the weapon of choice for total immersion in the *Star Wars* universe.

Star Wars: Knights of the Old Republic
Xbox, PC, Mac; BioWare, LucasArts/ Activision; 2003

This wildly successful BioWare console RPG, is founded on the D&D mechanics of *Baldur's Gate* (see p.58). The plot, however, is set in the *Star Wars* universe thousands of years before *Episode I* and concentrates on early confrontations between Jedi and Sith. There are loads of characters to talk to, hours of dialogue and multiple routes through the game to explore, depending on your choices. The follow-up, *KotOR II: The Sith Lords* (2004), offers more of the same.

constant emphasis on story, which is maintained by a team of strong in-house writers that includes Drew Karpyshyn, author of several *Star Wars* novels.

In 2005, BioWare merged with Pandemic on the back of $300 million of venture capital from a holding company. This made it the largest independent developer in the world (though with completely separate brands), so it was a surprise to many that just two years later the super studio was sold to Electronic Arts for a whopping $860 million. Exactly what intellectual properties EA would gain from this was only partially clear, but with another rumoured *Star Wars* title in the pipeline and a few scattered hints about BioWare moving into the MMORPG world, it was clear that by making an offer it couldn't refuse, it was neutralizing a huge business threat.

Capcom

Developer and publisher, 1979–

Videogame software publisher Capcom began life in 1983, born from a company set up in Osaka, Japan, in 1979 to make and distribute arcade games. The name comes from Capsule Computer, the "cap" apparently signifying both a container of fun and a sealed unit to prevent piracy, and the "com" referring to the home computer that the company perceived as its main competition. In its early years, like all the other Japanese publishers, Capcom worked exclusively with Nintendo, starting with the arcade conversion of the vertical-scrolling wartime shooter *1942* for the NES in 1985, but went on to produce games for various Sega and Sony platforms. Over the decades, it's been responsible for some groundbreaking work, inventing whole genres, but equally hasn't been shy of milking a property for as long as possible. These days it's one of the most successful Japanese companies in terms of foreign sales, occasionally even producing games that do better in the US than Japan.

There's a sizeable fan community devoted to classic Capcom properties, such as the iconic fighting game *Street Fighter II* and its spinoffs (itself being a sequel to the original *Street Fighter* game that first hit arcades in 1987; see p.227). Other 1980s and early 90s hits included platformers *Ghosts 'N Goblins* (1987) and the notoriously hard *Mega Man* (1987) – Capcom's biggest property in Japan, which was originally designed by Keiji Inafune, Capcom's head of R&D. Both series are still seeing releases, but the original games can also be found on many a compilation disc. It's undoubtedly fighting games that Capcom is best known for, and aside from *Street Fighter*, it's been responsible for *Power Stone* and *Marvel Super Heroes* games, plus mash-ups such as *Marvel vs Capcom: Clash of Super Heroes*, which features a whole range of Capcom characters squaring up against the likes of Wolverine and Spider-Man.

Captain America and co. take on Capcom's own-brand fighters in the classic beat-'em-up clash, *Marvel vs Capcom: Clash of Super Heroes*.

In 1996, Shinji Mikami's PlayStation horror title *Resident Evil* was another landmark in videogames, kicking off an ongoing series, as well as – due partly to restrictive exclusivity agreements with Nintendo – spinoffs such as FPS *Resident Evil: Survivor* (PS, 2000)

Power Stone 2
DC; Capcom; 2000

This is an arcade conversion of a game with a distinctive gameplay style. Multiplayer battles are staged in bewilderingly complicated levels, ranging from oriental castles to battleships with fully functioning machine-gun turrets. Rather than the occasional wall to smash, interacting with the environment is the highlight of the game. There are also heaps of quirky pickups – as well as standard weapons, also to be found are mantraps, sonic blast megaphones and power stones (which create a super attacking version of your character).

Onimusha: Warlords
PS2; Capcom; 2001

Transported to medieval Japan, the *Resident Evil* formula translates incredibly well in terms of its looks, atmosphere and the more combat-oriented gameplay. The hero, Samanosuke (based on the motion capture of a famous Japanese actor), uses his cinematic moves to wipe out the undead. Samanosuke blocks, kicks, slashes and dodges his way through the story, which is dotted with some frustratingly tricky puzzles.

Viewtiful Joe
GC, PS2; Clover Studio, Capcom; 2003

At its core, this is a 2D side-scrolling action beat-'em-up, but with all the flair and polish of a Clover Studio game. The theme is movie superheroes, the artwork cel-shaded and the action challenging. Joe uses the various superpowers at his disposal, including slowing down and speeding up time, which comes in handy during fights and in puzzle sections.

and light gun shooter *Resident Evil: Dead Aim* (PS2, 2003), plus side episodes to the main storyline on PlayStation and Dreamcast, not to mention a trilogy of movies, and numerous imitators. Horror-themed games were nothing new (see box, opposite), but *Resident Evil* was the console game that popularized the nascent "Survival Horror" genre.

In its wake came other action titles such as *Onimusha: Warlords*, the first PS2 title to sell over a million copies, and *Devil May Cry* (see p.76), the latter famously beginning life as a *Resident Evil* game. After a restructure of Capcom's several development studios, the company's foremost creators (notably Shinji Mikami and Hideki Kamiya) ended up at Clover Studio in 2004, where they created inventive titles like *Viewtiful Joe* and *Okami* (see p.153); both men left the company when the studio was closed in 2007.

Using an in-house programming engine on the PC for all its development, Capcom ports all its games over to the relevant hardware for testing – a system that makes it easier to adopt the multiplatform strategy to which the company had committed itself. In the HD generation, for example, the Xbox 360 was blessed with two brand-new Capcom properties. The first, inspired by the 1982 John Carpenter movie *The Thing*, was a snow shooter entitled *Lost Planet* (later released for PC and the PS3), and the second a zombie action game, *Dead Rising* (2006). Nintendo had not been left behind either, with the DS getting, among other things, a series of stylus-based *Phoenix Wright* games.

But this lack of commitment to a single platform hasn't always gone down well with Capcom's hardcore fans, who were so dismayed about *Devil May Cry 4* appearing on Microsoft's machine that they launched a petition. Capcom, though, has resisted taking sides and therefore assured its longevity as a key player, poised to be at the forefront of whatever comes next.

SURVIVAL HORROR

As with most videogame genres, this one's becoming less than helpful – its edges are increasingly blurred, and arguments abound as to the criteria for a survival horror game. What isn't in doubt is its inspiration in movies, not just the George A. Romero *Living Dead* trilogy of low-budget zombie flicks, but also the Japanese horror film movement. The first *Resident Evil* game (see p.166) was heavily influenced by the 1989 game *Sweet Home*, itself based on a Japanese horror film of the same name, directed by Kiyoshi Kurosawa, and also released in 1989. But *Resident Evil*'s not the only kid on the horror block; first came the Lovecraftian *Alone in the Dark* (DOS, 1992), and afterwards Konami's chillingly adult *Silent Hill* series (which first surfaced for PlayStation in 1999; see p.179). Many other "survival horror" themed games have introduced themselves along the way, such as the splatterfest light gun arcade shooter *House of the Dead* (originally a 1996 arcade game), Capcom's *Onimusha* (PS) series, with its hordes of evil spirits, and the heart-stopping dinosaur shooter *Dino Crisis 2* (PS, 2000).

Incidentally, the scenario for the British movie *Shaun of the Dead*, an overt homage to the Romero trilogy, was first played out on the same team's *Spaced* TV sitcom, where hallucinations during a speed-fuelled *Resident Evil* marathon transformed Simon Pegg's neighbours into flesh-eating zombies.

Alone in the Dark
PC; Infogrames; 1992

Set in a spooky mansion in 1920s Louisiana, whose owner is presumed to have committed suicide, you play as either the man's niece, or as PI Edward Carnby, gradually uncovering the dark secret behind Hartwood's death. The game was innovative in its use of 3D, and makes excellent use of H.P. Lovecraft's *Cthulhu* mythos, including forbidden books such as the *Necronomicon*. There's lots of atmosphere, and not too much combat, but what there is can be deadly.

Dead Rising
Xbox 360; Capcom; 2006

Darkly funny zombie splatterfest set in a shopping mall, which inspired the *Dawn of the Dead* movie company to sue for copyright infringement. Playing as photojournalist Frank West, you have 72 hours to find out the truth, completing various missions to rescue folk, fight psychopaths and of course slaughter as many of the thousands of zombies as possible, using anything and everything that comes to hand.

Eternal Darkness: Sanity's Requiem
GC; Silicon Knights, Nintendo; 2002

A masterpiece of storytelling, centred on Alex Rovias, as she explores the mansion of her horrifically killed grandfather and finds the evil tome of the title. You play as twelve different characters in the family's past, from a Roman soldier to a 1950s psychologist. Like the *Call of Cthulhu* roleplaying game, the characters' sanity is affected by what they see; lose it and it affects not just the character but the gamer, too.

Never have so many zombies appeared on one screen at the same time: *Dead Rising* presents what must be the shopping trip from hell.

Electronic Arts (EA)

Publisher and developer, 1982–

The games industry has something of a love-hate relationship with EA. On the one hand, this is the publisher that helped pioneer the concept of developers as artists (its name, inspired by that of United Artists, is a reflection of that concept). On the other, that start-up publisher has since grown into a colossus in the videogaming world, gobbling up some of the most gifted independent developers in the (mostly) Western hemisphere and subsuming them into a corporate culture that has since been rejected by those very talents,

whilst staff toiled in overworked silence (see box, opposite). It certainly didn't help that when references to such controversies on its Wikipedia page were watered down in 2007 – by someone with an IP address registered to EA's Redwood City HQ – it simply announced that "Many companies routinely post updates on websites like Wikipedia to ensure accuracy of their own corporate information", apparently endorsing Soviet-style historical revisionism. In 2008, signs of perestroika were evident in CEO John Riccitiello's admittance that EA had made mistakes and would be allowing its acquisitions more latitude and autonomy in the future. In typical EA-style, however, this was swiftly followed by a (rejected) bid to buy Take-Two, publisher of triple-A titles such as *Grand Theft Auto* and *BioShock*, and owners of Firaxis (keepers of the Sid Meier franchise) and the 2K Sports range – had the bid succeeded, few seriously believed EA would allow the main competition to its EA Sports division to continue to breathe.

EA Sports' vision of cricket is as accurate as ever, though real-life spectators at the Oval tend to be rather more lively than they are here.

One of the odder alterations to the Wikipedia page had been the attempt to downplay the role of founder Trip Hawkins in EA's history, though his vision for the company was certainly in stark contrast to today's relentless takeover machine. An ex-Apple employee, Hawkins wanted to create an independent publisher that would uncover the best new developers around, such as Richard Garriot, and

EA SPOUSE: IT'S IN THE NAME

In late 2004, the gaming press was abuzz with chatter about a blog entry entitled *EA: The Human Story*. Addressed ultimately to Larry Probst, it was an erudite and impassioned plea from the anonymous EA Spouse for EA's CEO to recognize the human cost of having his staff work 90-hour-plus weeks for no recompense beyond their normal salaries. Spouse's heartfelt appeal immediately spilled out into the wider gaming development community, where such conditions were relatively common, inspiring something of a workers' rebellion. Coverage in the mainstream media in the *Wall Street Journal*, *Salon*, the *LA Times* and the *New York Times* generated such support that three successful multi-million-dollar class actions were launched against EA alone, with cases against Vivendi and SCE following. Spouse – actually one Erin Hoffman, wife of a former EA employee – went on to form Gamewatch.org as a kind of gaming watchdog. It's a pretty quiet site, but EA clearly hasn't forgotten the power of the people: in 2008, it loudly proclaimed the results on an internal survey that showed staff were far happier than they had been in previous years. The spokesperson was careful not to overplay EA's hand, though, stating simply that "We're not in a bad place on this survey. We were in a bad place three to four years ago."

by cutting out third-party distributors (a first in the industry) make games whose profits could be shared more justly with all involved. He also believed in the promotion of coders almost as pop stars, and early EA games featured LP-style packaging and artwork, accompanied by the biographies and photos of the programmers. After a name change from the lame-sounding Amazin' Software and an early display of its penchant for a catchy slogan in "We see further", EA's first titles went live in 1983 and included the home-computing games *Archon*, *Pinball Construction Set* and the seminal multiplayer *M.U.L.E.* Subsequent success was enough to invoke a change of philosophy to developing games in-house, starting with 1987's *Skate or Die!* This was also when Hawkins decided to make greater inroads into the console market, especially on the Mega Drive (Genesis) which he felt matched the processing oomph of contemporary PCs. Some seminal PC titles – including Molyneux's *Populous* – were ported over, whilst the popularity of the console

helped establish EA as the dominant sports game publisher, setting up its *NHL Hockey*, *NBA Live* and *FIFA Soccer* titles to become the sales behemoths they are today.

So convinced was Hawkins of the future of gaming on consoles, he left EA in 1991 to pursue development of the 3DO platform (see p.11). Left in the hands of business-minded Larry Probst, not only did EA's habit of releasing annual updates to its sports titles ramp up significantly, so did its acquisitions programme. Beginning with Distinctive Software (later to become SSX and EA Canada), throughout the 1990s and 2000s it hoovered up Richard Garriot's Origin (of *Ultima* and *Wing Commander* fame), Peter Molyneux's Bullfrog Studios, Westwood (*Command & Conquer*), Will Wright's Maxis (*The Sims*, *Spore*), Geffen and Spielberg's Dreamworks Interactive (of *Medal of Honor* fame), Digital Illusions CE (*Battlefield*) and BioWare and Pandemic (see p.226); and in 2005 they bought 19.9 percent of Ubisoft's shares.

Not all the mergers have been successful. Both Garriot and Molyneux left shortly after joining, and studios that have failed to meet financial targets – which have, in the past, been prioritized over quality – have been shut down. That the only other publisher to rival them, Activision, has also built itself up through acquisitions and faced similar accusations of stifling creativity and overworking of its staff speaks to the issues affecting all corporations that work in the creative field, but the outcome of the EA Spouse affair (see p.231), as well as Riccitiello's comments, shows that the hungry giant is at last showing some measure of reflection.

David Jaffe

Designer, c.1971–

Times are changing, but it's still the case that most game designers are more or less anonymous to anyone outside the industry. Not so David Jaffe. An employee of Sony Computer Entertainment America for nearly fifteen years before striking out on his own, he has become, through frequent interviews and his own outspoken, expletive-ridden blog, not just infamous, but extraordinarily accessible to the general gaming audience.

He's probably best known for the *Twisted Metal* series, a high-speed vehicular combat game that appeared on the PlayStation in 1995 and subsequently in various incarnations on PS2 and PSP, making it the longest-running PlayStation-exclusive series. By no means a straightforward racer, much like a beat-'em-up, each driver has their own story, the underlying premise being that a bunch of misfits have assembled to take part in a competition with the ultimate prize of a wish fulfilled by

Minotaurs are just one breed of mythical monster to meet a beautifully animated death at the hands of antihero Kratos in the *God of War* series.

the organizer Calypso. A maniacal clown driving an ice cream van is the iconic *Twisted Metal* character, but they include some normal-seeming contestants, too. Players (and it's a multiplayer game at its best) race around a variety of environments at breakneck speed, hunting down pickups, ambushing and blasting at each other in a kind of demolition derby. Jaffe has been involved in every game but *3* and *4*, which were handled by a different team using a different game engine, and are therefore not considered *Twisted Metal* canon.

The other outstanding game for which he's responsible is the spectacular *God of War* (see p.93), which Sony was at first reluctant to commission, since it wasn't considered innovative enough; this Jaffe has freely conceded, saying that the team deliberately rejected innovation in favour of making a game designed to provide unparalleled entertainment. Crowd-pleaser though it is, one of its underlying themes is the abandonment of family, mirroring the fact that the team worked so hard during development they scarcely saw their own loved ones. Not surprisingly, Jaffe was content to hand his directorial role on to Cory Barlog for *God of War II*, becoming instead creative director for Sony's Santa Monica studio in its entirety, a high-level role that involved varying levels of input into the studio's games.

His desire to create "pop songs", rather than the "opera" of *God of War*, led to the creation of *Calling All Cars!* in 2007, a multiplayer PlayStation Network car chase game that was small in scope (some said too small) and received mixed reviews. A couple of months later Jaffe left Sony to set up an independent studio, Eat Sleep Play, with Scott Campbell and other former Incognito staff who had worked on the *Twisted Metal* and *Warhawk* series for Sony. A significant move, it was however less risky than some other startups, since the new company had in place a deal with Sony for multiple titles, including a PS2 port of the PSP game *Twisted Metal: Head-On*, incorporating lots of extras. Quite possibly a casualty of Jaffe's shifting focus, the political game *Heartland*, a planned PSP title that posited the USA being occupied by China, was cancelled.

Whether he again aims for the dizzy heights reached in *God of War*, or sticks with smaller, less ambitious

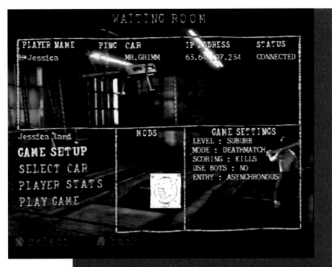

Twisted Metal: Black
PS2; Incognito, Sony; 2001

The only mature-rated game in the series, this one marks the return of the original development team, who invest the game with vast, ambitious levels ranging from standard arenas to a ship- and beach-based level. It's a fantastically dark (in both senses) experience, with an atmospheric soundtrack, stylized menu screens (see picture, above) and story endings that encourage playing through as the different characters. No easy ride, the game also offers a co-op mode.

projects, David Jaffe is certainly a developer to watch (and it would be hard not to). He provides a fascinating commentary on his own work, but more than that, his passion for and knowledge of videogames, coupled with a willingness to express even the strongest of opinions, makes for a uniquely personal take on the industry. Find out what he has to say for yourself at *criminalcrackdown.blogspot.com*.

Hideo Kojima

Designer, 1963–

"No one was home when I finished school. It was tough, I came home first, and had to spend the time alone – which I hated ... I still remember those feelings of solitude ... I put the TV on as soon as I enter the room, just to deal with the feeling of loneliness."

A direct window onto Kojima's emotions is rare. More normally, like his fabulously convoluted plots, you sometimes feel that something might have gotten lost in translation when he waxes lyrical – he once compared the PS3 to a big meal you have once a year, the Xbox 360 to a special weekend feast and the Wii to an everyday feed (possibly a reference to Ken Kutaragi's comment that the PS3 should be thought of as a fine dining experience, but with customary Kojima over-expansion). He has also confessed to feelings of ambiguity towards the US whilst acknowledging the lure of its pop culture, and along with loneliness these are qualities clearly present in Solid Snake: the lone wolf-style operative, composite character drawn from American films, comics and books, who has to hold his own in remote, unspecific places (his closest relationships being channelled through his codec).

Metal Gear, his first published game, released by Konami in 1987, was a hit across the MSX home-computing system and the NES. Regarded now as a work of contemporary genius, it didn't propel the man into the international spotlight, however (and Konami's *Castlevania* series, see p.236, was garnering more sales in any case). But then Kojima hadn't always aimed to end up in the industry, having wanted at various stages of his life to become an artist, a writer and a filmmaker. The financial difficulties of a relative in the arts put him off that particular line of work: whilst his attempts at writing for Japanese magazines were rebuffed thanks to his tendency to submit several hundred more pages than they wanted (no surprise there). The creative urge was strong enough, though, to go against the advice of family and friends, and, after completing a degree in economics, to join Konami as a designer. His initial unfamiliarity in programming the MSX system meant that his plentiful ideas were often overlooked, but *Metal Gear*'s success raised his profile within Konami and allowed him to go on to develop the acclaimed, Japan-only titles *Snatcher* (1988), *Metal Gear 2: Solid Snake* (1990) and *Policenauts* (1994). He's said that where this last game was his equivalent of an indie flick, the *MGS* series is his blockbuster series.

And what a blockbuster. With *Metal Gear Solid* (a title that references both Snake and the move to 3D; 1998) the world sat up and took notice of the man who had piled all his career ambitions – writer, artist, film director – into one of the most engrossing, cinematic and dialogue-obsessed titles ever developed. So much weight of expectation became attached to the series that games he developed in between episodes – including the *Zone of Enders* and *Boktai* series – inevitably failed to make the same waves. But they weren't what people really wanted from Kojima, something reflected in the remixed releases *MGS2: Sons of Liberty* (2001) and *MGS3: Snake Eater* (2004) received in the forms of *Substance* (2003) and *Subsistence* (2005) respectively.

Since the development of *MGS2*, though, Kojima has been saying that he wants to move on from Snake and leave his legacy in the hands of others – hence his decision to withdraw from the series after *MGS4* (see p.138). Konami has been wise to give him that latitude in creating a subsidiary company, Kojima Productions, which allows him to leave behind the political and strategic burdens of his former position as VP of Konami Computer Entertainment Japan. Now free to concentrate on designing games in a truly unshackled role, it remains to be seen whether he'll ever reach the blockbuster heights of *MGS* again – or whether he even wants to.

Konami

Developer and publisher, 1973 –

Starting out in 1969 as a jukebox rental and repair company in Osaka, Konami shifted into arcade gaming machines in the early 1970s and has been a key player in the worldwide videogames industry ever since. Its Konami Digital Entertainment divisions boast plenty of well-known, bankable series; meanwhile, the parent company is involved in various other enterprises, such as casino gaming machines, fitness equipment, toys and trading cards.

Perhaps Konami's most famous early success in Western arcades, *Frogger* (1981) was distributed by Sega, leading to disputes over the rights to release the game on other systems. As for the actual game, it's a top-down classic, featuring an amphibious hero negotiating traffic and then hopping across logs in a river full of alligators, all to reach the safety of its lilypad. It was immensely popular and far harder than its cute looks suggested. Konami also produced groundbreaking arcade games such as *Track & Field* (1983), a multidiscipline athletics game that invented exhaustingly fast button-pressing as a technique,

Frogger spawned onto numerous platforms in the early 1980s and beyond, sometimes credited to distributor Sega, although Konami originally developed the game.

and the ever-popular *Gradius* shooter (1985) with its Vic Viper spaceship. Both of these were converted for home consoles, Konami being one of Nintendo's most prolific and successful partners during the NES era. So successful, in fact, that its complaints about the annual five-game limit resulted in Nintendo allowing it a second licence under a second company name, Ultra Games, in 1988. Konami used this to take advange of the *Teenage Mutant Ninja Turtles* craze, with a licence to make games based on characters from the comic and TV series. In some ways, *TMNT* was a forerunner to

DEATH TO UNDEATH: CASTLEVANIA'S IMMORTALITY

One of Konami's self-proclaimed "signature brands", the legendary gothic horror adventure series *Castlevania* has a long, somewhat uneven history. Diehard fans may well lap up every incarnation, on any platform where it appears (and it's been on most), but there are some definite standouts amongst the *Castlevania* canon, which draws on Bram Stoker's *Dracula* for its plotline and ambience. The first game to appear outside Japan was *Castlevania* for the NES in 1987, followed by a number of sequels, but it was the 1997 PlayStation game, *Symphony of the Night*, that steered the series into a less predictable kind of adventure. Rated amongst the top games of the year, there was nonetheless something defiantly retro about a 2D adventure game released in the same year as *GoldenEye 007* and *Final Fantasy VII*.

The assistant director on *Symphony of the Night*, Koji Igarashi, took control of the series from then on. Each subsequent episode provided new characters, abilities, or gameplay elements, thereby refreshing an experience that otherwise follows a fairly strict template. Backed by atmospheric music, games feature a whip-brandishing vampire slayer, often with a playable companion, who in an attempt to prevent the dominion of the dark

Even when reduced to PSP size, the environments of Dracula X Chronicles exude the series' signature gothic look.

vampire lord, has to fight enemies such as bats, mermen and medusas, and learn new abilities and find new weapons in order to take on ever-tougher bosses. It's a game that's meant to be played in two dimensions, and intrepid ventures into the third (such as 1999's *Castlevania 64*) haven't always been successful. Faced with re-inventing a game that, like *Street Fighter*, is built around a now old-fashioned premise, the games have made a very successful transition to the next-gen handheld consoles (they've existed in portable form since the Game Boy), allowing a gripping game – one that's never been a sandbox, but about exploration of expertly plotted, claustrophobic 2D interiors – to really shine.

Castlevania: Symphony of the Night
PS; Konami; 1997

The PlayStation classic was first re-released on Xbox Live Arcade in 2007, with everything present and intact to fans' delight, even down to the dodgy voice acting. One of the things that marked this title out from its predecessors was the inclusion of more RPG elements as well as platforming standards,. It also moved away from a level-based structure, its world transformed into one that, like *Super Metroid*, involved backtracking and revisiting areas with the aid of new powers. Beat the game and achieve the right ending and you'll be presented with a whole new, upside-down castle to play through, doubling the size of the game and giving a new meaning to the term "replay value".

Castlevania: Portrait of Ruin
DS; Konami; 2006

The second DS title after *Dawn of Sorrow*, *Portrait of Ruin* takes place during World War II. Dracula's timeline (which Koji Igarashi has said he regrets making public) means an appearance around every 100 years. Two characters battle to prevent his resurrection, the regular slayer, using the regular whip, plus a spellcasting girl; all this and additional worlds reachable through portraits in Drac's castle. One of the best, though least exciting benefits of the DS is that a map remains conveniently onscreen at all times.

Castlevania: The Dracula X Chronicles
PSP; Konami; 2007

This is essentially the 3D reworking of a very old game, *Rondo of Blood*, which was only released in its original form in Japan for the PC Engine. Though it looks fantastic, it's somewhat strange to play a 2D game in 3D – even getting onto the staircases feels peculiar at first. However, there's more to the UMD than meets the eye: it actually contains three games, though you need to get through a few levels before you can access the unlockable and much more difficult original version of *Rondo*; plus yet another revision of *Symphony of the Night*, which in story terms is the sequel to *Rondo of Blood*.

the company's successful exploitation of the *Yu-Gi-Oh!* franchise today, producing games based on material originating in manga and anime.

As the console market became a three-way race, Konami developed a closer relationship with Sony, whose technology it used in some of its arcade machines, and it was for the PlayStation that some highly successful series made their debut. One example, though it drew on previous soccer games in Konami's catalogue, was *Winning Eleven* (first booted in 1995), long prefaced by *World Soccer* in North America, but now called *Pro Evolution Soccer* there as in most territories. The only significant competitor to EA's *FIFA* football franchise, it's never benefited from the latter's glossy representation of real players and teams, but is considered to evoke the feel of football more accurately (see p.157). Bigger than that, even, was Hideo Kojima's 1998 *Metal Gear Solid* (albeit technically a sequel; see p.234), while seeking to grab a bit of Capcom's dominance in the survival horror genre, *Silent Hill* (1999) managed to thoroughly trump *Resident Evil* in the psychological terror stakes.

Back in the arcades, Konami proved to be an innovator with both software and hardware, inventing a new style of gaming with its Bemani titles, products of an internal studio whose work started with *Beatmania* (1997), a rhythm music game featuring a DJ's turntable and keyboard. Going through numerous incarnations, it's influenced many a music-themed game, not least *Guitar Hero* (see p.104). Bemani games reached their undeniable peak of international fame in *Dance Dance Revolution* (1998), the start of a long-running series of arcade and home-console games played using a dance mat, which have encompassed every imaginable musical genre and theme, infiltrating the media way beyond expectation (see p.277).

In 2005 Konami underwent a restructure and bought *Bomberman* developer Hudson Soft, giving it another big name to add to the pile. Even though it has a host of reliable names with which to conjure games in the HD era – including the never-ending hit series *Castlevania* – and, like Capcom, has sensibly opted to work with Sony, Nintendo and Microsoft, it's to be hoped that sooner or later a new, worldbeating series will emerge from the company that over the years has published so many classic games.

LucasArts

Developer and publisher, 1982–

George Lucas's filmmaking empire entered the games business in 1982, with a project looking into the capabilities of Atari's computers, presumably with an eye to the potential afforded by the success of the first two *Star Wars* movies and more recent *Raiders of the Lost Ark*. Lucasfilm Games, as it was then known, wouldn't make its own *Star Wars* game for many years; perhaps not so surprising, considering the catastrophe that was the *E.T.* game (see p.7). In subsequent years, as Lucasfilm and its subsidiaries remained at the forefront of video, sound and special effects technology, developing ever more sophisticated CGI, games would become a vital, and lucrative, movie marketing tool. Back in the early 1980s, though, Lucasfilm licensed Atari and others to produce arcade and home computer games based on its film franchises, setting out instead to create new and original titles.

After the unmemorable first-person football game *BallBlazer* and space actioner *Rescue on Fractalus*, both published by Atari in 1984, Lucasfilm Games established itself at the head of a new genre – the graphical adventure game. This was spearheaded by self-published titles like Ron Gilbert's *Maniac Mansion* (1987), a point-and-click comedy-horror game for the home computers of the time, whose development included the invention of SCUMM (see p.143), and

which inspired a three-season-long TV show (plus a 1993 sequel, *Day of the Tentacle*). Gilbert went on to produce the groundbreaking *The Secret of Monkey Island* (1990), followed by *Monkey Island 2: LeChuck's Revenge* (see p.141), which again broke new technical ground with its iMuse engine, allowing in-game music to change, depending on the player's actions.

The first actual Lucasfilm spinoff would stick with the genre, with the point-and-click *Indiana Jones and the Last Crusade* in 1989, followed in 1992 by Hal Barwood's *Indiana Jones and the Fate of Atlantis*, an original premise with such a great script that it sparked rumours of a film spinoff; the next Indy film–game tie-in wouldn't be until 2008's *Kingdom of the Crystal Skull*. Meanwhile, the company's last great adventure title was 1998's *Grim Fandango* (see p.103), after which the genre appeared to fade away with the arrival of 3D. At that point LucasArts' focus was taken up, like its parent company's, with the prequel trilogy of *Star Wars* movies, beginning in 1999 with the release of *Star Wars Episode I: The Phantom Menace*. Although LucasArts' first *Star Wars* game as developer had been a side-scrolling platformer for the NES based on *A New Hope*, the franchise was then – as it is now – licensed to a number of other companies, resulting in games of varying quality. Until 2001, by far the most highly regarded was the outstanding *X-Wing* series for the PC (1993 onwards), developed by the same team (Larry Holland's Totally Games) responsible for LucasArt's excellent World War II air combat sims for PC: *Battlehawks 1942* (1988), *Their Finest Hour: Battle of Britain* (1989), and *Secret Weapons of the Luftwaffe* (1991), each set in a different battle theatre and each as historically impeccable as the others, boasting giant manuals to prove it.

No matter that the *Star Wars* prequels disappointed many hardcore fans, for a while the world went *Star Wars* crazy anyway and LucasArts put out a slew of

Indiana Jones and the Fate of Atlantis
Amiga, PC, Mac; LucasArts; 1992

A stay-up-all-night game, *Fate of Atlantis* is a brilliantly written puzzle-cum-action game, with a fork at one point allowing you to choose the path of puzzles, fighting, or a collaboration between Indy and his glam cohort Sophia (though you need to do all three to beat the game). In search of Atlantis, our hero crosses the globe in 256 colours, with settings ranging from Indy's university office to Atlantis itself. A (whip-) cracking adventure all around and one of the few games to feature a feisty crab.

Star Wars Rogue Squadron II: Rogue Leader
GC; Factor 5, LucasArts; 2001

Follow-up to the N64 game and the spiritual successor to the massively successful PC-only *X-Wing* series, allowing console owners to fly X-wings, Y-wings, even the *Millennium Falcon* itself in an superbly atmospheric arcade-style space shooter. The ten missions mainly from the original trilogy (including the Death Star) have you play as Luke Skywalker or Wedge Antilles, with the medals awarded opening up additional missions plus DVD-style extras.

Star Wars: Battlefront 2
PS2, Xbox, PC; Pandemic Studios, LucasArts; 2005

Battlefield-style squad-based shooting game set not in World War II but on snowy Hoth, lush Endor or swampy Degobah – in fact a full six movies' worth of locations – this is one of the bestselling games with the *Star Wars* name on it. Just a year after the first *Star Wars Battlefront* game, it filled out the gaps in what was already a decent experience, offering space combat too, though not as in-depth as say *X-Wing Alliance*. As you'd expect for a game like this, multiplayer is really where it's at.

games on the back of the films, ranging from the dismal *Obi-Wan* (Xbox, 2001) to the superb *Rogue Squadron* series (see below). In 2003 fans even got a chance to roleplay during the Galactic Civil War, thanks to the first *Star Wars Galaxies* game, a PC-only MMORPG produced by Sony. The following year, a company shakeup meant redundancies and a number of cancelled projects, including the sequel to the 1993 hit *Sam & Max Hit the Road*, a satirical adventure game starring the crime-fighting animal duo. The team who had been working on the game formed a new company, Telltale Games, with the aim of revitalizing the adventure genre; and it has done just that, with *Sam & Max* released in episodic form for PC download and compiled on disc for the Wii. Around this time even LucasArts' *Star Wars* games were ramped downwards for a while, though highlights from other developers included BioWare's *Knights of the Old Republic* RPG (see p.226).

A one-on-one wookiee–stormtrooper encounter takes place in one of *Star Wars: Battlefront 2*'s many ship-based settings.

As a publisher LucasArts has successfully straddled various genres, from the realistic shooter *Mercenaries* (Pandemic Studios, 2005) to *Lego Star Wars* (see p.126) and *Indiana Jones*, though the *Star Wars* brand is probably enough in itself to have carved out a prominent place in videogames history. All the more interesting, then, that as a developer, the LucasArts name is for many still synonymous with classic adventure games of the 1980s and 90s.

Mario

Intergalactic superstar, 1980–

Nintendo's mascot, the stout, heroic plumber who after nearly thirty years in the business is more famous than most movie stars, has starred in well over a hundred games in his own right, as well as making numerous guest appearances. In fact, every new console except the GameCube has launched on the

wings of a new Mario platform game, and although these represent the quintessential Mario experience – and a large slice of Nintendo's earnings – he's not been shy in venturing into other genres, too.

His earliest appearance was as the protagonist known as Jump-Man in the world's first platform game, *Donkey Kong* (arcade, 1980), in which he had to make his way up girders, jumping barrels, to the top of the screen to rescue his girlfriend Pauline from the gorilla. Ever since, Mario has sported the same cap, gloves, overalls and moustache. The number of pixels might have changed, but the fashion statement hasn't, even though these features originated as a means to demarcate the character's hands and mouth – and not have to deal with hair – when detailed features were an impossibility. But if anyone in the videogames industry values tradition as much as it does innovation, it's Nintendo, and so the moustache has stayed, becoming the butt of plenty of jokes (in *Super Paper Mario*). Elsewhere, the cap and overalls are abandoned only temporarily, to be replaced with super-powered items of clothing.

Donkey Kong filtered down to the Game & Watch and the NES, and spawned various sequels, but Mario eventually got his own name in the title, accompanied by brother Luigi, in the two-player *Mario Bros.* (arcade, 1982); this game was also the first to feature the turtles that would later evolve into Koopas. In 1986, *Super Mario Bros.* for the NES was groundbreaking as the first side-scrolling platformer, boasting a total of seven worlds to conquer. It is still the bestselling game of all time, partly down to being bundled with the console; it was succeeded by more of the same in *Super Mario Bros. 2* (NES, 1988). Then came *Super Mario Bros. 3* (NES, 1990), a thorough revision that introduced a less linear structure, with a map from which to enter and re-enter levels; it also had the first powered outfits for Mario – for example a frog suit.

Launching the SNES, *Super Mario World* built on this 8-bit foundation (see below).

Mario missed the GameCube launch, his usual spot filled by *Luigi's Mansion*, and when *Super Mario Sunshine* was eventually released, six years after *Super Mario 64* (covered on p.190), it looked great but felt overwrought and disappointing in comparison with the genius of the first 3D platform game – a viewpoint that was confirmed by the Wii's superb *Super Mario Galaxy* (see p.192). Most of the games prior to and including *Super Mario 64* have been revisited for the DS and/or released on the Wii's Virtual Console, where they're consistently the most popular downloads.

Mario's not just an adventuring plumber, however, but an accomplished sportsman, too. In 1985 he served as umpire in the NES game *Tennis*, and ten years later got to play the game himself in the headache-inducing Virtual Boy's *Mario's Tennis*; *Mario Tennis* for the N64 wasn't just more accessible, it was incomparably more fun, with superb mechanics and multiplayer options to match the best tennis sims of the time. Golf is quite possibly Mario's favourite sport, though, with his first named appearance being *Mario Golf* on the NES, revisited for the N64, and leading on to the GameCube's *Mario Golf: Toadstool Tour* (2003), which features familar *Super Mario 64* levels as golf courses. Other sports to have featured Mario in the squad are baseball (*Mario Superstar Baseball*, GC, 2005), basketball (*Mario Hoops 3-On-3*, DS, 2006), and football (soccer), a career that spans *Super Mario Strikers* (GC, 2005) and the wacky *Mario Strikers Charged Football* (Wii, 2007). Mario holds joint billing in the official *Mario and Sonic at the Olympic Games* (Wii 2007, DS 2008), along with Sega's own mascot and entourage, in a collection of sporting minigames to mark the 2008 Beijing games. His most productive hobby, though, has to be the genre-inventing *Super Mario Kart* (SNES, 1992) and its sequels (see p.132).

Super Mario World
SNES; Nintendo; 1991

The game that launched the SNES and offered the first sighting of dinosaur Yoshi, *Super Mario World* is the consummate example of a 2D platform game. Even now its complexity means it still poses a challenge for speedrunners. For less ambitious players, the gameplay is just as absorbing as ever, with secret levels and discoveries galore in a vibrant, side-scrolling world. It's available via Wii Virtual Console, and there's also a pocket-sized version for the GBA.

Super Paper Mario
Wii; Nintendo; 2007

Is it an RPG, or is it a platform game? It's both, but weighted towards the platform end with the Wii remote used horizontally with regular platform-style attacks rather than *Paper Mario*'s turn-based battles. What defines the game is Mario's ability to temporarily flip the world into 3D; the fact that each place has a double existence is the key to negotiating levels. Aside from the action, the writing is fresh and funny with its metafictional jokes, the characters are weird and wonderful, and in RPG style there are plenty of them to meet and chat to for info or sidequests.

Finally, Mario's no slouch on the fighting stage, doing himself proud when pitted against his Nintendo colleagues in the *Smash Bros.* series, which has appeared on the N64, GameCube, and reached a climactic high with *Super Smash Bros. Brawl* for the Wii (see below).

Even though you wouldn't necessarily include Mario

TEN IN-GAME ICONS

Mario's merely one of the senior members in a pantheon of well-known videogame icons, characters that symbolize a unique gaming experience – even though some of them aren't even visible for much of the game. In the case of older icons, the actual character designs have changed with advancing technology, but designers have aimed to preserve the iconography while making the stars of their games more believably three-dimensional.

1. LARA CROFT Fending off all opposition, she's still England's favourite twin-pistol-firing treasure hunter, whether the top-heavy original (pictured bottom-right) or the newer, elegantly athletic model.

2. SONIC THE HEDGEHOG Sneaker-powered spiky blue bullet with a knowing wink, the 1980s survivor may be getting a restyle, but as visual shorthand he doesn't really need one.

3. MASTER CHIEF For millions of players around the world, the cybernetically enhanced, faceless warrior remains humanity's last hope.

4. LINK (pictured above-left) From a cute bundle of pixels to a detailed, adult man, blond-haired Link returns again and again to don the green tunic, sword and shield of Zelda's silent hero.

5. RYU Hadouken and shoryuken specialist, Ryu is the Street Fighter if ever there was one, having appeared – with best mate Ken – as the central character in every game to date.

6. PIKACHU Most famous of all Pokémon thanks to his role in the TV show, the lightning-tailed mascot is still catchable in *Pokémon* games and has been spotted in *Super Smash Bros. Brawl*.

7. PAC-MAN Yellow munching machine whose iconic status is rivalled by Blinky, Pinky, Inky and Clyde, probably videogaming's most familiar baddies.

8. GORDON FREEMAN Bespectacled former physicist and the epitome of the silent, first-person protagonist as he heads up the resistance in an alien-occupied world run by Black Mesa's military-industrial complex.

9. SOLID SNAKE (pictured left) Ruggedly ageing solo operative who's just as handy with a gun, a strange nuclear device or a cardboard box.

10. THE PRINCE (pictured top-right) Tiny but tireless when it comes to katamari-rolling.

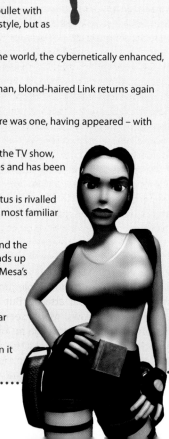

in the same sentence as, say, Cloud Strife, he's acquitted himself well in a handful of none-too-serious RPGs. The SNES had the first, unremarkable *Super Mario RPG* in 1996, which was followed by the N64's *Paper Mario* in 2001, which ingeniously put a paper-thin 2D Mario into a 3D environment. It featured the turn-based combat, hit points and usual paraphernalia of standard Japanese RPGs of the time, coupled with a funny script and the inimitable Mario personality. The sequel, *Paper Mario: Thousand Year Door*, came out on GameCube in 2004, later joined by *Super Paper Mario* (see p.240), as well as handheld titles in the *Mario & Luigi* roleplaying series.

Lastly, Mario has lent his star quality to various other genres, including puzzles (*Dr. Mario*, *Picross*, *Tetris*) and even computer painting games such as *Mario Paint* (SNES, 1992). Most impressively, Mario's musical themes inspired a title in the *Dance Dance Revolution* series (*DDR Mario Mix*, GC, 2005). Then there's the successful boardgame-themed, multiplayer *Mario Party* series, which has seen around ten iterations since its start in 1999 on the N64.

His career outside of games has been equally stellar, with a number of cartoon TV series, comics, and of course the live action *Super Mario Bros.* movie from 1993, starring Bob Hoskins as the red half of the duo. Offscreen, his face has appeared on countless items, from predictable T-shirts and lunchboxes to packets of macaroni cheese, a Mario-hat games rack, and even a shower-head. His fame knows no bounds, as befits a character who in his time has developed from 2D to 3D (and back again), from simple jump manoeuvres to remote-waving spin attacks. But however much he changes and grows, Mario seems to remain at the forefront of imaginative game design: from the first platform game to the first kart-racing game, this unassuming everyman has proven himself capable of world domination over and over again.

Sid Meier
Designer, c.1954–

With a name that appears in the title of most of his games, Sid Meier is a videogames brand if ever there was one. And it's a brand associated with some of the most influential computer games of all time, with *Civilization* (see p.176) standing as the flagship – a turn-based strategy game so absorbing that it can draw in anyone who owns a computer, gamer or not.

While working as a computer programmer, Meier founded a software business, MicroProse, with his colleague (and pilot) Bill Stealey, originally to make games for the Atari 800. MicroProse focused on combat flight sims such as *Spitfire Ace* (1982) first of all, graduating to submarines and military strategy titles like *Silent Service* (1985). However successful these games were, Meier must have got bored writing so many of them, as his next big creation was a pirate-themed game for the Commodore 64, released in 1987 as *Sid Meier's Pirates!* (presumably as a way to distance it from MicroProse's stock in trade). Like most Meier games, it's been remade since, most recently for PSP (see p.244).

Meier continued to work on projects that genuinely interested him, such as *Railroad Tycoon* (1990), a historical management-cum-strategy-sim that began a tide of similar "tycoon" releases. It was inspired by a board game published in the US by Avalon Hill, where Bruce Shelley, the developer who assisted Meier, used to work. The game's US-wide scope was minuscule, though, compared with the masterpiece *Civilization*, influenced by 1989's *Populous* and *SimCity* but intended (according to Meier) to be more fun to play. It was released in 1991 and performed far better than anyone had dreamed.

In 1996, Meier left MicroProse, where he'd long been working as a contractor, to join development studio Firaxis with fellow ex-MicroProse employees Jeff Briggs and Brian Reynolds. It was Reynolds who primarily designed the follow-up, *Civ 2* (1996), while Meier focused on new properties, such as the Civil War sim *Sid Meier's Gettysburg!* (1997). Reynolds was also largely responsible for the speculative sequel to *Civ*, *Alpha Centauri*, a space colonization game published in 1999.

Firaxis was bought by 2K Games in 2005, but Meier's company continues to develop new versions of his games, re-inventing them to take in new technology, while responding to the growing videogame market by giving them more global appeal. Most recently, the company has brought the quintessential PC game to a new console audience, an ambitious plan that's meant a complete re-envisioning of *Civilization*. Released in 2008 in versions for the Xbox 360, PS3 and DS, *Civilization Revolution* is a much speedier game that takes a fraction of the time to complete. Firaxis's maxim is to make "Games That Stand the Test of Time", and it seems that's exactly what they do.

In its most recent incarnation *Sid Meier's Pirates!* boasts a level of animated graphics that was unimaginable when the game debuted in 1987.

Sid Meier's Pirates!
PC, Xbox, PSP; Firaxis, Atari; 2004

This is a swashbuckling adventure/ strategy/sim in glorious 3D. Playing through the career of a pirateer in the Caribbean, you'll be engaging in ship-to-ship battles and sword fighting, wiping out other pirates while pacifying the region's political powers, and collecting lots of treasure. More repetitive than it sounds, it's especially suited to the short-attention-span PSP.

Sid Meier's Railroads!
PC; Firaxis, 2K Games; 2006

Another addictive iteration of an old game, although slightly simplified from previous versions. In the original *Railroad Tycoon* you had to build and maintain a railroad network across the nineteenth-century US, but more recent versions have allowed Europeans to travel by train too. Like most strategy-sim games, it can be as complex as you want to make it, offering a choice of era, and a variety of challenges, both fictional and real.

Shigeru Miyamoto

Designer, Nintendo, 1952–

Miyamoto-san captured alongside his most enduring creation.

He's regularly described as videogames' Steven Spielberg or Walt Disney, but comparing Nintendo's chief designer and general manager with the giants of children's filmmaking is ultimately futile. True, one of the characters he created is probably better known than Mickey Mouse, and yes, his games appeal to children and adults, just like *ET*, and he's probably won as many, if not more, respective industry awards than Spielberg, but these comparisons are superficial at best. More than anyone, Shigeru Miyamoto knows the difference between games and cartoons or movies, and uses his knowledge and understanding of the games medium in a way few others can.

Miyamoto didn't have any ambition to make games when he joined Nintendo in 1977; freshly graduated from an industrial design course, he wanted to design toys. But Nintendo offered him a job and he ended up working as an artist, designing console labels and cabinet artwork. When Nintendo ended up having to rustle up a game to fill redundant Radar Scope arcade game cabinets, Miyamoto created *Donkey Kong* (1981). From that point on, his games have been legendary, more often than not challenging expectations and providing revolutionary experiences. His secret then, as now, was that he wasn't asking what gamers wanted and trying to meet their demands, but producing work that he himself found new, exciting and fun to play. Back in the late 1980s and early 90s, when Nintendo dominated videogames, it was Miyamoto who was largely responsible, his games effectively selling the consoles needed to play them – it's really not too far of a stretch to credit him with much of the success of home videogaming.

So, how do you define a Miyamoto game? *Donkey Kong* was the first to boast proper characters and to offer a reason for the player to get to the end – but story in itself is one thing Miyamoto isn't interested in. While designers at other companies are working on interactive storytelling that engages the emotions as well as the fingers, Miyamoto's only use for story is as a motivating hook; after that, well, it doesn't matter that every *Mario* game has the hero rescue a princess, and every *Zelda* game also has the hero rescue a princess. The details are of course different, but the skeleton propping up the gameplay is generally the same. That's because Miyamoto is resolutely avoiding trying to compete with novels or films or manga, say, aiming always to provide a different kind of experience, one in which story, for him, isn't important. What does matter is the emotion released by playing the game, rather than following a story. Beating even part of a Miyamoto game is for that reason tremendously empowering, making the player feel like they've really achieved something. In *Zelda* games, this is done through ingenious dungeon structure, a building-block approach to puzzles that makes the player feel clever and, despite there being no character levels, that they're constantly improving.

Pikmin
GC; Nintendo; 2001

As the producer responsible for the concept, Miyamoto was apparently inspired by his own garden to create this delightfully loopy management/strategy/puzzle game. The action revolves around the tiny Captain Olimar, who crash-lands his spaceship on an alien, garden-like planet, with just thirty days to escape. To do this, he needs to grow and direct an ever-increasing army of carrot-shaped Pikmin creatures, devoted workers who will fend off other beasties and help him fix his ship and escape.

Wii Fit
Wi; Nintendo; 2008

Miyamoto claims to have come up with the idea as a result of becoming more concerned with his weight as he's got older. The ultimate in nongamer games, *Wii Fit* comprises a balance board – a scales and a balance monitor – with a variety of exercise programmes. There's yoga, jogging, pushups and, rather bizarrely, goalkeeping, with more to unlock as you progress. It also monitors your weight and offers encouraging feedback.

These three types of pikmin have distinct abilities, from water resistance to fighting, by way of some lightweight bombing.

to "upend the tea table" – a reference to a manga where a strict father would have the family rushing to put everything back together again. But interviews with the development teams describe exactly how much they learned from the master. For example, the need for every element in a game to be functionally valid – concentrate on the visual design first, and you can end up with a pretty but ultimately empty game. He rarely comments on other publishers' games, but has made it clear he's not interested in making games like *Halo* or *Grand Theft Auto*, which is perhaps one of the reasons he is sometimes underestimated as being simply a children's game designer.

As a sometime spokesman for Nintendo, Miyamoto has recounted his involvement in the development of the Wii and DS, using the famous "Miyamoto's wife test" as a litmus to determine whether a game will engage a nongamer. He's made it clear, though, that hardcore gamers won't be forgotten in the new era – he insisted on *Super Mario Galaxy* being made more difficult, for example – but his overriding aim is to get games back in the limelight, not for their violence or other negative headline-grabbing facts, but as the positive plaything they were in the days of the NES, a goal that with the Wii and DS, Nintendo seems well on the way to achieving.

Mario games are similar in that they're just tricky enough to keep you persevering, painfully aware that it's your own lack of skill rather than a flaw in the game that's holding you back.

In his higher level role, Miyamoto is involved in overseeing many games rather than simply focusing on one or two. He works with all the teams in Nintendo's Entertainment Analysis & Development division, where he seems to be if not feared then at least viewed with a healthy amount of reverence. The joke is that he is liable

Peter Molyneux

Designer, 1959–

Peter Molyneux's propensity for getting publicly over-excited about his bountiful ideas before they reach fruition has wrongfooted him more than once. *Fable* (see p.65), the capabilities of which he promoted with the enthusiasm of a school kid given the keys to a candy store, is probably the most infamous example of him jumping the gun. The final product left many critics only partly satisfied. (Some hoped-for elements would appear, however, in *Fable 2*, but even Molyneux has admitted that just as much had to be taken out of that game as was added in.) In another instance, as far back as 1984, he was so convinced of the success of his upcoming management sim *The Entrepreneur* that he told his mailman to expect vast volumes of orders and even enlarged his letterbox to cope with the expected deluge. The resultant deluge consisted of just two envelopes, one of which he suspected was from his mother.

   Whilst both incidences could indicate a huge ego and a propensity to deliver bad games, neither seems true. One of the most media-friendly and creative figures in gaming, you'd be hard pressed to finger any Molyneux title as substandard: even the highly uncharacteristic *Hi Octane* (PS; 1995), the rushed result of attempting to satisfy the deadline demands of new masters EA (see p.231), was solid as racers go. Instead, these *faux pas* can be seen as the mark of a boundless enthusiasm for gaming's possibilities. This is a man who holds an OBE, is a *Chevalier de l'Ordre des Arts et des Lettres*, is responsible for the god sim *and* goes to the unprecedented effort of apologizing to fans. Given all this, certain missteps can be allowed.

Never one to be knocked back for long, Molyneux founded the legendary Bullfrog Studios in 1987, which among its earlier titles included *Populous* (see p.248). Although recognized as a landmark title now, he had trouble attracting publishers' interest so foreign was its concept. But Electronic Arts eventually picked up the baton, and the resultant hit gave Bullfrog the confidence and finances to move on to a fistful of seminal titles including *Syndicate*, *Magic Carpet* and *Theme Park* (all covered on p.248). Despite breathing life into Bullfrog's success, however, EA's connection was ultimately to be the death of it. Purchasing Bullfrog in 1995 and imposing corporate demands on its creative minds resulted only in sequels to existing hits and precious little new material. *Dungeon Keeper*, a notable exception from 1997, was bettered by its sequel (see p.248), but by this time Molyneux had already resigned, if unofficially, due to the pressure and

Onscreen icons simplify the process of creating a film masterpiece in *The Movies*.

Dungeon Keeper 2
PC; Bullfrog, EA; 1999

Although he had left Bullfrog by the time of this sequel to his original *DK* title, *DK2* executed some vintage Molyneux ideas about sandbox gaming in a pre-*Sims* world. Siding with the thoroughly evil, the game's task is to create a subterranean lair that will attract an army of unsavoury creatures. Having amassed an evil army, tunnel through to a neighbouring dungeon (pictured below), preferably one belonging to some goody two-shoes hero, and put them in their rightful place.

Magic Carpet
PC, PS, Saturn; Bullfrog, EA; 1994

Going head-to-head with *Doom* with the advertising slogan "BFG=BFD" (the "D" referring to "deal") wasn't the wisest move as this completely failed to convey what *Magic Carpet* was about. Those who stayed to investigate, however, found technical marvels and gameplay delights in equal measure, with effects like fog and water reflections coming into play as you flew your magic-carpet-equipped wizard across a world of oceans and mountains. He can use an array of offensive and defensive spells – the terrific terrain-affecting ones were a clear nod to *Populous*.

Populous
PC, Mac, Amiga, Atari ST, GB, SNES, MD, SMS; Bullfrog, EA; 1990

The world went wild for the first ever god sim. You play as a righteous deity who must obtain theological domination of the world by empowering and expanding your base of worshippers and eliminating those of the rival evil god. With a timeline encompassing different civilizations, the tools at your disposal include the ultra-cool ability to terraform the landscape. Molyneux has since said this was included because he was too lazy to plan any set-piece maps: whether true or not, it would've been a completely different experience without it.

Syndicate
PC, Mac, MD, SNES, PSP; Bullfrog, EA; 1993

Cybernetic paramilitaries controlled by rival companies fighting for control of a series of cities (see below), the assassination of rival businessmen, control of the civilian populace, brainwashing and military-grade weapons research: this was *Populous* scaled up in maturity for *Blade Runner* fans.

Theme Park
PC, Mac, Amiga, Atari ST, GB, SNES, MD, SMS; Bullfrog, EA; 1994

It's not known whether being based near the UK's Thorpe Park and Chessington World of Adventures played any part in inspiring Bullfrog, but their version of this most US of concepts certainly started off in the UK. The aim is to build a theme park from scratch; keep the staff happy to prevent strikes; beware bankruptcy; and make enough cash to start up an international chain of such attractions. With echoes of *The Entrepreneur*, it was demanding and addictive, and since it ran in real time it was hard to find a good moment to stop playing.

lack of creative freedom. EA duly shut down Bullfrog in 2001, prompting an outpouring of community anger that was only officially acknowledged in 2008, when John Riccitiello admitted that EA had blown their management of the outfit (to which, in fairness, Molyneux responded "I was a bit of a prat").

The year Bullfrog croaked, however, also saw the first fruits of Molyneux's next venture, the independent Lionhead Studios that he had co-founded in 1997. *Black and White* (see p.64) was a stunning return to form. This game, coupled with follow-ups *Fable*, *Black and White 2* and *The Movies* (see p.182), did enough to catch Microsoft's eye: the US giant purchased the UK's primary independent home-counties developer in 2006. Unlike the EA deal, however, Molyneux has been overwhelmingly positive about the new relationship. He notes that "…being part of a family that truly wants to make great and innovational games is more important than being independent". But whether he'll ever find the fullest expression for his plethora of ideas, which includes secretive projects *Dimitri*, *Project X*, the cancelled *B.C.* and *Unity*, and the long-awaited *Fable 2*,

is another matter – not least because his grasshopper-like mind can't seem to stop coming up with new ones. What is more likely, however, is that Microsoft already has a large enough inbox to deal with those multiple orders.

Rare

Developer, 1982–

When Microsoft bought Rare in 2002 for a rumoured $375 million, it was investing in one of the most respected game developers around, a twenty-year-old business still headed up by its founders, Chris and Tim Stamper, and still based in a British village not far from the town where the company started. As Ashby Computers & Graphics Ltd, the brothers had made a name for themselves in home-computer games, with titles like *Jetpac* (1983) for the Sinclair Spectrum, released under the label "Ultimate – Play The Game". The consensus then was that videogames were a thing of the past, and the NES hadn't even appeared in the US let alone the UK, when Rare won a licence to make games for Nintendo. It went on to create dozens of games for every Nintendo system, including key titles such as 1991's notoriously tough *Battletoads* for the NES, and arcade beat-'em-up *Killer Instinct* (1994, SNES 1995).

Rare advanced to a new level of success with *Donkey Kong Country* (see p.251) in late 1994, a game whose stunning looks wiped the floor with every other 16-bit game around at the time – it had been created in 3D, on a much higher spec computer, and then converted to 2D for the SNES. It sold in its millions, keeping the doddering console going for a while longer, and doubtless contributing to Nintendo's unprecedented step of buying a 25 percent share of the company.

It was on the N64 – a platform built on the same technology that had been used to make *Donkey Kong Country* – that Rare's most consistently successful

TEN TRUSTY SIDEKICKS

Saving the princess, the universe or even just getting to the next save point can be a lonely job. Luckily, our gaming heroes can regularly count on having a devoted companion at their side. Help or hindrance, these sidekicks provide conversation and comic relief, along with a dose of common sense and an alternative take on the problem at hand.

1. LUIGI (pictured left) The younger half of the twin Bros., green-capped Luigi is taller, leaner and better at jumping than Mario. He's not as brave or as jolly, though, so even in a starring role (such as *Luigi's Mansion*, 2001) he can come across as second best.

2. MIDNA The cute, eye-patched imp from the *The Legend of Zelda*'s Twilight Realm, Midna is thoroughly annoying as she bosses Wolf Link around, but as Link's response to her changes, so does the player's.

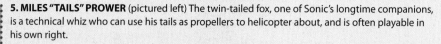

3. ALYX VANCE Faithful sidekick to *Half-Life*'s Gordon Freeman, Alyx is frequently at your side, occasionally flirting and making jokes with you, and of course doing her bit with a pistol.

4. CLANK (pictured top-right) In the series that takes their names, Clank is the highly intelligent robot companion to Ratchet. His role fluctuates in importance from game to game, though he's at his most influential in *Up Your Arsenal*, as the star of holovision show *Secret Agent Clank*.

5. MILES "TAILS" PROWER (pictured left) The twin-tailed fox, one of Sonic's longtime companions, is a technical whiz who can use his tails as propellers to helicopter about, and is often playable in his own right.

6. ISSUN Amaterasu would be rudderless without this tiny master calligrapher there to comment, guide and yammer annoyingly in the game *Okami* (see p.153). Issun accompanies Amaterasu in a bid to learn the celestial brush strokes for himself.

7. DAXTER (pictured right) Jak's wisecracking furry ottsel (half otter, half weasel) partner, having long ago sacrificed a return to humanity, has now sneaked into the limelight working as a bug hunter in his own self-titled PSP adventure.

8. AGRO *Shadow of the Colossus*'s Wanda couldn't beat half the colossi without the help of his trusty horse, but that's only half the story: companionship, specifically the nature of their master-and-friend relationship, makes up the rest.

9. KAZOOIE The red-crested breegul in Banjo's backpack can be of great assistance to the bear, not least as a missile weapon; then again, the trouble the pair encounter in the *Banjo-Kazooie* series is usually down to her mouthiness in the first place.

10. DOGMEAT Dogmeat may have been made of celluloid in *Mad Max*, but in *Fallout* the lovable (people-mauling) mutt makes a highly practical travelling companion for the Vault Dweller. He was so popular, in fact, that he was resurrected for *Fallout 2* and *3*.

Donkey Kong Country
SNES, GBA; Rare, Nintendo; 1994

Miyamoto gave Rare licence to thrill with his original characters, and they did just that, adding Diddy Kong to the mix, and investing the whole thing with amazing graphics, and a very British sense of humour. A traditional side-scrolling platformer it may be, but the fabulous jungly soundtrack and graphics still make it shine on the Wii Virtual Console more than ten years from its original release.

Perfect Dark
N64; Rare, Nintendo; 2000

With no readymade plot to hang the shoot-and-duck action on, Rare went for a noirish future of aliens and conspiracy theories, featuring cool protagonist Joanna Dark, an operative working for the Carrington Institute. As well as the familiar mission-based single-player game, spread across a variety of settings, there's also a *GoldenEye*-style multiplayer game, a two-player co-op mode, and the much less collaborative but perhaps more interesting counter-op mode.

Banjo-Tooie
N64; Rare, Nintendo; 2000

Banjo-Tooie is the sequel to the original platform title, piling more of everything into the mix, with the more or less silent duo exploring vast, varied levels: from claustrophobic mine caverns to a gorgeously rendered Maya temple, complete with talking statues. There are loads of new abililties to learn, stacks to collect, and fun minigames such as avian Wolfenstein complete with music. Witty, pretty, and superior to the GBA *Banjo* game.

Viva Piñata
Xbox 360; Rare, Microsoft; 2006

Four years in the making, its tremendously cute appearance belies a rather complex god game, where instead of a city or nation, the player has to create and tend for a garden. The idea is to attract various types of piñata, and make sure all their needs are catered for through judicious building, clearing, planting and watering, buying whatever supplies you need with chocolate coins. Breeding and naming new varieties of the little papier-mâché creatures is a delight.

Encouraging piñatas to pair up and produce offspring is a crucial part of any successful piñata gardener's role.

games were made: *GoldenEye 007* in 1997 (see p.95); action platformer *Banjo-Kazooie* (1998), which typified the off-the-wall humour and inventiveness of the Rare brand; the 3D action-platformer *Donkey Kong 64* in 1999; and what was essentially a follow-up to *GoldenEye*, the critically lauded *Perfect Dark* in 2000, which used the same engine but with an original, sci-fi-themed storyline (see box, above).

In buying Rare, Microsoft was effectively announcing a commitment to develop new console games (rather than simply releasing PC ports), and anticipation for what Rare would bring out was therefore high. For whatever reason, though, many of Rare's subsequent titles – such as the haunted house beat-'em-up *Grabbed by the Ghoulies* (2003) – seemed disappointingly mediocre compared to what had gone before. A couple of games that had been in the pipeline for years, the sequel *Perfect Dark Zero* and brand-new property *Kameo: Elements of Power*, shifted to the Xbox 360 launch lineup in late 2005, but neither was as successful as expected. The following year *Viva Piñata* (see p.251) was overshadowed by the attention given to *Gears of War*. And despite it being promoted by a kids' cartoon series, the game itself wasn't the child's play it appeared to be.

The Stampers parted company with Rare at the end of 2006, handing over the reins to other longstanding team members. The developer still produces games for Nintendo, though its console titles are made exclusively for Microsoft; ownership of various back catalogue titles is fairly complicated, however, meaning that *GoldenEye* has not yet appeared on either Xbox Live or Wii Virtual Console at the time of writing. Nostalgia's probably got something to do with it, but it's the games of Rare's past on which its reputation rests today. It remains to be seen whether it can still produce such significant (and playable) landmark games as it did in the 1990s.

Rockstar

Developer, 1998–

Rockstar's name speaks of both its founders' history and their ambitions. Formed in 1998 by ex-music industry execs as the new identity for the developers of the first *Grand Theft Auto* (see p.100), it certainly packed more of a punch than its erstwhile name of DMA (which, it was joked, really "Didn't Mean Anything").

Though Rockstar is nowadays most closely associated with the hoo-ha generated by every release of *GTA*, its several studios – all named after their locations, from Rockstar North (in Scotland) to Rockstar San Diego – have actually produced a clutch of wide-ranging quality titles. These range from the *Max Payne* shooters (see p.136) to racing titles *Smuggler's Run* (2000) and the *Midnight Club* series. They have even produced a music-mixer, *Beaterator* (the online version of which can be found at beaterator.rockstargames.com), and stepped into the dangerously unglamorous world of table-tennis sims, with the imaginatively titled *Rockstar Games presents Table Tennis* (Xbox 360, 2006).

But in the general press, coverage of Rockstar pretty much comes down to talking about the controversy, because it's the *other* titles people think of when its name is mentioned. The titles in question are *Bully* (see opposite), *Manhunt* (see p.33) and of course *GTA* – all produced by the studio formerly responsible for (virtually) blowing up cute rodents in the classic *Lemmings* (1991; see p.17). It speaks of what the series has done for videogaming's profile, that a *GTA* name check can become an instant reference point for the mass media, while the game has even come under fire from industry insiders such as Warren Spector (see p.254) for the high profile it gives to violence. But as its name suggests, Rockstar isn't averse to looking seductively dangerous.

It also befits Rockstar's moniker that the success it has enjoyed is ultimately down to a group of individuals with a vision of creating cool-as-hell lifestyle statements as much as games. Whilst the quality-obsessed brothers Sam and Dan Houser were heading up the development side of things right from the beginning, PR genius Terry Donovan has produced for Rockstar some of the most sophisticated marketing yet seen in gaming. As a lifestyle brand, Rockstar's frame of reference has reached well beyond the traditonal videogaming arena, with Donovan stating that the company wasn't competing with the likes of Konami, Hasbro or Mattel, but with Def Jam, Adidas and New Line Cinema. This was something that was backed up with campaigns that used the kind of fly-posters more normally associated with promoting bands. The company's distinctive "R*" logo is now commonplace thanks to their clothing line and, for the release of *Vice City*, a hilarious website written by the fictitious Kent Paul, the vain (and psychotic) former music industry insider, was employed to great effect.

Rockstar's pursuit of film and music touchstones went deep into the actual games too, which drew on a pool of voice actors – from Dennis Hopper and Timothy Spall to porn star Jenna Jameson and music legends such as Shaun Ryder, Ice T and George Clinton. A further indication of the game's place in street culture came in 2001, when a haul of ecstasy tablets bearing the "R*" logo were seized.

Several members have left the band, Donovan included in 2007, but the Houser brothers remained as the creative forces at the helm. By this point, expectations for the next incarnation of *Grand Theft Auto* were already so great that Take-Two (the owner of Rockstar) was able to bullishly reject an Electronic Arts takeover bid in early 2008, arguing that EA was significantly undervaluing Take-Two by bidding for them before the upcoming release of *GTAIV*. And they were probably right, with the game raking in over $500 million in sales in its first week of release. Whatever the eventual outcome for Rockstar, the irony is that the creators of the world's best-known game franchise don't actually own its licence, with it resting instead in the hands of Take-Two.

Bully (Canis Canem Edit) & Bully: Scholarship Edition
PS2, Xbox, Xbox 360, Wii; Rockstar; 2006

Despite being portrayed in some quarters as taking the worst aspects of *GTA* – no doubt to Rockstar's PR delight – and transposing them to a school, *Bully* is actually quite captivating. Dealing with topics long covered by teen movies, and providing an endearingly young perspective on high-school life, adults will appreciate this far more than children for having already lived through aspects of it.

Dumped at a new school by uncaring parents, Jimmy picks up numerous skills in the free-roaming environment of Bullworth Academy, including self-defence.

Warren Spector

Designer, 1955–

So pervasive is the influence and reputation of Warren Spector in games that the man and the myth often cannot be distinguished from one another. Even specialist press have been known to glaze over in admiration during the very moments he rails against this himself: "'There's a tendency among the press to attribute the creation of a game to a single person,' says Warren Spector, creator of *Thief* and *Deus Ex*", ran one completely oblivious headline. Perhaps that's because, as a fifty-something designer and developer, he's had the time, good fortune and better judgement to have been involved, at some level, with a number of seminal titles. The list is breathtaking: *Wing Commander* (1990); a slew of *Ultima* titles with Richard Garriot, on which he also met Ken Levine, whom he would work alongside on *System Shock* (Levine took the sequel; see p.76); and *Thief: The Dark Project* (see p.117). Then there was the game that, if it weren't for *Zelda*, would top many people's best-game-ever list. That game is, of course, *Deus Ex* (see p.74); and it's a mark of his modesty that Spector has never listed any of his own titles in his own favourites list, whereas a *Zelda* title has featured consistently.

Like Levine, "story" is important to Spector, but then storytelling, through the media of sound, vision and the imagination, has always been a part of his life: after graduating with a BS in Speech and an MA in Radio, TV and Film, his first job was with the paper-based RPG company Steve Jackson Games, where he worked on 1984's *Toon: The Cartoon Role Playing Game* before joining TSR in 1987, where he edited the second-edition *AD&D Dungeon Masters Guide*. With the perfect credentials to enter the world of PC RPGs, he joined Garriot's Origin in 1989 and embarked upon a career that would see him become part of the loose-knit elite group of game designers that continues to change the way games are perceived.

His take on how this can be achieved is refreshingly holistic, reaching out into the community whilst continuing to push from inside the industry. Spector is a firm supporter of fellow developer Ernest Adam's belief that games can only develop as an artistic medium where creators are schooled in other creative arts – to wit, "the ignorant developer createth only the derivative game". With this in mind, he has lectured on game design and narrative development in both the industry and academia. Similarly, he's passionate that this period in gaming history be captured on record so that the next generation of developers doesn't "…come to the medium with nothing but gaming experiences to draw from".

These are high standards that he holds, and he's had to defend himself in the past over accusations of elitism

Warren Spector's classic *Deus Ex* blends the RPG and FPS genres, while portraying the future as a dark and dangerous place.

and controversy. He has suggested, for example, that *Grand Theft Auto* doesn't do videogaming's image any favours by masking its amazing design behind its violence; and stated that it's the individual designer's responsibility to be creative when faced with endless sequels and franchises. He certainly walks the talk, though. Having formed the independent Junction Point Studios in 2005, he came full circle back to his *Toon* past when it was subsumed by Disney in 2007. Not only was the indie developer of some of the most sophisticated adult games ever working for the mother of all corporate franchises, but he was now creating games for the kiddies' cartoon icons. Sceptical observers wondered how he could possibly reconcile this environment to his outspoken belief in games as sophisticated art.

Spector responded in typically robust fashion, repeating his assertions that it's the job of the developer to search for the spark of creativity that makes a licence work and to translate it into a new medium. He's still modest enough to acknowledge that it may not come off, though, asserting frequently that "Fail gloriously" is his motto – not because he *wants* to fail, but because he thinks the only way to succeed is to take big risks.

Square Enix

Developer and publisher, 1980s–

"Squenix" officially came into being in April 2003 with the merger of the companies responsible for Japan's two main competing roleplaying series, both of which had been going for around twenty years. Square Co, home of the *Final Fantasy* games, was the name that meant the most to Western gamers; although Enix Corporation's *Dragon Quest* had sold something like 40 million games, most of them were in Japan. Ironically, since it was the merger with Enix that saved

Square from oblivion, the resulting company name remains pretty much synonymous with *Final Fantasy* in the US and Europe.

Square's previous games, such as *Rad Racer* for the NES (1987), had negligible impact compared to the leviathan of *Final Fantasy*. Like most console developers, Square produced games exclusively for Nintendo in the early years; its defection in 1996 to Sony – and the CD format's larger capacity for cut scenes and the like – left the two companies in a bitter standoff for years. Square's last game for Nintendo was *Super Mario RPG* for the SNES (1996), leaving the N64 bereft of a killer RPG, while the PlayStation's first RPG, *Final Fantasy VII*, was critical to its success, especially in Japan.

From *Final Fantasy VIII* (1999) onwards, Square continually pushed the boundaries, aiming for ever higher peaks of visual realism. Aware that its character designs and animation were superior to what could be seen in some animated movies, the company set up Square Pictures, a division helmed by *Final Fantasy* creator Hironobu Sakaguchi that would produce the feature film *Final Fantasy: The Spirits Within* (2001). Costing an estimated $137 million, it was a technical masterpiece, but its virtual characters lacked the heart of real actors and its plot was rather complicated; financially, it was catastrophic. Square had also invested heavily in the online *Final Fantasy XI* (2003) game – playable, uniquely, on PS2 and latterly Xbox 360, as well as PC. The previous title, *Final Fantasy X*, had been a huge seller, although not every fan was happy with the proportion of voice-acted video versus gameplay. That said, it was the first in the series to get a sequel, *FF X-2* (2004). In 2002 a new franchise began, *Kingdom Hearts*, with *FF* characters joining some of the best-loved characters in the world – the stars of Disney films old and new.

Meanwhile, Enix's early *Dragon Quest* games had been released in the US for the NES, under the title

Dragon Warrior; but the series stopped abruptly in the early 1990s and didn't appear again until 2001's *Dragon Warrior VII* for the PlayStation, followed by *Dragon Quest VIII* for the PS2 in 2005. This last game was well received, and is a great RPG in its own right (see p.24), but for many gamers used to years of *FF* iterations, adapting to a new series with its own systems and different quirky monsters felt too much like hard work.

The deal with Enix coincided with a change in Square's strategy, and Square's first game for Nintendo in years was a classic, *Final Fantasy Tactics Advance* (2003). What's more, the company was squeezing every last drop it could out of its valuable intellectual property – not a bad thing, as it's meant a re-release of all the pre-Sony *FF* back catalogue, on Game Boy Advance, on the DS and PSP. There's also been another movie, the thematic sequel to *FFVII*, *Advent Children* (released on DVD and UMD in 2006), a smaller film, more oriented to gamers and more enjoyable as a result. Finally, the company has a mobile division, too, which will no doubt take advantage of the catalogue of puzzle games from Taito, which it bought in 2005.

There were plenty of staff changes in the new era, with Sakaguchi leaving to form Mistwalker in 2004, a studio set up to write games for the Xbox 360; Yasumi Matsuno, creator of *FF Tactics* and *Vagrant Story*, meanwhile, left the following year, having laid down the story and direction for *FFXII*. Nobuo Uematsu, composer of some of the most memorable *FF* music (which he also performs with his band The Black Mages), also left in 2004. But there are still some brilliant creators working at Square Enix, including character designer Tetsuya Nomura, director of *Kingdom Hearts*, and who was also thoroughly involved in *FFXII* (see p.85). As a sign of the company's future, *FFXII*'s worldwide success can't be overestimated; its

launch was marked by, among other things, parties featuring cosplay competitions, and New York declaring October 11, 2006 to be "FFXII Day".

It seems that there's plenty of life left in this veteran yet, and every reason to look forward to future releases as well as indulging an affection for old games in new formats.

Chrono Trigger
SNES; Square; 1995

A last shout for the SNES, this was a historic melding of RPG minds, created by *Final Fantasy*'s Sakaguchi and *Dragon Quest*'s Yuji Horii, with *DQ*'s character artist and *FF*'s composer. The game's theme is, naturally, saving the world, but in this case it involves travelling across different time periods. The hero is a red-haired kid called Crono who teams up with various PCs; the game features lots of different endings, depending on the player's choices. Sadly, it has never been available in Europe.

Kingdom Hearts
PS2; Square; 2002

This is a cute action-cum-RPG that's in fact relatively challenging in gameplay terms, with real-time battles that are sometimes hampered by the camera. But the chance to fight the Heartless back to back with Goofy and Donald Duck isn't to be sneezed at, nor exploring the worlds of Tarzan, Alice and Aladdin, and watching your character Sora converse with Disney's finest.

Jiminy Cricket is one of many Disney favourites with a cameo in *Kingdom Hearts*, an ingenious collaboration with Square: the two character styles seem made for each other.

Yu Suzuki

Designer, Sega, 1958–

As head of development team AM2 at Sega, Yu Suzuki has played a significant role in videogaming's evolution, designing some of the best-known arcade games of the 1980s and 90s. A list of his greatest hits would include 1985's *Hang-On*, a motorbike racing game with a handlebar controller, and the shoot-'em-up *Space Harrier* (also 1985), both of which were later ported to consoles and computers. The following year, *OutRun* hit the arcades: the antithesis of F1-style racers – and an indication of Suzuki's own aspirations – it featured an open-top red Ferrari (complete with girlfriend in the passenger seat), which sped into the screen past scenes of mountains or palm trees, accompanied by cool, jazzy music. It subsequently appeared on the Sega Master System as well as various home computers. In 1993, however, came his most enduring title, *Virtua Fighter* (see p.208). It wasn't just the first beat-'em-up in 3D, but also pioneered the use of motion capture for more realistic character animation, and was so popular that the 1995 Saturn version was released as the system's killer launch game in Japan.

For the Dreamcast Suzuki attempted something equally ambitious, creating in *Shenmue* (2000) what he hoped would be an entirely new genre of entertainment. Marketed as an RPG, it was a long way from elves and dwarves. It had a plot styled more like a kung fu movie, with protagonist Ryo investigating his father's murder in a journey that takes him from small-town Japan to (eventually) China. Much of the game is spent trawling the streets of real-world-style towns, instigating conversations with the busy inhabitants, engaging in fights with enemies, all amidst continually morphing surroundings – streetlights come on as it gets dark, and a downpour means everyone's suddenly carrying umbrellas. These incredibly realistic environments even included an arcade, where you could play Suzuki titles of the past (*Shenmue* being set in 1986). It looked beautiful and boasted enough cut scenes – their direction inspired by the team watching dozens of kung fu and Western action movies – to be spliced into a movie to promote *Shenmue II* (2001). Typically for Suzuki, though, artistry was combined with technical innovation. For instance, in Quick Time Events, which involve rapid button-pressing according to onscreen prompts, designed to achieve cinematic fight effects without the honed skills of a *Virtua Fighter* player. Highly influential, QTE can be seen in adapted form in games such as *Resident Evil 4* (p.166) and *God of War* (see p.93).

Rumoured to cost in excess of $70 million, there weren't enough Dreamcasts out there to make the numbers work, even though around a fifth of owners bought the game. However, some of the cost was expected to be deferred over future episodes anyway (the story was to have 16 chapters and *Shenmue* covered just the first). So, *Shenmue II* for the Dreamcast – a console which had already officially ceased production – went ahead in Japan and Europe. Now that Sega's development studios were free to make games for other consoles, Suzuki leapt at the chance to transfer the sequel to the higher-spec Xbox. This platform's iteration of the game was eventually released in the US in 2002.

Despite Internet reports to the contrary, there's no sign yet of *Shenmue III*, although for a while *Shenmue Online*, a MMO set in Ryo's world, was on the cards. Sega was working on it with a Korean developer, and Suzuki had been reported as demonstrating screenshots at a Chinese games show in 2006. The project now appears to be cancelled, though, and there's been no word from Suzuki since. So this ambitious, epic project appears to have slipped finally into oblivion. Not that this stops a battalion of unsatisfied *Shenmue* fans from petitioning

Shenmue II
DC, Xbox; Sega; 2001

Starting with Ryo's arrival in China, the setting reflects Suzuki's original inspiration for the game: a visit to China in 1994 to research martial arts for *Virtua Fighter*. Many of the first game's flaws have been polished away, with a speeded up timeline meaning no more twiddling of thumbs while waiting for shops to open. There are hundreds of characters to engage with and plenty of fighting, but there's no getting away from the fact that it's a story without a real ending.

With its gorgeously detailed recreations of the 1980s cityscape, the *Shenmue* series is almost as much simulation as roleplaying game.

across the Internet for another episode. As far as Sega – and Suzuki – are concerned, their demands seem to be falling on deaf ears.

Will Wright
Designer, 1960–

Alongside Warren Spector (see p.254), Will Wright is one of the few game designers to frame his work as easily in intellectual terms as populist ones. His games, however, fall more into line with the sandbox-style work of his friend Peter Molyneux, though unlike Molyneux he tends to focus on a single major project at a time. His latest magnum opus, *Spore* (see below), shows a clean line of sight back to *The Sims* and *SimCity* (see p.182 & p.260), only this time concerning evolving creatures in primordial soup. Interestingly, he's said that *Spore* is a truer sequel to *Black and White* (see p.64) than Molyneux's own *Black and White 2* was.

That's not to say Wright doesn't have time for fun: well into his gaming career it transpired that he had once won the illegal US Express race, successor to the equally illegitimate Cannonball Run. He's also not averse to self parody, making appearances in his games as an evil character, and fittingly, in the *Sims* expansion pack *Makin' Magic* as a sleeping giant.

The first game designer to be given a front-page feature in the *Wall Street Journal* (in 2006) and a BAFTA fellowship (in 2007), Wright had already been hailed by the games industry in 2001, when he was presented with a "Lifetime Achievement" recognition by the Game Developers Choice Awards, and in 2002 when he was inducted into the Academy of Interactive Arts and Sciences' Hall of Fame.

The Sims' massively broad appeal owes a lot to the sedate pace of the game: simulated people gently going about their business in a simulation of the everyday world.

Jeff Braun to co-found the tiny development studio Maxis in 1987, giving him the support to endure two more years of banging on the big labels' door. A name change to *SimCity* and an adaptation of the gameplay to include goals saw Brøderbund finally agree, and despite initially poor sales on its 1989 release, word spread to such effect that even *Newsweek* would cover it. The results were a world apart from the initial reaction: not only did awards and plaudits roll in, but even the CIA called Maxis with a related request (though Wright has not revealed what). Sequels and spin-offs followed, including a nod to another of Wright's interests in *SimAnt* (1991). But his next really big hit was to be *The Sims* (see p.182). In keeping with this naming tradition, he wanted to call his next super-project *Sim Everything*, but a need for secrecy during development saw *Spore* suggested, and he has since said that the break with *Sim*-related terminology has been refreshing.

But Wright's early history shows the classic pattern of an initially unfulfilled genius, with his university years yielding no qualifications after he dropped out of three successive degrees. These were all, however, in subjects that would inform the principles of his classic titles: architecture, mechanical engineering and computers. His first game, *Raid on Bungeling Bay* (1984) also prefigured several ideas that would feature in his urban-planning game *SimCity*. In one particular way, *Raid on Bungeling Bay* was the direct inspiration for *SimCity*, for it was when designing its landscapes that Wright found he enjoyed their creation more than playing the game itself.

Though failing to convince the publishers of the viability of *Micropolis* (*SimCity*'s working title) as a game with no win conditions, Wright did succeed in persuading

Wright, who sold Maxis to EA in 1997, hasn't needed to work since *SimCity*'s success, saying that if he didn't have these labours of love his time would only be taken up with building robots (another passion of his). EA clearly recognized the value of his labours though, allowing him – unlike many others – the latitude to postpone *Spore* well after its original release date, and at an estimated development cost of $20 million. But if he ever decides he's had enough of the gaming industry, the robot reps will no doubt be queuing up at his door.

SimCity

Amiga, PC, Mac, SNES; Brøderbund, Maxis, EA, Nintendo, Superior Software, Acornsoft; 1989

Design and build a city based on residential, commercial and industrial zones, remembering to provide appropriate power grids and transportation systems whilst putting fiscally responsible programmes in place (including taxation). Guide its expanding population through time, but beware disasters – from earthquake to a nuclear-reactor meltdown. To keep things from being overly ordinary, Godzilla was also a concern in the Tokyo scenario.

Spore

PC, Mac; Maxis, EA; 2008

This should have been a canon entry, but having suffered numerous delays it remained unpublished at the time of writing. Referred to as a massively single-player game, it sees the player take control of the evolution of a species through a series of phases – tide-pool, creature, tribal, civilization and space – each of which has a distinctly different playing style. With ability to control or influence nearly every aspect of the game, Wright has said it could take 79 years to explore every aspect of it. Someone, somewhere, sometime, will presumably attain this goal.

Evolution takes a big step forward – graphically, too – in Will Wright's long awaited masterpiece, *Spore*.

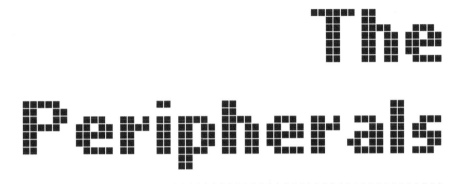

The Peripherals

Peripherals are rarely strictly necessary: not so much the main event as a complementary add-on designed to improve the experience in some way. In this section we cover topics that supplement our main Backstory, Canon and Players sections – the relationship between games and the movies, for instance. It's impossible to escape videogames' seeming obsession with the movies; many a bestselling title is launched on the back of a blockbuster film, even though the majority of film-based games are critically panned. Also covered here is an account of some of the peripheral equipment – some wonderful, some weird – that attempts to provide gamers with a new perspective on a game. Finally, there's our list of recommended further reading on the subject of videogames, both in print and online.

The movies

German director Uwe Boll (see p.267) may be responsible for some of the worst-received game-to-film adaptations in recent years, but videogaming has had a much longer, often inglorious relationship with the silver screen. The link between the two mediums was established fairly early, well before the cinematic pretensions of *Wing Commander* and *Metal Gear Solid* rammed them home. But whilst distinctions can be drawn between films based on games and vice versa, the latest incarnation of the relationship – machinima (see p.268) – has blurred the lines. It's not just about the symbiotic relationship between plots, settings and characters either: one of gaming's more academically minded players, Warren Spector, compares the developmental history of both mediums and sees the industry's current state of existence as paralleling that of cinema in the 1960s. Indeed, one of the earliest formal recognitions of these increasing and inextricable links came in 2002, when London's Barbican Art Gallery launched their globetrotting *Game On* exhibition – which included among its many venues the Australian Centre for the Moving Image (ACMI), the world's first major cultural centre to possess a dedicated gaming exhibition space in Game Lab, founded in 2005.

By the early 1980s, the waves created by the first golden age of videogaming were spilling into the mainstream. Some of the initial attempts at its portrayal were as undeveloped as the industry itself, using videogames as simplistic and formulaic plot devices, such as in *Joysticks* (1983) – a hackneyed tale of a businessman trying to shut down a small-town videogame arcade. But there were others that took the new medium more to heart, with Disney's *Tron* (1982) placing a game at its core and using cutting-edge computer graphics to tell its tale. Likewise, Lorimar's *The Last Starfighter* (1984) used a fictitious arcade game as its primary narrative device, bookending the story with the lead characters playing at the cabinet. The same year, MGM's *WarGames*, whilst ostensibly about NORAD's anti-ballistic missile system, used gaming frames of reference.

Joysticks aside, these films established games as a valid touchstone in celluloid fiction – albeit one that saw them as potentially threatening the status quo – and they have remained as such since, from films dealing with virtual reality (such as *The Lawnmower Man*, *The Matrix*, *eXistenZ* and even *Spy Kids 3-D*) to outright adaptations of gaming franchises.

Adapt or die

The gaming crash of 1984 brought an abrupt halt to any thoughts there may have been of adapting games into film. Nintendo's success in resurrecting console gaming did lead to Universal Pictures' dire *The Wizard* (also known as *Joy Stick Heroes*; 1989), a plug for the forthcoming *Super Mario Bros.* game; but it wasn't until the film *Super Mario Bros.* (1993) that a game was so directly ported across mediums. Despite starring Bob Hoskins and Dennis Hopper, it was awful, though it did at least leave a map of pitfalls future films might avoid.

Movie studios next concentrated on a games genre that had originally drawn its inspiration from film: the martial arts beat-'em-up. Across the mid-1990s, fans of *Fatal Fury*, *Mortal Kombat*, *Street Fighter*, *Tekken* and *Double Dragon* were fed live-action and animated iterations of their favourite game worlds, starring actors as diverse as Christopher Lambert, Jean Claude Van Damme and, puzzlingly, Kylie Minogue. But it turned out that gamers were a far harsher audience, often condemning the adaptations for deviating from already established backstories (the only one to fare well on this front, as well as commercially, was the first *MK* film, directed by Paul Anderson, who would go on to direct *Event Horizon* and the *Resident Evil* films).

Perhaps believing that only the creators of a game could have the vision to translate its concepts to screen, Chris Roberts brought his brainchild to the theatres with *Wing Commander* (1999); but even he fell foul of fans' relentless demand for perfect cinematic symmetry with the digital versions. Interestingly, there was synchronicity of sorts, albeit manufactured: later versions of the game and the accompanying novels would refer to the film's characters and events, bringing the film into the games' canon.

Pikachu and Lara save the day

By the late 1990s, the horses were well and truly on the track. Two of them in particular led the race by example. If you were of a certain age, then you'd probably already forked out pocket money to see Pikachu, Ash et al in 1998's *Poké-mon: The First Movie*, whose five (count 'em) box-office sequels and still-ongoing straight-to-TV releases have made the series one of the highest-grossing game-to-film adaptions ever. It was also the first game-based title to outperform *Mortal Kombat*'s global profit of just over $122 million, with *The First Movie* raking in nearly $163 million. The media, however, remained unimpressed, relegating it to the status of a kids' film rather than seeing it as a successful crossover.

It was left to plucky Brit Lara Croft to show how to make a really big financial splash, if not a critical one. Directed by Simon West of *Con Air* fame, *Lara Croft: Tomb Raider* (2001) would top box office charts on its way to earning over $250 million. Angelina Jolie's performance was judged by gamers to be OK, the *Indiana Jones*-style story adequate, and it gave them a chance to ogle the cinematic version of Lara from an angle other than one that focused on her behind. The trouble was, the press actually paid attention this time because the game had done such a good job of popularizing the brand, and reviews roundly condemned the film as all flash with little substance. Still, you can't argue with profits, and in that regard

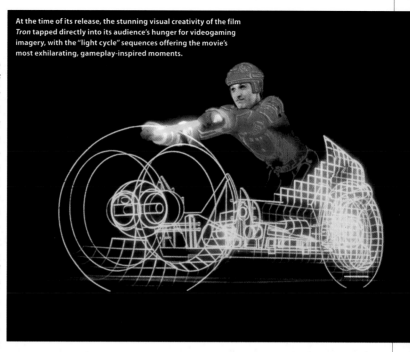

At the time of its release, the stunning visual creativity of the film *Tron* tapped directly into its audience's hunger for videogaming imagery, with the "light cycle" sequences offering the movie's most exhilarating, gameplay-inspired moments.

Lara Croft did provide a template for creating bona fide box-office smashes out of digital intellectual property. Namely: keep the finances sensible, tread a stylistic path already established in cinema, and whenever possible feature scantily clad sex symbols.

Gaming breaks cinematic cover

The same year that *Tomb Raider* was making strides into the mainstream, a very different sort of film, Square's *Final Fantasy: The Spirits Within,* took several steps back (see p.255). By now, however, *Tomb Raider*'s formula was being applied to a glut of gaming franchises, mostly without concern as to their critical

Many of the sets created for the movie version of *Tomb Raider* depicted a familiar environment of mechanical temples and ancient booby traps, and found Angelina Jolie performing the same kind of puzzle-solving gymnastics as appear in the games.

merit. From Paul Anderson's return-to-the-fold outing of *Resident Evil* (2002) to Uwe Boll's adaptations (see p.267), Corey Yuen's *DOA: Dead Or Alive* (2006) and *Hitman* (2007), the silver screen played host to an increasing number of hot babes in dumb films. The director of *Romeo Must Die*, Andrez Bartkowiak, attempted id's *Doom* (2005) and did at least gain recognition for aspiring to move beyond a straight adaptation, but it was universally regarded as otherwise uninventive. Even Christophe Gans, director of 2001's acclaimed *Brotherhood of the Wolf* and self-proclaimed gaming fan, couldn't turn *Silent Hill* (2006) into anything worthwhile.

All of which might indicate that videogaming fans don't have much to look forward to from Tinseltown, but it's worth bearing in mind Spector's observation on the youth of the industry. Almost as soon as a game is successful, talk of it becoming a film emerges, and as the list of titles in development and production companies and directors associated with them grows, so too, statistically, does the likelihood of a successful critical hit. So whilst few gamers hold out much hope for *The Sims* as directed by *Norbit*'s John Davis, the fact that Jerry Bruckheimer has taken on *Prince of Persia: Sands of Time*, that Legendary Pictures, producers of *Superman Returns* and *300*, are adapting *World of*

A LOAD OF BOLL

House of the Dead, Bloodrayne, Alone in the Dark, Postal and *In the Name of the King: A Dungeon Siege Tale*: ask any movie critic what these have in common and they will say first that they are indescribably bad movies based on games, and second that they're all directed by Uwe Boll. A serial gaming-rights buyer, it's rumoured that his box-office bombs are only financially viable as tax write-offs. But what's just as fascinating is how someone who clearly understands cinema and has a doctorate in literature could be so prolifically awful (there's even an online petition asking him to stop making movies). But whilst his films are (so far) well beyond the so-bad-it's-good mark, his apoplectic reaction to criticism and apparent conviction in his genius have proven priceless entertainment: he once went so far as to fight the naysayers in a boxing match in 2006, itself the subject of mini-documentary *The Manoeuvre in Vancouver*. Boll-bashers, though, have a more fitting epithet for the occasion: *Raging Boll*.

Warcraft, and that Peter Jackson has grappled with *Halo*, could well be encouraging signs. Indeed, in 2008 came the hopeful news that Take-Two have signed up no less that Gore Verbinski, the *Pirates of the Caribbean* director, for a *BioShock* (see p.62) adaptation, along with screenwriter John Logan of *Gladiator* fame.

Documentaries

Gaming has traditionally fared better in non-fiction arenas, but it's a far less populated playing field and one that tends to be restricted to TV, where occasional documentaries chart the history of videogaming in varying degrees of depth. There are a few worth hunting down, though.

Game Makers (also called *Icons*), the US show from G4, began as a series of programmes zooming in on videogaming's star players, from Miyamoto to Mario, before widening its focus to trendsetters in popular culture. Their first four series, which ran from 2002 to 2005, offer in-depth interviews and commentary

on the industry from its insiders. The Discovery Channel's 2007 *I, Videogame* (also entitled, more prosaically, *Rise of the Videogame*), is a five-part series chronicling videogaming's development at a level of depth lacking from similar attempts. For even greater detail, and a more anecdotal and tongue-in-cheek approach, there's the lovingly produced *Once Upon Atari* (Scott West Productions, 2007), which focuses exclusively on the people who helped make Atari the console giant it once was. Taking a different approach entirely, Marcin Ramocki and Justin Strawhand's *8-Bit* (2006) explores the relationship between art, games and music as interpreted by the first generation of kids to have grown up with gaming, although it can get academic at times.

More entertaining, and far less concerned about actual games – though it does contain a huge amount of trivia – is *King of Kong: A Fistful of Quarters* (2007). A documentary about the quest to win the *Donkey Kong* world record, the film captures the passions and rivalries of Steve Wiebe and Billy Mitchell through their running battle to either take the title or reclaim it, as well as referee Walter Day's struggles to moderate between them. Day has claimed that director Seth Gordon was deceptive in his portrayal of events, but the fact remains that as it stands, *King of Kong* is the first film with games at its core to achieve overwhelming critical success. That it transcends gaming to become an achingly funny parable of an unintentionally existentialist struggle may well have a lot to do with it.

MACHINIMA:
MOVIE MAKING'S SECOND LIFE

The debate over who's influencing who – filmmakers or videogames developers – understandably focuses on each medium's set-pieces: the slow motion, gravity-defying sequences from *The Matrix*, the camera angles of *Metal Gear Solid*, or the 360-degree camera angles of *300* to name just a few examples. But whilst these were the kind of touchstones that dominated most discussion right through the noughties, a mash-up form had been developing away from the limelight, and in the hands of the public, since the early 1990s: machinima.

The use of gaming engines in animation goes back to the demoscene of the 1980s, when people would use home computers to show off their audiovisual skills. But the first recognized machinima, as defined by today's standards, dates to 1996, when clan The Rangers used *Quake*'s in-game recording feature to create their *Diary of a Camper* vignette. The ability to capture in-game footage already existed, most notably in Disney's 1992 game *Stunt Island* and *Doom* (see p.17), but *Diary* was different. It wasn't made to broadcast the clan's gaming prowess. Instead, it told a simple, very short story using the game's pre-existing 3D modelling and animation options.

The response from the gaming community was overwhelming, and within weeks the broader online community had created dedicated editing and processing tools for the new form of entertainment. Perhaps because of its tendency toward cutting-edge graphics, the FPS (particularly *Quake* and *Unreal*), would remain the dominant machinima platform well into the 2000s, with coders providing ever more sophisticated in-game recording tools, leading to a slew of other short films.

The wonderful *Red vs Blue* series cast sporting the battle armour and gold reflective visors made so familiar by the *Halo* games franchise.

The epithet "Quake films" was initially used to describe this emergent entertainment. But in 2000, machinima.com (see p.284) launched, introducing a term that encapsulated the fusion of machine and cinema (a typo is supposedly responsible for the name – originally "machinema", the accidental new reference to anime was quickly adopted). A platform for the rapidly expanding medium, the website was a repository for the medium's early classics, from *Quad God* to Rooster Teeth's excellent *Halo*-based *Red vs Blue* shorts. The latter typify the movement's roots, combining wry, existential rumination, ostensibly on gaming but which transcends its trappings: it proved so popular that Rooster Teeth turned its sporadic output into five series spanning one hundred episodes, eventually being sold on DVD. In the meantime, other creators were focusing on feature-length machinima with the likes of *Anachronix: The Movie*, which won Best Picture at the world's first Machinima Film Festival in 2002.

Media awareness for the genre rose after praise from film critic Robert Ebert, and again after George Lucas and Steven Spielberg used the *Unreal Tournament* engine to storyboard the later *Star Wars* films and *Artificial Intelligence: AI*, respectively. In 2004, The History Channel used *Rome: Total War* (see p.171) to recreate historic moments in its *Decisive Battles* series (the game engine was also used in the BBC's *Time Commanders* a year earlier). Around the same time, machinima started appearing on MTV in the form of re-enacted music videos, and in 2006 a *South Park* episode, heavy with *World of Warcraft* machinima, won an Emmy. Even the "established" gaming industry began to get in on the act, with machinima being a large part of *The Movies* (see p.182), and companies such as EA hiring Rooster Teeth to provide broadcast-quality machinima ads.

A growing awareness and a similar process to movie making – with scripting and fully scheduled production phases – does not mean machinima is capable of rivalling film. It possesses some advantages: it's cheap or costs nothing to make, the editing tools are mostly free, and it's filmed in real time, making it much quicker to produce than traditional animation. But it's limited by the visual aesthetics of the game in which it's created and its highly dependent on the technology at hand.

The original *Gamer Tonight* was an animated fictional gameshow that satirized gaming stereotypes; the hilarious *WoW Gamer Tonight* episode took the joke a step further and posited the action within the *WoW* arena. See the whole thing at: youtube.com/watch?v=6oMbSKwLWLs

Games of films

The film industry has long treated videogames as part of the merchandising that accompanies any major release, and, as with the films themselves, they vary hugely in quality. Some are just good (or great, such as the Bond-themed *GoldenEye*, see p.95), others simply aren't (or are awful, such as *E.T.*, see p.7).

Like movies of videogames, games of their cinematic parents are often re-imagined versions, perhaps merely being set in the same world rather than working through the plot of the original movie. Or they might try and recreate one aspect of it: the premise of LucasArts' poor *Star Wars Episode I: Racer*

(1999) was based entirely on the ten-minute pod-racing scene from *The Phantom Menace* (for more on LucasArts games, see p.238). But this in turn was based on the precedent set by its forebear, the classic 1983 *Star Wars* arcade game that successfully shoehorned the whole *Star Wars* experience into the cinematic Death Star bombing run. Their best Indiana Jones games, meanwhile, went nowhere near the plots of the movies.

As evidenced by the failure of *Racer*, controlling the brand doesn't always equal quality games (rival franchise *Star Trek* has an even patchier history). Taking a different tack, Dreamworks Interactive, founded in part by Steven Spielberg, didn't attempt to create

While the *Alien Versus Predator* movie franchise has yet to produce a hit, the videogame boasts some genuine shocks, fast action and, in keeping with the original comic books, lots of razor-taloned aliens to do battle with.

a game from the parent studio's films, preferring instead to capture their atmosphere in titles such as *Medal of Honor* (see p.71). Then there are the games that turn out to be better than the films they're tied to: the long-running *Aliens Versus Predator* games, for example, have generally been far superior to the film adaptations of the comic-book series; likewise, Atari's 1983 laserdisc game of *Firefox* was an infinitely more exciting experience than Clint Eastwood's stultifying directorial misstep.

Aside from *Star Wars* and *E.T.*, some of the earliest Western film-to-game adaptations were, funnily enough, tie-ins to those very first films about games. *Tron*'s light-cycle and battle-tank 1982 game in particular proved so good that it outgrossed the moderately successful film: the arcade cabinet version is now a collector's item and sequels to the game were released in 1983 and 2003. Plans by Atari to release a game of *The Last Starfighter* (as promised in its closing credits) were never to be realized, although in 2007 *Last Starfighter* fans Rogue Synapse released their own version as freeware; whilst *WarGames* received two

Aliens Versus Predator
PC; Sierra & Fox Interactive; 1999

Actually based on the comics rather than the movies – but even as a humble game, it's a far superior experience to either of the franchise's cinema releases. Even if no one can hear you in space, you can still make a lot of noise screaming the place down.

Harry Potter and the Chamber of Secrets
PC, Mac, Xbox, PS2, GC, GBA, GBC; EA & Warner Bros; 2002

Both the film and the game confounded Potter sceptics by actually being quite alright. Broomsticks, Hogwarts and magic wands are all duly transferred to the small screen.

Lord of the Rings: The Battle for Middle-Earth
PC; EA; 2004

Not a genre breaker for sure, but marshalling the Riders of Rohan against Lord Sauron's forces in this RTS is pretty cool. Like the films, it's a surprisingly stirring slice of hocus pocus.

Peter Jackson's King Kong
PC, Xbox 360, Xbox, PS2, GC, PSP, GBA; Ubisoft; 2005

Many critics felt the production values employed in the game mirrored those in the film, making this a cinematic experience simply by dint of looking like its parent.

Featuring many of the battle scenes from the original movie (including this epic sequence where Kong scraps with a trio of dinos), the game works remarkably well as a companion piece to the film.

271

iterations, one in 1983 for the Colecovision and another in 1998 on the PC and PlayStation.

Fortunately, the oceans of generally average-to-poor titles pouring through the recently opened floodgates were easily forgotten. *Ghostbusters*, *Batman*, *Rambo*, *Predator*, *Alien* and even Michael Jackson's *Moonwalker*, among many, many others, all fell victim to pixilated mediocrity during the 1980s, a trend that continued into the 1990s with the dual release of *Street Fighter: The Movie* and its game (both were terrible). But the success of the PlayStation and genres like horror survival only encouraged pillaging of cinema's back catalogue, with Romero's classic *Evil Dead* being resurrected as a whole gaming series with absolutely no discernible gaming benefit to anyone. Likewise, game versions of *Scarface* and *The Godfather*, coming long after the movies themselves in 2006 and 2007, failed to impress. With such vast swathes to cut through, then, the boxes on this and the previous page contain a few movie-game tie-ins that not only don't suck, but actually cut some mustard.

Spider-Man
PC, Mac, PS, DC, N64, GBC; Activision; 2000

Spidey single-handedly revived the superhero videogame from being choked by the cold hands of the dastardly *Superman N64* and *Batman Forever* games.

Star Trek Voyager: Elite Force
PC; Activision; 2000

The last good *Star Trek* game to date, this action-adventure FPS presents a perfectly believable Trekker blast.

Tron 2.0
PC, Mac, Xbox; Buena Vista Interactive; 2003

The original was great for its time, but there's no need to party like it's 1982. Highly stylized (as illustrated by this digital diva), incredibly immersive and given a thorough noughties update, it's both original and a thorough nostalgia blast.

The Warriors
PS2, Xbox, PSP; Rockstar; 2005

Trust Rockstar not to stuff up anything that relates to violent movies. Here they dig back to 1979's gang-based cult hit set in New York. Unsurprisingly, brawling features heavily.

The kit

Extending the experience of gaming beyond the screen has always been a part of videogame culture, and the fetish for peripherals has long been catered to with an embarrassment of extraneous console gadgets and arcade innovations. Simulated motorbikes and snowboards, batting cages, a range of brightly coloured plastic weaponry – the list goes on. Some of these elements enhance the gameplay in obvious ways; others are more mystifying in their purpose; whilst a few are simply prohibitively expensive for what is ultimately just entertainment.

Cabinet fever

Installing a scaled-down Formula One racer in your den will hit your pocket hard, but these costs are easily circumvented by visiting the arcades, where manufacturers have traditionally indulged videogamers with pricey and space-consuming gear like multiplayer driving simulators, as well as testing out new-fangled concepts like dance games (see p.277). Never ones to undersell their products, they've also been pretty creative about how to pull in the punters, and the all-singing all-dancing affairs of today are the descendants of a long line of experiments in the name of fun.

Take Midway's *Sea Wolf* (1976), for example, which posited the player as a World War II submarine commander: what better way to view the game than through a periscope? Atari's *Battlezone* (1980), which used basic vector graphics to convey a 3D arena, one-upped the periscope idea by adding dual joystick controls, significantly adding to the experience of being a tank commander. That the game only had one fire button was easily overlooked because its *trompe l'oeil* dashboard artwork did such a great job of impersonating military-grade hardware. It was also a great re-use of a control system that Atari's amazing (for 1976) eight-player *Tank 8* had already utilized.

Other delights from early on included light guns (see p.274) that came in the shape of crossbows and

even bazookas, and control mechanisms that grew increasingly diverse across time. Joysticks with throttle controls abounded and steering wheels accompanied by gearshifts and gas and brake pedals proliferated. A set of handlebars even protruded from 1984's bicycle-riding *Paperboy*. The popularity of arcade light guns, in particular (actually pioneered by consoles), received another boost in the 1990s thanks to games like *Skeet Shot*, *Terminator 2* and the first iterations of Konami's *Lethal Enforcers*, Sega's *Virtua Cop* and *House of the Dead*, Namco's *Time Crisis* and Midway's *Area 51*.

But no matter how fancy-looking the controls, manufacturers have always been careful not to make them too complicated, remembering well the lessons of *Computer Space* (see p.4). Instead, they have gone to town on the aesthetics of the cabinets. Police vehicle-combat game *A.P.B.* (1989), for example, featured the aforementioned pedal-and-steering-wheel combo, but also had a button whose simple purpose was to sound an in-game siren while simultaneously triggering a bank of flashing lights on top of the machine. Other flippancies included Jaleco's *Arm Champs* (1988), an arm-wrestling game that saw the players wrestling with an electronic arm and Taito's *Sonic Blast Man* (1990), in which the player donned a boxing glove and laid out a series of villains (not including, despite the name, a hedgehog) by whacking an electronic punch bag.

Next in desirability were cabinets that came in special editions that you literally had sit to on, or in, to play. Fondly remembered titles in this category include Sega's helicopter blast-fest *Thunder Blade* (1987), whose sit-down version felt like a stripped-down Apache cockpit: moving the joystick tilted the chair, leaving every kid who played it with the feeling they'd just piloted *Airwolf*. Sega were also responsible for the 1985 motorcycle racer *Hang-On*, whose special edition looked for all the world like a Ducati with a gaming screen built into its windshield. That same year they launched the frenetic *Space Harrier* shooter, whose full-motion cockpit felt more like a jerky flight simulator than a game cabinet. Both games garnered such iconic status they would reappear in virtual form in their creator's *Shenmue* on the Dreamcast.

But the titles that hold the dearest spots in the hearts of arcade gamers are the ones that were truly immersive, like the fully enclosed *Sinistar* (1982), designed to look like a spaceship and featuring a cockpit hood that could be raised and lowered. Even grander were Atari's *Star Wars* and Bally's *Discs of Tron* (both 1983), which by dint of their physical design and use of audio transported players to their other worlds, blocking out most of reality as far as gamers were concerned. *Discs of Tron* was so big, in fact, that Bally often shipped it to arcades with half the cabinet sawn off, meaning that many, sadly, never got to experience that full *Tron* feeling. Atari managed to port the experience of racing with *TX-1* (1984), which whilst not fully enclosed did impinge upon the driver's peripheral field of vision with a bank of screens. Sega looked on and learned: their *After Burner* (1987) took things further by animating the enclosed cockpit of their aerial-combat game.

By the early 1990s it looked as though the next step towards total immersion was in virtual reality (VR) games. But despite a couple of attempts the medium never took off through a combination of prohibitive pricing and, presumably, feelings of embarrassment over standing around in public wearing lumpy headsets that made you completely oblivious to reality. Not that public modesty was to stop the success of *Dance Dance Revolution* or *Sega Bass Fishing* – although, notably, both made the transition to the privacy of the home console market.

Controller freaks

Where cabinets have led, the home-gaming scene has traditionally followed. That is except in one key area: light guns. In a not-so-tacit recognition that some genres just play better with the right kind of controls, the first-ever console, the Magnavox Odyssey (see p.6), came with the first-ever videogaming light gun. The concept would go on to great success in the arcades during the early 1990s, but it fell to the console market – Nintendo in particular – to develop it across the 1980s, most iconically with the NES Zapper (also known as the Famicom Light Gun). Sega returned fire with their Light Phaser for the Master System (Atari did too with the XG-1 for the Atari 7800, but by that time no one was paying them any attention).

It was the Zapper that would have the most enduring legacy. Packaged with the NES and a game named *Duck Hunt*, it wasn't supported by many quality games, but its

Based on the design of a weapon from a Japanese anime entitled Zillion, *the Sega Light Phaser looked enough like a real weapon to warrant concern from some parents.*

popularity led to Konami's hands-free headset-cum-light gun that clamped over your head, providing you with headphones, a HUD aiming system and a mic into which one yelled "Fire!". Following on, the SNES would receive the Super Scope and the Megadrive (Genesis) would get the Enforcer, both wireless and both looking for all the world like something the soldiers in *Tom Clancy's Advanced Warfighter* series would employ fifteen years later. Their success fed back into the arcades and duly turned full-circle with the PlayStation and PS2, which supported Namco's GunCon and Konami's Justifier with a raft of highly popular arcade ports. Most recently, "Zapper" resurfaced in the Wii Zapper, which is actually just a cradle for the Wii remote and nunchuk and came bundled with the *Zelda*-based *Link's Crossbow Training*.

In the late noughties, it was Nintendo's Wii that led the way in popularizing the more esoteric controllers designed to maximize a player's immersion (music and rhythm controllers are a whole other ball game, however: see p.278). The third-party sports kit available for *Wii Sports*, for example, which includes baseball bat, tennis racket and golf club adaptors, were the first in a line of extras that allowed gamers to pretend they were indulging in real-life activities. Unlike light guns, the usefulness of such peripherals tends to be very limited – it's difficult to see how a golf club can be used in any other fashion (*Grand Theft Auto* players may well differ on this). Driving and flying games, on the other hand, have long been catered to, with myriad sets of steering-wheel-and-

If you have trouble with a regular joystick, the *Steel Battalion* Controller probably isn't for you; though for that immersive I'm-driving-a-big-robot experience, it can't be beat.

pedals and joystick-and-throttle sets made available over the years, with the latter particularly popular on the PC for rendering flight sims more realistic. Things can get a little out of hand, though: Capcom's *Steel Battalion* controller (pictured below) featured three foot pedals, two joyticks, around forty buttons and the accordingly high price tag of $200. And it only supported two games.

The majority of titles, however, are designed to be played with a system's default controllers, so the sheer volume of niche peripherals can seem astounding, the result of either hopeless optimism or cynical marketing. It's debatable, for example, how many people were really willing to shell out for the *Resident Evil* chainsaw controller (which was, in fact, a standard controller in the shape of a bloody woodcutter), the *Onimusha* sword, a *Zelda* sword-and-shield kit or the Falcon (a kind of 3D joystick that has been trying to supplant the already perfected mouse-and-keyboard combo on PCs for some years now).

But at least those contraptions worked. Substandard products have long been fed to gamers, with a large number of them aimed at Nintendo's products. One of the earliest was their own Robotic Operating Buddy (ROB), whose sole purpose – to extend the gameplay beyond the screen to a mini robot – was seriously compromised by its inability to react to commands on time. But the most notorious was Mattel's officially licensed NES Power Glove, advertised blatantly throughout *The Wizard* (see p.264), whose line of dialogue "I love the Power Glove. It's so bad" was

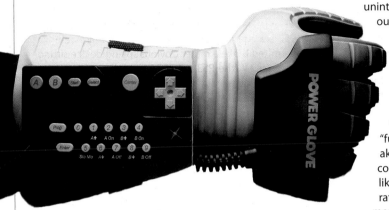

unintentionally right on target. Not to be outdone in the shoddiness stakes, Sega released the Sega Activator in the early 1990s, which they marketed with the line "You are the controller". The result was frustrated gamers flailing their limbs wildly in front of their TVs, though to be fair this truly was fulfilling Sega's other promise of "full body action." In this respect it was akin to another, earlier, hands-free NES contraption, the U-Force, which looked like a laptop and was supposed to accurately translate the player's arm movements into game commands. It didn't.

To date, the most successful mass-market hands-free devices are far more prosaic: the headsets gamers communicate with during online videogaming. True controller-free gaming, of a kind, was achieved in 2004 in a game called *Mindball*; developed by a scientist, the simple ball game is controlled by two players' brain waves. Whilst the big players are no doubt interested in that kind of future, it currently comes with a price tag even Ken Kutaragi would be reluctant to pass on to the consumer: $19,000. In the meantime, gamers with cash to throw around can take advantage of such off-the-wall products as the convoluted Dream Machine or Kilowatt devices, which function as much as gym workouts as they do controllers – though many may feel that to lose the couch-potato aspect of gaming is to lose its guilty pleasure.

The Nintendo Power Glove, which appeared in 1989, looked impressive, but only delivered limited functionality (and it was almost impossible to match with the rest of your outfit).

GOOD VIBRATIONS

When the N64's Rumble Pak brought force-feedback to gaming, no one could have fully predicted how far peripheral makers would go in embracing the rumbling technology. The flood of force-feedback joypads, joysticks and steering wheels was to some extent predictable, but the concept of gaming chairs in the home was relatively new and rather undermined the concept of a discreet console. Now relatively inexpensive, they vary from those using the kind of massage technology found in the Pak to incorporating high-powered subwoofers that impart a truly earth-shaking feeling. If that's not hardcore enough, videogamers can opt for devices that administer electric current instead. Not actually shocking, but perhaps intended to be (although Mizuguchi denies it), was the feedback peripheral released in support of *Rez* (see p.169), which deserves special mention for the uses certain gamers put it to whilst playing the game. It's name? The Rez Trance Vibrator.

Twist and shake?

To non-gamers, any shooting game, even one with a plastic gun aiming at balloon targets, fulfils the stereotype of the violent videogame; there are plenty of peaceful peripherals that are nonetheless potentially more damaging to the health, such as those designed to enable music and exercise games. The ten-year-old *Dance Dance Revolution* (aka *Dancing Stage* in the UK) remains the queen of dancing games, demanding of its players perfectly timed dance steps and allowing little room for error. Konami's disco-lit, booming and flashing units became an obsession in Japanese arcades from 1998, spreading across the US over the next two or three years. Despite the initial cost, they were rarely out of use, and their Japanese soundtracks were soon replaced with US-friendly songs.

Eventually home conversions became available, translated into demarcated dance mats to use with console versions of the games, which were not nearly as glamorous, but allowed even double-left-footers to dance their socks off in private before daring to show off in front of an audience – playing *DDR* well is a performance art, as witnessed by the crowds that gathered around the machines. Dozens of themed iterations later, it's still going, most recently on the Xbox 360, but it's no longer as popular as it once was, perhaps because of its ever-increasing difficulty; perhaps also because its calorie-burning trackers saw it being used in US high schools as gym exercise.

The energetic, skilful aficionados of DDR can probably get fit as quickly as a player of *EyeToy Kinetic* (2005), a PS2 exercise programme based around Sony's webcam peripheral. Like a rather obvious spying device sitting on your TV (the PS3 version is more hi-tech), EyeToy allowed you to watch yourself in-game, with real-time image processing applying the image to whatever was on the screen – quite disconcerting to find yourself the star of a game. The original PS2 EyeToy was famously advertised with footage of grannies boxing, making it a forerunner of the Wii not just in body gesture input, but also in trying to expand gaming outside its traditional confines. Now, of course, *Wii Fit* has usurped the exercise PR crown with its scales/balance board (see p.246), although EyeToy games still cover various sports and dance titles.

The *Dance Dance Revolution Mario Mix* mat, from 2005, was one of many devices that brought the experience of arcade dance machines into the home.

EyeToy has other uses too, including providing pictures to use with other PS2 games like *Buzz!*, which originally started as a music quiz (2005) but has developed into a series with themes including children's quizzes, sports and movies. Doubtless, it would have been no more successful than the quizshow games before it, if not for its iconic red-buzzer controllers. It's these contraptions, with their four colour-coded buttons, that provide its mainstream appeal. As the developer commented, "Sixaxis has 17 buttons … quite an intimidating interface." Excellent as a mainstream party game for the more cerebral type of show-off, the teasing comes as much from the irritating Australian host as any real-life opponents.

Even more off-screen entertainment can be had with a couple of mics and a large lung capacity. Genuine karaoke setups have always been out of range for casual *Pop Idol* wannabes, but with the *SingStar* series (which first appeared on the PS2 in Europe in 2004) anyone can be a diva with a proper microphone instead of a hairbrush – in private or in company. The ability to play back performances (which can be enhanced again by means of the EyeToy) to general hilarity means the humiliation can be stretched out even longer. Karaoke classics like "YMCA" and "Like A Virgin" have made way for the likes of R&B, rock ballads and even Bollywood themes. With the PS3 version, it's also become possible to download extra tracks and to upload your best (or worst) performances to a *SingStar* website.

Long before the individualistic warblings of karaoke, however, came simpler, rhythm-based games. Arcade veteran Sega produced a number of offbeat peripherals for the Dreamcast – for example a home version of Sonic Team's maraca-shaking Latin-flavoured game, *Samba de Amigo* (2000), which came with a pair of maracas and a floor sensor to monitor your shaking position. Sega and Nintendo decided that it was perfect for conversion to the Wii – though the mad-eyed dancing monkey keeps his place, the maracas are forever lost to eBay (sadly, shaking a remote just doesn't feel like *la vida loca*).

Other types of percussionist could get their beat on when Donkey Kong lent his name to *Donkey Konga*, a GameCube game (Namco, 2004) playable with a dual-conga drum with a microphone sensor, which allowed hand clapping as well as slapping the skins to a eclectic selection of cover versions with *Donkey Kong Country* backdrops. If you did manage to get hold of the drums, as well as two sequels, they also worked with *Donkey Kong Jungle Beat* (Nintendo, 2005), where they were bizarrely used to control the gorilla in an otherwise fairly conventional platform game.

As far as replica instruments go, the iconic mini Gibson SE from the original *Guitar Hero* (see p.104) is perfect for playing solo in the bedroom; there's no need for any audience other than the one that comes with Career mode. Still, brought together with another guitar, drums and a mic, it adds up to the ultimate party game: *Rock Band* (Xbox 360, PS2, PS3, Wii). Harmonix (creators of the *Guitar Hero* software), backed by their new owners MTV, were responsible for this must-have game of Christmas 2007 (in North America). It wasn't just the (pricey) kit that made it such a success, but its potential longevity, thanks to the availability of new downloadable tracks every week. With a full four-member band on the go, more than any other game it captures the feel of being a musician – selling out and bickering rock'n'roll egos included.

The information

For a form of entertainment that's outside the mainstream, videogames are the subject of hundreds of magazines and books – mainly game guides, technical manuals or academic studies. Magazines, however, are facing stiff competition these days from the Internet, where news and reviews are able to reach readers far more quickly. As technology develops, so do the sites covering games, from the earliest of Usenet groups to messageboards, from websites devoted to discussing games in all their forms, to gameplay videos, even video podcast shows, and of course blogs. We've picked out a handful of our favourite books, magazines and websites below – including some sites where you can actually play games – in what's inevitably a subjective list.

Print

The A-Z of Cool Computer Games

by Jack Railton (Allison & Busby, 2005)

An alphabetical trawl through gaming from the late 1970s up until the PlayStation, this is a uniquely entertaining and informative read, infused as it is with a British pop culture sensibility. Sections cover individual games like *Pong* and *Tron*, but also include the likes of the ZX81, pocket calculators, and dads (who lost their technologically dominant role to their kids with the advent of personal computers).

Dungeons and Desktops: The History of Computer Role-playing Games

by Matt Barton (A K Peters, 2008)

An engaging, exhaustively thorough history, from the story of early attempts at RPGs to the creation of the genre's current masterpieces, including games you know and plenty you probably won't. For a taster, check out the same author's articles on Gamasutra.com.

Edge

(Future Publishing)

Well designed, long-established monthly magazine focusing on the broader context of videogaming: previews and reviews, opinion columns and in-depth features on the industry, including plenty of technical stuff for insiders (and wannabes).

Electronic Gaming Monthly

(1UP, US)

Wide-ranging monthly magazine with news, previews, features, and of course reviews, which adopt a different approach to most, namely comprising three reviewers giving their personal response to each title.

Game Over: Press Start To Continue

by David Sheff and Andy Eddy (Cyberactive Media Group, 1999)

Compelling read about the life of Nintendo, from its humble origins as a playing-card manufacturer in late nineteenth-century Japan. It's not afraid to look beneath the surface either, recalling Nintendo's numerous legal entanglements with the likes of Atari and Sega.

gamesTM

(Imagine Publishing, UK)

A more recent challenger to *Edge* in the UK for its modern design, in-depth features as well as reviews and news, and dedication to representing game art in all its glory.

Grand Theft Childhood: The Surprising Truth About Violent Video Games and What Parents Can Do

by Dr Lawrence Kutner and Dr Cheryl Olson (Simon & Schuster, 2008)

Much-needed voice of sanity to counteract the media hysteria surrounding children and videogames. Using the findings of their own government-funded study into the effects of games on teens and preteens, the authors (both on the faculty at Harvard Medical School) explain the genuine issues that might arise, and offer advice on dealing with them. More than anything, they advocate better communication between the generations.

PC Gamer

(Future Publishing)

One of the bestselling PC mags, providing reliable games reviews, plus reviews and handy how-to articles on systems and hardware. Its website, along with Future stablemates *Edge* and *PC Zone*, forms part of the CVG network.

Phoenix: The Fall & Rise of Videogames

by Leonard Herman (Rolenta Press, 1997)

Worthy and even-handed account of videogaming history, though somewhat dry and told in strict chronological order, which serves to break up some of its long-running themes. Still with plenty to appeal to hardcore gamers or anyone nostalgic for the first home consoles.

Power-Up: How Japanese Video Games Gave the World an Extra Life

by Chris Kohler (BradyGames, 2005)

The Wired.com blogger's essential work on Japanese gaming, based on exhaustive research and first-hand interviews. Starting off with a university thesis on cinematic games and including sections on topics as diverse as games music and shopping in Tokyo's Akihabara, it's an entertaining read. Particularly recommended for avid *Mario*, *Zelda* or *Final Fantasy* fans.

Retro Gamer

(Imagine Publishing)

Resurrected old magazine devoted to anything and everything retro. Features reviews of games that appeared on ancient systems, "making of" interviews, and a hardware buying guide, all covered with the same meticulous attention to detail shown by stablemate *gamesTM*.

Rough Guide to the PlayStation Portable

by Nicholas Gilewicz and Sean Mahoney (Rough Guides, 2006)

Like Rough Guides' bestselling *iPod* book, this is an essential, user-friendly guide to getting the most out of the PSP. Along with sections on how to use it for watching non-UMD movies, surfing the Net via Wi-Fi and suchlike, it gets right under the hood to look at homebrew software and modifications.

Trigger Happy: Videogames and the Entertainment Revolution

by Steven Poole (Arcade Publishing, 2004)

One of the few books to feature Aristotle and Aliens on the same page (albeit in the index), this is an erudite examination of videogame aesthetics by book critic, musician and former *Edge* columnist Poole. Using examples from past, present and predicted future, the book discusses the issues at the heart of gaming, such as why Angelina Jolie was never going to match up to the real Lara.

The Ultimate History of Video Games

by Steven L. Kent (Three Rivers Press, 2001)

For a book subtitled *From Pong to Pokémon – The Story Behind the Craze that Touched Our Lives and Changed the World*, this weighty book is rather thin on detail when it comes to the world outside of the US. That said, it's refreshingly unbiased on what it does cover (which is plenty to be getting on with in any case), and the text is interwoven with quotes from interviews with key industry players, past and present.

Online

1UP

www.1up.com

The website from the house of *EGM*, although relatively new, is amongst the top general games sites on the Net. With content organized by platform or by the usual previews, reviews and cheats headings, it has a well-developed community feel, enhanced by blogs and messageboards. Its weekly podcasts – which come in both audio and video varieties – are well worth catching, too.

CVG

www.computerandvideogames.com

A site in its own right, with news and reviews of games and PC hardware, CVG is a portal to Future's other games sites, some of them related to magazines (*Edge/Next Generation*, *PC Zone*), others purely web-based, such as multiformat GamesRadar (www.gamesradar.com) and FileRadar (www.fileradar.net), a download site for patches, demos and mods.

"No F***ing Lightweights!"

The Escapist

www.escapistmagazine.com

Online magazine dedicated to quality writing on games and gaming culture, whose daily news updates supplement themed weekly issues. Reader numbers have leapt up with the addition of "Zero Punctuation", mordantly funny, fast-talking animated video-reviews by Ben "Yahtzee" Croshaw.

Eurogamer

www.eurogamer.net

A broad-ranging, easily searchable site, providing a huge database of well-written reviews, interviews and other features, a MMO-dedicated section and a community area – much of which is also accessible at the French (.fr) and German (.de) sites. It's a good source of reliable info on European release dates, and regularly boasts breaking news stories.

Gamasutra

www.gamasutra.com

Subtitled "The Art & Business of Making Games", this is the online home of the company responsible for the Game Developers Conference and *Game Developer* magazine. Unsurprisingly, it's the premier site for anyone who works in or studies videogames, while sister sites include the fascinatingly eclectic GameSetWatch blog (www.gamesetwatch.com).

GameFAQs

www.gamefaqs.com

With its exhaustive database of user-supplied plaintext FAQs and walkthroughs, accompanied by messageboards, system info and a daily poll, GameFAQs represents an incredible labour of love for many, including former site creator CJayC, who retired in 2007. Now part of Gamespot's network, other sites may carry much of the same content, but this is still the best one-stop destination for a stuck gamer.

Game|Life

blog.wired.com/games

Wired.com has one of the best general videogames blogs on the Net, its intelligent yet unpretentious posts covering a broad swathe of games and gaming culture, from Flash titles to MMOs, and from obscure Japanese trends to UK tabloid reports. Along with the author of *Power-Up* (see above), its team includes one of the top women games writers.

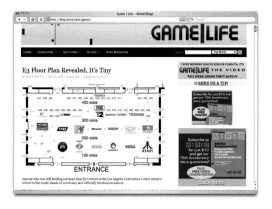

GamePolitics.com

www.gamepolitics.com

Dennis McCauley's excellent blog is subtitled "where politics and video games collide" – and it's a nasty smash-up. A valuable educational resource, the site offers a rather shocking eyeopener to the negative and often ignorant response to games by policitians and other opinion-makers. It also reports on videogames' more positive impact on society, and provides a long list of useful links.

TheGamesList

www.thegameslist.com

Social bookmarking meets free online gaming – it had to happen. The site offers hundreds of games and asks you to rate them once you've played them, in order to get unique recommendations based on your preferences. Members are also encouraged to add new games found elsewhere on the Net, all of which adds up to a continually growing community games site.

GameSpot

www.gamespot.com

Everything you ever needed to do with games: despite the rapid staff turnover in late 2007 and early 2008, it continues to provide incomparably detailed reviews, videos, podcasts, messageboards and will even host your blog. Separate editions for the US, UK and Australia mean that news and other location-sensitive info is geared to your own territory. Optional paid subscription gives you faster downloads and no advertising.

GameSpy

www.gamespy.com

IGN's stablemate, GameSpy isn't just a site devoted to regular games content, but a portal to all sorts of specialized sites covering genres and individual games as part of the Planet collection of sites. GameSpy itself is exceptionally good for online multiplayer gaming, the market it was originally designed to serve, and also hosts comic strips including John Kovalic's excellent *Dork Tower*.

GameTap

www.gametap.com

Subscription-based downloadable games for your computer, around a hundred of which are absolutely free. Much of the catalogue comprises what might be termed legacy console games (for systems like the Genesis/Mega Drive and Atari 2600), though there are a number of original titles available too. Non-Windows games work on Macs as well as PCs.

IGN.com

www.ign.com

Another of the big guns, IGN, now owned by NewsCorp, is almost as venerable as GameSpot and offers many of the same features, though its IGN Insider membership grants extra premium content such as high-definition video. Alongside the massive amount of games info, there are links to channels devoted to sports, cars, movies, comics and suchlike.

Inside Mac Games

www.insidemacgames.com

Long-running site supplying a growing niche of the gaming market with release dates, news and reviews. Though with the growth of MMORPGs and browser games, Mac owners have plenty to be getting on with while they wait for the latest PC game to be ported.

Jay Is Games

jayisgames.com

Blog site packed with reviews and walkthroughs for high-quality casual and browser games, plus design competitions, chat and more. Games can be downloaded here or at Casual Gameplay (casualgameplay.com).

Joystiq

www.joystiq.com

Originally an Engadget spinoff that's now a massive and evergrowing gaming news blog, with respected opinion columns and a useful daily summary of posts. Sister sites include WoW Insider (www.wowinsider.com), an unofficial blog covering the ubiquitous MMORPG.

Killer List of Videogames

www.klov.com

Searchable database of over 4000 arcade games, as provided by the International Arcade Museum website, an archive of research on coin-operated games, slot machines and other entertainment hardware. This is also a good starting point if you're thinking of buying your very own sit-in Atari *Star Wars* or *Hang-On* motorbike.

Kotaku

kotaku.com

Continual dripfeed of news posts for hardcore gamers, covering anything and everything gaming in idiosyncratic style. Alongside its irreverent take on regular gaming news, the site hosts an increasing number of home-grown interviews, in-depth features and reviews. Would-be commenters have to be approved before they're allowed to post.

Level Up

blog.newsweek.com/blogs/levelup

Newsweek's games blog is authored by journalist N'Gai Croal, who treats games as a valid subject for critical discussion, an approach no doubt influenced by his previous work as a film reviewer. Look out for collections of interviews with the various members of a game's development team, plus some unusually personal (and philosophical) email debates with MTV News' Stephen Totilo. Impeccably written and researched, there's nothing else quite like it.

Machinima.com

www.machinima.com

All your machinima needs in one place: channels dedicated to the most popular game sources; articles for wannabe filmmakers on how to create your masterpiece; help-wanted requests; and most importantly an endless supply of movies to stream or download, including Rooster Teeth's *Red vs Blue*, the long-running *Halo*-based series.

Miniclip

miniclip.com

This colourful site is currently the world's biggest browser games site, with 43 million users at the time of writing, making its founder one of Britain's most successful entrepreneurs. Around 400 free and more pay-to-download games are available in a number of languages.

MobyGames

www.mobygames.com

An enormous web project recording every published game in minute detail, this is probably the only place to find out the name of the supervising executive producer's assistant drone on 2001's *Magna Carta* (there's a random game button). There are also lots of community reviews written by members who really know their stuff.

Penny Arcade

www.penny-arcade.com

From the original, often outrageously funny webcomic devoted to gamers and games culture, Penny Arcade has become a multi-tentacled media machine, with its own adventure game, a digital distribution site, an annual games conference and even a children's charity. Still at the heart of it all are Tycho and Gabe (alter egos of its creators), stars of the thrice-weekly strip and authors of the accompanying blog.

PopCap Games

www.popcap.com

Probably the most successful casual gameplay developer, producing highly addictive games for systems ranging from mobile phones to the Xbox, PC and even iPod. PopCap is home to *Bejeweled*, the gem-linking game that's sold over ten million copies. Other titles include *Chuzzle* and *Peggle*.

Steam

www.steampowered.com

Leading the way in digital distribution of new PC games, Valve's neatly designed site sells its own titles plus those from other major publishers like Rockstar, Sega and Ubisoft. Once bought, games receive patches automatically and can be played on your own or any other broadband-connected PC.

What They Play

www.whattheyplay.com

In beta at the time of writing, "the parents' guide to video games", set up by former head of all 1UP's games media, John Davison, is an invaluable resource for responsible parents who want to know what's in a game and whether it's really suitable for their kids, beyond the box rating.

Glossary
& Index

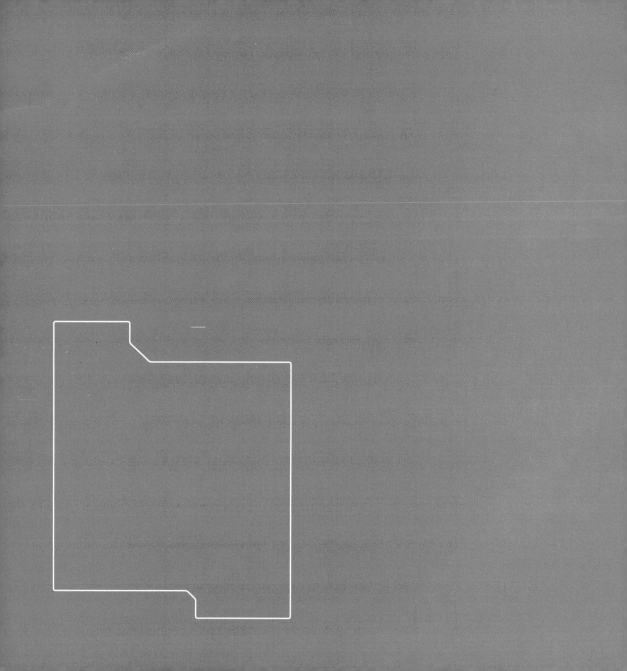

Glossary

action-adventure A broad game genre encompassing games that include combat or other perilous physical activity as well as exploration and puzzle-solving.

AI (artificial intelligence) Dictates the actions of anything in a game that isn't controlled by the player; great AI makes for more interesting and realistic behaviour by non-player characters or enemies.

analog controls Buttons or other mechanisms on a game controller that react to gradations of movement; an analog stick, for example, will allow you not just to move in a specific direction, but to move slowly or quickly depending on the level of pressure exerted; compare this with digital controls, which offer just two states: moving or not moving.

arcade cabinet A coin-operated games machine in an arcade.

beat-'em-up A genre of one-on-one fighting, often martial arts.

beta The stage in a game's development when an almost-finished version is submitted to user testing to iron out any problems.

boss An enemy at the end of a level which must be defeated in order to complete the level and move on to the next; they tend to be tougher than other opponents in the game.

cel shading Computer-generated artwork that resembles 2D cartoons in style, rather than aiming for photorealism.

console A game-playing system that is hooked up to a TV screen, for instance the PlayStation, Xbox or Wii.

cosplay The pastime of dressing up as characters from games at launches and other events; big in Japan, it's now become popular in the UK and US.

cut scene A non-interactive sequence that interrupts gameplay, usually designed to move the plot along.

developer A person (or more usually a vast team of people) who designs and produces games.

digital controls See **analog controls**.

d-pad A controller's cross-shaped directional button.

emulator Software that mimics the functionality of a console or other hardware, so that games can be played on a different system from that for which they were originally designed. See p.47.

engine The software backbone of a game, underlying programming that is often used across different games.

expansion pack Additional content for a game, extending its life.

first-party Used to describe a game developed by the same company that makes the console it's played on, for example Nintendo games for the Wii.

first-person Viewpoint whereby the player sees the action through the game character's eyes.

FMV Full motion video; see **cut scene**.

force feedback Technology by which a peripheral such as a controller responds to signals in the game and vibrates correspondingly; for instance, when the car you're driving crashes, when your character dies, or to signify recoil in shooting games.

FPS First-person shooter, a shooting game with a first-person perspective.

god game or **god sim** A strategy game in which you get to take control of the creation of a civilization or some other kind of human development such as a city.

handheld A portable gaming system with an integral screen, for instance the PlayStation Portable or Nintendo DS.

hit points A numerical representation of a character's capacity for damage, especially in RPGs; if a character is wounded in battle or falls off a ledge, hit points diminish. Other types of game use graphic life meters or bars, which drain or change colour to indicate health.

HUD Heads-up display; in a FPS it often gives information on health and available equipment.

isometric Viewpoint that allows you to see objects from three sides at once, used in RPGs and strategy games to give an overview of a broad area.

JRPG A roleplaying game produced originally in Japan. See p.23.

LAN Local Area Network; in games, this is usually used to refer to a small-scale multiplayer setup.

life meter See **hit points**.

localization The process of changing a game so that it appeals to a different territory from the one it was originally designed for, including changing the language and altering anything that might be deemed offensive in the new territory.

machinima An art form that uses in-game footage as the basis for filmmaking. See p.268.

minigame A short, usually simple game, either within a bigger game, or forming part of a collection of games often suitable for multiple players in a party setting.

MMORPG Massively Multiplayer Online Roleplaying Game; an MMO is simply any massively multiplayer online game.

mod (modification) Based on the code of an existing game, modding usually provides new levels for an old game and can even revise the gameplay setting beyond recognition. See p.38.

NPC A non-player character, controlled by the computer rather than the player.

PC A player character, controlled by the player.

peripheral Anything you connect to a console or PC to facilitate gameplay, for example a controller, a microphone or a steering-wheel.

pick-up An item picked up by a character that offers a usually short-term or one-off effect, for instance a weapon in a racing game, or a health potion in a platform game.

platform(er) A genre in which the player's character has to jump from 2D platform to 2D platform; the word is also sometimes used for the 3D version, in which characters have to traverse dangerous environments by means of accurate player control.

port A later version of a game revised to work on a different system from the one for which it was originally designed.

rhythm A generally music-based game in which fast and accurate responses to prompts are required. See p.278.

RPG Roleplaying game; a lengthy game (fifty-plus hours of gameplay is not unusual) in which the player assumes the role of a character or characters. It usually has a fantasy setting. See also **JPRG**.

RTS Real-time strategy game; a game in which the player's actions and the computer's reactions occur in real time.

save point A predetermined place in the gameworld where the player can choose to save progress for con-tinuing at a later time; some games have autosave points that do the same job. Often located before a boss or other perilous situation.

sim Simulation, a type of strategy game. The term is used in combination with whatever's being simulated, for instance a flight sim or a theme park sim.

spawn The reappearance of a dead character or defeated enemy. If Master Chief dies in *Halo*, for example, he'll respawn in a safe location.

third-party Used to describe games developed by one company for another company's hardware, for instance a Rockstar game designed for the PS3.

turn-based Describes a game or part of a game in which the action happens in a certain prescribed order; the computer will wait until a player has acted before taking its turn.

unlock To access a part of a game, or an item in a game, that only becomes available once certain criteria are fulfilled. In some games, completion unlocks a further level, for example.

walkthrough A detailed guide through a game, often written by fans.

Picture credits

The publishers thank the relevant copyright holders for providing the images used in this book. If for any reason any attribution is incorrect the publishers will correct the error on subsequent reprints once it has been brought to their attention: 1 Taito Corp., Midway Games; 4 Atari, Inc.; 5 Namco Ltd., Midway Games; 6 Atari, Inc.; 7 Atari, Inc.; 8 Activision, Inc.; 9 Nintendo Company Ltd.; 10 Nintendo Company Ltd.; 11 Nintendo Company Ltd.; 13 Sonic Team, Sega Corporation; 14 Midway Games; 16 Brøderbund Software; 17 Psygnosis; 19 Psygnosis; 20 Naughty Dog, Sony Computer Entertainment; 21 Nintendo Company Ltd.; 22 Square Enix Company, Ltd.; 22 Square Enix Company, Ltd.; 23 Game Arts, Sony Computer Entertainment Inc., Ubisoft Entertainment; 24 Mistwalker Corp., Microsoft Game Studio; 25 Namco Bandai Holdings, Inc., tri-Crescendo; 26 Sega Corporation; 27 Sony Computer Entertainment; 28 Microsoft Corporation; 29 Tecmo, Ltd.; 29 Bungie Studios, Microsoft Game Studios; 30 Sega Corporation; 32 Rockstar Games, Take-Two Interactive; 33 Rockstar Games; 34 Nintendo Company Ltd.; 35 Nokia Corporation; 35 Tiger Telematics; 36 Ensemble Studios, Microsoft Game Studios; 38 Relic Entertainment, Sierra Entertainment, Inc.; 39 Blizzard Entertainment, Vivendi Games; 39 Valve Software, Vivendi Games; 40 NCsoft; 42 Nintendo Company Ltd.; 43 Office Create, Majesco Entertainment, 505 Games; 44 Sony Computer Entertainment; 45 Noobz.eu; 45 Microsoft Corporation; 46 Microsoft Corporation; 47 SNK Playmore; 48 Sony Computer Entertainment; 50 Darxabre, Sold Out; 51 Traffic Games; 52 Nintendo Company Ltd.; 53 Nintendo Company Ltd.; 57 Nintendo Company Ltd.; 59 Black Isle Studios, Interplay Entertainment Corp., BioWare Corp.; 61 EA Digital Illusions Creative Entertainment AB; 63 2K Games; 64 Lionhead Studios, EA Games; 66 Revolution Software, Virgin Interactive; 68 Criterion Games, EA Games; 70 Infinity Ward, Aspyr, Activision, Inc.; 73 THQ Inc., Relic Entertainment; 77 Capcom Co., Ltd.; 79 2 K Games, Bethesda Softworks, LLC, ZeniMax Media Inc.; 80 Quantic Dream, Atari, Inc.; 82 Black Isle Studios, Interplay Entertainment Corp.; 84 Square Co. Ltd., Sony Computer Entertainment; 86 Square Enix Company, Ltd., Ubisoft Entertainment; 88 Sega Corporation, Sports Interactive; 89 Sports Interactive; 92 Epic Games, Microsoft Games Studios, People Can Fly; 94 Sony Computer Entertainment, SCE Worldwide Studios; 96 Rare Ltd., Nintendo Company, Ltd.; 97 Polyphony Digital Inc., Sony Computer Entertainment; 98 Microsoft Game Studios; 100 Rockstar Games; 103 LucasArts Entertainment Company LLC, Tim Schafer; 105 Hamonix Music Systems, RedOctane, Activision, Inc.; 106 NanaOn-Sha, Sony Computer Entertainment; 109 Valve Corporation, Vivendi Universal Games, EA Games; 110 Bungie, Microsoft Game Studios; 112 Bungie, Microsoft Game Studios; 113 2K Czech, Rockstar Games, Take-Two Interactive Software, Inc.; 114 Ubisoft Entertainment; 117 IO Interactive, Eidos Interactive; 118 Team ICO, Sony Computer Entertainment; 121 1c Company, Ubisoft Entertainment; 122 Nintendo Company Ltd.; 124 Nintendo Company Ltd.; 126 Eidos Interactive, LucasArts Entertainment Company LLC; 127 Eidos Interactive, LucasArts Entertainment Company LLC; 129 Ubisoft Entertainment, Bandai Co., Ltd., Q Entertainment; 130 EA Sports, EA Tiburon; 132 Naughty Dog, Sony Computer Entertainment; 133 Nintendo Company Ltd.; 134 BioWare Corp., Microsoft Game Studios, EA Games; 135 BioWare Corp., Microsoft Game Studios, EA Games; 136 Rockstar Games, Remedy Entertainment ; 138 Konami Corporation, Kojima Productions; 140 Nintendo Company

Page references to game reviews are highlighted in bold.

D: Rough Guide
DIRECTIONS for
short breaks

Available from all good bookstores

Morocco
South Africa, Lesotho &
  Swaziland
Tanzania
Tunisia
West Africa
Zanzibar

Travel Specials
First-Time Africa
First-Time Around the World
First-Time Asia
First-Time Europe
First-Time Latin America
Make the Most of Your Time
  on Earth
Travel with Babies & Young
  Children
Travel Online
Travel Survival
Ultimate Adventures
Walks in London
  & SE England
World Party

Maps
Algarve
Amsterdam
Andalucia
  & Costa del Sol
Argentina
Athens
Australia
Barcelona
Berlin
Boston & Cambridge
Brittany
Brussels
California
Chicago
Chile
Corsica
Costa Rica
  & Panama
Crete
Croatia
Cuba
Cyprus
Czech Republic
Dominican Republic
Dubai & UAE
Dublin
Egypt
Florence & Siena
Florida

France
Frankfurt
Germany
Greece
Guatemala & Belize
Iceland
India
Ireland
Italy
Kenya & Northern Tanzania
Lisbon
London
Los Angeles
Madrid
Malaysia
Mallorca
Marrakesh
Mexico
Miami & Key West
Morocco
New England
New York City
New Zealand
Northern Spain
Paris
Peru
Portugal
Prague
Pyrenees & Andorra
Rome
San Francisco
Sicily
South Africa
South India
Spain & Portugal
Sri Lanka
Tenerife
Thailand
Toronto
Trinidad & Tobago
Tunisia
Turkey
Tuscany
Venice
Vietnam, Laos
  & Cambodia
Washington DC
Yucatán Peninsula

Phrasebooks
Croatian
Czech
Dutch
Egyptian Arabic
French

German
Greek
Hindi & Urdu
Italian
Japanese
Latin American
  Spanish
Mandarin Chinese
Mexican Spanish
Polish
Portuguese
Russian
Spanish
Swahili
Thai
Turkish
Vietnamese

Computers
Blogging
eBay
FWD this link
iPhone
iPods, iTunes
  & music online
The Internet
Macs & OS X
MySpace
PlayStation Portable
Website Directory

Film & TV
American Independent Film
British Cult Comedy
Chick Flicks
Comedy Movies
Cult Movies
Film
Film Musicals
Film Noir
Gangster Movies
Horror Movies
Sci-Fi Movies
Westerns

Lifestyle
Babies
Ethical Living
Pregnancy & Birth
Running

Music Guides
The Beatles
The Best Music
  You've Never Heard

Blues
Bob Dylan
Book of Playlists
Classical Music
Elvis
Frank Sinatra
Heavy Metal
Hip-Hop
Led Zeppelin
Opera
Pink Floyd
Punk
Reggae
The Rolling Stones
Soul and R&B
Velvet Underground
World Music

Popular Culture
Classic Novels
Conspiracy Theories
Crime Fiction
Cult Fiction
The Da Vinci Code
Graphic Novels
His Dark Materials
Poker
Shakespeare
Superheroes
Tutankhamun
Unexplained Phenomena
Videogames

Science
The Brain
Climate Change
The Earth
Genes & Cloning
The Universe
Weather

For more information go to **www.roughguides.com**

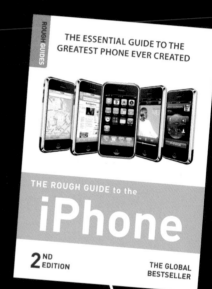